CHILDREN'S BRITANNICA

CHILDREN'S BRITANNICA

Volume 10
Instinct to Lesotho

Encyclopædia Britannica, Inc.

AUCKLAND / CHICAGO / GENEVA / LONDON / MADRID / MANILA
PARIS / ROME / SEOUL / SYDNEY / TOKYO / TORONTO

First edition 1960
Second edition 1969
Third edition 1973
Fourth edition 1988

International Standard Book Number: 0-85229-237-6
Library of Congress Catalog Card Number: 92-72908

*Printed and bound in Great Britain by
BPCC Hazells Ltd
Member of BPCC Ltd*

INSTINCT see ANIMAL BEHAVIOUR.

INSURANCE is a way of protecting people against unexpected losses. The cost of a fire or other disaster usually is too great for one person, whereas it can easily be met by many persons together. To take part in this kind of self-protection, each person regularly pays a specific amount of money, which in insurance terms is called a *premium*. All the premium money is combined into a fund which nowadays is managed by all sorts of different insurance companies. If any person insured with an insurance company suffers damage, or a loss, payment is made to that person by drawing on this vast fund.

Insurance is issued by an insurance company in a written agreement. This agreement is called a *policy*, or a *contract*. It describes the protection that is provided for the person who is insured. There are many types of policies. Life insurance, health insurance, fire insurance, personal insurance, and motor vehicle insurance are among the most common. If an insured person suffers a loss, that person will be paid money up to the maximum amount stated in the policy. Payment is seldom more than the loss.

History

Insurance probably was first used by Babylonian traders five or six thousand years ago. Goods were loaned to the traders at an interest rate equalling around 25 per cent of the value of the vessel and its cargo (see INTEREST). If the goods were stolen or some other misfortune caused a loss, the trader did not have to pay anything. The high rate of interest was, in a sense, the trader's payment for insurance.

This insurance practice was carried over into sea trade by the Phoenicians whose ships travelled the Mediterranean Sea. The loan made to finance a voyage did not have to be paid if the voyage failed because of piracy or other misfortune at sea. Insurance for the vessel itself was also provided. The Phoenician papers are the earliest records of insurance.

The Greeks and Romans also used this kind of insurance. Because it concerned commerce at sea, it was known as marine insurance. Merchants of Italy brought marine insurance to England in the 12th century.

During the 17th century in England, one of the popular meeting places of shipowners, seafaring men, and merchants was a coffeehouse in London owned by Edward Lloyd. Much business was conducted here. By 1688, Lloyd's had become a kind of club for businessmen who were willing to give insurance against risks at sea. They passed around a paper with the name of a ship that was about to sail, the name of the captain, the ship's destination, and the cargo it carried. If they thought it was a good risk—one in which the goods would get

S. & O. Matthews

Fire marks like this showed early firefighters that the building was insured with their company.

a good return and the voyage would succeed—these businessmen wrote under the details of the trip their names, and the amount of money for which each would be responsible if the voyage failed. This is how the term *underwriting* came into use. From the 18th century, Lloyd's became famous for its marine insurance, and today it is a centre for shipping news collected from all over the world. The latest movement of over 18,000 ocean-going vessels are kept track of at Lloyd's. It also handles every kind of insurance that you could possibly think of.

In the field of life insurance a great contribution was made by the English mathematician, Edmund Halley, who first calculated the orbit of a comet. His contribution to

The sinking of the *Amoco Cadiz* off the Brittany coast in 1978 caused the world's worst oil spillage and the then largest insurance claim for a loss.

Popperfoto

insurance was a mortality table, which he presented in 1693 to the Royal Society of London. It showed insurers the average number of years that persons of a certain age could expect to live. On the basis of these averages, insurers could figure how much people of different ages should pay for insurance. (See HALLEY, EDMUND.)

Probably the first company formed solely to insure lives was the Amicable Society for a Perpetual Insurance Office, founded in London, England, in 1706. In the United States, the first insurance company was the Presbyterian Ministers' Fund of Philadelphia, Pennsylvania, chartered in 1759. It was founded to care for the survivors of Presbyterian ministers.

The first fire insurance companies were formed after the Great London fire of 1666 (see FIRE OF LONDON). These companies kept their own fire fighting departments. The companies gave their policyholders metal emblems that were fixed to the outsides of the buildings insured. These were called fire marks. If a building had no fire mark and happened to catch fire, it is said that firemen just stood by and watched it burn.

The first American insurance group was founded in 1735 by storeowners seeking to share the risk of fire destroying their wooden buildings. The first fire insurance company in the United States, the Philadelphia Contributorship, was formed in 1752 by Benjamin Franklin (on whom there is a separate article). Many insurance companies came to be based in Hartford, Connecticut, and today it is known as the insurance capital of the United States.

Types of Insurance

In insurance terms, the insured, or policyholder, is the person who wants protection against loss, and the insurer, or underwriter, is the organization that pays for losses. The premium is the amount of money that the insured pays to the insurer for protection. For example, the rate of the premium is the amount of money that the company charges for each 1,000 dollars (or pounds, or whatever currency is involved) of insurance. The *beneficiary* is the one who receives the money paid out by the insurer. The policy is the written contract between the insured and the insurer.

Life Insurance can do several things. First, by paying the beneficiary the amount of the policy when the insured dies, it can make up for loss of future earnings caused by unexpected death. (The beneficiary in this case is usually the husband or wife of the person who has died.) Many life insurance policies also have value as money.

The three main kinds of life insurance are whole life insurance, term life insurance, and endowment policies. Whole life insurance protects for an entire lifetime. With limited-payment life insurance, the payments of premiums stop after a specified number of years, but the person is insured for the remainder of his life. Term life insurance gives protection only for a certain period of time— five or 10 years, for example—and the premiums increase each time the policy is renewed (because of the higher risks of death as the policyholder grows older). Endowment policies are the kinds of plans that emphasize thrift. They provide payment for the amount of the policy to the beneficiary if the endowed person dies during the endowment period. If that person is still living at the end of that time, the full amount is paid out to him.

An *annuity* is a sort of reverse life insurance policy. Instead of paying a certain amount when a person dies, it pays a guaranteed income as long as that person lives. Some people invest a single, large lump sum in an annuity and start collecting income immediately. Others invest a small sum each month for some years and at retirement collect annuity income, usually on a monthly basis. The total amount a person receives may exceed the cost.

Health Insurance is the most common insurance in the United States, Canada, Australia, and New Zealand. Most people in these countries have some form of health insurance, either policies they buy themselves or policies that they get by joining group plans where they work. All these, and other countries too, also operate a free national health service for those living below a certain economic level. In Britain, this system extends to everyone so health insurance is not really necessary. However, many companies and individuals do take out private health insurance as additional health protection. The various health insurance policies may cover hospital expense; surgical expense; regular medical expense, which covers nonsurgical physician care; and major medical expense, which helps to pay for most expenses during serious and prolonged illness or disability. Disability income insurance helps to replace income that is lost because of illness or injury.

Property Insurance. This is the modern form of the old fire insurance that was sold by early insurance companies. The name has changed because houses are now covered for far more than just fire. The effects of violent storms, flooding, theft, vandalism, and other dangers are the other major risks included. The value insured is normally what it would cost to rebuild a new property.

House interiors are also protected by contents insurance, which protects against theft or damage to household furniture, jewellery, cash, televisions and videos, family antiques, and so on.

Motor Insurance. This can seem the most complicated type of insurance to the individual. A driver can be covered for any accident to his vehicle or injury to himself, or he can just protect the vehicle against fire or theft. By law, motorists are required to hold some minimum form of motor insurance which at least covers any injury or damage done to another driver or vehicle. The premium is fixed according to the type of vehicle, driver's age, occupation, and previous driving record (whether he has been in any accidents, in which case the cost is higher).

There are many other types of insurance designed to cover special risks; for example insurance to cover injury to workers in a factory, and so on.

INTELLIGENCE. Intelligence can be described as the ability to think and learn quickly, to grasp difficult ideas, and to find solutions to problems. Only creatures with advanced brains can think (see BRAIN); and human beings have the most highly developed brains of any animal. Intelligence can be shown by different people in many different

CEPHAS Picture Library/Mick Rock

Intelligence tests for the very young make use of simple puzzles, such as the one illustrated here.

ways, and also by people with little education.

Intelligence tests may be given to school children and are usually given to a group, like an examination. They take the form of a number of short questions to which the answers have to be given in a limited time. The questions become more difficult towards the end. Intelligence tests can test how well we understand words, numbers, shapes, and how things work. But, as in all examinations, *personality* affects the way people do the tests; in other words, some people perform very well every time, while others (just as intelligent) become nervous and so do less well. Individual intelligence tests may also be given, for example, by an educational psychologist to a child with learning difficulties.

By testing large numbers of children, psychologists (see PSYCHOLOGY) have worked out the marks that an average child would be expected to get at varying ages. For example, if someone aged 10 gets the marks expected of a child of 11, he or she is said to have a "mental age" of 11. Mental age divided by the actual age, in this case 11 divided by 10, gives the Intelligence Quotient, or "I.Q.". This fraction is multiplied by 100 so as to give the answer as a percentage. So in this case the I.Q. would be 110. "Attainment tests" can be used to measure a child's reading age, or his or her standard in other subjects.

Today most people think it is more useful and accurate to measure particular abilities or special "aptitudes", which together make up general intelligence. In schools a "verbal reasoning" test can show the aptitudes a child possesses. Similar tests are used to help students choose suitable courses or careers. There are also tests of originality or inventiveness, called "creativity tests".

It is no longer thought that intelligence is a general quality, underlying all behaviour and inherited wholly from our parents. Intelligence is improved by learning. Some people are born with greater possibilities or "potential intelligence" than others. But this potential may not develop unless it is encouraged and stimulated by the influences surrounding the child from birth. What we *inherit* from our parents and ancestors (see HEREDITY AND GENETICS) and what we gain from the conditions in which we are brought up, our *environment*, together contribute to the development of our intelligence.

Much animal behaviour, which often appears intelligent, is actually the result of instinct (see ANIMAL BEHAVIOUR). But some animals possess the ability to learn and can apply what they have learned (their experience) to different situations. This is a form of intelligence.

INTEREST. When people borrow money they have to pay something extra for doing so, and the extra is called *interest*. Most people borrow money to buy houses, and many people borrow smaller sums of money to buy cars or household items. People then pay back this loan for the house, or car, over a long period on a regular basis, usually monthly, and this regular payment will include some interest added as well. See also BANKS AND BANKING; INVESTMENT; MONEY.

You can also make money by investing it in government savings bonds, in a bank deposit account, in a building society or savings and loan association, or in many other schemes. You are in effect lending money to these organizations and you therefore receive interest for doing so.

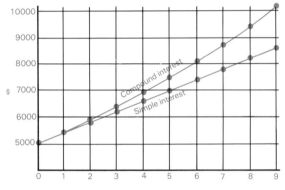
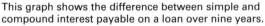

This graph shows the difference between simple and compound interest payable on a loan over nine years.

Suppose a man inherits a sum of money. For the sake of this example, we will work in dollars, but we could use any currency. Let's say that our man has $5,000. He can invest this at an annual rate of interest of $8\frac{1}{4}$ per cent (written $8\frac{1}{4}$% p.a.) (see PERCENTAGE). The abbreviation "p.a." stands for *per annum*, which is Latin for "through each year". This means that the organization with which he invested the money would then pay him, at the end of every year, $8\frac{1}{4}$% of his $5,000. On a calculator you can work this out by keying in the following expression:

$$5000 \times 8.25 \div 100$$

and this comes to $412.50. This kind of interest is known as *simple interest*. It is not very common nowadays, but years ago, rich people would invest a large amount of money, and the interest taken out each year would be enough to live on, so that they did not have to earn a living.

The more usual form of interest is *compound interest*. This is where you do not take out the

annual interest but leave it in the account so that it too earns interest. For the amount above it would work like this. After one year the money (sometimes called the *principal*) would be worth $5,000, plus $412.50. On a calculator with a % key this can easily be keyed in as:

$$5000 + 8.25\%$$

and this comes to $5412.50. This new amount now becomes the principal for the second year, at the end of which we add 8.25% again. The amount the money is worth after successive years can be seen in the following table.

No. of Years	Amount ($)
0	5000
1	5412.50
2	5859.03
3	6432.40
4	6865.65
5	7432.07
6	8045.21
7	8708.94
8	9427.43
9	10205.19

Thus in nine years at this rate of interest the money has more than doubled. The total interest earned is $5205.19. At simple interest nine payments of $412.50 would only earn $3712.50. These figures look even more striking on a graph. See the illustration with this article.

Generally the more money you have to invest, the higher the rate of interest. To borrow money always costs more than lending it earns, otherwise we would all be able to make a profit by borrowing money and then lending it to someone else. Banks and other financial or investment organizations in fact do do this, since they make their money by borrowing it, from ordinary investors, and lending it to businesses or governments at higher rates of interest. They can do this partly because the sums they lend are very large.

Some people think that interest may have begun as a sort of penalty payment demanded from a borrower who was late in repaying a loan. Gradually, the charging of interest came to be recognized as part of a business deal. Individuals became very rich by lending money at high rates of interest. The United States philosopher Benjamin Franklin wittily described the idea of charging interest in one sentence: "Money makes money, and the money money makes makes more money."

With the growth of industry on an international level during the 19th century, large amounts of money began to be borrowed for starting new businesses. Governments in many countries now borrow money from ordinary investors. They use the money, together with revenue raised from taxes, to pay for various projects, such as defence programmes, road building and repairs, welfare schemes, and so on. Governments pay ordinary investors a certain rate of interest. Depending on the type of government in power, this rate may be fixed by official policy or may be determined by existing economic conditions, often described as "market forces".

See also ECONOMICS.

INTERIOR DECORATION. The words

"interior decoration" are most often used to describe the design and decoration of the inside of a building such as a house—wall, floor, ceiling, windows, doorways, and furnishings. We can trace the history of interior decoration in Western civilization to classical times. The classical art and decorations of Ancient Greece and Rome have been very important to European design since the Middle Ages. Many of the styles of this early period had experienced revivals in fashion at different times through the centuries. Present day architects and designers continue to borrow styles from the past.

Classical

Almost nothing remains of Greek houses or furniture. What we know about Greek design comes from the Romans, who copied and adapted Greek designs. In the 18th century complete Roman houses with furnishings were discovered under layers of lava deposited when Mount Vesuvius in Italy erupted in AD 79 (see POMPEII). The walls of these houses and the statues and furniture were brightly painted and the floors covered with colourful mosaic pictures and patterns.

The Middle Ages

A cathedral built in the Middle Ages has colourful round rose windows, pointed arches and windows, and a tall spire pointing towards heaven. This was called the Gothic style.

Those houses built between the 12th and 16th centuries which can still be seen today are in the main houses built for fairly rich people. (The houses of the poor have not survived the passage of time.) We can tell too from descriptions and illustrations of the time what medieval houses looked like, and how people lived in them.

In a large house, most people lived, ate, and slept in a large room called the great hall. In the middle of the floor a pile of logs blazed, supported on iron bars which were called fire dogs. Sometimes cow-dung and seaweed were used as fuel instead of wood. The smoke escaped through a hole in the roof above, though in bad weather the rain and wind came in, blowing the smoke into the room. The roof itself was supported on gigantic, oak, exposed beams.

The windows were not very large and often had wooden shutters rather than glass to keep out the cold. Unfortunately they also shut out the light. Artificial lighting was inadequate, as it was supplied only by a few candles or oil torches.

The floor was made of earth, wood, or stone, and was often strewn with rushes which became very dirty. Sometimes the floor would have patterns painted on it or drawn into a thin layer of sand. In the houses of the wealthy, the floors might be covered with tiles. Floor coverings, such as carpets, were rare. In medieval and Tudor Britain, carpets were imported from Flanders and the east but were used to cover tables rather than floors.

Walls were panelled with wood to keep out the cold. An alternative way of keeping out the draughts was to cover the walls with tapestries, which were made by hand with coloured silks and wools. They showed scenes of

Courtesy, Metropolitan Museum of Art, New York, Rogers Fund 1903

Above: Frescoed room from a villa at Boscoreale near Pompeii, 1st century AD, in the Metropolitan Museum of Art, New York City. **Right**: 15th-century Flemish interior with Gothic-ornamented furniture: *St. Barbara* (oil on panel), attributed to Robert Campin, 1438, in the Prado, Madrid. **Below**: Elaborately carved and painted gallery typical of French Renaissance design: Palais de Fontainebleau, Galerie de François I, *c.*1533–45.

Courtesy, Museo del Prado, Madrid

Giraudon/Art Resource

Courtesy, Metropolitan Museum of Art, New York, acquired with funds given by Mr. and Mrs. Charles B. Wrightsman

Left: Michelangelo's ceiling and wall frescoes in the Sistine Chapel, Rome (1508–12; 1533–41) help to create a vivid effect in a simply-designed interior. **Above:** Delicate and decorative Rococo panelling and furniture in this Louis XV-style room from the Hôtel de Varengeville, Paris (*c.*1735), now in the Metropolitan Museum, New York.

Scala/Art Resource

country life. The walls of some of the Tudor palaces were decorated with paintings. Wallpapers were also sometimes used in larger houses. The earliest piece of wallpaper which has been found was made in 1509, but wallpaper was rare, even for the wealthy.

The poorer people at this time lived in small "wattle and daub" (sticks and mud) houses which they built for themselves. Inside, these houses had earth floors, and plaster walls which were sometimes decorated with patterns.

The Renaissance

The Renaissance began in Italy in the early 15th century (see RENAISSANCE). The Italians were very interested in the classical styles of Ancient Greece and Rome, and wanted to make Italy as great as it had been in Roman times. So they copied ancient styles in their architecture and paintings. The Renaissance style spread throughout northern Europe and Britain, and it replaced the earlier Gothic style of the Middle Ages.

In the 16th and 17th centuries, interior ceilings and walls were richly decorated, with ornamental plasterwork or carved woodwork. Woodwork was also sometimes panelled or painted, for example, with flowers. Windows were much larger and had glass, often coloured, in them. Curtains of velvet or satin were hung on each side. The fireplace was heavily decorated with columns, coats of arms, and other motifs.

These styles were taken over to North America by the colonists in the late 17th century.

There they built houses exactly the same as the ones they had left in Britain. In the south, wealthy planters imported the latest fashions from Europe to their houses.

The 17th and 18th Centuries

The Baroque style developed in Italy out of the Renaissance style in the 17th century. It was much more ornate and flamboyant than the Renaissance style. In Baroque interiors, there was a lot of marble and wood carved into huge sweeping curved forms. A great deal of the ornament was painted gold. The walls were frequently hung with large mirrors, especially above the fireplace. The ceilings were heavily decorated with plasterwork, and sometimes had scenes painted on them. Staircases were also heavily carved. The Baroque style soon spread from Italy to France, where King Louis XIV used it in his palaces, such as the Palace at Versailles.

In the middle of the 18th century, a lighter and more delicate style of interior decoration emerged in France. This was called the Rococo style. Like Baroque, Rococo interiors were decorated with mirrors, gilding, and painted scenes on ceilings and walls, but the overall colour of the rooms was much paler than it had been previously—pale blue and white were especially popular. The fashion for the Rococo style spread to Britain.

At the same time as the fashion for Rococo style grew, the earlier Gothic style and the new Chinese style were also popular in Britain. Wallpapers were imported from China, illustrating scenes of Chinese life.

Gradually, wealthy people tired of the ornate and busy Baroque and Rococo styles. They sought a calmer, more restrained style for decorating the interiors of their homes. Their imagination was captured by the uncovering of the remains of the Roman towns Pompeii and Herculaneum (buried by Vesuvius). They became very interested in Greek and Roman architecture, with its straight lines, symmetry, and classical details. This became the latest fashion, called neoclassicism.

One person who worked in the neoclassical style was Robert Adam (see ADAM, ROBERT).

A. F. Kersting

Early neoclassical-style dining room at Saltram House, Devon, designed by Robert Adam in 1768.

He not only designed the building and its interior for each of his patrons but also designed pieces of furniture to match each room. Adam paid great attention to ceilings and floors; he often designed them so that the pattern on the ceiling was exactly the same as the pattern on the floor.

Ceilings and walls at this time could be decorated with panels—oval, circular, or square, which were sometimes filled in with a scene painted by a famous artist. Fireplaces were smaller and less ornate than they had been in the Baroque and Rococo period. Mirrors above the fireplace went out of fashion. Rooms were very light because they had large sash windows, with painted wood frames. They had satin or velvet curtains. The houses were lit at night by candles, either placed in chandeliers hanging from the centre of the ceiling or in brackets attached to the wall, often with a small mirror behind to reflect the light from the candle.

Above: Interior view of the Glass House, New Canaan, Connecticut, designed by Philip Johnson, 1949; this provides perfect harmony of landscape, architecture, and interior design. **Right:** The attraction of the Christ Lutheran Church in Minneapolis, US, designed by Eliel and Eero Saarinen, 1950, lies in its simplicity.

Russ Kinne/Photo Researchers (left)   *Balthazar Korab (above)*

The 19th Century

By the middle of the 19th century, the factory machinery introduced during the Industrial Revolution was producing an effect on the houses of ordinary people. For all sorts of products for the home—such as furniture, wallpapers, and carpets—could now be made in large numbers and at a price that many could afford for the first time. Cheap books and magazines showed people how they could decorate their houses in the latest fashion— dark red and green flowery wallpapers were particularly popular at the time.

Because things were cheap, people's houses became very crowded with all sorts of objects— such as stuffed animals, fans, pictures, glass domes. Most of the daylight was shut out by long lace curtains and heavy velvet ones; in front of the window would be an aspidistra in a pot. The chimneypiece was covered in velvet drapery, with a fringe along the edge.

In the 19th century, there were lots of styles in fashion at the same time. Many of them were revivals of styles from earlier periods in history, such as the Gothic. Some of the styles copied those from far-off exotic places, such as Japan. People often decorated each room of their house in a different style.

These styles also reached America, where colonists used them in their houses. Earlier in the century, an American religious sect called the Shakers produced very simple designs for interiors and furniture, and these were also popular. The Shakers started to produce their furniture commercially. Other manufacturers produced similar designs.

Some people in Britain grew to disapprove of all the different styles, the clutter in houses, and the shoddiness of cheap machine-made goods. One such person was a man called William Morris, who founded the Arts and Crafts Movement in the mid-19th century (see MORRIS, WILLIAM). He thought that the best architecture and furniture had been produced in the Middle Ages when things were made by hand. So he and some friends started to make furniture, wallpapers and so on, to show people what good design should look like. His ideas had a great influence on designers at the time and later on too. One person he influenced was the American architect Frank Lloyd Wright (see WRIGHT, FRANK LLOYD). In his buildings, Wright used a lot of stone and wood and designed furniture to go with a particular building.

People gradually began to simplify design in their homes and remove all the clutter. By 1900, electricity was coming into use in houses. It was a much cleaner fuel than the gas light which had been used throughout the 19th century, and so walls could now be decorated in lighter colours because they did not get dirty so quickly.

The 19th-century designers were great imitators. The only unique 19th-century art style was Art Nouveau ("the new art"), with its sinewy lines and flowing plant and flower forms. Designers working in this style included the Belgian Victor Horta, Spain's Antonio Gaudi, C. R. Mackintosh in Scotland, and L. C. Tiffany in America. *Liberty's*, a famous London department store, designed fabrics and furniture in this style.

The 20th Century

In 1919, a school of art, architecture, and design was founded in Dessau, Germany, by the architect Walter Gropius. It was called the Bauhaus and was to have a very important effect on 20th-century architecture and design. The Bauhaus developed the idea that buildings and objects should be very simple in design, with little or no ornament. The way these buildings and objects looked should depend on what they were to be used for. That is, they should be functional. These ideas

formed the basis of an influential movement called "Modernism".

Most people's houses in the 1920s and 1930s were decorated in a mixture of the Modernist style and other styles which were in fashion at this time. One of these was called Art Deco, which originated in France. Art Deco combined ideas from all over the place into a style which was recognizable by its zigzag and rising sun shapes and its yellow, orange, and black colour schemes. All sorts of things such as light fittings and carpets were designed in this style. At the same time in the United States, a style emerged called Streamlining. This style derived from studies made of birds in flight, and after it had been applied to aeroplanes, boats, and trains, it was also applied by designers to many other objects, from refrigerators to interior fittings to pencil sharpeners.

After the hardships of World War II, people in the 1950s wanted jolly, colourful homes to live in. This was made possible by all the bright new plastics which had been invented during the war. Acid yellows and greens and bright reds were popular for interiors. Scientific investigation into the structure of atoms and molecules influenced forms in interior decoration; thin spikey forms and coloured

ZEFA

A modern European interior from the 1980s makes the most of available light. The living area in this German house is sparsely furnished; walls and furniture are white, and decoration is kept to a minimum.

baubles began to appear on carpets, wallpapers, and curtain materials. Wooden furniture and interesting new designs for light fittings from Scandinavia became very popular in the 1950s. In America, Charles Eames and Eero Saarinen were influential architect-designers, who, like William Morris and Frank Lloyd Wright, designed buildings and all the furniture inside.

Since the 1950s, there have been various fashions for interiors. For example, Pop in the 1960s used bright colours and bold shapes. High Tech in the 1970s drew its forms from factories and machinery. Also, an interest in styles of the past resulted from a concern with restoring old buildings and preserving the past. Post-Modernism is a recent phenomenon in architecture and design and has many different styles within it, many of which look back to styles of the past such as Classicism.

See also ARCHITECTURE and FURNITURE. You will find more information about other subjects mentioned in this article by turning to the Index volume.

INTERNAL COMBUSTION ENGINE. The internal combustion engine is one that burns fuel inside its working parts, unlike a steam engine which burns its fuel under a separate boiler. Internal combustion engines are of three main types. First, petrol engines, used chiefly in cars, motor cycles, scooters, and some small aircraft. Second, diesel engines, used chiefly for driving heavy machinery, ships, railway engines, buses, and heavy trucks, but also, increasingly, for light goods vehicles and cars, especially in countries where lower taxation makes the fuel much cheaper than petrol. (See DIESEL ENGINE.) Third, gas turbines or turbojets, most of which are used in jet aeroplanes. In all of these types, the fuel is burnt so that it heats air. The air therefore expands, or swells (see HEAT), and thus exerts a thrust, which either pushes a piston down a cylinder or blows on a turbine to turn it like a windmill.

The earliest internal combustion engines used as their fuel ordinary coal gas. The first engine of this kind was made in 1860 by the Frenchman, Etienne Lenoir. He was followed by the Germans Nikolaus Otto and Eugen Langen who sold 50,000 of their "silent" gas engines between 1867 and 1884. Another German, Gottlieb Daimler, was the first to make a fast-turning engine using liquid fuel such as petrol, and put one in a bicycle in 1885 and in a motor car in 1886. Another German, Rudolf Diesel, made the first diesel engine work in 1894. Gas turbines were built by several inventors early in the 20th century, but did not come into use until World War II (1939–45).

Petrol Engines

The petrol engines in cars and some aeroplanes have four or more cylinders whose pistons are connected so as to turn a single crankshaft. The pistons work up and down rather like the knees of a person pedalling a bicycle, and are connected to the crankshaft in much the same way. To explain the working of the engine, one cylinder only need be considered. The connection between piston and crankshaft can clearly be seen in the illustration together with the valves—mushroom-shaped pieces of steel which move to open and close ports, or holes, at the top of the cylinder. The valves are opened at the correct moments against springs trying to keep them shut by machinery driven from the crankshaft. Each movement of the piston from one end of the cylinder to the other is called a stroke. In a "four-stroke" engine, only one stroke out of four does work. Taking the four strokes in turn:

1. *Intake or Inlet Stroke.* The piston moves down the cylinder and as the inlet valve is opened air is sucked into the cylinder through the inlet port. On its way to the inlet port the air passes through the carburettor or fuel injection equipment where a fine spray of petrol mixes with it, so that a mixture of petrol and air fills the cylinder (see CARBURETTOR). When the piston reaches the bottom of the cylinder, the inlet valve shuts and traps the mixture in the cylinder.

2. *Compression Stroke.* The piston returns

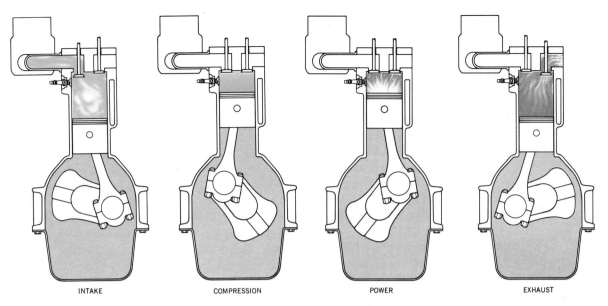

| INTAKE | COMPRESSION | POWER | EXHAUST |

Above: The four-stroke cycle. Piston descends on the intake stroke while inlet valve is open. It ascends on the compression stroke with both valves closed; ignition takes place at the top. The power (or expansion) stroke forces piston down again; both valves are closed. On the exhaust stroke piston ascends again and forces spent products through exhaust valve. **Below:** The rotary engine. Intake begins (A) and ends (B) with chamber at maximum volume. Compression begins (C) and chamber volume decreases. Charge is fully compressed (D) when ignition takes place, causing gas to expand and producing clockwise thrust on rotor (E). The moving rotor uncovers exhaust port and waste gases are expelled (F).

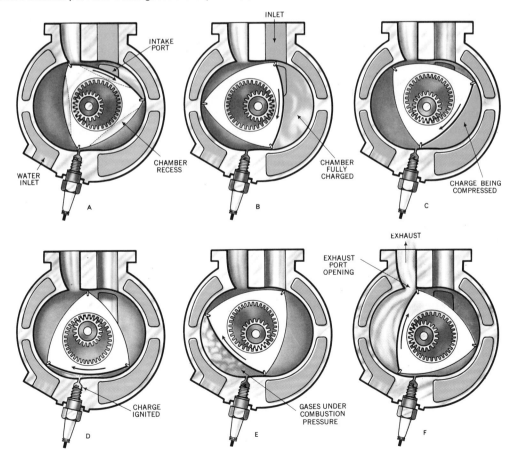

up the cylinder and as both valves are shut the mixture is compressed, or squeezed.

3. *Power or Expansion Stroke.* As the piston reaches the top of the compression stroke, it is arranged that an electric spark jumps across between the points of the sparking plug screwed into the top of the cylinder. The spark ignites, or lights, the mixture of petrol and air, which burns rapidly and expands, pushing the piston down the cylinder. The burning mixture becomes very hot, so that arrangements must be made for cooling the cylinder.

4. *Exhaust Stroke.* At or just before the end of the power stroke, the exhaust valve is opened. Thus as the piston moves up the cylinder again, it pushes the burnt gases out past the open exhaust valve, which is made to close at the end of the stroke. The piston has now made four strokes and its fifth stroke is a repeat of the first.

Some of the smaller petrol engines, especially those in light motor cycles and scooters, are of the kind known as "two-stroke" engines, in which one stroke out of two does work. The transfer and exhaust ports are in the cylinder walls towards the lower end, the transfer port being connected to the crankcase below. As the piston rises, the suction behind it draws a fresh charge of the petrol and air mixture from the carburettor into the crankcase, while compressing the previous charge into the upper part of the cylinder. As in the case of the four-stroke engine, a sparking plug in the top of the cylinder ignites the mixture as the piston reaches the end of its stroke. The burning gas expands, driving the piston down and compressing the fresh charge of mixture in the crankcase below the piston. When the piston uncovers the exhaust port the burnt gases rush out, and a little later the piston uncovers the transfer port on the other side of the cylinder. This allows the compressed mixture in the crankcase to rush into the cylinder through the transfer port, pushing out the last of the burnt gases. The piston now begins to rise again, covering the two ports as it does so and compressing the fresh charge above it. Thus every downward stroke is a working stroke. The two-stroke engine

needs no valves and is therefore simpler than the four-stroke kind. Although it gives nearly twice the power of a four-stroke engine with a cylinder of the same size, it is a little less efficient because it uses more petrol to do just the same amount of work.

The rotary-piston engine developed in Germany by NSU-Wankel is different from any other internal combustion engine. Instead of pistons it has a triangular orbiting rotor which turns inside a closed chamber. The sequence of intake, compression, power, and exhaust is completed during one turn of the rotor. The engine is very smooth-running because the only moving parts are the rotor and the output shaft.

In petrol engines the sparking plug is supplied with electricity at high voltage either from an *induction coil* connected to the battery (see BATTERY, ELECTRIC) or from a *magneto*, which is a small dynamo driven by the engine (see DYNAMO). By the principle of electromagnetic induction, which is described in the article TRANSFORMER, the induction coil changes the low voltage of the battery into the high voltage needed to make the spark.

The petrol either flows to the carburettor through a pipe from the tank above it, or, if the tank is lower than the carburettor (as in most motor cars) the petrol is pumped to it by an engine-driven or electric pump. The stream of petrol is changed into petrol-gas by passing through a nozzle with a tiny hole (called a jet) so that it comes out as a very fine spray to mix with the air sucked into the cylinders. In the passage between the carburettor and the inlet valve of the engine there is a valve called the *throttle*, which is opened or closed by the accelerator pedal in order to allow more or less mixture to pass. In this way it controls the engine speed. With fuel injection, pressure on the accelerator is detected electronically, and fed to a microprocessor which controls the length of time (measured in milliseconds) for which fuel is injected at each inlet stroke.

The engine is cooled by one of two methods, air cooling and water cooling. Air cooling is used for many of the smaller petrol engines, whose cylinders are made with a number of fins on the outside. A finned cylinder has a much bigger surface area than a plain one and therefore the heat can escape from it to the surrounding air more readily. The larger engines are water-cooled, their cylinders being surrounded by an outer jacket, or casing, containing water. The jacket is connected by pipes to a radiator, in which the water passes through tubes or passages designed to have a large surface area. The heat is taken away from the radiator by air blown through it by the fan.

All internal combustion engines require lubrication, which means oiling. Unless the friction (rubbing) between the moving parts is reduced by oil, they grow very hot and may even *seize*, or bind together. The oil is sent by a pump to the working parts through small pipes and sometimes through holes drilled in the parts themselves, and afterwards trickles down to the *sump* at the bottom of the crankcase. The oil from the sump may be passed through a separate radiator to cool it before it is pumped round the engine again. In some small two-stroke petrol engines, about 62 millilitres of oil are mixed with every litre of petrol (or about half a pint of oil with each gallon of petrol). The oil is therefore drawn through the carburettor and enters the cylinder in tiny droplets which do not burn like the petrol-gas and air mixture but lubricate the engine. This is called "petroil" lubrication.

Diesel Engines

The second large class of internal combustion engines, called diesel engines, is taken to include all engines in which the mixture in the cylinder is ignited by the heat caused in compressing it. This is explained in the article DIESEL ENGINE.

Gas Turbines

Engines with pistons that move up and down tend to vibrate because the pistons are continually reversing their direction of movement. In a turbine, the rotor, or moving part, turns in one direction only and the movement is smooth and free from vibration. The gas turbine is also simpler than the petrol and diesel

engines, as well as being smaller and lighter for the same power.

A gas turbine has three main parts: the compressor, the combustion chamber, and the turbine. The compressor is situated at the front behind the air intake. It consists of a spinning fan with a number of blades arranged in several rows. It draws in air from outside and compresses it. The air is heated by being compressed and is led into one of several combustion chambers. Liquid fuel such as paraffin (kerosine) is injected, or squirted, into the combustion chamber, where it burns, expanding the air by heating it. The hot gases rush out of the combustion chamber and blow on to the blades of the turbine, making it turn like a windmill. The shaft of the turbine is connected to that of the compressor. After the hot gases have left the turbine they can be made to turn a second turbine whose shaft is connected with that of the aeroplane propeller. An engine of this type is called a *propeller turbine*, or *turbo-prop*. In other gas turbines, the turbine drives nothing except the compressor and the hot gas escaping from it rushes out through a nozzle in a powerful jet backwards, thus driving the aeroplane forward. This is explained in the article JET PROPULSION. Turbines of this kind are called *turbo-jets*. Gas turbines have been used for driving machinery on the ground, ships and even railway locomotives but are most often found in aeroplanes. This type of engine is not suitable for small sizes such as those used in motor cars and motor cycles.

The gas turbine appeared much later than other types of internal combustion engine because of the difficulty of finding materials for the working parts (especially turbine blades) that would stand up to the very high temperature of the burning gas without melting or weakening.

INTERNATIONAL LAW is made up of the rules and customs that deal with the relationships between different countries and citizens of different countries. This kind of law is usually divided into two sections—*private* and *public*. Private international law deals with the rights of individuals in international situations; it is sometimes known as conflict of laws. Public international law deals with the rights of independent nations dealing with each other.

Private International Law

In private international law the individual may be a person, a corporation, or even a nation, since a nation may wish to buy, borrow, or sell as an individual. For the individual, private international law is necessary because a traveller cannot take his own law into a foreign country. For instance, if a United States citizen is a student in London or Paris, he or she is no longer living under United States law. If he or she does something illegal, dies, or marries a foreigner, international law determines which set of laws will apply.

Merchants and travellers depend upon private international law. They buy and sell in foreign markets knowing that they can expect the protection of private international law. Under such protection, merchants invented bills of exchange. They set up banks as aids to commerce, and learned to transfer credits from one country to another. Money and currency became more stable and reliable. (See BUYING AND SELLING.)

Public International Law

Public international law grew out of customs and agreements between independent states who traded with each other. The ancient Greeks and Romans had such understandings. For example, piracy was disliked and feared. By agreement among countries, pirates were always hanged when captured. (See PIRATES AND PIRACY.) Treaties between states usually had rules for carrying on commerce and for enforcing commercial contracts. It was profitable for states to be friendly with each other. A diplomatic service for political matters and a consular service for business affairs developed. (See DIPLOMATIC SERVICE.) Through diplomats and consuls, agreements were made between nations. Several nations might agree that no foreign vessel could come

within a certain limit of their coastline. Any vessel in a storm might signal for help by a signal agreed to by all nations. Duties (taxes) to be paid on goods to be imported might be agreed upon in advance by the trading countries. (See CUSTOMS DUTY.) International business and international law are necessary to each other.

International law has not been as successful in politics as in business. Each nation may insist upon its own rules, because each is absolutely independent. This situation often prevents agreement. The strong nation may try to control a weaker one by threat of force. The weaker nation may have to give in to the bully. To avoid this, nations of the world began to agree upon a fair set of rules before beginning discussions of business or of politics. The group of rules accepted and followed for the past 200 years is called the *law of nations*, or international law. Besides these rules, nations also bind themselves to accept others by signing treaties with one another. (See TREATY.)

A Dutch scholar and statesman, Hugo Grotius, is considered the father of international law. His book *On the Law of War and Peace*, published in 1625, said there was a natural law more important than the sovereignty (independence) of any state.

In 1668 at Aix-la-Chapelle, the then important nations signed a treaty ending a war between France and Spain. They recognized and accepted the law of nations as the basis of international relations. Great powers assembled again in Paris in 1856 to make the Declaration of Paris, and at Geneva in 1864, for the Geneva Convention. Efforts were made to put international conduct on a level with private conduct, that is, to expect good behaviour from nations as well as from individuals. Important meetings of the great nations were held at The Hague in 1899 and in 1907.

Most of these agreements were broken when World War I began in 1914. At the end of the war (1918), the League of Nations was planned to settle international disputes peaceably. The United States did not join the League. Other great powers accepted the

League, but limited it very much. This condition made the League an influence for good, but it did not have the power to enforce the demands of its members.

World War II (1939–45) was not prevented by international law. People again realized a need for a set of international rules that would work. Before the war ended, the United Nations Organization (UN) was set up. After World War II, the UN began the task of trying to establish rules between nations that could be enforced. (See INTERNATIONAL RELATIONS; UNITED NATIONS.)

INTERNATIONAL RELATIONS are dealings between nations. At the level of individual people, if there is argument between families, the local court settles the dispute and the town police see that the court's ruling is enforced. On the national level, disputes between individual states or provinces are settled in national courts. The courts may use armed forces to see that these decisions are obeyed.

In the world today there are more than 170 independent nations. These nations differ from the other groupings of people. One of the differences is that a nation is not controlled by any higher authority. It is independent, and can do what it wishes. It has what is called external sovereignty.

The study of international relations includes the ways in which these independent countries deal with each other. To handle many matters one nation must have a way of working with other nations. These matters include such problems as trade, exchange of money, refugees, tourists, boundaries, communications, and the sharing of scientific information.

In the United States, the Department of State handles most of the government's relations with other nations. The similar department in other countries is often called the Ministry of Foreign Affairs. Ambassadors or High Commissioners are sent from one country to another to look after a nation's interests. Treaties of friendship, military alliances, and commercial agreements may be signed between two or more countries. Many nations often take part in international conferences to settle matters. (See DIPLOMATIC SERVICE.)

Two thousand years ago there was no such thing as international relations, because there were few independent nations. The Roman Empire included most of the civilized world. The provinces, such as Britain, Turkey, Egypt, and Switzerland, had relations with the government in Rome. But there was little communication among the various conquered countries except through Rome.

The Nation

With the decline of the Roman Empire in the 5th century AD, Europe broke up into many small principalities (kingdoms). Each of these was controlled by a prince or king. During the next 1,000 years, these units joined together into larger groups through conquest, or by marriage of members of ruling families.

By 1700, Europe was made up of many nations. Each considered itself to be special and unique. It usually had its own language, flag, music, and literature, a common religion, and its own great heroic traditions. The people felt they owed no loyalty to any power other than that of their own country.

The most important aim of a nation has always been the protection of its own people. Each nation decides what is a threat to its existence and how best to meet it. The decisions are based largely on what it feels other countries may do; on its own physical power, its armies, economic resources, and on the strength of its allies. But equally important in any decision are things which cannot be measured. Such things may be the philosophy of the government and the way its people think.

Since there is no higher authority to keep order, nations have developed many ways of survival. Some nations have found that their best protection was isolation, thus keeping away from the quarrels of others. Some have felt that working through alliances with others was the better way to protect their own interests. One policy usually works well in one place and at one time, and a different policy will prove more successful elsewhere at a different time.

Balance of Power

In order to survive, a small country may sign an alliance with a large country that will promise to protect it. Sometimes, a group of small countries will agree to protect each other from a major threat. Many times two or more large powers become partners to defend their interests against other powers.

Since the 1500s, the European nations have used the balance of power system to help keep peace. If one or more nations started to become too powerful, other countries became allies to keep the first nation or nations in balance. It was hoped that in this way no one country or group of countries would become strong enough to attack another.

The European balance of power diplomacy helped the United States. During the American Revolution (1775–83), Britain could not spare the soldiers needed to defeat the colonial uprising without weakening her forces in Europe. Once the United States was independent, it adopted a policy of staying out of European affairs, or isolationism. It was not until 1899 that the United States had to become interested in the actions of European nations. This came about after the Spanish–American War, when the Philippines were ceded to the United States.

There were many failures in the balance-of-power system. Napoleon Bonaparte built a huge empire, and early in the 1800s held most of Europe under his control. But in 1814 he was defeated, his empire collapsed, and the major European powers restored the balance. For the next 100 years there were no major European wars, although there were many small wars. World War I (1914–18) marked the end of the old balance-of-power system, and the beginning of a search for new ways to prevent war. When talking stops, wars begin, and this is why "summit" meetings take place from time to time, bringing world leaders together for talks, with the aim of easing tension in international relations.

Collective Security

Unlike earlier conflicts, World War I was a total war. It affected all people in the warring nations, not just soldiers. New weapons caused more death and destruction than ever before, and forced countries to consider new and better ways of avoiding wars. The League of Nations was formed in 1920, with the idea of collective security. It was hoped that all the peace-loving nations would unite to stop any one country from attacking another. But the League had no army and could not stop Italy from conquering Ethiopia in 1935.

The League collapsed with the outbreak of World War II in 1939. This war caused even greater destruction, and brought a terrifying new weapon – the atomic bomb. It made nations try again to find peaceful solutions to their problems. To do this, the United Nations (UN) was formed in 1945, at the end of the war. The UN has no permanent international army, but the Security Council can call upon member states to provide troops for a peace-keeping force, and this has been undertaken at various times, for example in Cyprus and Lebanon. (See UNITED NATIONS.)

The World After 1945

The world after 1945 was very different from that known before 1940. No longer were there large groups of major powers that could be balanced against each other. Instead, there were two powerful groups of nations with opposing political views on how its citizens should be governed and what freedoms they should have. One power, the USSR, gathered around itself the then communist countries of eastern Europe and Asia. The other power, the United States, formed military alliances with many nations, the most important grouping being NATO. Each group of nations, using political, economic, military, and propaganda weapons, tried to expand its own influence, or weaken that of its opponent.

Between these two groups were many nations of Africa and Asia. These countries, which totalled over 100, did not want to get into a struggle between the major powers. They were called the *non-aligned* nations, because they wished to be left alone to work for their own development. In international relations they acted as a check on the actions of the major powers.

The group of communist countries began to dissolve in the late 1980s with the relaxation of control from the Soviet Union.

An international grouping of a regional nature, the South Pacific Forum, was formed in 1971 by Australia, New Zealand, Fiji, Papua New Guinea, and other countries in the Pacific, to discuss common problems, such as nuclear testing in the Pacific. Another group, the Caribbean Community and Common Market (CARICOM), was formed in 1973, to work for economic co-operation in the Caribbean.

Protection of their own interests has always been the main goal of all nations in their dealings with others. This does not mean that selfish considerations are always most important. Enlightened self-interest may show a country that by giving up certain rights and claims it may be helping itself in the long run by the friends it gains. Many nations have realized that it is impossible for a few countries to remain wealthy when millions of people are starving. The Third World is an expression used to describe these poorer developing countries. The nations of the world are now so closely connected that each country is affected by the problems of others.

Trade and Trade Agreements

Economics also play a part in international relations. No country grows everything its people need. None has all the minerals needed by its industries, or manufactures all the items its people buy. A country wishing to buy from other countries must sell some of its products or provide services, such as tourism, to other countries to pay for foreign purchases, unless aid is given in the form of a gift.

International trade has always been important to international relations, especially as most countries are not self-supporting in raw materials and other needs. Nations enter into trade agreements among themselves to decide what goods can be sold to each other. For many centuries these trade agreements were bilateral, or between only two nations at a time. In this century the need for international trade has become so important that many countries enter into multilateral (between many nations) trade agreements.

Today, most trading nations have entered into a General Agreement on Tariffs and Trade (GATT, which is a specialized agency of the UN). These nations meet to draw up trade treaties. From time to time a country or a group of countries may decide to avoid trading with another country to try to influence that country's actions, which are strongly disapproved of. When such steps are taken they are known as sanctions.

International Co-operation

The Geneva Conventions of 1864, 1906, 1929, and 1949 made rules for the treatment of prisoners of war. Although some countries have not always obeyed these rules, the treatment of prisoners has generally improved.

In the day-to-day activities of nations there are many examples of international co-operation. Modern science and industry would come to a halt if all activity stopped at a nation's border. In many areas, it has been in the best interest of all countries to agree on uniform rules and standards.

In 1874 the Universal Postal Union was founded at Bern, Switzerland. It sets up uniform postage rates for international mail, establishes standards for postal services, and draws up regulations for publishers wishing to send magazines to other countries. The International Telecommunication Union, founded in 1865, helps assign radio frequencies, and seeks to set the lowest possible rates for international radio, telephone, telegraph messages, and satellite communications. In 1878 the World Meteorological Organization was started. It helps set up weather stations throughout the world, and assists in the rapid exchange of weather information.

Since the end of World War II in 1945 several important organizations aiming at international co-operation have been established, including the International Atomic Energy Agency (established 1957), which encourages research into the peaceful use of atomic energy and establishes standards of safety at nuclear plants, because an accident at one of these plants may well cause problems for countries thousands of miles away.

Other organizations include the Food and Agriculture Organization (FAO) founded in 1945, and the World Health Organization (WHO) founded in 1948, both being specialized agencies of the UN.

International co-operation may take the form of a small group of countries getting together with the aim of more than just the improvement of international trade. In 1957 six leading countries of Europe formed the European Economic Community (EEC), also known as the Common Market. In 1986 membership was increased to twelve. The Community attempts to make it easier for goods, people, and money to pass over national boundaries. Most important of all, the twelve countries can speak as one in international affairs. (See EUROPEAN COMMUNITIES.)

International Court of Justice

At various times nations have tried to set up international courts to settle disputes among themselves. The Hague Peace Conference of 1899 planned the Permanent Court of International Arbitration. This court was to some extent replaced in 1922 by the Permanent Court of International Justice. In 1946 the UN took it over and it is now known as the International Court of Justice. (See INTERNATIONAL LAW.)

Nations may bring their disputes with other nations before the Court, but they cannot be forced to do so. Also, there is no way to make a country obey a court ruling which it dislikes. But world public opinion often makes a country accept a decision against itself.

INTESTINE. The digestive tract, from the end of the stomach to the anus, is known as the intestine. The intestine is tube-like in shape and lies within the abdominal cavity, or what is mistakenly called the "stomach". It has two main divisions, the small intestine and the large intestine or colon. The parts are named

for their width or diameter, not for their length. In humans, the small intestine, which is about 6 to 7 metres (20–23 feet) in length, is longer than the large intestine, which is about 1.5 to 2 metres (5–7 feet) in length. (See DIGESTION.)

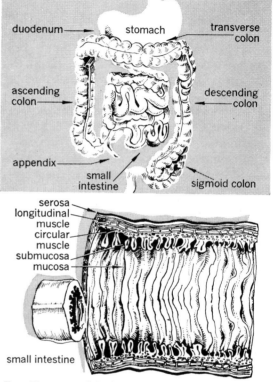

Top: The parts of the intestine.
Above: Cross-section of the small intestine.

The small intestine is divided into three parts, the *duodenum*, the *jejunum*, and the *ileum*. Each part has a special type of fold and is larger than the one before. Food from the stomach passes into the duodenum, on through the rest of the small intestine to the large intestine. (See STOMACH.)

Between the small and large intestine lies a small, saclike structure, the *caecum*, to which is attached the best-known part of the intestine, the appendix. The appendix has no obvious use in human beings, but in herbivores such as rabbits it is very large and helps to digest tough plant material.

The large intestine is also divided into three parts, the *ascending colon*, the *transverse colon*, and the *descending colon*.

The major job of the small intestine is to continue digesting the food and to absorb the useful parts through its lining into the body. The large intestine absorbs water from the remaining, undigested food and stores it, ready for elimination from the end of the tract.

After the partly digested food leaves the stomach, it must be changed further, before it can be completely absorbed by the body. This is done by substances called enzymes (see ENZYME), and by bile. The enzymes are manufactured by glands of the small intestine, or are added to the intestine by the glands of the pancreas. The bile comes from the liver by way of the gall bladder. These substances enter the duodenum through a passageway known as the common bile duct.

The inner part of the small intestine is called the *mucosa*. The mucosa has many folds, which are called *villi*. The villi increase the surface area of the intestinal lining so that as much food as possible can be absorbed. Underneath the mucosa are blood and lymph vessels, which take away food that has been absorbed.

The intestine has very active muscles that help to move undigested food through its two parts. The intestinal muscles are in two layers. The first circles the intestine, and can make it larger and smaller. The second, or outer layer, runs the length of the intestine. The outer surface is covered by a thin, shiny, transparent membrane, the *serosa*.

INUIT see ESKIMO.

INVESTMENT. Every summer the fields are full of tractors and combine harvesters gathering in the farmers' crops. The hay, wheat, and other cereals gathered are taken to barns and silos for storage. These machines and buildings are the farmers' *capital*. The important thing about capital is that it is not really wanted for its own sake (most people are not really interested in having a silo in their garden) but rather because it is producing other things. From time to time it is necessary to increase the number of tractors or improve some buildings and this addition to capital is what we call *investment*.

Investment takes place all around us and not only on farms. Giant firms, such as Ford or General Motors producing motor vehicles and trucks, invest vast sums in factories, body presses, paint shops, and engine assembly plants. They also invest in research so that the motor vehicles they produce in the future will be safe, efficient, and of a type people want to own. On a smaller scale, people invest in improving their homes by adding rooms, building garages or installing central heating. In all these cases the amount of capital is being increased so that the farmer can produce more wheat in the future, the car maker can manufacture more vehicles, and the house owner enjoy more comfort.

To invest in a new tractor, a factory, or central heating is very expensive. In some cases the firm or household has saved money for this purpose. People make *savings* when they decide not to spend all their income (see INCOME) when they receive it but keep some of it for use later. Firms save by keeping back some of their profits. People are not the only creatures which save. Squirrels, for example, save up nuts in the summer and hide them away to eat in the winter, and dogs bury bones to eat another day. The important difference is, however, that people make use of savings to invest in factories and machines which eventually produce *more* than the money they cost. This is known as the return on capital and is the main reason people invest. A squirrel only gets back the nuts that have been buried (if it can find them).

Some money lies idle as people and firms save up for an investment they wish to make in the future while others wishing to invest immediately have insufficient savings to do so. This is where banks play an important role. They collect up savings from those with long-term investment plans and lend it to those who wish to invest immediately but cannot afford to do so. The borrowers have to pay back the loan in time for the savers to complete their long-term investment plans. In fact, there are so many savers and investors that a careful bank always keeps enough money in reserve to meet these needs (see BANKS AND BANKING).

To encourage savers to keep money in a bank a small sum of money or *interest* is paid every year. In olden days, before banks were developed, it was common for people to keep their savings at home—hidden under the bed or buried in the garden. But by offering interest, the banks attract money which can then be transferred to useful investments. People borrowing from a bank to invest pay a slightly higher rate of interest for this than the amount received by the lenders. This higher interest is charged both to allow the bank to pay for its staff and offices, and also to make sure the business investors are going to use their borrowings wisely. If interest has to be paid, the borrowers will be careful to select the best possible investments to ensure that there is a profit (see also PROFIT AND LOSS).

Another way in which savers' money is invested by companies is through stock markets. Companies issue stocks and shares and these are bought by people, using their savings. Again, the companies pay the savers' annual interest for the use of these funds. (See EXCHANGE AND EXCHANGES for an explanation of stocks and shares.)

In some cases governments too invest, such as in roads and schools. They do this mainly because it is important to ensure that adequate transport and education is available to everyone. They may pay for these investments from the taxes (see TAXES) they collect but they also often borrow from savers, just like manufacturers and farmers. Governments issue bonds and savings certificates (which are similar to stocks and shares) and in some countries they operate their own banks.

IODINE is one of a group of chemicals known as the *halogens*, or salt producers. It is never found free in nature, which means that it always has to be extracted from something else. Certain seaweeds contain a great deal of iodine, and can be burnt to form ashes known as kelp, from which the iodine is extracted. Nowadays, however, the chief sources of supply of iodine are saltpetre beds in Chile and certain oil-well brines.

The human body needs a small amount of iodine to keep it healthy and in most parts of the world drinking water together with the plants used for food contain as much iodine as is necessary. In some regions, however, they do not, and unless iodine is taken in some other way, a condition known as goitre, or a swelling of the thyroid gland in the neck, occurs. Nowadays goitre is easily prevented by taking iodine usually mixed with salt (iodized salt). If pure iodine is swallowed, however, it is poisonous.

Iodine and an iodine compound called iodoform are also used as antiseptics to kill germs, although they sting when put on cuts. Scientists use iodine as a test for starch, since it turns any substance containing starch a deep blue, as can be seen by dabbing it on a raw potato. When iodine is sprayed on to clouds it causes rain. Pure iodine is a nearly black solid which *sublimes* at room temperature to give a deep-violet vapour from which the element gets its name, *iodes* being Greek for "violet". Iodine was first discovered in 1811 and identified by the French scientist Gay-Lussac in 1815.

ION. An ion is an atom, or group of atoms, which has had one or more electrons added to it or taken away from it and which, therefore, carries an overall (net) electrical charge. In the article ATOM it is explained that every substance is made up of tiny particles called molecules which are composed of atoms. Each atom consists of a central "nucleus" or core carrying a positive charge of electricity, surrounded by one or more electrons each carrying a negative charge of electricity. Ordinarily, the size of the charge carried by the nucleus is equal but opposite to that carried by the electrons, so that the whole atom is electrically neutral, or balanced. If an atom loses one or more electrons from its outermost shell a positively charged ion (*cation*) is formed. If an atom gains one or more electrons into its outermost shell, a negatively charged ion (*anion*) is formed. In writing chemical equations ions are shown by a superscript to the symbol for the atom, or group of atoms, which

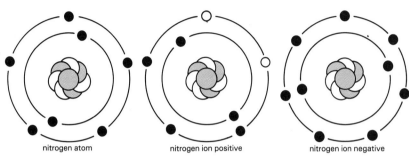

nitrogen atom   nitrogen ion positive   nitrogen ion negative

When electrically balanced, a nitrogen atom has seven protons in its nucleus and seven electrons surrounding it. If, in a chemical reaction, the atom loses any electrons, it becomes a positive ion. If it gains any extra electrons, it becomes a negative ion.

indicates the size and nature of the charge. Thus Na^+ is the symbol for a sodium atom which has lost one electron to become a sodium ion which carries a single net positive charge; a calcium ion, Ca^{2+}, is formed by the loss of two electrons from a calcium atom; and the negatively charged chlorine ion, Cl^-, is formed when a chlorine atom gains one electron. (See CHEMISTRY.)

Molecules are said to be *ionized* when they are split up into ions. This often happens when a substance is dissolved in water, as the water weakens the attraction between the ions. If, for instance, common salt (sodium chloride) is dissolved in water, it is split into sodium ions and chlorine ions. If the two terminals, positive and negative, of an electric battery are dipped into the salt solution, they attract the opposite electric charges on the ions and the result is that an electric current passes between the wires through the solution. Molten ionic compounds can be used for the purification of metals by electrolysis. (See ELECTROLYSIS.)

To ionize a gas, a fairly large amount of energy is required. It can be done by heating the gas to an extremely high temperature or by directing rays of electrons on to the gas. These rays may consist of X-rays, cosmic rays, ultraviolet rays or the gamma rays from radioactive substances (see RADIOACTIVITY). The gas is made conductive – that is, will allow an electric current to pass through it – by being ionized. This important effect is made use of in the instrument called an ionization chamber, which is used to measure how radioactive a gas is. It does this by measuring the size of the electric current sent through the gas inside it by a battery. The more radioactive a gas, the more ionized it is, and therefore the larger the current that flows. Such instruments are used to measure radiation in nuclear power stations, and also when prospecting (searching) for radioactive minerals such as uranium.

High up in the Earth's atmosphere there is a zone called the "ionosphere" in which the air has been ionized by radiation from the sun (see ATMOSPHERE). Fortunately for us, the ionosphere soaks up much of the ultraviolet radiation that would otherwise burn our skins severely. The ionosphere also acts as a kind of mirror to reflect radio waves and the fact that its height above the Earth varies with the position of the sun is the cause of the "fading" of distant radio signals. If there were no ionosphere the waves would travel on into space without being reflected back to Earth, and long-distance radio messages could only be sent by "bouncing" signals off communications satellites, which is the method used to send television programmes across the world.

IOWA is "the tall corn state". It can rightfully boast of itself as first in the United States in corn (maize), and pigs, and third in cattle. Most of Iowa is gently rolling prairie covered with black loam. About 90 per cent of the state is used for farming. Many of the state's 3,500 manufacturing establishments are in agriculture-related businesses, such as food processing and the making of farm machinery. Only about one-fifth of the population is employed in industry, and most industries are in the major cities.

Location

Iowa is in the north central part of the United States. Its eastern border is the Mississippi

River, and its western border is formed by the Big Sioux and Missouri rivers. To the north is the state of Minnesota and to the south Missouri.

The state is roughly a rectangle. Its greatest east-west length is 483 kilometres (300 miles), and its greatest width, north to south, is 322 kilometres (200 miles). Iowa ranks 25th among the 50 states in size.

The glaciers of the Ice Age transformed Iowa into one vast, level plain. There is only one natural region, the Central Lowland. The highest point in the state is 509 metres (1,670 feet), near Sibley in the northwest corner. The lowest point in the state, 146 metres (479 feet), is in Lee County in the east. There are only two substantial breaks in the level plain. In the northeast, about Dubuque, steep cliffs rise from the Mississippi. In the southwest there are low mound-like bluffs in the area around Council Bluffs.

In spite of the overwhelming use of land for farming, Iowa contains about 600,000 hectares (1.5 million acres) of forests. These tracts produce a vast amount of hardwood timber every year. The chief commercial trees are oak, hickory, maple, elm, black walnut, and wild cherry.

Iowa has a continental climate, with hot summers and cold winters. The summer growing season for crops is about 150 days. The spring and autumn growing seasons for hardy grains such as oats range from 40 to 50 days. Rainfall is evenly distributed. Most of the state receives from 780 to 810 millimetres (30 to 32 inches) of rainfall annually.

The People

Several Indian tribes were living in Iowa when the first white settlers arrived. Among them were the Omaha, Oto, Missouri, Sauk, Sioux, Fox, Winnebago, and Iowa. (The name "Iowa" means beautiful land.) The first Europeans to arrive were explorers and fur traders from Spain and France.

Most of the early settlers were from the eastern states, but in the 1840s immigrants began arriving from England, Ireland, Germany, Holland, Scotland, Sweden, and other countries. One group was a German religious society, the Amanas, that had originally settled in New York. In Iowa, 800 members formed a community in the northeast part of the state, near Iowa City, the former capital. Today the Amana colonies are a business co-operative and a popular tourist attraction.

There are other ethnic and religious enclaves (settlements) as well. The Dutch settled Pella in the 19th century. Many Czech immigrants went to Cedar Rapids. Groups of Amish (an austere Christian group that live and work without telephones, motor vehicles and most other modern equipment) live south of Iowa City and around Independence. When the Mormons were migrating from Illinois to Utah, a colony remained behind at Lamoni. A large number of Norwegians settled at Decorah. Quakers settled in the West Branch-Springdale area. West Branch is the birthplace of President Herbert Hoover and the site of his presidential library.

Most of the state's present population is descended from the original stock of American settlers and immigrants. Blacks make up less than 2 per cent of the population, and these are mostly concentrated in the cities, especially Des Moines and Waterloo. There are about 5,500 Indians remaining in Iowa. There is a small Indian reservation near Tama.

The Economy

Agriculturally, Iowa specializes in the feeding and selling of livestock. In the early 1980s Iowa ranked second among the states in the total value of all livestock. The state also ranked first in maize for animal feed, second in soya beans, and third in oats and hay. The state annually produces more than one thousand million bushels (36 million cubic metres) of maize.

Iowa produces about a quarter of the nation's pigs, and it is usually second only to Texas in beef cattle. Iowa imports feeder cattle, "unfinished" beef cattle, to be fattened on maize. Most of these come from ranches in the west or southwest. Sheep are raised for meat and wool. Dairying is a major agricul-

Iowa State Development Commission

Iowa is America's supreme farming state. It ranks among the top three in crops and livestock production. **Above:** Iowa's state capitol, in Des Moines, was built in the classical style, between 1871 and 1896.

ZEFA

tural activity in the northeastern part of the state.

Iowa is located at the western fringe of the American manufacturing belt. Much of the industry is farm-related. The Quaker Oats factory in Cedar Rapids is the world's largest cereal processing plant. There are meat-packing plants in Des Moines, Sioux City, Ottumwa, and other cities.

While agriculture is the main economic activity of the state, other products including electronic materials, refrigeration equipment, pens, tyres, and rolled aluminium are manufactured in Iowa. Portland cement and gypsum are the main mineral resources that have been exploited. Geologists have found huge coal reserves in the eastern part of the state. Both the Missouri and Mississippi rivers support commercial fisheries.

Transport

When the Iowa Territory opened for settlement in 1838, several military highways were built across the state to connect the forts. In the 20th century, with the coming of the motor vehicle, it was largely over these roads and early wagon trails that Iowa's modern high-

way system was built. There are now about 180,200 kilometres (112,000 miles) of road, tenth in the nation for total mileage.

Both the Missouri and Mississippi rivers are navigable for freight shipping. Iowa's goods can go by water through Illinois to seaports on the Great Lakes (see GREAT LAKES) or down the Mississippi to the Gulf of Mexico. Barge traffic accounts for most of the shipping on both rivers.

Education

The public (state) education system was established in 1858, and a compulsory education law was passed in 1902. To provide for the rural population, the state once had many one-room schoolhouses situated at regular intervals. School district reorganization has eliminated many of these schools, and pupils are transported by bus to town schools.

The main state-supported colleges and universities are the University of Iowa, at Iowa City; Iowa State University of Science and Technology, at Ames; and the University of Northern Iowa, at Cedar Falls. Private schools include Drake University, at Des Moines.

History

Iowa was included in the Louisiana Purchase of 1803, in which the United States acquired all French land west of the Mississippi. The Iowa Territory was created in 1838.

In 1832 the Indian chief Black Hawk was defeated by white settlers at Rock Island, Illinois (see BLACK HAWK). The last Indian outbreak was in 1857 at Spirit Lake.

Iowa was strongly anti-slavery. About 75,000 of its citizens served in the Union Army during the American Civil War (1861–65).

FACTS ABOUT IOWA

AREA: 145,752 square kilometres (56,275 square miles).
POPULATION: 2,795,000 (1991 estimate).
CAPITAL: Des Moines 193,187.
CITIES: Cedar Rapids, 108,751; Davenport, 95,333; Sioux City, 80,505; Waterloo, 66,467; Iowa City, 59,738; Dubuque, 57,546; Council Bluffs, 54,315.
HIGHEST POINT: Ocheyedan Mound, 510 metres (1,673 feet).
PRODUCTS:
    Agriculture: Maize, soya beans, hay, oats, eggs, poultry, grain, pigs, beef cattle, sheep, milk, butter, popcorn, sorghum.
    Mining: Stone, sand and gravel, cement, gypsum, clay, coal.
    Manufacturing: Farm and garden machinery, general industrial machinery, meat products, prepared feeds, dairy products, agricultural chemicals, drugs, soaps, cleaning and toilet goods, electric and electronic equipment, household appliances, newspapers, commercial printing.
STATE EMBLEMS. Flower: wild rose. Tree: oak. Bird: Eastern goldfinch.
JOINED THE UNION: Iowa became the 29th state in 1846.

IRAN (formerly Persia) is a country in southwest Asia. It is named after the Aryan people who once lived there. It is bounded by Azerbaijan, Armenia, the Caspian Sea, and Turkmenistan to the north, by Turkey and Iraq to the west, and by Afghanistan and Pakistan to the east. On the south are the Persian Gulf and the Gulf of Oman.

Iran is surrounded by mountain ranges. In the north are the Elburz Mountains, rising to over 5,600 metres (18,300 feet) in the Peak of Demavand. In the west are the broad ranges of the Zagros Mountains, and in the east rise the ranges of Khurasan and Baluchistan. In the centre is a tableland some 1,220 metres (4,000 feet) above sea-level, broken by high

mountain ridges. Between these ridges much of the land is a desert of sand dunes, bare rock, muddy marshes, and salty lakes. There are lowlands near the head of the Persian Gulf and along the Caspian shore.

The summers are humid on the coasts and dry inland, but very hot. Autumn is brief and winter severe. Rainfall is heaviest in the northwest and on the Caspian coast, most of it falling in winter. The northern slopes of the Elburz Mountains and, except in the south, the higher parts of the Zagros ranges are fairly well wooded with oaks and other trees. The Caspian coast has almost tropical vegetation, but elsewhere are only shrubs, tamarisks, and camel thorn. Along the Persian Gulf grow date-palms.

Leopards, wolves, and bears live in the mountains, and lynx and jackals are common, as well as deer and wild pigs, goats, and sheep. The many birds include the bulbul, the Persian nightingale. The Caspian Sea is rich in fish, especially sturgeon (see CASPIAN SEA).

People and Towns

Although more and more Iranians now live in towns, there are still large numbers of nomads. These wandering herdsmen move with their sheep and goats between summer and winter pastures, living a tribal life in tents. Those who are settled usually live in villages and most of the townsfolk are traders, merchants, or industrial workers. There are a

ZEFA

Above: The 17th-century shrine of Fatimah at Qom is a centre for Islamic study and a place of pilgrimage. **Left:** Iran has very cold winters with snow in the mountains.

J. Allan Cash

number of Armenians and Jews in the main towns. Persian is the main language, but Kurdish, Luri, Turki, and Baluchi are also spoken in some parts and Arabic is used along the Persian Gulf. Many adults have learned to read and write as part of the government's education programme. But many children in rural areas never get the chance to attend schools, even though primary education is

FACTS ABOUT IRAN

AREA: 1,643,510 square kilometres (634,562 square miles).

POPULATION: 51,225,000 (1988).

GOVERNMENT: Islamic republic.

CAPITAL: Tehran, 6,022,078.

GEOGRAPHY: A treeless plateau surrounded by mountains; most mountainous in the south and west, less than half the country is suitable for agriculture.

CITIES: Mashhad, 1,466,018; Esfahan, 1,001,248; Shiraz, 848,011; Ahvaz, 589,529.

ECONOMY. Products and exports.

  Agriculture: Wheat, sugar-cane, barley, potatoes, grapes, rice, water melons, sheep, goats, cattle.

  Mining: Iron, copper, kaolin, barite, chrome, zinc, lead.

  Manufacturing: Machinery, textiles, chemicals, iron and steel.

  Exports: Petroleum and petroleum products.

EDUCATION: Compulsory education for all children, although there are few schools in rural areas.

compulsory. Those who cannot read or write make up 30 per cent of the population. There are several universities and a number of scientific and technical institutes. Health and sanitation remain poor and many diseases bring high death tolls.

The capital of Iran is Tehran (see TEHRAN). Tabriz, where fine carpets are made, is an important industrial and trade centre in the northwest. Carpet weaving is the country's second largest export industry after petroleum. Tabriz was once famous for its Blue Mosque, now a ruin. Mashhad (Meshed) in the northeast is a city sacred to Muslims. Many go there on pilgrimage to the magnificent shrine of the Imam Riza, whom they regard as a saint. At Qom, both a centre for religious studies and an industrial city, in the central province, there are other Islamic shrines. About 320 kilometres (200 miles) south of Tehran is Esfahan (Isfahan), a city containing a number of beautiful buildings. These include the royal mosque, covered with brilliant blue and purple tiles and dating from 1611, the former royal palace, and the great cathedral mosque with its superb domed chambers. (See MOSQUE.) Northeast of Shiraz are the remains of Persepolis, the ancient capital city of Persia, which was captured and partly destroyed by Alexander the Great in the 4th century BC.

Agriculture and Industry

For thousands of years the country had been a land of peasant farmers and herdsmen. Only a small part could be cultivated because over half its area is wasteland, most of which is desert. Apart from dams and wells, a favourite way of irrigating the land was by means of *kanats*. These are long underground water channels made by sinking vertical shafts in a hillside and tunnelling between the bottoms of the shafts until water is reached far beneath the slope. The water then runs down the kanat. Some kanats are more than 40 kilometres (25 miles) long.

In 1908 petroleum was found near Masjid-i-Suleiman in southwest Iran. The British first developed the oilfields and from 1954 the oil industry was run in partnership between the Iranian government and a consortium (group) of Western oil companies. The oil industry was taken over by the Iranian government in 1979. The main oilfields are north and east of Abadan, and oil has also been found offshore in the Persian Gulf. Pipelines carry the oil to Kharg Island in the Gulf, where there is a huge terminal for super-tankers. Although oil is the most valuable export, production has fallen off dramatically because of the Iran-Iraq War and low demand for oil world-wide.

Apart from oil, the country also has large reserves of natural gas and minerals. Hydro-electric power has been used to speed an industrial revolution which has changed the lives of many of the people. There is a steady drift of people from the countryside to the growing towns. At Esfahan is the largest steel mill in the Middle East. Other products include cement, petrochemicals, textiles, and a wide range of factory-made goods. Iran is famous for its carpets and rugs, most of which are hand-woven (see RUG AND CARPET).

However, farming is still important, and much is being done to modernize agriculture. Autumn-sown wheat and barley are the chief grain crops, except in the Caspian coastal belt, where rice is grown. Fruit and crops such as sugar, tea, and cotton are produced. Some silk is also produced. There are large herds of cattle, sheep, goats, horses, and camels. In the forests young trees are being planted to replace the many cut down for timber or fuel.

The chief railway runs from the Caspian Sea to the head of the Persian Gulf, a magnificent feat of engineering which involved building 125 tunnels in a stretch of 207 kilometres (129 miles). Lines have been built linking Tehran with Turkey and Mashhad. The main roads fan out from Tehran to the provincial capitals. Country roads are poor by Western standards. The chief seaports are Bandar Khomeini (Bandar Shahpur) and Bandar Abbas. The former ports of Khorram Shahr and Abadan, which lay at the head of the Gulf on the Shatt al-Arab water, between Iraq and Iran, were badly damaged and cut off from the Gulf as a result of the war.

Modern History

For the story of the rise and fall of the Persian empire, see the separate article PERSIA, ANCIENT. In the Middle Ages, the country we now call Iran was ruled by the Seljuk Turks and then by the Mongols under Genghis Khan (see GENGHIS KHAN) and his grandson Hulagu Khan. Later it was conquered by Tamerlane. From the 1500s Iran was ruled by emperors, called shahs, and in the 1700s trade and other links with the West began to increase.

Throughout the 1800s Iran was the cause of conflict between Russia and Britain. The Russians wanted to expand southwards, while the British wanted to protect their empire in India and the East, and so sought to keep Russian influence away from the Persian Gulf. Iran suffered from this outside interference. Large sums of money borrowed from abroad were wasted by weak and dishonest governments. In 1909 there was a revolution, and a parliamentary system of government was set up. But the governments continued to be feeble and in 1921 an army officer, Reza Khan, seized power. In 1926 he had himself crowned shah.

He brought in reforms to modernize the country. However, his friendship with Nazi Germany led to his downfall. British and Russian troops occupied Iran and in 1941 Reza Khan gave up the throne. He was succeeded in 1945 by his son, Mohammed Reza Pahlavi.

Mohammed Reza decided to use Iran's enormous oil wealth to "westernize" the country. In 1951 the British-run oil fields were taken over and nationalized. During the 1960s Iran underwent great changes. There were land reforms to divide farmland among the peasants; dams and power stations, factories and roads were built. But the shah ruled as a dictator. Opponents of the government were imprisoned or exiled. Nevertheless, by the mid-1970s Iran had progressed so quickly that it seemed about to challenge the West as an industrial power.

However, the religious leaders in Iran were opposed to such rapid changes. Chief among them was Ayatollah Ruhollah Khomeini. ("Ayatollah" is the top rank among Islamic mullahs, or holy men.) Khomeini was an old opponent of the shah, and had long been in exile. In 1978 there were riots and strikes against the shah's government. The army could not keep order and in 1979 the shah was forced to give up the throne and leave Iran. A revolutionary Islamic republic was set up, with the Ayatollah Khomeini, supported by other religious leaders, running the country. Work on new industrial projects (such as nuclear power stations) was stopped. Despite worldwide protests, Iran held 53 Americans hostage in an attempt to force the return of the shah for trial. Khomeini was opposed to both the West (that is, the United States) and communism (the USSR). He wanted to return to the fundamental laws and customs of the Islamic religion. (See ISLAM.)

The revolution brought changes to all aspects of daily life. Islamic justice was introduced. Banks no longer paid interest to depositors. Women were made to wear the veil. Tens of thousands of Khomeini's political opponents were imprisoned or executed.

In 1980 Iraq invaded Iran to get back territory on the eastern bank of the Shatt al-Arab waterway. Known as the Gulf War, the conflict developed into a series of attacks first by one side and then by the other, both using sophisticated weapons. Only in 1988, when Iran found itself politically isolated and unable to pay for the war, did Khomeini agree to a ceasefire under United Nations supervision.

Iran suffered deeply from the Gulf War. As many as one million were killed or wounded in the fighting. The economy was ruined.

After Khomeini died in 1989, Hojatoleslam Rafsanjani became the country's new president. (A *hojatoleslam* is a religious leader of the second rank.) Rafsanjani wished to seek help from the West to rebuild Iran, but he was opposed by the hardline religious leaders. In 1990 a terrible earthquake near the Caspian Sea added further to the country's problems. Such was the devastation, Iran was forced to accept help from Western governments and aid agencies.

IRAQ occupies a central position in the Middle East. It is bordered by Turkey to the north, by Syria and Jordan to the west, and by Saudi Arabia and Kuwait to the south. Iraq has a short coastline where the Shatt al-Arab flows into the Persian Gulf. The Shatt al-Arab is formed by the Euphrates and Tigris when they join about 190 kilometres (118 miles) from the Persian Gulf. For some time Iraq was called Mesopotamia, from Greek words meaning "between the rivers", the Euphrates and

Tigris, which run from one end of Iraq to the other. (See EUPHRATES RIVER; MESOPOTAMIA; TIGRIS RIVER).

Although it has been independent only since 1932, Iraq is called the cradle of civilization. The Sumerians, one of the earliest civilized people known, had settled there by 4000 BC and their civilization was followed by those of Babylon, Assyria, and Persia.

South and west of the Euphrates the land rises gradually to the barren tableland of the Arabian plateau. North and east of the Tigris are fertile uplands rising to the jagged ranges of the Kurdish mountains. Between the two rivers lies a flat plain, covered with fertile soil brought down by the rivers as silt. However, the wide stretch of upland between the upper courses of the Euphrates and Tigris in northwestern Iraq, called Al Jazirah, is mostly desert.

The climate of Iraq is severe. In summer the days are intensely hot, with a dry northwest wind called the *shamal* which sometimes brings dust storms. It grows cooler at night, but near the coast the damp heat is almost unbearable. The winters are cold, with heavy snow in the Kurdish mountains and chilly north winds sweeping across the country right down to the Persian Gulf. Little rain falls except in the northeast.

FACTS ABOUT IRAQ

AREA: 438,317 square kilometres (169,235 square miles).
POPULATION: 16,630,000 (1988).
GOVERNMENT: Single-party republic.
CAPITAL: Baghdad (4,648,609).
GEOGRAPHY: A central plain watered by the Euphrates and Tigris rivers. Desert lies to the west of the Euphrates. The northeast is mountainous. There is a short coastline on the Persian Gulf.
CITIES: Basra, 616,700; Mosul, 570,926; Irbil, 333,903; As Sulaymaniyah, 279,424; Kirkuk, 200,000; Amara, 80,000.
EXPORTS: Foodstuffs, rubber, paper, fertilizer.
EDUCATION: Most children attend secondary and primary schools.

Little natural vegetation grows on the dry plains except small bushes and thorny plants. The marshlands are covered with long grasses and rushes and near the rivers grow willows, poplars, and liquorice plants. There are forests of oak in the Kurdish mountains. The wild animals include jackals and hyenas, and among the marshes and streams live otters and many water birds such as pelicans, storks, and herons.

The People

Most of the Iraqis are Arabs, their language being Arabic and their religion Islam (see ISLAM). In the northeast, however, live the Kurds, a fiercely independent people also found in Turkey and Iran. They speak a language like Persian. There are many different religions in Iraq. An interesting one is that of the Yezidis, who combine many features of other religions in their worship. There is still a shortage of schools and teachers, but standards of education have improved.

The most important cities of Iraq are the capital, Baghdad (see BAGHDAD), and Mosul, both on the Tigris; the river port of Basra; Amara on the lower Tigris; and the oil town of Kirkuk in the northeast. The word "muslin" comes from Mosul, although the material itself is no longer made there.

Keystone

An Iraqi woman and child in the ancient city of Irbil, where a settlement has existed for over 5,000 years.

Remains of ancient civilizations are scattered over the plain, the positions of the old cities such as Babylon, Nineveh, and Ur being marked by huge mounds called "tells". Most of our knowledge of these civilizations comes from excavations made here. One of the most famous buildings in Iraq is the ruined remains of the palace at the deserted city of Ctesiphon (near Baghdad).

Agriculture and Industry

The chief occupation of the people is farming. In the desert fringes of the country are to be found tribes of wandering Arabs called Bedouin, who live in small groups each under a sheikh, or head man. They go from one oasis to the next, breeding sheep, goats, and camels, and living in mud huts, or tents made from goat hair.

In the north, agriculture depends on natural rainfall but elsewhere it relies on irrigation. The ancient rulers of Iraq took great trouble to dig canals for distributing the water from the rivers, but they were neglected by the Turks and the Mongols when they came to power in the Middle Ages. Only within the last 50 years has irrigation on a large scale been taken in hand in the form of barrages. These are big dams built across the Euphrates and Tigris that trap the water in huge reservoirs, from which it is pumped into channels leading to the fields. The barrages also help to prevent the rivers from overflowing in the spring.

The most important crops of the plains are wheat, barley, and maize. Rice is grown in the marshy lands of the lower Euphrates and Tigris, and some cotton near Baghdad and Kut. In the foothills of the Kurdish mountains tobacco, fruit, such as water melons, tomatoes, and grapes, are grown. Iraq is one of the world's largest producers of dates. Millions of date-palms grow in well-watered plantations in a belt that extends on each side of the Shatt al-Arab. Many sheep and cattle are reared and Iraq exports wool and meat.

Oil is even more important to Iraq than agriculture. Most of the country's wealth comes from the huge supplies of petroleum obtained from oilfields near Kirkuk, Zubayr (near Basra), and Ayn Zalah in the extreme north.

Oil and natural gas are Iraq's richest mineral resources. The oil is pumped through pipes to Saudi Arabia. Most is crude oil and has to be sent abroad to be made into petrol, paraffin, and diesel fuel, although there is a large refinery for doing this near Baghdad.

Before the 1950s, Iraq had very few industries. Today it produces petroleum products, bricks and cement, fertilizers, textiles and carpets, and refined sugar. There is a steel mill in Baghdad. The Tigris River and its tributaries provide hydro-electric power. Timber is imported.

Iraq is linked by rail with Turkey and Syria and by road with Jordan, Turkey, and Iran. In the more primitive parts of the country camels and donkeys are the only means of transport. There are two sea ports, Basra on the Tigris, and Umm Qasr near the Kuwait border. Both were damaged in the war with Iran and in the Gulf War. Small boats can sail up the Tigris as far as Baghdad, and beyond to Mosul.

History

Iraq formed three provinces of the Turkish Empire until World War I when Turkey was defeated and Iraq was taken by British troops. After the war, Britain was responsible to the League of Nations for the government of Iraq. With the agreement of the people, Faisal, son of King Hussein of the Hejaz, who had started an Arab revolt against Turkey in 1916, was chosen as king of the new country.

Oil was found in 1927, and in 1932 Iraq joined the League of Nations as an independent country. When World War II began, Iraq broke off relations with Germany, but in 1941 there was a revolt which was put down with British help.

In 1958 the kings of Iraq and Jordan proclaimed the union of their countries as the "Arab Federation". Later that year, however, there was a revolution in Iraq and the country became an independent republic. In the Arab wars with Israel in 1967 and 1973 Iraq supported Egypt and Syria, but took little part in the fighting.

In 1980 war broke out over Iraq's claim to the east bank of the Shatt al-Arab and during

8 years of fighting much damage was done to the country's cities and industries. The war lasted until 1988 and cost more than 500,000 Iraqi lives. In 1990 Iraq invaded Kuwait, and declared that it was now part of Iraq. The United Nations (UN) demanded an immediate withdrawal and supported a trade embargo and naval blockade of Iraq. In February 1991, after 6 weeks of war, Iraq was expelled from Kuwait by a combined UN force from 28 nations, under the leadership of the United States. Uprisings followed among the Shiite population in the south and the Kurds in the north. These were put down by the Iraqi government. "Safe havens" were set up in the north under UN supervision to protect the Kurds from Iraqi reprisals.

IRELAND, NORTHERN. Northern Ireland is part of the United Kingdom of Great Britain and Northern Ireland. It has a population of 1,578,000 (1989). In 1921, following a guerrilla war between Irish nationalists, who wanted Ireland to be an independent country, and the British, Ireland was divided into two parts. Northern Ireland remained part of the United Kingdom, while the rest of the island became first the Irish Free State, later Eire, and finally the Republic of Ireland. (See IRELAND, REPUBLIC OF.) Sometimes Northern Ireland is called Ulster, the ancient name of that part of Ireland, although the old Ulster included areas that are now in the Irish Republic.

For local government purposes Northern Ireland is one region divided into 26 districts. In the past, it was made up of six counties – Antrim, Armagh, Down, Fermanagh, Londonderry, and Tyrone. All except Fermanagh touch the shores of Lough Neagh, the biggest lake in the British Isles. Fermanagh is in fact south of Donegal, which is one of the counties of the Irish Republic.

Land and Climate

Northern Ireland has some outstanding scenery, including the dramatic Giant's Causeway in County Antrim. The Bann, Northern Ireland's longest river, rises in the Mourne mountains in County Down and flows through Lough Neagh, finally entering the sea at the north coast. The land round Lough Neagh is flat and low-lying, but there are groups of hills forming a distant ring round it. The Antrim hills are in the north and east, the Mourne mountains and the hills of Armagh in the south, and the hills of Tyrone and the Sperrin mountains in the west. County Fermanagh contains many lakes and much hilly country.

At its nearest point to Scotland, Northern Ireland is divided from it by only 21 kilometres (13 miles) of sea, and on a clear day a person in Antrim can look across the sea and see houses in Scotland.

The climate of Northern Ireland is rarely hot and is not as rainy as western Britain. There is usually a little snow each winter but it seldom lies long. The wildlife of the countryside is much like that of northern England, but there are no snakes or toads.

Population and Economy

Most of the land of Northern Ireland is used for farming and is divided into many thousands of small farms, which are usually owned by the farmer and the farmer's family. Over 60,000 people work in agriculture. The fields, like the farms, are usually small, giving the countryside a patchwork appearance. Most farmers carry out mixed farming; that is, they grow crops and also keep animals. A quarter of the bacon produced in the United Kingdom comes from Northern Ireland, and there is much poultry farming.

The crops are mostly barley, oats, and potatoes, with small amounts of root crops and kale which are used for feeding animals. Some wheat is also grown and much fruit in some districts, particularly in County Armagh.

Belfast, Londonderry, and other towns have large textile and clothing industries mainly based on cotton and man-made fibres such as nylon and rayon. There is also a considerable manufacture of linen goods, but most of the flax for the linen is now imported. In 1990 over 29,000 people were employed in the textile industry. This amounts to 30 per cent of Northern Ireland's manufacturing work force. At

The Mourne mountains in Northern Ireland provide some cattle and sheep grazing, as well as reservoirs supplying water to Belfast.

Courtesy, Northern Ireland Tourist Board

Belfast's huge shipyards some of the largest tankers and merchant ships were once built. The shipbuilding industry, once Northern Ireland's largest industrial employer, has declined in recent years and now employs less than 5,000 people. An aerospace factory is now the province's largest single employer, with a workforce of 7,200. Both civil and military aircraft are built at Belfast, plus parts for other aircraft built in the USA and the Netherlands. The other industries of Northern Ireland include heavy and light engineering, the manufacture of mineral waters, tyres and rubber products, whiskey, tobacco, footwear, furniture, carpets, plastic articles, electrical equipment, and optical goods.

Northern Ireland's electricity is generated by coal and oil-fired power stations. The largest is at Kilroot, near Carrickfergus. There are no coal mines in the province, but large reserves of lignite (brown coal) have recently been discovered in County Antrim and County Armagh. Total lignite reserves may exceed one billion tonnes.

During World War II Northern Ireland was important as an air and naval base, protecting the Atlantic approaches to Britain, and its shipbuilding, aircraft, engineering, food, and clothing industries were of great value to the rest of the United Kingdom. Because of its wartime importance, Belfast was heavily bombed.

With so many manufacturing industries, the value of goods exported from Northern Ireland is very high, being as great as that from many much larger countries and larger than that of the Republic of Ireland.

Tourism supports 9,000 jobs. In 1989 150,000 people visited Northern Ireland. The province has many attractions, but the continuing violence discourages visitors from overseas.

Just over half the people of Northern Ireland live in towns and more than a third of them are in or near Belfast. The city stands at the head of Belfast Lough, a broad inlet of the sea surrounded by pleasant hills. It is the chief port of Northern Ireland. It has a university and its own broadcasting station with radio and television programmes, and also has two busy airports, Aldergrove 20 kilometres (12 miles) northwest of the city and Belfast City airport which is only three kilometres (1 mile) from the city centre, on the east side of Belfast docks. (See BELFAST.)

The largest city after Belfast is Londonderry, also known as Derry, in the northwest beside the broad waters of the River Foyle. Next come Newtownabbey, a new town on the north side of Belfast, and Bangor, a seaside town in County Down. There are a number of smaller industrial towns, including Lurgan, Portadown, Lisburn, Larne, Bally-

Northern Ireland Tourist Board
Dundrum Bay, County Down, Northern Ireland

mena, Newtownards, Newry, Coleraine, and Carrickfergus. The new city of Craigavon in County Armagh takes in Lurgan and Portadown.

The People and Government

Two-thirds of the people are Protestants and the rest, mostly in Fermanagh and Tyrone, are Roman Catholics. The people speak with an accent that is similar in some ways to that of Southern Scotland. Lowland Scots and English surnames are the most common, showing where many of the people's ancestors came from. Unhappily, relations between Protestants and Catholics have been beset by suspicion and fear. This division, complicated by other problems (such as economic decay), brought about the serious troubles which afflicted Northern Ireland during the 1970s and 1980s and affected the way in which the province was governed.

Northern Ireland is part of the United Kingdom and is represented by 17 members of parliament at Westminster. Until 1972 it also had its own separate parliament. Before it was prorogued (temporarily suspended) in 1972, this parliament was responsible for health services, schools, farming, factories, road transport, police, and other concerns of Northern Ireland. There was an elected government with a prime minister and a small cabinet of ministers. The parliament of the United Kingdom kept responsibility for such matters as the armed services and overseas trade.

In Northern Ireland there are two main kinds of school: voluntary schools mainly under Roman Catholic management, and controlled (state) schools run by the area education and library boards. Secondary education consists of grammar and technical schools. Besides Queen's University in Belfast, there are the New University of Ulster in Coleraine, and Magee University College in Londonderry.

The first parliament of Northern Ireland was opened by King George V in June 1921. The civil war which broke out in the Irish Free State overflowed into Northern Ireland. Not enough work could be found for the people at first. Later, new industries were set up and the region became more prosperous.

However, Roman Catholics felt that they were not getting their fair share of council houses and opportunities for employment, and that voting arrangements in local elections prevented them from being fully represented. Many Protestants, on the other hand, feared that if Roman Catholics became a majority in Northern Ireland, the constitution would be in danger. They believed that many Catholics were also republican; in other words, in favour of union with the Republic of Ireland.

A "civil rights" campaign sought fair voting, an end to discrimination (unfair treatment) in jobs and housing, and also an end to the Special Powers Act. (This Act allowed the government of Northern Ireland to arrest people without a warrant and detain them without trial.) Rioting followed the civil rights demonstrations.

In 1969 the British Army was called in to restore order in Northern Ireland, although the Northern Ireland government at Stormont remained responsible for security. Distrust and fear grew between Roman Catholics and Protestants. Streets were barricaded and gun battles were fought between soldiers and terrorist gunmen. The Irish Republican Army (IRA) played an active part in the fighting, supporting the Catholics and calling for the destruction of the government of Northern Ireland. In turn, Protestant terrorist groups also waged a campaign of violence.

Efforts were made to improve relations between the Roman Catholic and Protestant communities but the violence grew steadily worse. In 1971 Major Chichester-Clark resigned and was succeeded as Prime Minister by Brian Faulkner. Tougher action taken by the government of Northern Ireland included the internment (detention without trial) of people suspected of terrorist activities. Civilians, police, and soldiers alike were killed and wounded. Opposition members of parliament left Stormont and the government's reform programme could make little headway.

As a result of the increasing violence the British government suspended the Northern Ireland parliament in 1972 and thereafter Northern Ireland was ruled directly from Westminster. A Secretary of State for Northern Ireland was appointed and the government of Northern Ireland resigned.

In 1973 a majority of people voted in favour of retaining Northern Ireland's links with Britain. Local government elections were held. A new Assembly of 78 elected members and a new coalition executive (government) was formed, led by Brian Faulkner.

However, many Protestants were opposed to the agreement. Early in 1974 a general strike paralysed the province and the executive collapsed. In 1975 an elected Convention suggested a return to the old way of government in Northern Ireland but this was not acceptable to the British parliament. So the province continued to be ruled directly from London, through the Secretary of State for Northern Ireland. An attempt was made to revive the Assembly in 1982, but this failed.

Both the British and Irish governments are trying to put an end to terrorism, and to find a peaceful solution acceptable to all the people of Northern Ireland. In 1985 an agreement, known as the Anglo-Irish Agreement, was signed between the governments of Britain and the Irish Republic giving the republic an official position in Northern Ireland as a con-sultant in helping to solve the province's problems. This development was seen as interference in the internal affairs of Britain by some Ulster Unionist politicians.

In 1991 another attempt was made to start talks between the opposing political parties in the province, and British and Irish government representatives, with a view to deciding Northern Ireland's political future.

IRELAND, REPUBLIC OF. The Republic of Ireland occupies about 85 per cent of the island of Ireland which lies off the coast of western Europe. In all, Ireland has 32 counties, of which six – Antrim, Armagh, Down, Fermanagh, Londonderry, and Tyrone – have since 1921 been governed separately as Northern Ireland, which is part of the United Kingdom (see IRELAND, NORTHERN).

Bord Fáilte Photo

The Four Courts, Dublin (1786–1802), was rebuilt after heavy damage during the fighting of the early 1920s.

Ireland used to contain four provinces – Munster in the south, Leinster in the east, Connacht (Connaught) in the west, and Ulster in the north. Northern Ireland is sometimes known as "Ulster", though three of the Ulster counties (Donegal, Cavan, and Monaghan) are part of the Republic of Ireland. Dublin is the capital of the Republic. The name for Ireland in the Irish language is Eire.

To the west and south, the coasts of Ireland are surrounded by the Atlantic Ocean. On the east are the narrow North Channel, dividing Ireland from Scotland, and the Irish Sea, which lies between England and Ireland. Further south, St. George's Channel separates Ireland from Wales.

The centre of Ireland is flat, like a dish, surrounded by low ranges of mountains on the coasts. In the northeast are the Mourne mountains and the hills of Antrim in Northern Ireland, and in the northwest are the rugged mountains of Donegal and Sligo. In Connacht, facing west towards America, where so many Irish people have gone, are the mountains and rugged cliffs of Mayo, Galway, and Clare, sometimes rising to nearly 600 metres (2,000 feet) of sheer cliff beside the sea. Southwest below the long estuary (mouth) of the River Shannon, is the mountainous region of County Kerry, which includes the Macgillycuddy's Reeks and Ireland's highest mountain, Carrantuohill, 1,078 metres (3,537 feet). At the southwestern corner of Ireland the mountains and long deep harbours of west Cork extend into the Atlantic. The harbours include Berehaven and Bantry Bay, a deep water terminal for oil tankers.

Bord Fáilte Photo

Cork has one of the best harbours in Europe, the site of one of the world's first yachting clubs (1720).

FACTS ABOUT THE REPUBLIC OF IRELAND

AREA: 68,895 square kilometres (26,600 square miles).
POPULATION: 3,553,000 (1988).
GOVERNMENT: Independent republic.
CAPITAL: Dublin.
GEOGRAPHICAL FEATURES: A central plain, averaging 75 metres (246 feet) above sea-level,surrounded by broken mountain masses. Carrauntoohill is the highest peak at 1,078 metres (3,537 feet).
CHIEF PRODUCTS: Wheat, barley, oats, potatoes, sugar beet, turnips, livestock, milk.
CHIEF EXPORTS: Machinery and transport equipment, meat, dairy products.
IMPORTANT TOWNS: Dublin, Galway, Cork, Limerick, Dun Laoghaire, Waterford.
EDUCATION: Most primary and secondary schools are privately owned, aided by government grants.

The southern coast, with Cork harbour in its centre, has other fine ranges of low mountains. The Galtys, Knockmealdowns, and Comeraghs extend eastward to Waterford and Wexford, which have constant sea traffic with ports in Wales and southern England.

The east coast south of Dublin includes the massive granite range of the Wicklow Mountains. Dublin lies at the wide opening into the great central plain (see DUBLIN).

Much of the plain is so waterlogged that it cannot be cultivated. The wide bogs of the midlands are full of peat, which, when cut in sods and dried, forms a solid fuel and gives out much warmth. Since about 1930 great progress has been made in draining the bogs, and cutting and drying peat by machine.

The Shannon is the longest river in the British Isles. From its source in County Cavan in Ulster it flows for 260 kilometres (160 miles) to just below Limerick where it forms an estuary, 113 kilometres (70 miles) long.

Around the Irish coasts are many islands. Achill Island off Mayo and the Aran Islands off Clare are inhabited and the islanders speak Irish.

There is always much rainfall on the Atlantic coast, where the incoming clouds let fall their moisture when they are forced upwards by the western Irish hills. Elsewhere, however, the Irish climate is not very rainy, and there is no great heat or cold. There is, however, enough moisture for the rich grass growing on the limestone that forms much of the country to be a vivid green.

There are few wild animals in Ireland, apart from foxes, rabbits, and hares, and there are no snakes. It is said that St. Patrick drove snakes from the country in the 5th century. A great variety of sea-birds is found on the western and southern coasts during their seasonal flights to and from Europe, and fish are plentiful. Many rare plants grow wild in the west.

Agriculture and Industry

As it has a fertile (rich) soil and a mild climate, Ireland is a farming country, though the number of very small farms has decreased because of the many people who have left Ireland for other countries or gone to work in the towns. Farms are larger in the rich grazing districts of the midlands and eastern counties, but few people work on them. The farms in the west, such as Connemara, are small and poor.

Traditionally, Irish farming depended on raising cattle for beef, milk, and butter, although sheep are kept and pig-keeping (the Irish used to be thought a nation of pig-keepers) still goes on around Limerick and Cork. Great changes took place after the Republic of Ireland joined the European Economic Community (see EUROPEAN COMMUNITIES) in 1973. Membership provided more money for farm produce, so more could be spent on new methods and machinery. Pig production has increased and more land is being used to grow grain and root crops, including potatoes and sugar beet. Beet provides most of the sugar used in Ireland. Potatoes were the chief crop grown in Ireland until 1845, when a potato blight caused the loss of the crops and a terrible famine in 1847. After this tragedy few potatoes were grown until recently. Irish horses, both for racing and hunting, have been famous for many years, and both greyhound breeding and horse breeding provide an important export trade.

The industry of the Republic is mainly centred round Dublin, Cork, and Limerick. Irish brewing and distilling (notably of stout and whiskey) are world famous.

Recently, valuable minerals have been discovered in Ireland. These include zinc, lead, and copper. Natural gas has been found offshore in the south, and also limited amounts of petroleum. This is important because Ireland has little coal or iron ore. There is still great reliance on hydroelectric power produced by the Shannon. Electricity is also generated by power stations burning peat as fuel.

History of Ireland

The Romans never invaded Ireland but many other peoples did, among them the Milesians, who are said to have come from Asia Minor (now Turkey) and Egypt to Spain, and from thence to Ireland. The Greek geographer Ptolemy of Alexandria in about AD 150 mentioned the Iverni among the tribes of Ireland, and the Romans later gave their version of the name, Hibernia, to the whole island.

Early Ireland, also called Erin, was divided among tribal kingdoms, with five main provinces—Meath, Ulster, Connacht, Leinster, and Munster. Meath was the central province, and there the High King, who had power over all the provinces, had his hall at Tara.

The Irish had druids, who were pagan priests and wise men, until St. Patrick came in 432. He had been taken prisoner and kept in Ireland before, and after his escape he dreamed that he heard the Irish calling him to come to them. Patrick converted many people to Christianity. He was followed by saints

Bord Fáilte Photo

The Vale of Glendalough in County Wicklow is wild, desolate, but beautiful country with many forests.

such as Brendan and Bridget of Kildare who founded monasteries and built churches in Ireland.

After the Roman Empire fell, Europe went through a turbulent period, when the ancient civilizations were overrun by nomadic tribal peoples. Ireland, however, was not overrun, and it kept the flame of Christian learning alight, becoming known as "the land of saints and scholars". St. Columba crossed the sea from Ireland to Scotland and settled on the island of Iona, where he became one of the founders of the Christian Church in the north of Britain. Other Irish missionaries went to France, the Netherlands, Germany, Italy, and Switzerland.

In the 8th century the Norsemen invaded Ireland and seized the chief sea ports, Dublin, Waterford, Cork, and Limerick, besides the more western ports of Galway, Sligo, and Derry. After years of vain struggles against them, King Brian Boru gathered together the Irish and drove out the Norsemen at the Battle of Clontarf in 1014.

The English in Ireland

In the 12th century King Henry II of England sent an army to invade Ireland, and so began the troubled history of English rule. Settlers from England (and later Scotland) were given land that had belonged to the conquered Irish. The English settlers became known as Anglo-Irish. ("Anglo" means English.) The Anglo-Irish had more privileges than the native Irish and they had little to do with them.

Until the time of the Tudor kings the English had authority over the Irish only in the territory around Dublin, and this was known as the Irish Pale. In 1492, in the reign of Henry VII, the first of the Tudor kings, a law was passed decreeing that no Irish parliament could meet without the consent of the English king, who must also approve of all the subjects it discussed. Henry VIII, after quarrelling with the pope, took possession of Church property in Ireland, although Ireland remained Roman Catholic. Later, Elizabeth I carried out a thorough conquest of all Ireland, and under her and her successor, James I, swarms of

English and Scottish settlers took over the land, especially in Ulster.

When the Civil War broke out in England in 1642 most of the Irish supported Charles I. Because of this, the Parliamentary general Oliver Cromwell landed in Ireland with a large army, destroyed and burnt towns, and laid waste the country. He took possession of the rich midland and southern counties and drove the Irish to the poor lands of the west.

When King James II, who was a Roman Catholic, fled from England in 1688, the Irish supported him in his attempts to return to the throne. It was in Ireland, at the Battle of the Boyne (1690), that he was defeated by William III. James fled hastily from the battle and from the country.

William III and Queen Anne brought in laws to prevent Catholics from owning or buying land. They could not even have schools, and Catholic priests were made outlaws. The Irish parliament was made up entirely of Protestant landlords or people who agreed with them and Catholics could not vote at elections. The landlords made their tenants pay high rents for their small, miserable farms. The tenants had to live in mud huts with thatched roofs and their animals often shared the shelter with the family at night. Meanwhile, the landlords either went abroad or built for themselves fine mansions to live in. Dublin became a city of splendid buildings, many of which still stand.

In time, however, the landlords spent far more money than they could afford, and some of the Catholic families became rich again by trading, especially with France and Spain. The Irish parliament in 1782 declared its right to make laws independently of England, and the people began to rebel against their unjust laws. In 1793 Catholics were allowed to vote, but they were still unjustly treated and rebelled five years later. This rebellion was severely crushed, and in 1800 the Act of Union was passed, abolishing the Irish parliament and providing for Protestant Irish members of parliament in London.

The Catholic Irish, however, found a leader, Daniel O'Connell, and in 1829 he won the right of Catholics to become members of the English parliament. He was convinced, however, that this was not enough, and that Ireland needed a parliament of its own.

Most of the Irish at that time lived on potatoes, and even milk was a rare luxury. In 1845 a plant disease, the potato blight, appeared in Ireland and spoiled the crop. The next two years were far worse, and more than a million people died of starvation and of an illness, famine fever, that followed it. About 1,500,000 people left Ireland in despair, and there were only 5,500,000 people in Ireland in 1855, as compared with about 8,500,000 ten years earlier.

The British government took measures to relieve the famine, but these were late and badly organized. After the famine the Irish were more bitter than ever. A new movement was started called the Fenians, or Irish Republican Brotherhood. It wanted Ireland to become a republic completely separate from Britain. Another party was formed, seeking only "home rule" for Ireland; that is, a parliament for Ireland to look after the country's affairs.

Home Rule for Ireland

The Irish members of parliament who were trying to get home rule were led by Charles Stewart Parnell (see PARNELL, CHARLES STEWART). Gladstone, the British prime minister, partly agreed with Parnell and wanted to grant Ireland home rule, but his party, the Liberals, did not, and neither did the House of Lords. The Conservative party, when in power at the end of the century, helped the Irish people in the western districts and made it possible for the tenants to buy their farms from the landlords.

When the Liberal government of Britain finally agreed to bring in home rule in 1910, there was fierce opposition by the Unionist party in Ulster and in Britain. Northern Ireland was mostly Protestant, for many of the people there were descended from Scots who had crossed the narrow sea from Scotland. Because of the outbreak of World War I (1914–18) the question of home rule had to be put aside for a time.

In 1916 a group led by the Fenian Irish Republican Brotherhood caused an uprising in Dublin. They seized the Post Office and other buildings, where they were bombarded until much of the city centre was destroyed. The Easter rising was soon put down, but the people of Ireland sympathized with the leaders, many of whom were put in British prisons. A movement called Sinn Fein (which means "Ourselves Alone") gathered support quickly, and at the end of the war Sinn Fein won nearly all the seats in the Irish elections, except for those in east Ulster. In January 1919 the members of Sinn Fein met in Dublin and proclaimed Dail Eireann, the parliament of an independent Irish Republic.

The Irish then refused to obey the British courts and laws. The Irish Republican Army (IRA) (see IRISH REPUBLICAN ARMY) attacked British troops and police and lay in ambush for them. The British armed forces finally burnt large parts of several towns, including Cork city.

At last, however, the Anglo-Irish war, as this period was called, was brought to an end and a treaty was signed in 1921. Under this the Irish Free State was set up and given the same rights within the British Commonwealth as Australia, New Zealand, Canada, and South Africa. The northeastern counties of Ireland, however, remained part of the United Kingdom

The Irish Free State

The leader of the Sinn Fein party, which was by far the biggest Irish party at that time, was Eamon De Valera (see DE VALERA, EAMON). He wanted the whole of Ireland to be an independent republic outside the British Commonwealth. Nevertheless, Dail Eireann, the parliament of "southern" Ireland, agreed to the settlement by a small majority, and so De Valera became leader of a party in revolt against the government. Sinn Fein objected to the setting up of a separate government and parliament in Northern Ireland and to having a governor-general representing the British monarch. They wanted Ireland to become a republic and also objected to having British naval bases in Cork and in Lough Swilly in the north.

As De Valera had disagreed with the new government, Arthur Griffith became president in his place, and the government won the next general election. Fighting broke out between the government and the Irish Republican Army in 1922. Griffith died suddenly and ten days later Michael Collins, who commanded the government forces as Minister for Defence, was shot in an ambush. Collins had become a national hero as the brave and skilful organizer of the struggles against British rule, and he had been the chief Irish delegate, with Griffith, when the settlement was reached in London.

The new president of the Irish Free State was William Cosgrave, one of the oldest of a group of very young men who had to set to work to reorganize the state and crush the Republican rebellion. At the end of 1923 there was peace again, and the government was able to carry on and reorganize the country's work, controlling the civil service and encouraging industry and trade.

Meanwhile, De Valera and his followers refused to join the government, but in 1926 they quarrelled among themselves and a year later a group under De Valera, known as Fianna Fail, entered the Dail. They aimed, among other things, to reunite Ireland, to bring the appointment of governors-general to an end and to stop paying Britain the annual sum for land which had been bought with the help of loans.

The Irish Republic

Early in 1932 De Valera came to power and forced the governor-general to retire. He also abolished the oath of allegiance (the promise of loyalty) to the British crown. In 1937 the Irish Free State became known as Eire (Gaelic for Ireland), with an Irish president instead of a governor-general.

However, the refusal to pay land money to Britain led to trouble, and Irish trade with Britain was upset. It was realized that British trade was necessary to Ireland, for the "econ-omic war" was making Irish farmers poorer, and at last De Valera met the British prime minister, Neville Chamberlain, in 1938 to discuss the situation. He asked Britain to withdraw its fleet from Cork and Lough Swilly in Ireland. Britain agreed to this. It was also agreed that Eire should settle all its financial debts to Britain. De Valera promised that Ireland should never be used by enemies of Britain. When World War II broke out Ireland did not enter it on either side, remaining neutral. However, Irish farmers helped relieve Britain's food shortage by selling food to Britain, and many Irishmen fought in the British armed forces.

De Valera remained prime minister after the war, but in 1948 he was defeated and succeeded by John Costello, who led a government made up of politicians of various parties. Under Costello, Eire became a republic, changed its name to the Republic of Ireland and left the Commonwealth. This happened in 1949.

Ireland Today

Although Ireland is no longer part of the Commonwealth, citizens of the Irish Republic are in most matters treated as British citizens when they travel to Britain or to Commonwealth countries. For example, Irish citizens living in Britain can vote in British elections. Nevertheless, the division of Ireland into two parts has for years been a cause of unhappiness and unrest.

Relations between the Republic of Ireland and Britain were strained as a result of the violence in Northern Ireland which began in 1968. Many people lost their lives in riots and bombings, during the campaign of violence waged by the Sinn Fein through its military wing, the Irish Republican Army. The Irish government took firm action against the IRA and co-operated with Britain in efforts to bring about a peaceful solution to the troubles in the north.

In the Republic there has been a large majority of Catholics for centuries, and the proportion of Protestants has fallen steadily since the British connection was broken. The

Protestants, who form about five per cent of the population, live mostly in the eastern province of Leinster and especially in Dublin. The Republic of Ireland is one of the most strongly Roman Catholic countries in Europe. A notable event was the visit to Ireland of Pope John Paul II in 1979.

Since the great famine of the 1840s and the continuous emigration which followed, the population of the western counties has become steadily smaller. In the past 100 years, only the province of Leinster has shown a slight increase in population, but fully half of its 1,790,000 people live in greater Dublin and its suburbs. Dublin is the only big city in Ireland, with some 1,003,000 people. Next in size is Cork with about 402,000 and then Limerick (162,000) and Dun Laoghaire (54,000). (See DUBLIN; CORK; LIMERICK.) Almost all the small market towns have declined, through emigration or the drift to bigger towns.

There are marked differences of accent and speech between the four provinces of the Irish Republic. The Irish language is now spoken constantly only in certain small areas, mostly in the west. However, the tone and accent of the Irish speech persist in English. (For more about Irish, and Irish writing, see IRISH LANGUAGE AND LITERATURE.)

Primary schools are free and compulsory. Secondary education is given in private schools, many of which are run by priests, monks, and nuns. Many of the classes are taught in the Irish language, especially to younger children. The oldest university in Ireland, founded by Queen Elizabeth I, is Trinity College, Dublin. The National University of Ireland, with its flourishing colleges in Dublin, Cork, and Galway, was founded in 1908.

Eamon De Valera, the founder of the Fianna Fail republican party, was returned to power in 1951 and again in 1957. From 1959 to 1972 he was president of the republic. Later presidents were Erskine Childers, Cearbhall O'Dalaigh, and Patrick Hillery.

Emigration has been the cause of much anxiety to Irish governments in the past. (See MIGRATION, HUMAN.) Irish people left Ireland for the United States, Canada, Australia, and Britain. However, with the expansion of Ireland's industries in recent times, this population loss became less of a problem, until it reappeared as a less severe but worrying factor in the 1980s. Under successive governments led by Sean Lemass (Fianna Fail, 1959–66), Jack Lynch (Fianna Fail, 1966–73) and Liam Cosgrave (Fine Gael/Labour, 1973–77), Ireland grew more prosperous. The economy flourished after Ireland joined the European Economic Community in 1973, although unemployment worsened in the 1980s. Ireland's unit of currency (money) is the punt, or pound.

In 1977 Jack Lynch again became taoiseach, or prime minister. He resigned in 1979 and was followed by Charles Haughey, who was prime minister until 1981. In the 1980s Ireland faced economic problems and successive governments tried vainly to improve matters. They were led by Garret FitzGerald (Fine Gael/Labour, 1981–82), Haughey (Fianna Fail, 1982), FitzGerald again (Fine Gael/Labour, 1982–87), and most recently by Charles Haughey (Fianna Fail, 1987–90).

In the Irish parliament there are two assemblies: the Dail (House of Representatives) and the Seanad (Senate). There are 166 members of the Dail and 60 of the Seanad. The head of state, the president, is elected for a term of seven years. In 1990 Mary Robinson, a lawyer, became the first woman president.

IRIS. This flower, related to the crocus and the gladiolus, is named after the Greek goddess of the rainbow, because there are so many species of different colours.

The iris has six parts which look like petals but are called perianth segments. Three are turned downwards (the falls) and three stand upright in the centre (the standards). The shape of the flower makes certain that it can be pollinated only by pollen brought by an insect from another flower. The iris is beautiful both wild and as a garden plant. Some of the most attractive species come from the Mediterranean and Central Asia. For example, the Spanish iris (*Iris xiphium*) is violet with yellow

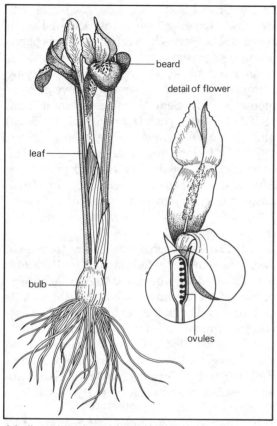

beard

detail of flower

leaf

bulb

ovules

A bulbous iris, showing sword-like leaves and large flower. The flower has upright petals, and bearded bent-over sepals known as falls. The closeup shows the ovary containing the ovules, future seeds.

or yellow-spotted falls and grows in damp, sandy places.

Another lovely wild iris is the pale blue *Iris florentina*, which grows in Tuscany in Italy. Its violet-scented rhizome is ground to make orris (iris) root powder for perfumes and medicine. Rhizomes are swollen underground stems that store food. These work their way to the surface, where they are baked by the sun. The rhizomes of cultivated plants should be broken up every three years about six weeks after they have finished flowering in late spring. Then, if the strongest pieces, with "eyes" from which leaves grow, are put back with only the fibrous root covered by the soil, the flowers will bloom all the better next season.

Garden irises are all kinds of colours—purple, lilac, white, cream, yellow, reddish-

violet, and grey. In some varieties the falls are a different colour from the standards, while others have veins (narrow stripes) brown or blackish in colour, or are spotted.

Best-known cultivated forms are the large bearded iris, especially hybrids of the German irises, pale blue, purple blue, and yellow. There are also the larger bloomed hybrids of *Iris mesopotamica*. Japanese irises of many varieties are grown on the edges of pools and dwarf irises are charming rockery plants. The yellow flag (*Iris pseudacorus*) is a swamp plant of Eurasia; the blue flag (*Iris versicolor*) is a similar wetland plant of North America. Irises vary from 22 centimetres (8.5 inches) to 1.5 metres (5 feet) in height and are good flowers for borders.

In the past irises were prized as cures for coughs, bruises, fits, dropsy, and snake-bite, as well as bad temper.

IRISH LANGUAGE AND LITERATURE.
The people of Ireland are famous for their clever and beautiful use of words. Throughout their long history they have developed an interesting and attractive literature, first in the Irish language and more recently in English. This article begins with a brief description of the Irish language and goes on to describe briefly the work of the most famous Irish writers in both Irish and English.

Many of the people mentioned here have separate articles of their own. You can also find information on them in the Index volume.

The Irish Language
Irish is a Celtic language (see CELTS). Like Scots Gaelic and Manx (the speech of the Isle of Man), it belongs to the Goidelic branch of Celtic, and its earliest surviving written records date from about the 4th or 5th century AD. These early examples of written Irish take the form of inscriptions on stone using a form of script known as Ogham. With the spread of Christianity throughout Ireland, Ogham was replaced by the use of the Latin alphabet in a specially adapted form. This type of Irish script is still occasionally encountered today.

C. M. Dixon

Ogham inscriptions were notches cut on either side of the edge of a stone. This one, from County Clare, has a runic translation carved above it.

Since the 12th century, when the Anglo-Normans first came to Ireland, both Irish and English have been in use in Ireland. In the course of time English replaced Irish as the language of the town-dwelling educated part of Irish society, but Irish still lived on among farming communities, especially in the western part of the country. However, in the 19th century, when famine and emigration caused a decline in the rural population, Irish almost reached the point of disappearance. In the late 19th century, when Irish political nationalism was growing, an organization was founded to preserve the Irish language and culture. This was the Gaelic League, set up in 1893. Today, though still not as widespread as English, Irish is an official language of the Republic of Ireland and is taught in state-run schools there. A knowledge of the Irish language is required for certain Civil Service posts and for jobs in the teaching profession.

Irish is a more complicated language than English, partly because its grammar is similar to that of Latin (both languages show case forms, for example), and partly because the way words are spelled rarely gives a true indication of the way they are pronounced. This is because the spellings, though modernized in the 1940s, still lag behind the changes that have taken place in Irish pronunciation. Thus Baile átha Cliath, the Irish name for Dublin, is pronounced something like *blaw* KLEE *ah*, with the emphasis on the syllable in capital letters. Another important feature of Irish is the fact that in certain circumstances the first letter of a word can be altered according to special rules. Thus the Irish for "the well" is *an tobar*, while that for "my well" is *mo thobar*.

Irish Literature

Poets have always had a special place in Irish life. In ancient Ireland the poets were called *filid*, which meant "seer". Second only to the priests, the druids, in importance, it was their sacred task to memorize and pass on all the many myths and legends of the Irish people, and to make up new poems about the events of their own time. They were allowed to criticize their rulers in verse, and so had great power. They were highly trained and protected by special laws.

Early Irish literature is full of tales of gods and heroes, of bloody battle scenes and tragic love stories, as well as adventures in the magical world of elves and fairies. All of these stories were collected and written down by Christian monks in the 12th century AD in the *Book of the Dun Cow* and the *Book of Leinster*. Another collection, adding later stories, was made in the 16th century. This was called the *Book of the Dean of Lismore*.

These books arranged the stories into groups which were called "cycles", according to the subject of the tale. There are four of these cycles: the Ulster, the Mythological, the Historical, and the Fenian. The Ulster cycle contains some of the earliest stories, including *The Cattle Raid of Cooley*, the great tale of the battle of the people of Connacht and their queen, Medb, against the people of Ulster, led by their king, Conchobar, and the warrior hero, Cu Chulainn. Many of the other tales in

Makers of 20th-century Irish literature 1. (left to right) The author and playwright Augusta, Lady Gregory; the essayist and poet George William Russell ("Æ"), and the dramatist Sean O'Casey.

Brown Brothers   *Bettmann Archive*   *Brown Brothers*

the Ulster cycle are about the adventures of Cu Chulainn, who was gifted with strength and wisdom beyond the powers of ordinary people. *The Wooing of Emer* tells of his love for the beautiful Emer, who also is the subject of many tales. The tragic story of Deirdre and her doomed lover is another famous story in the Ulster cycle.

The stories of the Fenian cycle, which were made up at a later date, are about two other Irish folk heroes, Finn McCool and his son Oisin (also spelled Ossian).

After Christianity came to Ireland, legends grew about the lives of the saints, especially the miracles which they were said to have

worked. These too became part of Irish folklore. The story of St. Patrick driving the snakes out of Ireland is a well known example.

As well as preserving early Irish literature, the Christian monks produced illuminated manuscripts. The *Book of Kells*, an illuminated manuscript of the first four books of the New Testament of the Bible, was completed at the monastery at Kells in County Meath in the 8th century. The *Book of Kells* combines a style of calligraphy (handwriting) known as Irish majuscule with delicate, complicated patterns and pictures, which often include people, animals, and birds. It is often called the most

De Cou from Ewing Galloway

Dublin's Abbey Theatre, where fine modern Irish plays were staged. Fire destroyed it in 1951.

Makers of 20th-century Irish literature 2. (left to right) The poet and playwright Padraic Colum; the poet and novelist James Stephens; and the dramatist John Millington Synge.

beautiful book in the world. (See MANUSCRIPT, ILLUMINATED.)

The monks of Ireland also wrote some of the most beautiful nature poetry in the Irish language.

From about 1200, during the Middle Ages, professional poets called "bards" were employed by noble families to celebrate their deeds and importance in verse. Like the *filid* who came before them, bards were carefully trained.

The older tales were still told as well. The first mention of leprechauns, the magic "little people" of Ireland, appears in the 14th century, in a retelling of an older story.

The Annals of the Four Masters (1616), a collection of all the stories ever written about the history of Ireland, was among the last major works to be written in the ancient Irish language until the end of the 19th century.

Anglo-Irish Literature

Irish literature written in English, often called Anglo-Irish literature, can boast of some of the greatest authors to write in the English tongue. Among them are the wit and satirist Jonathan Swift (1667–1745), the dramatist William Congreve (1670–1729), the political thinker Edmund Burke (1729–97), the playwrights Oliver Goldsmith (*c.*1730–74), Oscar Wilde (1854–1900), and George Bernard Shaw (1856–1950), and the novelist James Joyce (1882–1941).

In the 19th century the poet and singer Thomas Moore (1779–1852) made himself a national hero by putting new English words about the political wrongs of Ireland to old Irish melodies. The novelist Maria Edgeworth (1767–1849) wrote about Irish problems in *Castle Rackrent* (1800).

Irish Literary Revival

The Irish Literary Revival, also called the Celtic Renaissance, began in the last years of the 19th century. Its aim was to create once again a national literature written in the Irish tongue. People began translating and retelling the old myths and legends, and the stories excited the imagination of many other authors. The poet and playwright William Butler Yeats (1865–1939) was a leading figure in the revival. His *Fairy and Folk Tales of the Irish Peasantry* (1888), *The Celtic Twilight* (1893), and his plays such as *Land of Heart's Desire* (1894) and *The Wind among the Reeds* (1899), as well as many other works, took themes from the old literature.

John Millington Synge (1871–1909), in his plays *The Shadow of the Glen* (1903), *Riders to the Sea* (1904), and *The Playboy of the Western World* (1907), tried to catch the poetic rhythms, the wit, and the humour of peasant speech.

Sean O'Casey (1880–1964) attempted in such plays as *Juno and the Paycock* (1926) and *The Plough and the Stars* (1926) to give a realistic picture of the Dublin tenement districts during the revolution against British rule in the early years of the 20th century.

Brown Brothers   Irish Times   Brown Brothers   Erich Hartmann/Magnum

Makers of 20th-century Irish literature 3. (left to right) The writer and biographer Sean O'Faolain; the short-story writer Frank O'Connor; the novelist Liam O'Flaherty; and the dramatist Brendan Behan.

These three authors and many others, including Isabella Augusta, Lady Gregory (1854–1932), wrote for the Abbey Theatre, opened in 1904. Lady Gregory wrote and directed many plays such as *Spreading the News* (1904). She also wrote the story of the Abbey Players in her book *Our Irish Theatre*. The Abbey Theatre was the very heart of the Irish Literary Revival.

The list of poets who took part in the Irish Literary Revival is long and distinguished. Some of the best-known of these poets were George W. Russell, or Æ as he was called (1867–1935), Lionel Johnson (1867–1902), and Padraic Colum (1881–1972).

In the novel, George Moore (1852–1933) was outstanding. His 3-volume novel *Hail and Farewell* (1911–14) gives an account of the revival. The novelist James Stephens (1882–1950) is usually regarded as the most typically Irish. In *The Crock of Gold* (1912), his most widely known book, he tells of the curious adventures of tinkers, philosophers, and leprechauns. The humour of this book appeals to both children and adults.

James Joyce is probably the most famous Irish novelist. His genius stands alone but works such as *Dubliners* (short stories) and *Ulysses* show that his writing is rooted in Irish life.

Other writers in Irish of the 20th century include Sean O'Faolain, Frank O'Connor, and Liam O'Flaherty. Brendan Behan's (1923–64) autobiographical book *Borstal Boy* (1958) and

his play *The Hostage* (1958) are among the best known of his works. In the late 20th century the poet Patrick Kavanagh (1905–67) is highly respected, as are the novelists Iris Murdoch, Edna O'Brien, Molly Keane, and William Trevor.

The Irish-born Samuel Beckett, who was awarded the Nobel Prize for Literature in 1969, went to live permanently in France in his early life. He wrote most of his plays and poems first in French, and then translated them himself into English. His most famous play is *Waiting for Godot* (1955).

IRISH REPUBLICAN ARMY (IRA) is a semi-military organization which was formed to fight for an independent united Ireland. Since the late 1960s it has carried out many acts of terrorism in Northern Ireland in an attempt to force its unification with the Republic of Ireland. As with other terrorist organizations, its membership and activities are kept secret (see TERRORISM).

The IRA was founded in 1919 as an offshoot of the nationalist party Sinn Fein (see SINN FEIN; and the history section of IRELAND, REPUBLIC OF), though it has in general operated independently of political parties. During Ireland's fight for independence from 1919 to 1921 the IRA organized many attacks and sabotage operations against the British. Eventually Britain was compelled to set up the Irish Free State. A part of the British Commonwealth, it comprised 26 counties with a predominantly Catholic population, while the mainly Protestant six counties of Northern Ireland remained part of the United Kingdom. The more militant members of the IRA, known as the "Irregulars", refused to accept this partition. The Irregulars were defeated in the civil war of 1922–23, but did not dissolve their organization.

After a number of violent incidents the Free State declared the IRA an illegal organization in 1931. Nevertheless it carried out a number of bombings in England in 1939 and continued terrorist activities during World War II. The Free State took severe measures against those found guilty, executing five of the leaders and imprisoning many others.

In 1948 the Irish Free State left the Commonwealth and became the Republic of Ireland. The IRA then concentrated on a campaign to break Northern Ireland's connection with Britain and bring it into a unified Irish republic. Its efforts had little success until the late 1960s when the half a million Roman Catholics in Northern Ireland began to complain increasingly bitterly about discrimination in jobs and housing against themselves and in favour of the Protestants. Demonstrations and counter-demonstrations became so violent that in 1969 the British government sent troops to keep order. Later that year the IRA split into "official" and "provisional" wings.

Since then the Provisionals, or "Provos"

Topham

IRA members, disguised by dark glasses and masks, illegally wear uniform to attend a funeral.

have carried out many acts of terrorism. Soldiers, policemen, and civilians have been killed or injured in shootings, bombings, kidnappings, robberies, and ambushes since the IRA re-emerged as a terrorist force in the late 1960s. Well-publicised attacks included the murder of Lord Mountbatten when his boat was blown up in Donegal Bay in 1979, and the murder of a senior English MP (Member of Parliament) in his car at the Houses of Parliament in London. The latter was one of many terrorist atrocities which the IRA committed on the British mainland from the mid-1970s, which included placing bombs in shops, bars, parks, and cars, so that the maximum damage would be caused. The IRA came close to murdering the British Prime Minister and her ministers when they exploded a bomb at the Grand Hotel, Brighton, in 1984.

Many IRA members have been caught, tried in the courts and imprisoned. But the IRA claim prisoners should be treated as political prisoners, not as common criminals. IRA prisoners took part in hunger strikes (and some died from starvation) in an attempt to get this status. In the United States, suspected IRA men wanted for questioning back in Britain can be extradited (taken out of the country to face charges in British courts). Negotiations between the English and American governments is also helping to stop the flow of arms and cash that the large Irish community in the United States (many of whom are sympathetic to the IRA cause) send overseas. Violence by the IRA has been matched by the terrorist acts carried out by numerous Protestant paramilitary groups.

IRON AGE is the name given to a period in the early history of mankind when people began to use iron to make sharp knives to kill animals, axes for cutting wood, and swords with which to fight. The Iron Age came after the Bronze Age (see BRONZE AGE) and just before the period in which we are still living. Iron ores (the rocks and earth from which iron is extracted) are found in many parts of the world and are more easily obtained than

Left: British Museum. Right: Crown Copyright

Left: Bronze shield found in the River Thames in London. The people of the Iron Age still used bronze for many purposes. **Right**: Reconstruction of an early Iron Age farm at Little Woodbury in England.

copper (from which bronze is made) as they are normally found nearer the surface. Iron ore could be obtained and smelted (made into iron) locally, so it soon replaced bronze for use in tools and weapons. Bronze was kept for ornaments, rings, armlets, brooches, and pins as well as for many household goods such as buckets and dishes. Iron was smelted on charcoal fires and needed very little equipment so that it could easily be prepared by charcoal burners working in the forests.

The earliest people to discover how to use iron lived around or near the eastern shores of the Mediterranean Sea. The people in this area built cities and great palaces and temples long before those in the northern part of Europe. Iron was used in Asia Minor from about 2300 BC. Between 2000 and 1200 BC a remarkable people called the Hittites ruled much of Asia Minor and it is known that they also used iron (see HITTITES). An iron dagger was found in the famous tomb of the Egyptian pharaoh Tutankhamun, who lived in the middle of the 14th century BC.

Very slowly the knowledge of iron and its uses spread to the west, until at last it reached the island of Britain about 500 BC, a hundred years after it reached China. Iron was brought by traders travelling long distances to find markets for their goods or by tribes looking for fresh lands to cultivate. These peoples gradually moved west across Europe, and arrived in Britain between the 5th and 3rd centuries BC.

Iron Age Britain

These early Iron Age people have left many remains which can be seen today. Traces have been found of wooden huts and of hearths where the food was cooked and where blacksmiths worked to supply all the axes, sickles, and harnesses needed by the farmers who worked in the small, square fields near by.

At the time when these people were living peacefully in the south of England other iron-using people were settling down among the bronze-using people of Scotland, who were not used to the quiet farming life of the south. They all lived in hill forts, the walls of which were made with large stones and beams set crosswise. When set alight, the timber in these walls burned so fiercely that the stones were fused, or melted, together and became like glass. These forts are known as "vitrified" forts, from a word meaning glass-like. A large number of these forts were built along the western coasts of Scotland.

During the 2nd century BC other people settled in Britain, and these made even better use of iron than the first people. They decorated their brooches, mirrors, terret-rings (for threading the reins of horses), swords, and shields with beautiful designs.

The new invaders seem to have come up the Bristol Channel to the River Severn and the Welsh Marches (borders) and from there on to the west coast of Scotland. It may be that some of them traded with the inhabitants of Cornwall, who mined tin. Metal and pottery objects made by the new people have been found in the Cornish Iron Age villages of Chysauster and Carn Brea.

These people wore brooches which fastened rather like safety-pins and were often decorated. The brooches show that the invaders, who probably came from Brittany, western France, and Spain, brought with them the fashion of using brooches such as the swan-headed pins used by the first Iron Age people, to fasten their clothes instead of buttons.

The villages in Cornwall were small and usually had a group of houses set around a courtyard. Most of them were important centres of trade. In the Welsh Marches the settlers found they had to fight a good deal with the people who were living there when they came. They therefore built hill forts in which they could live in peace and security. Their camps were larger and with better fortifications than the camps in the south of England, which were surrounded by a ditch with a berm, or flat space, on the inner side and then a rampart with a timber facing. The rough countryside near the high Welsh mountains needed something stronger, however, and so high ramparts were built round the tops of the hills with two and sometimes three ditches outside. The earth thrown up from the last ditch was another obstacle to the enemy. The people who built these camps lived beneath the shelter of the ramparts in the hollow left when the rampart itself was made.

At Glastonbury and Meare in Somerset there were more homes of the same people, but instead of being protected by a rampart and ditch they were built on wooden posts driven into the marshes, like the lake dwellings of Switzerland. The objects found in these two sites show that they were very important trading centres to which goods came from long distances. The rounded pottery bowls with a design of curved and crossed lines were probably copied from metal bowls. Bone weaving-combs and many metal objects have also been found.

Iron Age Burials

An important Iron Age custom was that of burying an important man in a grave with his chariot. In tumuli (large mounds used as graves) in the Seine valley in France and in England, graves have been found containing two skeletons, one of a man and the other of his driver, in a crouching position, with the bones of a horse lying between the metal remains of the wheels of a wooden chariot. These finds show that it is possible that the Parisii people from France could have sailed across the North Sea to find new homes in England.

Courtesy, British Museum/ E. N. Kitson

Coins were first made in Britain shortly before the Romans came. The coin at top left has a portrait of Cunobelin (Cymbeline).

These movements were to get away from the Romans, who had conquered the tribes of Spain, the Alpine regions, and North Africa. The south of France was already ruled by the Romans, and they gradually made their way to the north, which was conquered by Julius Caesar in 60–58 BC. It is quite likely that the tribes who crossed over to Britain in the second Iron Age invasion did so to avoid being overcome by the Romans. They were probably closely related to the people already living in Britain.

These last invaders were the Belgae from northern France, who went to southeast England. The kings of the Atrebates, who settled in Hampshire, and of the Catuvellauni of Hertfordshire, had coins made with their names on them. The discovery of these coins in various parts of England shows how much fighting there was between these little kingdoms. These people lived on fairly high ground protected by a ditch and rampart, but in larger communities than had been known before.

As well as all the usual iron objects these people learnt how to make iron ploughshares with which they could cultivate heavier clay soil. They made their pottery on a wheel and as a result it was harder and better made than that of the earlier people. They buried their dead by burning their bones and placing the ashes in urns of remarkable shapes, and bronze figures and little statues were buried with them. These objects were ornamented in rather the same way as those of the Romans. This was a sign that the original Iron Age was coming to an end and with it the times that we call prehistoric, although in the sense that iron is still a valuable material in everyday life, we are still living in the Iron Age today.

IRON AND STEEL. Iron is one of the most common and useful metals. Steel, which is made from iron, but differs from it in chemical composition, strength, and toughness, is even more useful. Steel is the main building material for ships, railways, and cars. Without its strength, tall buildings and long bridges could not be built. What is more, people would have to live without electricity because iron and steel are the only commonly available inexpensive magnetic materials. Dynamos depend on ferro-magnetism (see DYNAMO), and heat-resisting steels are used to make boilers and steam turbines. In fact very few manufactured goods are made without the use of iron and steel machines.

Iron is one of the most abundant elements in the Earth, forming nearly 5 per cent of its crust. Scientists believe that the molten centre of the Earth itself is predominantly iron. It is found in all living organisms and is a component of haemoglobin in the blood and chlorophyll in green plants. Metallic iron is a silvery-white, fairly soft metal and is magnetic. It is rarely found in nature, except in the form of meteorites (see METEOR AND METEORITE), when the iron is usually found to be alloyed with about 7 per cent nickel. Iron freely oxidizes in moist air and therefore the iron in the Earth's crust is combined with oxygen as iron oxide, a red or black, hard, heavy mineral. The discovery of how to separate metallic iron from the mineral made possible the Iron Age in which we still live.

When the mineral form, iron ore or ironstone, contains more than about 20 per cent iron it may be worth mining. The world's main sources of iron ore lie in Russia, Australia, Canada, Brazil, India, the United States, South Africa, Sweden, and China. Other countries with important reserves are Venezuela, Spain, and Gabon. The deposits that are of most use are those that are nearest supplies of coal for smelting or near places where iron is needed. In Britain there is iron ore from Yorkshire to Dorset, and though the ore is not rich, the deposits are still worked because there is coal, and a market for the iron, close at hand.

Iron ore contains sand, clay, and water as impurities, together with other elements such as phosphorus and sulphur which are disadvantageous in steel and so must be removed.

Smelting Iron

Iron is separated from the ore by smelting in a blast furnace. The blast furnace is a very large steel tube, or stack, set on end and lined with fire-resisting bricks. The stack is fed continuously with a carefully blended mixture of ore, coke, and limestone, some of which has been heated together previously to form a clinker or "sinter".

Near the bottom of the furnace hot air is blown in through a pipe and a number of nozzles called *tuyères*. The coke burns fiercely as the hot air passes up through the "burden" combining with oxygen to form carbon monoxide which removes the oxygen from the iron ore. As the oxygen is removed, the iron melts and trickles down to collect in the bottom of the furnace as a molten pool on the hearth. The limestone "fluxes" the sand, clay, and other earthy impurities from the charge by reacting with them to form a liquid slag which floats on top of the iron in the hearth. It can also react with sulphur and phosphorus and remove a large proportion of these harmful elements.

The hot gases produced at the bottom of the furnace pass upwards through the stack. The gas (coal gas) emerging from the top of the stack is useful. It is hot and contains carbon monoxide which can be burnt to heat the in-going air blast, to generate steam power for blowing or pumping the air blast, and in some plants to generate electricity.

About every five hours molten iron is "tapped" or run through a tap hole into ladles or conveying vessels. It is then transferred either to steel-making furnaces in its liquid form, or to pig-casting machines where the molten iron is poured into moulds to make small blocks called "pigs". Slag is tapped approximately every two hours through a hole a little higher than the tap hole. Blast furnace slag is a useful by-product. It can be used for roadstone and railway ballast, some is "foamed" with steam for brickmaking, and some is granulated for cement manufacture.

Once lit, a blast furnace is kept going con-

Courtesy, British Steel

A 300-ton basic oxygen furnace being charged with molten iron.

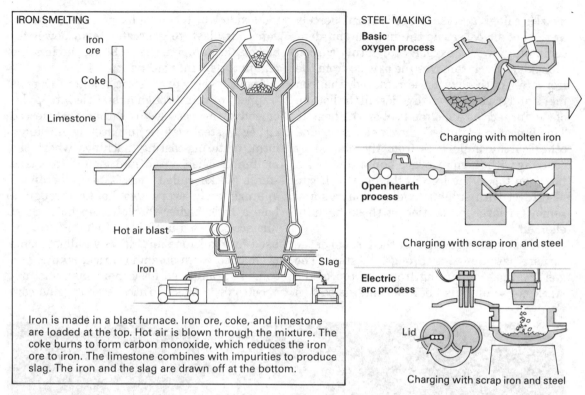

IRON SMELTING

Iron ore

Coke

Limestone

Hot air blast

Iron

Slag

Iron is made in a blast furnace. Iron ore, coke, and limestone are loaded at the top. Hot air is blown through the mixture. The coke burns to form carbon monoxide, which reduces the iron ore to iron. The limestone combines with impurities to produce slag. The iron and the slag are drawn off at the bottom.

STEEL MAKING

Basic oxygen process

Charging with molten iron

Open hearth process

Charging with scrap iron and steel

Electric arc process

Lid

Charging with scrap iron and steel

Iron smelting and the three principal methods of steel making today (above and page 57).

tinuously for up to six years or more. After this time its stack needs relining with heat-resisting bricks, mainly because of wear from the descending burden.

A rapid improvement in blast furnace technology has taken place. In 1930 the record production for any plant was about 1,000 tonnes (1,100 US tons) per day; in 1960 it had reached 3,000 (3,300 US tons); in 1970, 7,000 (7,700 US tons); in the 1980s a single furnace is designed to produce up to 10,000 tonnes (11,000 US tons) per day. To produce such large quantities of iron, the furnace has to be fed at great speed with enormous amounts of raw material. Modern furnaces have their air blast enriched with oxygen, steam or fuel in the form of oil or pulverized coal.

Pig Iron and Cast Iron

Most of the molten iron produced by the blast furnace is taken directly to the steel-making furnaces, and is not allowed to solidify. Some iron is required, however, for iron foundries (see FOUNDING), and therefore some molten iron is taken to pig-casting machines. These have a large number of metal moulds carried on an endless chain. Each mould is filled with molten iron and then is carried along the chain, being spray-cooled with water as it goes. As the mould tips over at the end of the track, the cast pig is tipped into a waiting railway wagon. The mould returns below the track to the start, being sprayed with white-wash on the way.

Pigs are the raw material for remelting in the *cupola*, the standard melting unit of an iron foundry. The cupola is rather like a blast furnace except that it is charged with pig iron and coke at the top. The hot gas is also allowed to burn or escape at the top. Remelting refines the iron to some extent, improving its quality. But even after casting into sand moulds, cast iron is still rather brittle. It is used for castings for domestic boilers and cookers, lawn mowers, motor car engine cylinder blocks and brake drums, ingot moulds for steel, rolls for rolling mills, and manhole covers and fire grates.

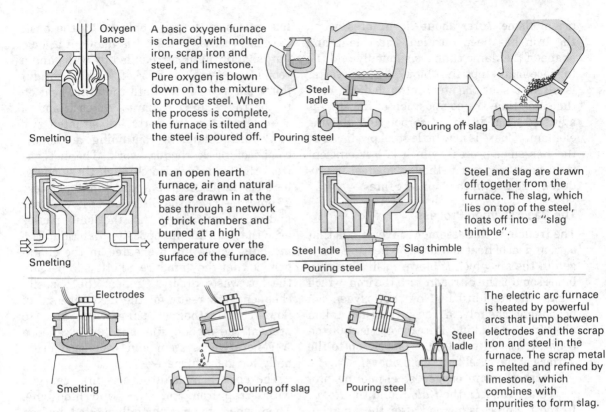

A basic oxygen furnace is charged with molten iron, scrap iron and steel, and limestone. Pure oxygen is blown down on to the mixture to produce steel. When the process is complete, the furnace is tilted and the steel is poured off.

Oxygen lance

Smelting

Steel ladle

Pouring steel

Pouring off slag

In an open hearth furnace, air and natural gas are drawn in at the base through a network of brick chambers and burned at a high temperature over the surface of the furnace.

Smelting

Steel and slag are drawn off together from the furnace. The slag, which lies on top of the steel, floats off into a "slag thimble".

Steel ladle

Slag thimble

Pouring steel

Electrodes

Smelting

Pouring off slag

Pouring steel

Steel ladle

The electric arc furnace is heated by powerful arcs that jump between electrodes and the scrap iron and steel in the furnace. The scrap metal is melted and refined by limestone, which combines with impurities to form slag.

Steel and Steel-Making

Steel is iron containing between 0.05 per cent and 1.5 per cent of carbon. The degree to which a steel can be hardened depends on its carbon content. The higher the carbon level, the harder and more wear resistant the steel can be made by heat treatment (see page 61.)

Most of the steel made is a simple mixture of iron and carbon and is commercially known as carbon steel. By mixing (alloying) carbon steel with other elements such as manganese, nickel, chromium, silicon, and molybdenum, alloy steels with special properties are made. High strength or hardness, shock or wear resistance, corrosion or heat resistance are examples of special properties of alloy steels. Most stainless steels contain 12 to 18 per cent of chromium and some nickel. The properties of steel depend not only on its composition, but also on its heat treatment. (See also ALLOY.)

Steel is made from molten pig iron by reducing the carbon content to the exact amount required, at the same time removing other impurities. Steel-making is therefore a refining process. Modern industrial society produces a lot of scrap iron and since scrap is easy to remelt it is an important commercial material for steel-making.

The Bessemer Process

The first bulk method of steel-making from molten iron was invented in 1856 by an Englishman, Henry Bessemer. (See BESSEMER, SIR HENRY.) An American, William Kelly, developed a similar process at about the same time. The principle of the Bessemer process is simply to blow air through molten iron for about 20 minutes. The molten iron is poured into a pear-shaped vessel (the converter) mounted on pivots which allow it to be tilted for filling, blowing, and emptying.

Air is blown into the molten iron through a series of nozzles or *tuyères* in the bottom of the vessel, and the oxygen of the air oxidizes, or burns out, the carbon and other impurities in the iron. The gaseous oxides produced rush out of the top of the vessel, burning with a bright flame. After about 20 minutes, when the iron has been purified, the colour and shape of the flame changes suddenly and the furnace man stops the "blow". The converter is tilted to pour the steel into a ladle, and at the same time the composition of the steel is adjusted by additions of carbon and alloying elements. There is now little steel produced by the Bessemer process, which is less efficient than more modern methods. No steel is produced this way in the United States.

The Basic Oxygen Process

The trouble with Bessemer converters is that a great deal of heat is wasted on heating nitrogen in the air which is blown in. It also combines some of the nitrogen with the iron, which makes the steel brittle. Now that oxygen can be bought cheaply, a revolution has taken place in steel-making. Pure oxygen is squirted by water-cooled nozzles or "lances" on to the surface of the steel bath from above.

The three main oxygen steel-making processes are the *LD*, the *Kaldo*, and the *Rotor*. In the LD process, named after the Austrian towns Linz and Donawitz where it was first developed, oxygen is injected at high pressure on to the surface of the steel bath in a huge container. Rapid refining takes place and in modern furnaces a 350-tonne (390-US ton) charge of 70 per cent molten iron and 30 per cent scrap can be converted to steel in 40 minutes. The process is relatively inexpensive. High phosphorus irons can be refined by the LD method if lime injection is combined with the oxygen. The lime produces an alkaline slag which absorbs the oxidized phosphorus from the metal. This slag is also a valuable phosphate fertilizer. The LD or basic oxygen furnace (BOF) is the primary steel-making unit of the world, making over 60 per cent of all steel produced.

The Kaldo and Rotor methods use the same principle as the LD furnace except that the vessels rotate slowly.

The Open Hearth Process

For almost a century the open hearth furnace was the main steel-making process but it has now been largely replaced by the basic oxygen process. The steel is made in a long, flat, shallow bath surrounded by walls and a roof of heat-resisting brick work. A bright flame passes over the bath radiating heat on to the raw material charge. At each end of the bath below the ports are situated two brickwork chambers containing a "honeycomb" of brick chequer-work. The hot gas from the furnace is led through these chambers before passing up a tall chimney. Every 20 minutes or so the direction of flow of gas and air is reversed so that the flame passes over the bath in the opposite direction. The incoming gases are preheated in the chambers so that they produce a hotter flame, and the hot waste products reheat the opposite chequer work ready for the next reversal of flow. This method of using waste heat to preheat the ingoing fuel and air is called a "regenerative" system and was used originally for glass furnaces.

The open hearth furnace is first charged with scrap iron and steel, and limestone. Then, when this has partially melted, molten iron is poured in. The oxygen for refining is supplied to the furnace by feeding in iron ore or mill scale, both of which are primarily iron oxide, or by injecting oxygen gas through water-cooled lances. (Mill scale is the outer skin that flakes off hot steel during rolling or forging.

When the steel reaches the correct carbon content it is "tapped" into a ladle, together with the slag which floats to the surface and overflows into a smaller ladle alongside. Alloying additions are thrown into the ladle as the metal runs out of the furnace tap holes. Open hearth furnaces of 350 tonnes (390 US tons) capacity may have a melting time of up to 10 hours, making it a slow process.

The Electric Arc Process

When steel of a high alloy quality is required, it is usually made in electric arc furnaces. The furnace may hold about 180 tonnes (200 US tons), and is a round shallow bath surrounded by a refractory wall. It has a domed roof which

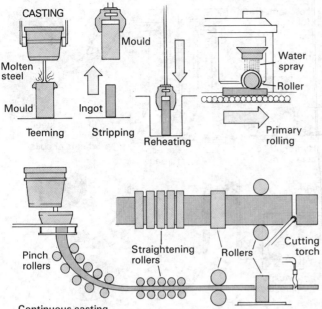

CASTING

Molten steel

Mould

Mould

Ingot

Teeming

Stripping

Reheating

Water spray

Roller

Primary rolling

Continuous casting

Pinch rollers

Straightening rollers

Rollers

Cutting torch

Casting steel. **Top:** Steel is cast into moulds to form ingots. When cool, the moulds are stripped off. The ingots are reheated and given a primary rolling before being taken to the rolling mill. **Bottom:** In continuous casting, molten steel is fed directly to a caster, which forms the steel into a continuous slab as it cools. The slab is then cut into billets.

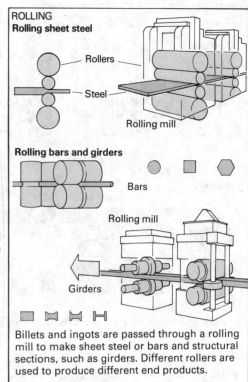

ROLLING
Rolling sheet steel

Rollers

Steel

Rolling mill

Rolling bars and girders

Bars

Rolling mill

Girders

Billets and ingots are passed through a rolling mill to make sheet steel or bars and structural sections, such as girders. Different rollers are used to produce different end products.

can be removed so that the cold scrap metal can be charged directly from above. The charge is heated by electric arcs from three carbon electrodes which are lowered through the roof. The lower ends of the electrodes do not touch the steel but the electric current jumps across to the steel in continuous sparks, or arcs, whose intense heat rapidly melts the scrap. The impurities of the steel are removed in much the same way as in the other processes. After taking samples to check the composition of the steel, and raking or pouring off the slag, the furnace is tilted to pour out the molten steel into a ladle.

The electric arc furnace is better for making high quality steels, because the heat source is independent of the chemical reactions in the steel bath and, being electrical, is easily controlled. It is possible to add larger quantities of alloying elements to the furnace than to the ladle and thus almost all high alloy steels, such as stainless steel, are made in this way. The process is now used also for large tonnages of more widely-used steels.

When extra purity is required, as for example in bearings, the steel is often tapped into a ladle in which it is then treated in a vacuum unit to extract dissolved gases.

Another type of electric furnace is the induction furnace. This is used mainly for special tool steels and as a small melting unit in foundries making steel castings. The melting pot, about the size and shape of a dustbin, is surrounded by a copper coil through which is passed a powerful electric current. Selected scrap and other pure raw materials are added to the pot where they are heated, melted, and mixed by electrical induction (see TRANSFORMER). Induction furnaces are often operated inside vacuum chambers to produce special heat resisting steels and nickel-chromium-cobalt alloys for gas turbines.

Shaping Steel

When the molten steel has been run off into a ladle it is then ready for the next stage – "teeming" or "casting". Some steel is poured

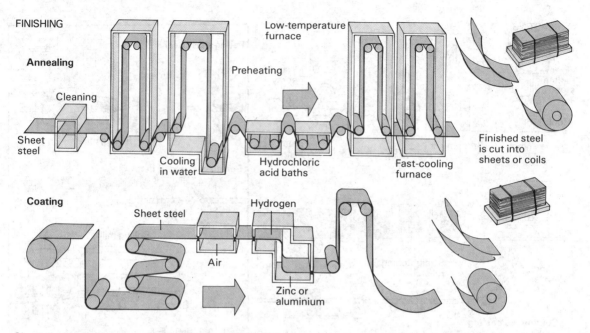

FINISHING

Annealing

Cleaning

Sheet steel

Low-temperature furnace

Preheating

Cooling in water

Hydrochloric acid baths

Fast-cooling furnace

Finished steel is cut into sheets or coils

Coating

Sheet steel

Hydrogen

Air

Zinc or aluminium

Sheet steel is finished by annealing (top), during which it is heated and cooled slowly to make it less brittle. The steel may also be coated (bottom) with zinc or aluminium, for example.

into prepared sand moulds to make steel castings. The remaining steel is "teemed", or emptied into metal moulds to produce ingots or billets for rolling and forging. Ingots are made by teeming into thick-walled cast iron moulds, and may vary from a few hundred kilograms (or pounds) to several hundred tons. The shaping of hot ingots by squeezing or hammering is described in the article FORGE.

Ingots intended for the rolling mill are usually less than 30 tonnes (33 US tons) in weight, the average size for making small bars, wire, and narrow strip being about 6 tonnes (6.5 US tons), while wide or thick plate ingots are usually about 25 tonnes (27 US tons) in weight.

A newer continuous casting method is used to produce small billets and slabs suitable for rolling. The molten steel is teemed into water-cooled copper moulds open at the top and bottom. As the steel solidifies in the mould it is withdrawn from the bottom in a continuous length. It can then be fed directly into the rolling mill.

More than 90 per cent of all the steel produced is shaped in rolling mills by passing hot ingots or billets through rollers arranged like those of a wringer. With smooth rollers the steel can be rolled into slabs and sheets; usually there are several sets of rollers, each set squeezing the sheet thinner. Thin sheet steel for tin cans is rolled in this way. By shaping the rolls with grooves and ridges they can be made to roll the steel into a great variety of long thin shapes. Examples are railway rails, girders for buildings, and round, square, and hexagonal bars for the engineering industry. In special cone-shaped rolls, set at an angle with a pointed rod called a mandrel between them, seamless tubes can be made. It is easy to shape hot steel and also to improve its properties, so that hot rolled or forged steel is tougher than a steel casting.

As the hot rolled section gets thinner it cools more rapidly, and to reheat it would require time and cost money. Many small sections are easily cold worked. Large quantities of thin gauge strip are cold rolled, rods are drawn through dies in wire manufacture, and large quantities of tubes are cold drawn. Cold-worked products are more accurately sized than hot rolled sections, and their surface finish is smoother and brighter.

Heat Treatment

Steel responds dramatically to heat treatment. After heating to red heat and very slowly cooling it is softened or *annealed*. To remove internal stresses left after casting or forging it can be heated and air cooled or *normalized*. Both these processes toughen the steel so that it can be bent or stretched without breaking, but they do not make it stronger. They are therefore also used to restore toughness and malleability after or between cold working operations.

Rapid cooling from red heat (800–900°C) (1470–1650°F) by *quenching*, or cooling, in brine, water, or oil hardens steel. The severity of the quench used depends on the type of steel and the hardness required. The most rapid quench is obtained in iced brine; less severe quenching is done in oil. A slow quenching is given by hot oil or molten lead baths. Some highly alloyed steels will harden by air cooling.

After quenching, most steels are too brittle to be useful, so they are reheated to a lower temperature (250–650°C) (480–1200°F) and cooled slowly to obtain a desirable combination of hardness, strength, and toughness. This treatment is known as *tempering*.

Sheet steel can be coated to prevent it from

All pictures courtesy, British Steel

Above: Molten iron being transported from a blast furnace in a "torpedo ladle" to a steel-making plant. **Right:** Steel being drawn down through a continuous caster. It passes through a water-cooled mould, which shapes it. Rollers support it while it cools.

Left: Steel being formed into structural sections, or girders, by being passed through a rolling mill when hot. **Above:** Very thin sheet steel, or steel strip, produced by cold rolling, is coiled up before being sold or taken to be coated.

rusting. A wide variety of substances are used including paints, varnishes, enamel, and a number of metals. The metals used are principally zinc, aluminium, chromium, tin, and lead, which is used mixed with tin; the steel is coated either by passing it through a bath containing the molten metal or by electroplating, which gives it a thinner coating (see ELECTROPLATING).

History

Iron objects have been discovered in many archaeological sites such as Ur of the Chaldees and within the Egyptian pyramids. The ancient Chinese, Indians, Greeks, and Romans knew about iron. The Greek poet Homer describes the heat treatment of iron in the *Odyssey*. The evidence suggests that the first iron was meteoric iron, highly prized for weapons and jewellery, and that the secret of smelting iron ore was not discovered before about 1500 BC. Iron was being worked in Britain before the Romans came, although the method of smelting was still very crude, and was surrounded by secrecy and magic.

The differences between iron and steel were only vaguely understood until the early 19th century. Before then the iron smelting furnace was simply a hearth above which extended a short chimney. The hearth was covered with charcoal up to the level of the blowhole, and a mixture of iron ore and charcoal was piled above (see CHARCOAL). After setting the charcoal alight the hearth was "blown" with a strong draught of air from bellows. The charcoal, being almost pure carbon, combined with the oxygen in the iron ore to form the gas carbon monoxide. A large, hot, pasty lump or "bloom" of iron and slag formed on the hearth and this was removed from the furnace and hammered into shape. The slag would be forced out of the "bloom" during forging. From time to time the forged bloom would be reheated before being beaten into bars. Iron made in this way contained many impurities, but it was valuable for making tools.

This iron was generally soft and not very suitable for weapons. Blacksmiths discovered by accident how to "steel" iron, by occasionally producing a batch richer in carbon than usual, and therefore capable of being hardened by quenching in water, then toughened by tempering. Forged bars were heated in beds of charcoal until by trial and error the process of *cementation* was evolved. The sword makers of Toledo, Damascus, and Japan learned to forge together bars of low and high carbon steel to produce sharp, tough blades capable of slicing through bronze and iron weapons and armour.

Early in the 18th century the English "ironmaster" Abraham Darby and his son developed the forerunner of the modern blast furnace. They used coke as the fuel and source of carbon, and steam engines to produce a higher blast of air to the furnaces. Coke is a good source of carbon, the impurities having been driven off in coke-making as gas, and it was also strong enough to support the iron ore and limestone in the furnace burden, creating a porous stack through which a fierce blast could be driven. Higher temperatures and faster melting rates were made possible, and the quantity of coke-iron produced in the world increased from a tiny amount to more than 100 million tonnes (110 million US tons) a year in the 19th century. Iron castings replaced wrought iron, wood, copper, and brass for many uses. By the beginning of the 19th century there were few charcoal furnaces left and the British iron and steel industry had moved to the coalfields of south Staffordshire, South Wales, and south Yorkshire.

In about 1740 Benjamin Huntsman discovered a way of melting steel in small quantities and casting ingots. He was able to make a clay mix which could be moulded into crucible pots strong enough to contain bars of blister steel produced by cementation while they were melted by heat from a charcoal furnace. The crucible was then lifted out of the furnace by hand tongs and had to remain intact until the liquid steel was teemed into cast iron moulds. Melting the steel removed the inconsistencies, and Huntsman's steel was a great improvement on the bars made by the cementation process. Huntsman kept his method secret for many years, but eventually his process became known, and was eagerly used by the cutlers and tool-steel makers of Sheffield in Yorkshire.

In 1784 Henry Cort devised the puddling furnace in which molten pig iron was stirred with rods to mix air and slag into it. The puddling operation removed silicon, manganese, and most of the phosphorus impurities before the carbon reacted with air to escape and burn as a gas. The stirred pasty mass left in the hearth was removed from time to time and passed to a water powered "shingling hammer" to be forged. The iron made was almost pure, and was softer and less brittle than cast iron. It was used for building bridges, ships, and machines and for making railway rails with another of Cort's developments, the rolling mill.

Bessemer's converter (1856) was the first method of making steel in bulk. It was first introduced into the United States in 1864 at Wyandotte, Michigan. A later development was the open hearth furnace, invented in England by William Siemens and his brother Friedrich in 1857, but developed in France by Emile and Pierre Martin. This process was especially successful in the United States as the iron ore found there has a higher phosphorus content and it cannot be so well refined in the Bessemer converter.

Another way to make use of this kind of ore was introduced by the English engineers Percy Gilchrist and Sidney G. Thomas, who in 1877 lined a Bessemer converter with dolomite and added limestone to the melt in order to remove the phosphorus.

In 1954 the first vessels for use with the basic oxygen process were installed in the United States at the McLonth steel plant in Detroit. The world's leading producers of crude steel and pig iron are Russia, Japan, and the United States.

IRRIGATION is the process of supplying water to land to help crops grow on it. In some countries, such as Egypt, no crops can grow without irrigation, and all Egyptian farms have to be irrigated. In other countries, irrigation is needed to grow particular crops. For example, the world's most important cereal crop, rice, is usually grown in flooded paddyfields. Nearly 65 per cent of the world's total irrigated land is in Asia, and most of it is used for producing rice. In many countries irrigation is used to increase yields of crops that could be grown without irrigation. Irrigated land may give double the amount of crop that can be obtained from land that is not irrigated.

The ancient civilizations of Egypt, India, China, Assyria, and Babylon depended on irrigation, which must have developed from the natural overflow of rivers. On monuments 4,000 years old there are pictures of people scooping water out of the Nile to pour over their fields. The Greeks irrigated their land and the Romans began the splendid irrigation systems of Italy, now among the best in the world.

When the Arabs swept through the lands along the Mediterranean Sea, many hundreds of years ago, they introduced irrigation to all the countries they conquered. In Spain, for example, canals and reservoirs built by the Moors are still in use. When the Spaniards conquered Mexico they found that the Indians there already knew about irrigation.

How Irrigation Developed

The simplest form of irrigation is the diversion of water from a stream or river into a channel which carries it on to cultivated land. The irrigated land must be lower than the river so that the water can flow down on to it. Ancient irrigation systems were often based on the annual flood of rivers after the rainy season or when the snow melted in the mountains. In the valley of the Tigris and Euphrates you can still see the remains of large irrigation canals built more than 4,000 years ago to catch the floodwaters that pour down from the mountains every May. (See TIGRIS RIVER and EUPHRATES RIVER.)

In the course of time, people found that more water could be saved by building a dam across a river to catch and hold the water. Unfortunately the ancient engineers were not able to build dams strong enough to withstand severe floods and they were usually washed away after a few years.

In irrigation, water often has to be lifted from its normal channel to a higher level from which it can run over the surrounding countryside. At first, people baled the water out of the streams by hand with buckets or clay pots and poured it on the ground or into little ditches, which ran honeycomb fashion over the fields.

But soon this method was replaced by labour-saving devices such as the Archimedean screw, said to have been invented by the Greek scientist Archimedes in Syracuse about 200 BC. It consists of a long wooden tube with a screw or spiral coil inside. One end of the tube is placed in the river or canal and the other on the bank. Turning the tube round forces the water up the spiral and out at the top. Variations of the Archimedean screw are still used in Egypt and India to lift water up to about 1.3 metres (4 feet). It is man powered and has the advantage of being portable.

The next stage was to invent water-lifting devices that could be driven by animals. The water wheel was the most successful of these and is still used throughout the developing world. It looks like an old-fashioned mill wheel, but it scoops up water in buckets as it turns, instead of being turned itself by the water. As the scoops reach the top of the wheel, the water runs out at the higher level and into the irrigation channels. The water wheel is connected by a series of gears to a big horizontal wheel which is turned by an ox or donkey walking round and round in a circle.

Water-lifting systems changed little until the development of engines powered by steam, oil, and electricity in the 19th and 20th centuries.

Modern Irrigation

It is easier, of course, to irrigate fields near the river, or whatever the source of water is, but canals can be dug to carry water to land further away. Sometimes, as in China and Italy, these canals are big enough for boats, so that they serve two purposes. They make the land

fertile and they act as waterways for barges to carry away crops from the farms.

In places where the rain falls heavily only at certain times of the year water is stored until it is needed. The most efficient way of storing water is to build a dam across a river so that the water collects in a reservoir behind it. Dams are constructed in upland areas, usually where a river valley narrows between hills and where as much water as possible can be held behind the dam in a reservoir. The water can then be run off in canals to the surrounding country. (See also CANAL; DAM; RESERVOIR.)

India and Pakistan have monsoon climates in which most rain falls during late summer and autumn. Water conservation and irrigation are therefore vital and it is not surprising to find that these countries have some of the largest dams ever built. The Mangla Dam on the Jhelum River in Pakistan, for instance, is more than 3 kilometres (2 miles) long.

Egypt is a desert country and relies entirely on the Nile for water. Until recently the flow of the Nile was regulated by barrages (dams of low height but great length), that controlled the river's annual flood. But these did not allow much water to be stored. Not until the completion of the Aswan High Dam could the Nile's waters be stored in a huge man-made lake.

Irrigation in North America

Whereas in much of the world irrigation is government sponsored, in Canada most of the irrigation work has been handled by private individuals and private companies. By far the largest project is that developed by the Canadian Pacific Company in Alberta, by which water can be supplied to more than 160,000 hectares (400,000 acres) of land. An important part of the development of this project was the building of the Bassano Dam. There are also large areas in Saskatchewan and British Columbia which have been made available for agriculture by means of irrigation.

In the United States little was done in the way of organized irrigation work until the last

ZEFA

Spectrum

ZEFA

ZEFA

ZEFA

Forms of irrigation. **Top left**: An irrigated plantation in Thailand. **Top right**: An Archimedean screw being used to raise water out of a river. **Above left**: Cattle-driven water wheels are common in such countries as Egypt. **Above**: Clay pots used on a water wheel in India to scoop up water. **Left**: Water from a pipe being fed directly into irrigation ditches.

Right: Border dyke irrigation is practised by a farmer on oat and alfalfa crops in North America. A small wooden gate regulates the water flow.
Below: Water flows from an irrigation ditch into an underground pipe, through which it is carried to the farmlands beyond.

Courtesy, B. C. McLean – Soil Conservation Service (right); US Department of Agriculture (below)

part of the 19th century. At first there was so much land that was naturally suitable for farming that there seemed no need to develop the arid regions. But as settlers arrived and advanced further west, the need for irrigation was felt. The Mormons, who settled near the Great Salt Lake in 1847, were pioneers in setting up a system of irrigation.

After 1901, when Theodore Roosevelt became president, much attention was given to the irrigation needs of the country. Public money received from selling lands in western states was used to construct irrigation work and the government built the necessary dams and canals to deliver the water to the farmers. The farmers paid for the water that they used, and the money received was used to build more irrigation works.

Many American dams were built wholly or partially for irrigation purposes. These include the Hoover on the Colorado River, the Grand Coulee on the Columbia River in Washington, and the Shasta on the Sacramento River in California.

After a dam has been built and the water has been stored, canals must be constructed to carry the water where it is needed. The building of these canals often presents difficult engineering problems. In order to carry the water on the most direct route, tunnels are pierced through mountains. Where the canals pass down steep slopes, it is frequently necessary to build bulkheads along their courses to keep the water from flowing so fast that it will wash away the banks. In other places the water is led down one steep slope and up another by means of siphons (see SIPHON).

From an engineering standpoint, the Colorado-Big Thompson project is one of the most spectacular ever undertaken in the development of the water resources of the West. The outstanding feature of the development is the 20-kilometre (13-mile) Alva B. Adams Tunnel under the Rocky Mountains. It was designed to divert surplus water from the western slope of the Rockies to water-deficient areas on the eastern slope. The transfer of water through this tunnel provides extra irrigation for about 290,000 hectares (720,000 acres). Power plants at the dams and along the main canals generate electricity for farms and for irrigation pumping.

Australian Irrigation

Early settlers in Australia diverted the course of the Murray, Loddon, Campaspe, and Goulburn Rivers to provide irrigation. An important step was taken by the government of Victoria when they persuaded the Chaffey brothers of California, who were experienced irrigators, to establish new projects in Australia. About ten per cent of cultivated land in Australia relies on irrigation. Some of the main schemes are centred on the Murray-Darling Basin (Victoria), the Murrumbidgee (New South Wales), the Dawson Valley (Queensland), and the Preston Valley (Western Australia).

Methods of Irrigation

When irrigation water reaches a farm, there are three main methods a farmer can use to get it to his crops: surface, sub-surface, and overhead irrigation.

Surface irrigation. The most commonly used type of surface irrigation is flood irrigation. Crops are flooded in level basins surrounded by small earth banks. Rice is the main crop irrigated in this way. Here the basins are known as paddy fields. Flood irrigation is also used for fodder, cereals, cotton, groundnuts and orchards.

Another surface method is furrow irrigation, where the water runs along gently sloping furrows and soaks into the earth. This method is the most widely used for all crops that can be grown on ridges between the furrows. Potatoes, sugar beet, maize, and orchards can be irrigated in this way.

Trickle irrigation is another method of surface irrigation. It is used for market garden produce such as lettuces and tomatoes that are grown in rows. It is very expensive and only used for crops that have a high value. Small pipes with nozzles at intervals along them are placed along the rows and water at low pressure trickles into the soil over the roots. The nozzles have to be kept clean so that they do not become clogged.

Sub-surface irrigation. In sub-surface irrigation porous pipes or pipes with holes in them are buried in the soil near crop roots and supplied with water at low pressure. This, too, is an expensive method and the holes in the pipes often get clogged.

Courtesy, Bill Mann – US Department of Agriculture (left), E. E. Hertzog/Bureau of Reclamation, US Department of the Interior (right).

Surface irrigation, such as that supplied by a sprinkler rig (above left) or by a system of furrows (above right), is normally used where the land is sloping, so that there is adequate drainage.

Overhead irrigation. Here the water is sprayed or sprinkled over the crops. It is pumped by pipe to various types of sprinklers which throw the water out in droplets like rain. The pressure of the water makes the sprinklers revolve, so they can cover a very wide area. Overhead irrigation is probably the most effective system for farmers growing a variety of crops since it is very flexible. Like an Archimedean screw the rigs can be moved about and used where the farmer needs them, even on relatively steep slopes.

A farmer can sometimes save his crop from being killed by frost by turning on the sprinkler system, because the water can thaw the soil, if the frost is not too severe.

Drainage

Whatever system of irrigation is used, it is important to drain the land well, otherwise the soil becomes waterlogged. There are very few areas where the natural drainage is good enough to deal with the extra water introduced by irrigation. Some schemes, in which the drainage was not properly considered, have brought about smaller instead of larger crops and a few have caused the land to be abandoned.

This is because in dry areas the alkaline salts (see ALKALI) that rivers and ground water contain naturally are left behind when the water evaporates and over a period become concentrated in the soil. This makes the land useless for agriculture. Good drainage allows the water to drain away, instead of evaporating, carrying away the salts with it.

At present, just over a quarter of the land in the world is cultivated. Much of the rest cannot be cultivated by present methods, but there are still large areas that could be opened up by modern methods, including in many cases irrigation and drainage. (See also DRAINAGE.)

IRVING, Sir Henry (1838–1905), whose original name was John Henry Brodribb, was one of the most famous English actors of all time. He was born in Somerset, England, the son of a salesman. After leaving school in London, Irving became a clerk and spent his free time going to the theatre and acting in an amateur theatrical company. He spent a small legacy from an uncle on wigs, swords, and theatrical costumes.

Irving's first stage success was in an amateur production of *Romeo and Juliet,* whereupon he decided to give up his clerical job and become a full-time member of a theatrical company which toured all over Great Britain and Ireland. At first he acted only in non-speaking roles. In the course of three years, Irving played over 400 parts in 330 plays, and received a thorough theatrical training. He continued with this company for ten years, and scored his first success in 1866 in a London play called *Hunted Down.* In the years that followed, Irving emerged as one of the leading actors of his day.

In 1878, Irving became the manager of the

Sir Henry Irving as Shylock in *The Merchant of Venice* (1878). This was one of his greatest performances.

Lyceum Theatre in London, and created a strong and loyal company around him. He spent huge sums of money on elaborate costumes and stage sets. Ellen Terry, the actress, joined Irving's company as the leading lady. This was the start of one of the most famous partnerships in the history of the English stage, a partnership which lasted 24 years. They performed together in many plays, including *Hamlet* and *The Merchant of Venice*, and people thronged to the Lyceum to see them. Irving's company toured America, and in the years that followed its success grew and the repertoire expanded.

A young critic, George Bernard Shaw (see SHAW, BERNARD) criticized some of the plays that Irving put on. He regarded them as being without literary merit and felt that a great actress like Ellen Terry was wasting her time acting in them. Shaw tried to persuade Irving to put on his play, *The Man of Destiny*, and a work by the serious Norwegian playwright, Henrik Ibsen (see IBSEN, HENRIK), but Irving was not interested. He was successful and had no intention of changing his policy. In 1895, Irving became the first theatrical person to receive a knighthood for his work.

In 1897 a devastating fire burned most of the stored stage scenery in the Lyceum Theatre and the insurance did not cover the losses. A year later Irving fell seriously ill and the company was forced to tour without him. As a result fewer people came to their performances. During the next four years this great and popular company declined and finally went into liquidation in 1902. Irving was penniless when he died at 68, after a performance at the Theatre Royal in Bradford.

IRVING, Washington (1783–1859), was one of the first United States authors to win fame in Europe. He is remembered for his humorous stories, essays, books of travel, and biographies. His best-known stories, "Rip Van Winkle" and "The Legend of Sleepy Hollow", are among the most treasured American literary works.

BBC Hulton Picture Library

The American writer Washington Irving, creator of "Rip Van Winkle" and "The Legend of Sleepy Hollow".

Irving was born in New York City, the 11th and last child of a wealthy merchant. As a boy he spent much of his time reading. Later he began to study law, but he liked writing and the social life of the city better than studying. At 19 he wrote some humorous articles for his brother Peter's newspaper, the *Morning Chronicle*, signing himself "Jonathan Oldstyle, Gent".

To improve his health, Irving travelled in Europe for two years. When he returned in 1806, he was admitted to the New York bar as a lawyer. But instead of practising law, he spent his time writing. With the help of his brother William and a friend, J. K. Paulding, Irving wrote 20 humorous sketches on the literary, social, and political life of New York, which were published in a book called *Salmagundi* (1808).

In 1809 Irving published *A History of New York, From the Beginning of the World to the End of the Dutch Dynasty, by Diedrich Knickerbocker*. He wrote this comic history of New York as a Dutch city to make fun of the style of writing then used by historians. The book also poked fun at old Dutch customs and people, and at some of the politicians of Irving's own time.

As a partner in his brothers' business, Irving went to Liverpool, England, in 1815. Three years later, when the family firm went bankrupt, Irving decided to earn his living as an author. During 1819 and 1820 he published a series of stories and sketches which he called *The Sketch Book of Geoffrey Crayon, Gent.* Although most of *The Sketch Book* was made up of essays on English life and manners, it contained "Rip Van Winkle" and "The Legend of Sleepy Hollow". The book was widely read, highly praised, and made Irving famous in North America and in Europe.

Irving followed this success with a similar book, *Bracebridge Hall* (1822), and *Tales of a Traveller* (1824), which contained stories and sketches gathered during a tour of Germany. From 1826 to 1829 he was part of the United States legation (embassy) in Spain. Using official documents, he wrote *A History of the Life and Voyages of Columbus* (1828). From his years in Spain he also wrote *The Conquest of Granada* (1829) and *The Alhambra* (1832).

Having served as secretary of the United States legation in London for two years, Irving returned to the United States in 1832, after an absence of 17 years. He was welcomed warmly as the first United States author to gain international fame. In 1835 he travelled to the Western frontier of America and later published several books based on the West. The following year he settled at Tarrytown, New York, on the Hudson River.

In 1842, Irving accepted an appointment as minister to Spain. After living abroad for three years, first in Madrid and then in London, he returned to his home, which he called Sunnyside. There he lived the rest of his life, and finished his huge five-volume biography, *The Life of George Washington* (1855–59), which he felt was his most important work. He was buried at Sleepy Hollow, near Tarrytown.

ISLAM is the name that the prophet Muhammad gave to the religion of the Muslims. It is an Arabic word which originally meant "submission" and has come to mean "submission to God". There are over 550 million Muslims in the world, nearly all of whom live in the continents of Asia and Africa. From its origins in Arabia, Islam has spread to North Africa, the Middle East, Pakistan, and Indonesia. Far smaller numbers of Muslims live in Australasia, China, North America, most European countries, and in the southern part of the USSR.

Like Christians and Jews, Muslims are monotheistic, which means that they believe in the existence of only one God, whom they call Allah. (In Arabic this means "the God".) These three religions (Christianity, Judaism, and Islam) have other links as well, for they share many of the stories and traditions that are told in the Old Testament of the Bible. Adam, Noah, Abraham, Ishmael, Moses, and David are all mentioned in the Muslims' holy book. Some of the Jewish and Christian prophets are prophets of Islam also. Jerusalem is a holy city to Muslims, as it is to Christians and Jews. Muslims have the story of Jesus Christ in their holy book, but they regard him as a prophet, not as the Son of God.

Muslims believe that the greatest and the last of the prophets was Muhammad (see MUHAMMAD). He was born about AD 570 in Mecca (Arabia), which has become the holy city of Islam. According to Muhammad, God revealed himself to man through his chosen prophets; among the major ones were Adam, Noah, Abraham, Moses, Jesus, and, finally, Muhammad. God gave the Law to Moses, the Gospels to Jesus, and the Koran to Muhammad. The *Koran* or *Qur'an* is the holy book of Islam. *Qur'an* comes from an Arabic word meaning "recitation". (See KORAN.) It governs the whole of a Muslim's life, for it describes how a Muslim should live. It sets out the duties of parents to their children, of masters to their servants, and of the rich to the poor. One section contains the laws of marriage and divorce, and says how possessions are to be divided when the owner dies.

The Koran lays down five main duties for all followers of Islam. They must recite the creed, which says, "There is no god but Allah; and

Muhammad is the prophet of God" at least once in their lifetime. They must pray five times a day: at dawn, just after noon, before sunset, just after sunset, and during the early part of the night. A Muslim washes his face, hands, and feet before he prays, and faces in the direction of Mecca while he prays. He prays wherever he is and need not necessarily go to a place of worship. (A Muslim place of worship is called a mosque; see MOSQUE.) Friday is the Muslim holy day, and in place of the prayer just after midday there are services in the mosques during the afternoon. The third duty of Muslims is to give alms (gifts of money) to help the poor. The fourth is to fast during the month called Ramadan, for this month is associated with God's giving of the Koran. Muslims must not eat or drink between sunrise and sunset during Ramadan. People who are ill or making a journey are permitted to eat at the normal times, but should fast when they are better or have finished their journey.

The fifth duty is to make a pilgrimage to Mecca. The Koran says that every Muslim should do this once in his life "if he is able"; that is, if he has enough money and is strong enough to make the journey. The pilgrimage, called *hajj*, is described in the article MECCA. When the religious ceremonies in Mecca are completed the pilgrims often visit Medina, further north, where Muhammad spent part of his life and where he was buried.

These Islamic duties are based on the writings of the Koran and the *sunnah*. The *sunnah* are the sayings and deeds of Muhammad that were collected together after his death by some of his followers.

Most Muslims belong to the orthodox, or Sunni, branch of Islam, so called because they believe in the accuracy of the *sunnah*. A smaller number, called Shiite Muslims, reject the *sunnah* and follow the teachings of Muhammad's son-in-law, Ali, who they believe was Muhammad's rightful successor. The majority of Shiites live in the Middle East, particularly in Iran, Lebanon, Iraq, and North Yemen.

To Muslims, Islamic Law, or the Shariah, is of fundamental importance. It was laid down by early Islamic teachers, and sets out not only how men and women should behave in their dealings with other people and towards the country in which they live, but also how they

IPA Picture Library

Pilgrims encircle the Ka'bah, in the Great Mosque in Mecca. The Ka'bah is an ancient shrine, which rests, according to legend, on foundations built by Abraham and Ishmael. Muslims believe it to be the holiest place on Earth.

ZEFA

Nigerians worshipping at a mosque in Kano. Almost half the people of Nigeria are Muslims.

should conduct their private lives and how they should worship god. Some countries, such as Saudi Arabia and Iran, are governed according to Islamic Law.

In recent years, Islam has been one of the fastest-growing world religions. In some countries, Muslims have resisted changes brought about by Western ways. For example, in Iran religious leaders brought about an "Islamic revolution" (see IRAN). In developing nations as well as in oil-rich lands such as Libya and Saudi Arabia, Islam has a strong influence on government as well as on the everyday lives of believers.

ISLAMABAD is the capital of Pakistan. The name means "city of Islam" or "city of peace". The city's area is compact, covering some 65 square kilometres (25 square miles). The seaport city of Karachi, chosen as the capital when Pakistan was founded in 1947, was found unsuitable and a new site was found in the north of Pakistan about 15 kilometres (9 miles) northeast of Rawalpindi. The name Islamabad was chosen in 1960. Building began in the following year and all the ministries, or central government offices, were moved there by 1969. The city combines tra-

ditional Islamic architecture with modern western office and administrative buildings.

Islamabad lies nearly 610 metres (2,000 feet) above sea-level. It is drained by the Kurang River (a tributary of the Indus) and a dam forms a clear lake in the area set aside as a national park. An expanse of natural terraces and meadows surrounds the city.

Besides areas for government buildings and national institutions, Islamabad is divided into housing zones each forming a self-contained township, as well as industrial and trading zones. There are also two universities, the Grand National Mosque, and the President's House.

The population of Islamabad is about 77,000, which is well below several other Pakistani cities, which have populations of over one million.

ISLAND. Any piece of land, large or small, with water all round it, is an island. The largest of all islands is made up of the three continents of Asia, Africa and Europe, while the second largest is formed by North and South America. However, when people speak of islands they are usually thinking of smaller pieces of land than continents, and of these Greenland is the biggest.

Islands are of two main kinds, called continental and oceanic islands. Continental islands are really portions of larger lands which have been cut off by the sea. This can happen for two reasons – the sinking of the level of the land or the rising of the level of the sea. During one period, for instance, England was joined to the continent of Europe. Then the Earth's crust sank and the North Sea and the English Channel spread until they joined, and so Great Britain became an island. If the sinking land is mountainous, the valleys may be covered and the ridges changed into peninsulas and islands. This is how the many islands off the west coasts of Canada and Scotland were formed. Continental islands are, naturally, very like the mainland from which they have been separated.

Oceanic islands rise from the depths of the oceans far from the continents. Examples of this kind of island are Ascension and St. Helena in the Atlantic Ocean and the countless islands of the South Pacific Ocean. They usually have few kinds of land plants and animals. Birds and insects are often the chief animals, while the plants are those whose seeds have been carried there by birds or by ocean currents. (See COCONUT, for example.) Oceanic islands are often the crests of high mountain ridges rising from the ocean floor. Some are the tips of underwater volcanoes, while in warm seas many are made of coral built by tiny animals. (See CORAL REEF.)

ISRAEL. The republic of Israel on the south-eastern shore of the Mediterranean Sea was founded in 1948. It is bounded on the north by Lebanon, on the east by Syria and Jordan, and on the south by Egypt. As well as a Mediterranean shore, Israel has a short coastline on the Red Sea.

In the north are the hills of Galilee (see GALILEE) The lowlands on the west coast widen into the fertile plains which border the Mediterranean. The southern half of the country is a dry sandy area called the Negev.

In the east the River Jordan forms part of the frontier between Israel and Jordan. It rises in Jordan and flows from Israel's northern border southwards into the Sea of Galilee (also known as Lake Tiberias) and finally into the Dead Sea, which lies about 400 metres (1,300 feet) below sea-level.

Israel has hot dry summers and cool

ZEFA

The foothills of the Samarian mountains seen from the Jordan valley. This territory, on the west bank of the River Jordan, is disputed with Jordan but has been occupied by Israel since 1967.

winters. The highland and coastal areas in the north receive more than 400 millimetres (16 inches) of rain annually, but rain in the desert regions of the south is very sparse.

Forests of oak and pine once covered much of the country but were cut down for timber in ancient times. Only recently have more trees been planted on the slopes. Wildlife includes gazelles, wild boars, and gecko lizards.

Peoples and Economy

Most of the people of Israel are Jews (see JEWS AND JUDAISM). Jews from all over the world have settled in the country since 1948 and even today only about 57 per cent of the Jewish population were born in Israel: the remainder are immigrants from Europe, the United States, Asia, and Africa. The official language is Hebrew, but Arabic is also spoken, because there are about 600,000 Arabs living in Israel. Most of the Arabs are Muslim (see ISLAM). There are also smaller Christian communities, who mainly speak Arabic. Many of the Jewish immigrants from Europe and North America are technicians and scientists, and they have helped Israel

to become one of the most highly developed countries in the world.

Israel is a democratic republic, with an elected parliament called the Knesset. The head of state is the president, but the government is led by the prime minister. Since 1950 the capital of the country has been Jerusalem, but this has not been recognized by other countries, and will not be until Arab-Israeli disputes are settled. Other large cities are Tel Aviv-Yafo and Haifa, both on the Mediterranean. (See JERUSALEM; TEL AVIV-YAFO.)

Road transport is more important than rail. Israel has three deep-water ports: Haifa and Ashdod on the Mediterranean, and Elat on the Red Sea. The international airport at Lod handles the flights of El Al, Israel's airline.

Israel is a larger exporter of agricultural products, especially citrus fruit such as oranges, grapefruit, and lemons. Other crops include tomatoes, cotton, wheat, potatoes, apples, sugar-beet, and grapes. Vegetables are grown as an early season crop for export to European markets. Turkeys are also a major export, and sheep and cattle are raised.

Agriculture has been increasingly mechanized, and the desert region of the northern Negev has been irrigated. Many farms are organized as *kibbutzim*. These are large settlements, where the workers share the earnings equally among themselves. They include social centres and schools and increasingly are earning money from tourism and high-technology industries. Fish are caught in the Sea of Galilee and also in the Mediterranean.

FACTS ABOUT ISRAEL

AREA: 20,700 square kilometres (7,992 square miles).
POPULATION: 4,563,000 (1989).
GOVERNMENT: Independent republic.
SEAT OF GOVERNMENT: Jerusalem, 482,700 (1987).
GEOGRAPHY: In the north is a plateau crossed from north to south by mountains and broken by great depressions. Along the coastline is a fertile plain. Most of the southern part of the country is desert. The Great Rift Valley runs through the country.
CITIES: Tel Aviv-Yafo, 319,500; Haifa, 223,200; Ramat Gan, 115,600; Bat-Yam, 132,800; Holon, 143,600; Petah-Tikwa 132,100; Beersheba 114,600.
ECONOMY. Products and exports.
    Agriculture: Fruit, vegetables, cotton, wheat, cattle, sheep, goats, chickens, timber, fishing.
    Minerals: Coal, petroleum, natural gas, phosphate, potash, phosphoric acid.
    Manufacturing: Cement, flour, polyethylene, paper and cardboard, ammonium sulphate.
    Exports: Machinery and electronics, diamonds, agricultural products, textiles and clothing, processed food, beverages, tobacco.
EDUCATION: Education is free and compulsory between the ages of 5 and 15.

Minerals include potash, phosphates, copper, and salt from the Dead Sea. (See DEAD SEA.) About a fifth of Israel's fuel comes from oil and natural gas in the Negev. In recent years industry has grown rapidly; the chief industries include electronics, food processing, the cutting and polishing of diamonds, and the manufacture of textiles, clothing, cement, chemicals, and military equipment. Tourism is another important money-earner; the country receives over 1 million visitors a year.

History

Israel was founded in 1948. The long history of the Jewish people before that date is told in the article Jews and Judaism. After World

Hutchison Library

The city of Haifa, on the Mediterranean coast, is Israel's principal port. It has important oil refineries.

War II, in which more than 6 million Jews died at the hands of the Nazis, the Jewish people fought more strongly than ever for a country of their own. In 1947 it was agreed by the United Nations that the area called Palestine should be divided into two states, one Jewish and one Arab, and that British rule (on behalf of the United Nations) should end. The Arabs would not accept this decision.

As soon as British rule ended in May 1948, Israel proclaimed itself an independent country with Chaim Weizmann as president and David Ben-Gurion as prime minister. At once it was attacked by the neighbouring Arab states of Lebanon, Syria, Iraq, Jordan, and Egypt. A fierce and bitter war ended in 1949. When peace was made, Israel was left in possession of several areas that the United Nations had agreed in 1947 should belong to the Arabs. Nevertheless Israel was admitted to the United Nations in May 1949.

In 1950 the parliament of Israel passed a

law that declared every Jew had the right to come and live in Israel. Many Jews came from abroad, and were first settled in camps, while roads and houses were built rapidly. The position of Jerusalem, which was supposed to be an international city, remained unsettled, for Israel ignored the agreement and adopted the city as its capital.

Israel has faced enmity from its Arab neighbours ever since its creation. There have been three Israeli-Arab wars; in 1956, 1967, and 1973. In 1956 Israel invaded the Egyptian territory of Sinai and captured the Gaza Strip. A cease-fire was arranged and early in 1957 a United Nations Emergency Force replaced the occupying Israeli troops. Then in 1967 the Egyptians ordered all UN forces out of the Egypt-Israel border region and war broke out between the two countries. It was known as the "Six-Day War" because within six days the Israelis had defeated the forces of Egypt, Jordan, Syria, and Iraq. Israel captured the Sinai Peninsula and the Gaza Strip from Egypt, the West Bank of the Jordan and east Jerusalem from Jordan, and the Golan Heights from Syria. When Egypt and Syria tried to recapture their territories in the "Yom Kippur War" of 1973, they were again defeated.

Israel has continued to occupy most of the territory it gained as a result of these victories.

Today it occupies 18,000 square kilometres (7,000 square miles) more than was allotted to it by the United Nations in 1947. Many Palestinians had to leave their homes and live in refugee camps, and Palestinian guerrillas have fought a terrorist campaign against Israel (see PALESTINIANS).

After the 1973 war, Israel and Egypt became more friendly, and in 1982 Israel completed its withdrawal from Sinai. But there was little sign of a peace agreement with Israel's other Arab neighbours. Unrest in Israel's northern neighbour Lebanon and an uprising among Palestinians living in the occupied territories added to the problems. For more about the troubled history of the area, see the article Middle East.

ISRAELITES see JEWS AND JUDAISM.

ISTANBUL is by far the largest city in Turkey, and its chief port and centre of trade. It was formerly known as Constantinople and lies on the shores of the Bosporus, which divides Europe from Asia (see BOSPORUS). Southwards it looks on the inland Sea of Marmara. Few cities anywhere have such an historic and strategic setting.

Originally the place was a Greek town called Byzantium. In AD 328, the Roman

Hutchison Library

The Galata Bridge crosses the Golden Horn and links the oldest part of Istanbul, on the south side, with the later parts, to the north. The level below the roadway has shops and restaurants. The tower at the top of the picture is the Galata tower, on the north side of the Golden Horn.

Emperor Constantine (see CONSTANTINE THE GREAT) chose it as the new capital of his empire. In 330 he called it Constantinople. The Turks conquered the eastern Roman Empire in 1453 and renamed the city Istanbul – a name obtained from Greek words meaning "in the city". However, the name Constantinople continued to be used by western countries until 1923, when the capital of Turkey was moved to Ankara. (See CONSTANTINOPLE.)

At the southern end of the Bosporus a long inlet called the Golden Horn runs inland on the European side. The Golden Horn, a fine natural harbour, which is, however, too shallow for modern ships, divides the old part of the city from the new. Old Istanbul stands on the promontory south of the Golden Horn, and contains many mosques whose great domes and tall slender towers called minarets stand out against the skyline (see MOSQUE). The Sultan Ahmed mosque is the finest of these. There is also the magnificent building of St. Sophia, once a great Christian church, later a mosque and now a museum; and the Topkapi Palace which sits at the tip of the southern promontory and was once the palace of the sultans. It houses many historic relics.

There are many manufacturing industries in the city, including textiles, cement, glass, and leather goods. Shipbuilding and repairs also go on. Banking is important, as is the tourist industry.

Bridges across the Golden Horn lead from the old city to the high promontory of Galata and Beyoglu (formerly Pera), where the main business and shopping centres and hotels are situated. The Bosporus itself is spanned by two of the world's largest suspension bridges. On the Asiatic shore is Üsküdar (Scutari), where Florence Nightingale nursed the sick and wounded soldiers in the Crimean War. South of Üsküdar is Haydarpaza, the terminus of the railway into Asia.

Higher up the Bosporus on both shores lie suburbs of Istanbul, with old wooden houses, modern villas, apartment blocks, castles, cafés, and mosques set above the water in hilly country.

The population of Istanbul is 5,476,000 (1985).

ITALY. The long peninsula of Italy in south central Europe sticks out into the Mediterranean and looks rather like a boot. The country includes the large islands of Sardinia and Sicily, on which there are separate articles. It is bounded on the north by the curved mountain barrier of the Alps (see ALPS), on the far side of which lie France, Switzerland, Austria, and Yugoslavia. Across the Adriatic Sea lie Albania, Greece, and most of Yugoslavia. Across the Mediterranean lies the North African shoreline. Italy is a mountainous country: the Maritime Alps on the frontier between it and France continue south in the form of the Apennine chain, which runs the whole length of the country. (See APENNINES.)

FACTS ABOUT ITALY

AREA: 301,277 square kilometres (116,324 square miles).
POPULATION: 57,436,000 (1989).
GOVERNMENT: Republic.
CAPITAL: Rome, 2,817,227.
GEOGRAPHY: Italy is a long boot-shaped country stretching from central Europe into the Mediterranean Sea. The Alps form the northern boundary. The Apennine mountain range runs through nearly the whole length of the country. In the north is the large, fertile plain of Lombardy. The islands of Sicily and Sardinia are mountainous.
CITIES: Milan, 1,478,505; Naples, 1,200,958; Turin 1,025,390; Genoa, 722,026; Palermo, 728,843; Bologna, 427,240; Florence, 421,299.
ECONOMY. Products and exports.
  Agriculture: Sugar beet, grapes, wheat, maize, tomatoes, olives, apples, barley, soya beans, oranges, rice, sheep, pigs, cattle, poultry.
  Mining: Rock salt, potash, feldspar, asbestos, barite, zinc, magnesium, lead.
  Manufacturing: Cement, iron and steel, fertilizers, sulphuric acid, plastics, caustic soda, textiles, wine, olive oil, motor vehicles, electrical goods.
  Exports: Machinery, chemicals, motor vehicles and transport equipment, clothes, shoes, metals and metal products, petroleum products.
EDUCATION: Children must attend school between the ages of 6 and 13.

Italy is poor in natural resources. Most of its surface is mountainous or hilly and the mountains do not contain rich stores of

metals or coal to make up for their barren soil. There are some coastal lowlands, but the chief lowland is the great plain in the north which is drained by the River Po and its tributaries (see Po River). Many other Italian rivers are swift streams, which in winter become roaring torrents washing away soil and trees, but for the rest of the year shrink to mere trickles. The climate of Italy differs greatly from place to place. In the north it is like that of most of the continent of Europe, with hot summers, cold winters and sufficient rainfall. Generally speaking, the winds bearing rain come from the west, so that most rain falls on the western side of the mountains and much less to the east of them. South of Naples the climate is more like that of North Africa, with hot dry summers and rain mainly in the winter.

Poplar trees grow in the Po Valley, cypress, beech and ilex (holly) in central Italy, and pine trees on the west coast and in the north. On the slopes of the Apennines are forests of beech and chestnut trees. As Italy is short of coal, much wood used to be cut for fuel, and this heavy cutting of trees had serious results in the south by laying bare the soil which causes it to erode. Bears and wolves are sometimes seen in the mountainous parts of the Abruzzi district in central Italy and there are still some wild boars in the forests and deer on the hills. National parks, in the Abruzzi for instance, have been created to protect places of natural beauty and areas which contain unusual geological features, rare animals, trees or flowers. Lizards are very common, and several dangerous species such as poisonous centipedes, scorpions, and tarantula spiders are found in the country. The rivers are rich in fish, and in the sea around Italy are found anchovies, sardines, and tunny, which are caught for food.

Hutchison Library

Left: The ancient city of Siena, in the Tuscany region. **Right:** The cathedral at Amalfi, near Naples.

ZEFA

People and Cities

During the last 2,000 years Italy has been invaded by Huns, Goths, Lombards, Normans, Arabs, Spaniards, Frenchmen, Austrians, Germans, the British, and the Americans. The people are from very mixed origins, but more than those of any other country they can claim descent from the ancient Romans and are proud of it. The geography and history of their country in the past prevented the Italians of different parts of the country from mixing much, for the barriers formed by the mountains combined with centuries of foreign rule to keep them apart. A person from Turin in the north may feel that the people of Calabria in the south are more foreign than French people, and in general people in the wealthier, industrial north have very different lifestyles from those in the poorer agrarian south.

Most Italians are Roman Catholics, and they take a delight in the religious processions held on saints' days, when many of the people wear picturesque local costumes. Italian cooking, with its variety of dishes, is popular in many countries. The main meal, usually at midday, often begins with soup, which may contain rice, pasta (flour made into macaroni, spaghetti or vermicelli) or greens. This is followed by meat or fish, cheese, and fruit. In parts of the Po valley, *polenta*, or cooked maize, is common and a lot of barley and chestnuts are eaten. Most cooking is done with olive oil and with their meals people drink local wine, as grapes grow all over Italy.

Italians are very fond of soccer and other popular sports are cycle racing, and motor racing.

The Italian language is spoken everywhere except in some districts near the Austrian frontier where some people speak German. Children must attend school between the ages of 6 and 14. Primary schools are free but the secondary schools, although cheap, are not free. There is a shortage of schools in parts of Italy and some older people cannot read and write. However, 97 per cent of Italians are literate. Italy has many universities and anyone who takes a degree becomes a *Dottore* (which means "doctor" in the sense of a learned person). The capital of Italy is Rome on the River Tiber. In the western part of Rome is the Vatican City which is the headquarters of the Roman Catholic Church and where the Pope lives. It is an independent state. (See ROME; TIBER RIVER; VATICAN CITY.) Other important cities are Milan, Naples, Turin, Genoa, Palermo, Florence, and Venice. (See FLORENCE; GENOA; MILAN; NAPLES; VENICE.) Life in Rome and the northern cities is modern, but in the country towns – particularly in the south – people live in much the same way as they have done for generations. Many of the towns were built on hill-tops to escape the dangers of fever, flood, and invasions.

Italy is probably richer than any other country in its artistic treasures, buildings, and historic remains. These attract millions of foreign visitors every year.

Agriculture

About one tenth of Italian workers are occupied on the land. Many farmers rent their land

Burt Glinn/Magnum

Houses crammed on the steep slopes of Positano, a resort on the Gulf of Salerno, southern Italy.

(rather than own it) but there are laws to protect them from eviction. In southern Italy and Sicily there are still a few big estates owned by landlords who let out the land in tiny strips to the peasants. Often the landlord does not himself live on the land but puts the management in the hands of a *fattore*, or agent, and this arrangement has often resulted in the ill-treatment of the peasants. Since 1950 the Italian government has taken over many of the big estates and divided them among the farm workers.

Farming conditions and methods vary enormously in the different parts of Italy. In the Alpine valleys there are good dairy farms, and in the Lombardy Plain there are big modern farms using machinery. As the Italians eat much bread and pasta, wheat is an important crop in all areas. Most of the wheat and maize is grown on the northern plains and in Apulia and Sicily. Rice is grown in the Po valley and olives and vines in all districts. Lemons, oranges, figs, grapes, tomatoes, almonds, and walnuts from the south and islands are sent abroad in large quantities, as well as apples, peaches, pears, cherries, chestnuts, and grapes from the northern Alpine regions. There is also a large production of sugar beet, tobacco, and hemp (used for making rope and twine). Cattle are reared mainly in the north, as there is little good meadow-land elsewhere, and sheep and goats are kept on rough pasture, especially in Sardinia and Sicily.

Industry and Transport

Factories were late in coming to Italy, partly because it was not a united country until 1870 and partly owing to the shortage of iron, coal, and raw materials. There are now large industrial towns producing goods for export. The chief minerals are bauxite in the south, used for making aluminium, mercury obtained near Siena, lead and zinc in Sardinia, and sulphur in Sicily. The rushing streams in the mountains, particularly in the Alps, give a good supply of water power for making electricity; the Italians call water power "white coal" because it does the work

A roof-top view of the centre of Verona, in northern Italy.

of coal without the dirt and smoke. Supplies of a natural gas called methane that comes out of the earth and can be burnt as fuel are found in the Po valley and small amounts of oil have been found near Ragusa and Gela in Sicily.

Nearly a half of the working people are engaged in industry, most of which is in the great northern cities of Milan, Turin, and Genoa. Naples and Taranto are the most important factory centres in the south. The area around Milan is famous for its furniture, lighting, and fashion design and manufacture, and products are exported worldwide. The machinery manufactured includes vehicles and electrical goods, machine tools and printing presses. Large quantities of office machinery such as typewriters and computers are sent abroad. Many new oil refineries have been built in recent years and

there is a large chemical industry. Textiles are important and the Italians make rayon and other artificial materials as well as cotton, wool, and silk goods. Fashion clothes are also made, and the fashion houses of Rome, Florence, Milan, and Venice have rivalled those of Paris. The manufacture of ornamental glass has long been carried on in Venice, and pottery and glass are made in Tuscany and Umbria. Shoes are a speciality of the Marche region.

Many of the country people in the south are "subsistence" farmers; that is, they grow only enough food to feed themselves, and have no surplus left over to sell. Italy is not rich in raw materials and has to import most of its petroleum, coal, oil, iron, steel, copper, timber, wool, cotton and other raw materials, as well as meat and other foodstuffs such as coffee and maize. In general these goods, Italy's imports, cost more than the value of the goods Italy sells abroad. The balance has to be made up from the money brought in by foreign tourists and by carrying goods in Italian ships. Italy has a large fleet of merchant ships. The chief seaports are Genoa, Augusta, Trieste, Taranto, Naples, and Venice. The chief Italian airport for international traffic is that at Rome, followed by Milan.

Life in rural areas is often hard and some people are very poor. Many have emigrated to North America, Australia, and northern European countries. The money that these people send back to their families helps to boost the Italian economy.

There is a good railway network. In the north, Milan and Bologna are the main railway junctions. There are four main north-south lines: Turin to Rome, Milan to Naples (with a ferry connection to Palermo, Sicily), Brennero to Rome, and Tarvisio to Lecce. The main east-west railway lines are Turin to Trieste, Ancona to Rome, and Naples to Foggia. Much of the railway system is electrified.

The main roads are good. Italy has thousands of kilometres of modern highways called *autostrade*. The so-called consular roads follow the ancient Roman roads. They radiate out from Rome to all parts of Italy. The most famous are the Via Aurelia, linking Rome and Genoa; the Via Cassia, from Rome to Genoa by way of Florence; and the Via Appia, which runs from Rome to Brindisi.

History

More than 2,000 years ago, Italy was united under the government of the Romans, who brought civilization to a great part of Europe (see ROME, ANCIENT). Most of this civilization perished during the centuries of invasion by northern barbarians. The ruins of Roman architecture and the remains of Roman roads and Roman law were all that was left of a great heritage. For some time, northern Italy was part of the Holy Roman Empire, on which there is a separate article, and for many years there was a struggle for power between emperors and popes.

During the Middle Ages some Italian cities and towns became small but powerful states in their own right. Milan, Pisa, Florence, Genoa, Verona, Venice, Bologna, Amalfi, and Perugia are important examples. They traded with Africa and the East as well as the rest of Europe, and had their own armies – and sometimes navies – to protect them. They took sides in any war that was going on if they thought it would help them. As they grew rich and powerful, they became flourishing centres not only of trade but also of art, for the rulers and merchants encouraged architecture, painting, sculpture, and literature. The great revival of interest in the arts, known as the Renaissance, was nowhere stronger than in the Italian city-states (see RENAISSANCE).

The power of the city-states dwindled towards the end of the 15th century, when France invaded the country. Although a large region in central Italy called the Papal States was under the rule of the Pope, much of the rest of the country changed hands between France, Spain, and Austria. In 1805 the great French general, Napoleon Bonaparte, had himself crowned King of Italy, and although his kingdom vanished with his defeat, the idea of a united Italy remained.

In 1831 Giuseppe Mazzini founded a movement which aimed at making all Italy into a single republic. The revolts that he himself plotted were failures, but the struggle for independence continued under the leadership of Count Camillo Cavour, a great statesman. By 1860 most of northern Italy had been united, and the south was added to it when Giuseppe Garibaldi led his thousand red-shirted followers through Sicily and southern Italy to meet the victorious army of the north at Naples. (There are separate articles on these three men.)

Italy remained for some years a weak and poor country, although towards the end of the 19th century it established some African colonies. In 1912 some lands in North Africa, were taken from Turkey, together with the Dodecanese Islands in the Aegean Sea.

Italy fought on the same side as France and Great Britain in World War I, but obtained less than it expected from being on the winning side. In the period of disappointment and disorder that followed, Benito Mussolini and his Fascist party came to power. Then for nearly 20 years Italy was ruled by this dictator who stifled all criticism by imprisoning or exiling his critics. (See MUSSOLINI, BENITO; FASCISM; DICTATOR.) Mussolini brought Italy into World War II on the side of Germany, and was thrown from power by his own people when British and American soldiers invaded in 1943. Great damage was caused by the fighting in Italy, and after the war the Italian colonies were taken away, except Somalia (now part of the Somali Republic) where Italy remained responsible for the government until 1960.

After World War II Italy became a republic. It joined the defensive alliance called the North Atlantic Treaty Organization (NATO) in 1949 and the United Nations in 1955. Italy was also a founding member of the European Economic Community (see EUROPEAN COM-

The town of Assisi sits in the hills of Umbria, in central Italy. The region is prosperous agriculturally. The valleys are intensively cultivated.

Greg Evans

MUNITIES). Industry recovered quickly after the war, but no government managed to stay in power very long. Unemployment and poverty, particularly in southern Italy, were serious problems. The government tried to improve matters by starting new industries and Italy is now a mainly industrial country, with a reasonably high standard of living. Politically, however, Italy has been unstable. Few Italian governments in modern times have been able to last long and the rivalry between the Roman Catholic Church and the Italian Communist Party has continued.

Art, Literature, and Science

Few peoples have contributed so much to the arts as the Italians. All over the country there are beautiful churches, palaces, town halls, bridges, and market squares, many of them built in the style of the Italian Renaissance and with fine examples of Baroque architecture in the south particularly. (See ARCHITECTURE.) Modern Italians have restored with care many of the beautiful buildings damaged during the war.

Sculpture abounds in the museums and art galleries as well as in the churches. The father of Renaissance sculpture was Niccolo Pisano (1220–83), and the great painter Giotto (see GIOTTO) was also a skilled sculptor. Donatello, on whom there is a separate article, made many of his sculptures for churches and often chose children as his subjects. Andrea del Verrocchio (1435–88) made a bronze figure of a soldier on horseback which is so lifelike that the horse looks as if it is moving. A pupil of his was the great genius Leonardo (see LEONARDO DA VINCI). Benvenuto Cellini (1500–71) was chiefly a goldsmith but is celebrated for his bronze figure of Perseus, and Giovanni Bernini (1598–1680) was particularly famous for his fountains. The greatest of all sculptors was Michelangelo (see MICHELANGELO BUONAROTTI).

Painting is the art for which Italy is best known. During the Renaissance, almost every city had its own school of painting and its workshops where young artists were trained by the great masters. The best-known schools are those of Florence and Venice, and you can read more about Italian painters in the article PAINTERS AND PAINTING.

Since World War II Italian film-makers have gained a worldwide reputation. Among them are Roberto Rossellini, Vittorio de Sica, Michelangelo Antonioni, Federico Fellini, Pier Paolo Pasolini, and Luchino Visconti. Italians are also at the forefront of furniture, fashion, and industrial design.

Italians have composed many beautiful pieces of music. Giovanni da Palestrina (1526–94) wrote music chiefly for the church. Antonio Vivaldi (*c.*1678–1741), one of the finest violinists of his day, wrote concertos for the violin and other instruments. Much of his work was almost forgotten until the 20th century. Today's violins are copied from those developed at Cremona by Nicolo Amati (1596–1684) and his pupil Antonio Stradivari (1644–1737). Modern opera began with Claudio Monteverdi in the 17th century and became one of the most popular forms of music in Italy, particularly in the hands of composers such as Gioacchino Rossini, Giuseppe Verdi, and Giacomo Puccini in the 19th century. (See VIOLIN FAMILY; OPERA.)

The best Italian literature belongs to the age of the city-states. First and foremost is Dante (1265–1321), whose finest work is the *Divine Comedy*, a poem describing a journey to hell and heaven. This poem served as a model for all users of the Italian language. (See DANTE ALIGHIERI.) Francesco Petrarca, better known to English-speaking people as Petrarch (1304–74), was another great poet with a deep love of Italy. Giovanni Boccaccio (1313–75) wrote short stories that became famous over all Europe and were often imitated, as, for instance, by Geoffrey Chaucer in England. Niccolo Machiavelli (1469–1527), wrote about history and political ideas and was the greatest prose writer of the age. (See BOCCACCIO, GIOVANNI; MACHIAVELLI, NICCOLO.) Alessandro Manzoni (1785–1873) wrote beautiful poetry but he is chiefly remembered for his novel *The Betrothed*, a tale of Milan in the 17th century.

Many famous scientists and explorers have been Italian. Among the scientists was Galileo (1564–1642). the first astronomer to make use of the telescope (see GALILEO GALILEI). Luigi Galvani (1737–98) and Alessandro Volta (1745–1827) were important pioneers in electricity, one of whom is remembered in the instrument called a galvanometer and the other in the unit of electrical pressure called the volt. Guglielmo Marconi (1874–1937) was the chief inventor of radio (see MARCONI, GUGLIELMO), Marco Polo (*c.*1254–1324) was a great Venetian explorer who travelled across Asia as far as China (see POLO, MARCO), and Christopher Columbus (*c.*1451–1506), who discovered America, was born and bred in Genoa. General Umberto Nobile was the first man to fly over the North Pole, which he did in the airship *Norge* with Roald Amundsen in 1926. Italian climbers were in 1954 the first to reach the top of the world's second highest mountain, the peak called "K2" at 8,610 metres (28,248 feet) in the Karakoram Himalayas in Kashmir.

IVAN THE TERRIBLE (1530–84) was the first tsar, or emperor, of Russia and became known as "the Terrible" because of the violence of his reign.

When he was three Ivan succeeded his father as Grand Duke of Muscovy, and when

National Museum, Copenhagen

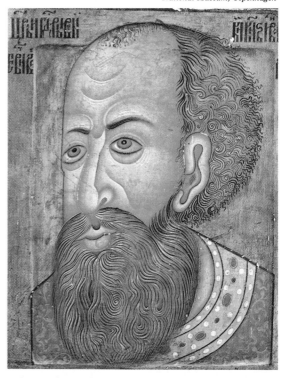

A 16th-century icon painting of Ivan the Terrible, first emperor of Russia.

he was 14 began to govern the country himself. Muscovy was a small state in northeastern Russia, with the city of Moscow as its capital. Until the second half of the 15th century it had been under the control of Tatar overlords. (See the history section of the article RUSSIA.) The two Grand Dukes before Ivan had extended their territory and had freed Muscovy from the Tatars (see TATARS). Ivan therefore claimed the title "Tsar" instead of "Grand Duke" and "of all Russia" instead of merely "of Muscovy", and at the age of 17 was crowned Tsar.

Ivan was a capable, energetic man and worked very hard. In the early years of his reign he appointed an advisory council, and promised his people to rule wisely and justly. He made many improvements in the government of his country, and tried to improve its rather backward methods of manufacturing goods. He made Russia still bigger by conquering Kazan in the east and Astrakhan in the south, driving the Tatars out of those lands.

The second, and violent, part of Ivan's reign began about 1560. His wife and eldest son died, his one great friend deserted him and political problems worried him. Some historians think that Ivan began to go insane, believing everyone to be against him. He had always hated the *boyars* – a powerful group of landowning noblemen – for they had treated him very badly while he was young, and he now began to take his revenge. He had many of them tortured and executed, seizing their lands and possessions. He had always preferred the merchant classes and the ordinary people who, in turn, liked him. However, the boyars were by no means his only victims, for anybody who displeased him suffered. In 1569 Ivan was told that the citizens of the city of Novgorod were plotting against him. He ravaged all the land round the city and then the city itself, massacring a great many of its inhabitants.

In 1580 Ivan quarrelled with his eldest surviving son, whom he loved dearly, and struck him a blow that killed him. Ivan himself died in Moscow on 18 March 1584.

BBC Hulton Picture Library

The American composer Charles Ives, photographed towards the end of his life.

IVES, Charles Edward (1874–1954).

The United States composer Charles Ives wrote some of the most original music of the 20th century. His work foreshadows many of the musical trends that have formed an important part of modern music. Yet for most of his life, music was only a hobby for Ives. During the week he ran a successful insurance firm and composed only at weekends. Illness forced him to retire from the insurance business in 1930 and later from the composition of music. His compositions only started to become known near the end of his life. Many of his works lay unpublished until after his death.

Ives was born at Danbury, Connecticut, and received his first music lessons from his father, George Ives. George, who was a local bandmaster, was a keen experimenter in music and sharpened Charles's ear by getting him to sing "Swanee River" in one key, while he accompanied him in another. In the 1890s Charles Ives studied composition with a famous United States composer, Horatio Parker, and in 1898 went into the insurance business in New York. He helped found his own insurance company in 1916.

Ives's compositions are full of references to

American culture and reflect his upbringing in New England. Virtually all his works contain quotations from popular American tunes, well-loved hymns, or barn-dance melodies. Alongside these are references to European music, such as that by Beethoven, Brahms, or Tchaikovsky. But Ives also used many adventurous techniques. He was one of the pioneers of microtonality, the use of very small intervals between one note and the next in a melody. Many of his pieces are very complicated, written in several parts using many different keys and rhythms all at the same time. Typical of this style is the second movement of his *Three Places in New England* (1903–14), in which the listener hears the effect of two bands marching past each other, each playing its own tune in its own key and rhythm and at its own speed.

Among Ives's other major compositions are *The Unanswered Question* (composed before 1908), an instrumental work in which a trumpet repeats a questioning phrase; the *Concord* piano sonata (1909–15), which includes a part for solo flute and has movements named after famous New England writers; and his *String Quartet No. 2* (1911–13), which is meant to be thought of as an argument between the four players. The argument is eventually settled amicably. Ives also wrote symphonies and choral works.

IVORY AND IVORY CARVING. The white, smooth, solid substance called ivory comes mainly from the tusks of elephants. It can also be obtained from the tusks or teeth of walruses, wild boar, hippopotamuses, sperm whales, and narwhals (a species of whale). Elephant tusks, however, are the most valuable because of their great size.

Some of the most beautiful objects ever made by human craftsmen are carved in ivory. It is durable, easily worked with wood-working tools, and polishes beautifully. But the demand for ivory has caused the near extinction of some of these tusk-bearing mammals. Elephants are now "threatened" or "endangered" (see ENDANGERED SPECIES).

The African elephant is in most danger because its ivory has greater density and whiteness, and this makes it more valuable than the ivory of the Indian elephant. In 1989 experts estimated that Africa's elephant population numbered around 10 million in the 1930s, 1.2 million at the start of the 1980s, and by 1989 had been reduced to between 300,000 and 750,000 animals.

Campaigning by conservationists led to the introduction of export quotas by the African exporting nations – that is, only so much ivory could be exported by each country, depending on the size of its elephant population. But the quota system did not work, mainly because African governments were not able to prevent poaching and illegal exports. In 1989 the United States and a number of European nations including Britain agreed to impose a complete ban on the import of ivory.

The History of Ivory Carving

The very first artists who carved on ivory were probably the people of the late Stone Age, who scratched pictures on the tusks of mammoths, which were great animals like elephants that roamed over many parts of the world. One mammoth tusk that was discovered in France had the outline of a reindeer carved on it.

When the mammoth became extinct, about 3 million years ago, the tusks of the elephants of India and Africa began to be used instead. (There is still some fossil ivory from mammoths which comes from Alaska.) The ancient Egyptians used ivory for ornaments, sometimes combined with precious stones, and the ivory throne of King Solomon which is mentioned in the Old Testament was overlaid with gold. Ancient peoples of the Near East mainly used hippopotamus ivory, which is extremely hard and had first to be soaked in acid to remove the outer layer of enamel.The Romans made dentures, or false teeth, from this ivory.

Centuries before the birth of Christ, Phoenician traders were carrying ivory to Greece where it was used for carving and also for painting, for as well as being easy to

Courtesy, the Victoria and Albert Museum

Courtesy, the British Museum

Top: A Phoenician ivory carving made about the 8th century BC. **Below**: Norse chessmen, carved from walrus ivory in the 12th century AD.

carve, ivory forms a good ground for colour. It is particularly beautiful when painted with transparent colours, since the fine grain, or marking, of the ivory itself shows through. Not many Greek ivory carvings still exist. Greek writers described colossal statues of gods and goddesses, such as Zeus and Pallas Athene, made of ivory and gold.

From the beginning of Christian times, many ivory carvings were made that survive and can still be seen today in churches, art galleries, and museums. Some of the early ones were in the form of a *diptych* or a *triptych* – that is, two or three tablets of ivory bound together. On the flat, oblong leaves of ivory were carved delicate and lifelike pictures of figures and scenes, mostly taken from the New Testament.

At a later stage, articles carved from ivory were often made for use in churches, and the artists chose subjects such as the birth of Jesus, or miracles, or legends of the saints. During the reign of Charlemagne, who was crowned Emperor of Rome in AD 800, ivory was used a great deal for book covers. The carvers used the same kinds of design as the illuminators who decorated the parchment pages inside the books.

In the Middle Ages, towards the end of the 13th century, ivory carvings were very popular and rich nobles liked to have articles made of ivory in their homes. Paris became the centre of an ivory industry. New Testament scenes were still popular, but for objects such as the jewel caskets, mirror cases, and combs for ladies' dressing tables, the carvers often took their ideas from the stories and poems of the time about love and adventure. The elegant little figures, with gracefully curved bodies, were very different from the solemn and sometimes rather stiff-looking carvings of the past.

Later on, from the 16th century, carvers in Europe took to making miniature versions in ivory of larger sculptures in marble and stone. Many of these are wonderful examples of the skill of the carvers, whose signatures were often put on their works. (In earlier carvings there was usually no indication of who had carved them.)

From the 19th century onwards ivory came to be used for more practical objects because there were now machine tools to allow mass production. Umbrella and knife handles, combs, piano keys, and billiard balls were all made of ivory. In the second half of the 20th century, cheap substitutes such as plastics and vegetable ivory from the South American ivory nut palm became available and these were used instead.

Eastern Carving

In India, China, and Japan craftsmen have for centuries laboured patiently to make beautiful tiny objects of ivory, carved so delicately that

ZEFA

Hong Kong is one of the leading centres of ivory carving in the world. The over-hunting of elephants, which has brought about international restrictions in the trading of ivory, has put the livelihoods of these craftsmen at risk.

you would hardly think a human hand could do the work. This kind of work includes chessmen from India, miniature pagodas (temples) and little "puzzle balls", consisting of many balls one inside another, from China, and small toggles called *netsukes*, to be fastened to a purse or tobacco pouch, from Japan. *Netsukes* are often in the form of tiny figures of gods and heroes from old legends, their expressive faces no bigger than a little finger nail. They are usually carved from walrus or narwhal ivory.

The Chinese also used ivory for fans, some of which are made of plaited ivory threads and carved flowers and birds. The workshops of the city of Canton produced models of palaces with carved roofs, peopled by tiny figures and surrounded by trees and walls, all of ivory.

The craftsmen of the East did not only make such tiny and complicated things. They also carved simple figures of gods and animals, and used ivory to decorate couches, tables, and chairs.

The Eskimos in Siberia and North America have been carving in ivory for over 2,000 years, and continue to produce decorative and religious objects of ivory, tooth, and bone (see ESKIMO).

IVORY COAST (Côte d'Ivoire) is a republic on the west coast of Africa. It covers an area of over 300,000 square kilometres (115,000 square miles) and is bordered by Liberia to the southwest, Guinea to the northwest, Mali and Burkina Faso to the north, and Ghana to the east. The Gulf of Guinea forms its southern border.

The land rises from a low coastal plain to a higher plateau with some hills and mountains. The climate is hot and steamy, especially near the coast. The northern region is drier.

FACTS ABOUT IVORY COAST

AREA: 320,763 square kilometres (123,847 square miles).
POPULATION: 12,135,000 (1989).
GOVERNMENT: Republic.
CAPITAL: Abidjan, 1,850,000.
GEOGRAPHY: A narrow coastal strip with rocky formations, lagoons, and sand. Inland is rainforest in the southwest, and to the north is a savanna plateau.
CITIES: Bouaké, 220,000; Yamoussoukro, 120,000; Gagnoa, 93,500; Daloa, 59,500.
EXPORTS: Cocoa, coffee, petroleum, wood, chemicals, cotton, pineapples.
EDUCATION: School is compulsory between the ages of 7 and 12, but not all children go to school.

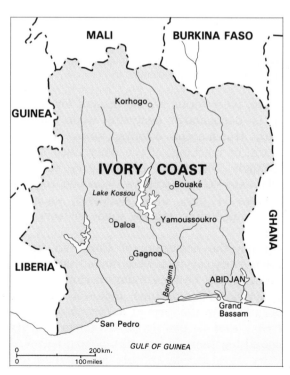

A market place outside the Palace of Congress in Abidjan, capital of the Ivory Coast, West Africa.

The southern part of the country was once covered by dense equatorial rain forests, containing valuable hardwoods such as mahogany and teak. But in recent years large areas of the eastern part of the forests have been cut down to provide land for agriculture. On the northern plateau the vegetation consists of savanna grassland which is favourable for grazing cattle. Animal life includes elephants, antelopes, lions, monkeys, snakes, crocodiles, and manatee, or sea cow (see MANATEE).

The people of the Ivory Coast belong to 60 different groups which have their own languages and customs. There are Christians, and followers of local religions, but Muslims form the largest religious group.

Farming is the most important occupation. The country is the world's largest producer of cocoa. Coffee and timber are the next most valuable exports, but pineapples, bananas, cotton, rubber, and palm kernels are also important.

Ivory Coast's mineral reserves are small, but since 1980 oil has been extracted from the Gulf of Guinea. There are now three offshore oil wells and a petroleum refinery. Other industries include flour milling, food canning, brewing, textile and plastics manufacture, and sawmills.

Although Ivory Coast is one of the most developed countries in black Africa, it is still very poor. Large numbers of people suffer from diseases such as malaria and tuberculosis. Only about three-quarters of the children go to school. Classes are overcrowded and there are not enough teachers.

History

European traders in slaves and ivory (which gave the country its name) visited the Ivory Coast from the 15th century onwards. Later the French established trading posts there and in 1893 Ivory Coast became a French colony. In 1947 the northern section became the separate nation of Upper Volta (now Burkina Faso).

Ivory Coast became independent in 1960. Since then it has been governed by Félix Houphouët-Boigny, the country's president and leader of the ruling political party.

IVY. The glossy, evergreen leaves of the ivy (*Hedera*) with their three- or five-pointed lobes make it the easiest of climbing plants to recognize. Ivies belong to the family of tropical twining plants, Araliaceae, although ivy itself does not use tendrils or its stems to wind round supports. It clings to walls and trees by means of little roots that grow out from the stems. There are about five species; the most common is the English ivy (*Hedera helix*).

Ivy may climb up to 30 metres (100 feet), but its lower branches often trail along the ground and these have much smaller leaves. The greenish-yellow flowers bloom in the autumn and are a rich source of nectar to insects such as bees, wasps, and moths. The black fruits should not be eaten by people, although many kinds of birds feed on them throughout the winter.

Ivy is bad for trees because it smothers them by growing all over them and by taking the

A–Z Collection

An ivy plant, supported by roots that grow out from its stem, climbs up the rough bark of a tree.

nourishment from the soil. It is often grown on walls as an ornamental plant, but its roots attack the masonry, weakening the wall. Many kinds of ivy are cultivated and some are grown in pots indoors. These sometimes have leaves that are green and yellow.

JACANA is a tropical bird that has remarkably long toes and toenails. Its name is of Brazilian origin. The jacana is a distant relative of the plover. Jacanas live in open marshes where they pick up their food of insects and other small animals. Their extremely long toes enable them to walk or run over lily pads and other floating vegetation.

There are seven species of jacana. All live in tropical and subtropical regions. One species, the Central American jacana (*Jacana spinosa*), ranges from Central America north-

ward into Texas. This bird is about 23 centimetres (9 inches) long, with a moderately long bill and short tail. It has a bare, yellow-orange fleshy area on the forehead and a sharp spur on the bend of each wing. The plumage is black and reddish with a brilliant yellow patch on each wing. The jacana gives a harsh cry, or cackle.

When the birds pair and nest, the male does most of the incubating (sitting on eggs) and caring for the young. The saucer-like nest is placed on floating vegetation. The four eggs are brownish with dark lines and scrawls.

The lotus bird is the name of the Australian jacana (*Irediparra gallinacea*). Unlike some of its relatives, its tail is very short, and when flying, the long feet and toes are used for steering. It is coloured black, brown, and white, and has a bright red "comb". It is found from New Guinea south down the east coast of Australia as far as Sydney.

The pheasant-tailed jacana (*Hydrophasianus chirurgus*) of India and the Philippines, is a handsome, black, yellow, and white bird that acquires long tail feathers in the breeding season.

NHPA/ANT

A comb-crested jacana or lotus bird settles on its floating nest. It lives in coastal swamps in Australia.

JACKAL. Like wolves, jackals belong to the dog family, but they are much smaller, up to 95 centimetres (37 inches). Their muzzles are also longer and more pointed than those of

Courtesy of the San Diego Zoo

The black-backed jackal, distinguished by its dark back and reddish flanks, lives in East and South Africa.

wolves and they have bushy tails. Like the fox, jackals have a strong body smell, produced by a gland at the base of the tail.

The fur of the common or Asiatic jackal (*Canis aureus*) is greyish-yellow, darker on the back and lighter underneath. It lives in eastern Europe, India, and parts of Africa. In Africa there also lives the black-backed jackal (*Canis mesomelas*), which has reddish sides, and the side-striped jackal (*Canis adjustus*), which is greyish with indistinct stripes on the sides.

Jackals hide in their burrows or in dense brush thickets during the day and come out at night, when they can be heard making a strange and frightening cry, something between a bark and a howl. They usually live and hunt in packs, and roam round the outskirts of a town or village, turning over rubbish heaps in their search for food. They eat fruit, birds' eggs, small mammals, and the dead and rotting flesh of prey killed by other animals such as lions. Sometimes a pack of jackals will attack and bring down larger prey such as sheep and antelope.

JACKDAW. The jackdaw (*Corvus monedula*) is a small member of the crow family, about 33 centimetres (13 inches) long. It has a wide distribution, from Europe east to Central Asia. Eastwards it is replaced by the white-breasted, white-collared Daurian jackdaw (*Corvus dauuricus*). The jackdaw can be easily distinguished by the grey on its face and on the back of its neck. The rest of its plumage is black, and it has clear, pearly-grey eyes. It is a very smart and perky-looking bird, and it struts along when walking on the ground.

Jackdaws, or "daws", move about in groups and are often seen in company with rooks, either feeding on the ground or flying in flocks with them. Wooded farmland and cliffs, both on the coast and inland, are the places where jackdaws are found. They are also very fond of towers and old buildings, such as cathedrals and castles, and wheel up in clouds from them, uttering their loud, harsh cry, which sounds rather like "jack". Their food includes insects and other creatures found on the ground and berries.

John Markham

The jackdaw is a handsome member of the crow family, distinguished by a greyish patch on its head and neck.

The jackdaw nests in holes in trees, buildings or rocks, and sometimes in rabbit holes. The nest is made by both the male and female, and four to six greenish-blue eggs spotted with brownish-black are laid.

Jackdaws often steal small bright objects and hide them. This habit inspired the poem "The Jackdaw of Rheims" in Richard Barham's *The Ingoldsby Legends*. The poem tells how the Cardinal's ring was stolen and how he put a curse on the thief, which proved to be a jackdaw.

JACKRABBIT see HARE.

JACKSON, Andrew (1767–1845) was the seventh president of the United States. As a former Indian fighter and a hero of the War of 1812, he was one of the most colourful presidents in the country's history. Courageous and hot-tempered, blunt yet shrewd, he was truly popular with the people, who nicknamed him "Old Hickory". Along with Thomas Jefferson, he is usually considered a founder of the Democratic party. (See POLITICAL PARTIES for an explanation of the United States Democratic Party.)

Early Life

Jackson was born on 15 march 1767 in the backwoods settlement of Washaw, now in North Carolina. During the American Revolution his brother Hugh was killed and he himself was struck by the sabre of a British officer when he refused to clean his boots. He carried the scar for the rest of his life and this probably explains Jackson's hostility to the British.

By the age of 14 Jackson had lost all his family. After a period as a teacher he began to study law in Salisbury, North Carolina. In 1788 he was appointed prosecuting attorney at Nashville in what became Tennessee. He boarded in the house of a Colonel Donelson and married the colonel's daughter Rachel Roberts. When Tennessee became a state in 1796 Jackson was a member of the convention that wrote its first constitution. He was elected to the United States House of Representatives and later became a senator. In

1802 he was elected major-general of the Tennessee militia.

Military Career

The War of 1812 with Britain gave Jackson his chance for fame. He first showed his military ability when he crushed a rising of the Creek Indians at 1814. His victory against the British at New Orleans made Jackson a national hero. Three times they attacked and three times he threw them back. In 1818 he chased some Indian raiders into Spanish-held Florida, embarrassing the government but shortly bringing about the acquisition of Florida of which Jackson was the first governor.

Leet Brothers

Andrew Jackson, US president, 1829–37.

Jackson retired in 1821 but only briefly. He again entered the Senate in 1823 and was persuaded to become a candidate for the presidency in 1824. He received more votes than any of the other three candidates but did not have an overall majority. The House of Representatives had to make the decision and at the urging of the speaker Henry Clay the members chose John Quincy Adams (see

ADAMS, JOHN). Jackson's supporters thought their hero had been robbed and put all their efforts into the 1828 election. The Jackson men took the name Democratic Republicans while Adams's friends called themselves National Republicans. Jackson won an overwhelming victory. Except for secretary of state Martin Van Buren his cabinet was not outstanding. He relied on his political friends for advice and they came to be known as the "Kitchen Cabinet".

United States President

The Union was less than 40 years old when Jackson took office. The states wanted to retain as much power as possible. Jackson's first test came when South Carolina felt so strongly that the nation's tariff (a trade barrier) on imported goods was too high that it declared the tariff law unconstitutional. This created a crisis over states' rights and the preservation of the Union. Jackson agreed the tariff was too high, but did not believe a state could simply reject it. On his appeal Congress issued a "force bill" giving the president the power to use the army and navy to enforce the federal laws, while also lowering the tariff. South Carolina thereupon accepted a lower tariff act and withdrew its former legislation against the tariff. Jackson had won a victory for the Union by his strong stand.

Jackson followed a harsh policy towards the Indians. In 1830 Congress passed the Indian Removal Act which allowed the removal of tribes from their lands within the states to land in the unsettled West. Jackson fought an important political battle over the Bank of the United States, which was private but had a charter from Congress. He questioned whether the bank was constitutional. His opponents rushed through a new charter, which he promptly vetoed (rejected). It was an important issue in the 1832 election campaign but Jackson succeeded in winning a second term.

Jackson was also successful in the field of foreign affairs. Trade with the West Indies began again when Britain withdrew its ban on it. Jackson put pressure on the French to pay compensation owed to those whose ships had been seized by France before the War of 1812.

As Jackson's second term ended he ensured the nomination of vice-president Van Buren as his successor, and then "Old Hickory" retired to his house, the Hermitage, near Nashville.

JACOBITE RISINGS.

JACOBITE RISINGS. The word "Jacobite" comes from the Latin word for James, which is *Jacobus*. People who continued to support James II after he had been deposed from the throne of Great Britain in 1688 were called Jacobites.

James II lost the throne because he had tried to change Protestant Britain into a Catholic country. He died in 1701 and the word "Jacobites" came to be used for people who supported his descendants.

In 1715 the Jacobites rose in rebellion against King George I, and in 1745 against his son George II, attempting on both occasions to win back the throne of Great Britain for James Edward Stuart, son of James II.

The Jacobites felt that George I and George II, who were Protestants and ruled Britain between 1714 and 1760, had no right to be kings of Great Britain. They supported the claim of James Edward Stuart, the son of James II, who was a Roman Catholic and living in exile in Europe. A number of British supporters joined him there and others were working for him in England and Scotland. At Perth (eastern Scotland) on 6 September 1715, the Earl of Mar, a Scottish nobleman, proclaimed James Edward king of England and Scotland, and the first serious Jacobite rising began. Scattered revolts in Scotland and northern England followed. On 13 November a confused battle was fought near the Scottish town of Stirling; the Earl of Mar claimed to have won it, but failed to advance further south towards England. In December James Edward himself landed in Scotland but this brought no extra support, and he and Lord Mar fled to France. The 1715 rising thus ended in failure.

The Jacobite cause was finally lost at Culloden in 1746, when the Highlanders, tired and starving, were defeated by the army of the Duke of Cumberland.

Thirty years later, in 1745, James Edward's son, Charles Edward Stuart, hoped for better luck. He is often called Bonnie Prince Charlie because of his great charm (see BONNIE PRINCE CHARLIE). The Scottish chieftains had advised him not to try another rebellion, but once he was in Scotland many of them flocked to his side. He raised his father's flag on 19 August 1745. With Scottish support, he took the city of Edinburgh and defeated the English at the Battle of Prestonpans (near Edinburgh) on 20 September. Two days earlier he had proclaimed his father king of Scotland and had held court at Holyroodhouse, the old home of the Scottish kings.

Charles Edward then set out to invade England. By the end of November he was in Manchester and a week later reached Derby, further south. In London there was a panic, and George II is said to have been preparing to leave England for Germany. However, Charles's officers were already advising him that it was impossible to carry on with the invasion: the English had not risen in revolt against King George, none of the expected help had been sent from France, and the Scottish army was sandwiched between two of King George's armies. Charles Edward was bitterly disappointed but was forced to turn round and head back for Scotland. This was really the moment of defeat, although defeat in battle did not come until the following year.

Charles marched back through Scotland, fighting as he went. His small army, exhausted, half-starved, and weakened by desertions, was at last completely overwhelmed at the Battle of Culloden Moor, near Inverness, on 16 April 1746. Charles went into hiding and until September was hunted by troops and spies of the government. At last he took refuge in the Scottish islands of the Hebrides, and his companion sought the help of a girl named Flora Macdonald. She obtained a pass giving her permission to travel to the mainland of Scotland with a manservant and a maid named Betty Burke. The "manservant" was Charles's companion and "Betty Burke" was Charles, disguised as Flora MacDonald's maid. From Scotland, Charles sailed to France, where he landed on 29 September 1746. He lived in France and then Italy, where he died in 1788.

These uprisings became known as the "Fifteen" and "Forty-five" after the years in which they took place. Both rebellions failed, and after 1745 Jacobite influence soon came to an end. After the rising the Highlanders (people from the north of Scotland who had given most support), were treated very severely and felt great bitterness towards England.

JADE. The word "jade" is used to mean one or other of two valuable ornamental stones, jadeite and nephrite. The two minerals are similar in appearance but are made up of different substances. Both stones are very hard and exist in a great range of colours, of which the greens and browns are the most usual. Jadeite is found in only a few places, and the best comes from mines in the Myitkyina district of northern Burma. For centuries nearly all of it has been sent to China to be carved, mainly at Guangzhou (Canton) and Shanghai. The most sought after jadeite is emerald-green in colour and semi-transparent; the lavender,

blue, and russet stones are also highly valued. Nephrite has been found in many countries, especially in the northwest part of China, Siberia, North America, and New Zealand, either as deposits in the mountains or in the form of huge boulders, sometimes a tonne or more in weight, in the beds of rivers. Favourite colours of nephrite are spinach-green, yellow, black, and the translucent white that the Chinese call "mutton fat".

Jade is especially connected with China, where it has been prized above all other stones. In early days the Chinese believed that it had magical powers to keep the body in health during life and to preserve it from decay after death. They therefore buried jade with the dead, and they used it for making objects connected with worship and with royal ceremonies. As time went on it began to be used more generally and was carved into beautiful ornaments and jewellery, as well as into vessels and statuettes. Some of the Chinese jade carvings, now carefully preserved in museums and private art collections, were made more than 2,000 years ago.

The Chinese, however, were not the only people who valued jade. There is proof that prehistoric inhabitants of Europe used it, in days before metals were known, to make cutting implements such as chisels because of its

Courtesy, Trustees of the British Museum

Left: An ancient Chinese ritual object called a ts'ung. It symbolises Mother Earth. **Right:** A Maori hei-tiki pendant from New Zealand. Both are of nephrite.

Top left: A nephrite belt hook, about 2,000 years old, carved in Japan. **Left**: This jadeite table from Teotihuacan, Mexico, is probably Mayan and over 1,000 years old. **Right**: A 2,000-year-old disc from China.

hardness. These tools have been dug up at ancient settlements.

The ancient Mexicans and the Maya people of Central America also treasured jade and carved it into ornaments, but after the Spanish conquest in the 16th century the craft died out. The Spaniards called the stone *piedra de ijada*, "stone of the flank", because they believed that wearing the smooth stone at the waist would cure pains in that part of the body. This is the origin of our word "jade". The Maoris of New Zealand made tools, weapons, and ornaments of jade until recent times.

Jade is too hard to be cut by metal, and is shaped by grinding with abrasive sands carried on tools of iron, wood, or bamboo. Jade carving is a skilful but slow and laborious process.

A green jadeite water vessel.

JAGUAR. The jaguar (*Panthera onca*) is the fiercest and largest of the great cats of America. It lives mostly in the South American forests and in the pampas of Argentina, where it is called *tiger*. Once it was common in the southern parts of the United States, but it is becoming rare there and in Mexico.

The jaguar is larger than the leopard (see LEOPARD), nearly 2 metres (6.5 feet) long, with a further 60 centimetres (24 inches) of striped tail. It looks rather like the leopard but is more heavily built, with short, very strong legs and a large and heavy head. The jaguar's coat is usually golden-brown with black markings. Along its back and on its sides these markings are in the form of rosettes, but on the head, legs and underpart of the body they are black spots. Some jaguars have a yellow or almost white coat with black spots, and some are nearly black, but these are very rare. Female jaguars have one litter of two to four cubs each year.

In the forests jaguars hide in the trees to spring on birds and monkeys, or capture turtles on the river banks and fish from the water. Sometimes they track and kill animals such as the tapir. On the plains they prey on sheep and cattle. Their roar, which is usually made at night, has been described as being between a cough and a growl. Because of the loss of its forest habitat and because it has been hunted for its fur, the jaguar is rare in many parts of its range.

There is also a much smaller South Amer-

ARDEA

The jaguar is a native of North and South America, but is now rare in the north.

ican wild cat called the jaguarundi which has a long slender body and resembles a large weasel. It may be either grey or reddish-brown in colour.

JAI ALAI is one of the world's fastest games. It is a ball game something like handball but played on a larger court. It is the national ball game of the Basques, a people who live in the Pyrenees Mountains in France and Spain. The name, adopted by the Cubans, means "merry festival" in the Basque language. In Spain the game is called *pelota*, which means "ball". The French call it *la pelote*.

Jai alai is played indoors and outdoors in a so-called *fronton*. The *cancha*, or court, is 53.3 metres (175 feet) long, 15.2 metres (50 feet) wide, and at least 12.2. metres (40 feet) high. It is enclosed at both ends and on one side. Along the open side sit three umpires and a referee who makes all final decisions. Behind them are the spectators, protected by a screen.

Two or four players make up a side. Each player wears a *cesta*, which is bound to one wrist with a leather thong. The cesta is a curved, basket-like scoop, about 0.76 metres (2.5 feet) long. It is used to catch and throw the ball, which must always be kept in motion. The ball is about the size of a tennis ball. It is made of tightly wound rubber covered with two layers of goatskin. Jai alai balls have been timed as travelling at over 240 kilometres (150 miles) per hour.

The wall which the ball is thrown against is called the *front wall*. The wall across from it is called the *rebounding wall*. A line is drawn across the front wall somewhat above the playing surface. The ball must always rebound from above this line. Another line, called the *service line*, is drawn across the playing surface 9 metres (29 feet) from the front wall.

The game begins by "serving" the ball. The server stands between the service line and the front wall, drops the ball, and catches it in the cesta on the bounce. Then he hurls it against the front wall so that it will rebound (bounce back) over the service line before touching the playing surface. If it does not, a point is scored against the server's side.

A professional jai alai player leaps high to snare a ball that is travelling at about 240 km (150 miles) per hour. Many professional players are of Basque origin.

If the serve is good, opposing players take turns in catching the ball with the cesta on the first bounce and immediately hurling it against the front wall until one of them misses a shot. This is a point for the other side. The ball may also be played on the first bounce when bouncing back from the rebounding wall. It may also be played before the first bounce from either wall. When a player on the side that is serving misses a shot, the other side wins one point and the right to serve. The side losing the point leaves the game and is replaced by another player or players.

Outside the United States the game score is between 10 and 40 points. In the United States a game has one less point than the number of players. For example, if eight players play, the game will be seven points. The side that reaches the game point first is the winner.

JAKARTA is the capital, largest city, and chief port of Indonesia. It is on the northwest coast of the island of Java, at the mouth of the River Ciliwung. It lies on a flat plain that is prone to flooding, and the climate is tropical and very humid.

In the city are three sections: the old city, lying along the mouth of the river; the new city, on higher ground to the south; and the port called Tanjungpriok, which is 10 kilometres (6 miles) to the east. There are many industries in the old city, including iron foundries, tanneries, sawmills, textile mills, printing, and chemical plants. Jakarta is the banking and commerce centre of Indonesia. Javanese, Chinese, and Arab peoples live in overcrowded residential quarters, and Oriental houses contrast with Dutch colonial buildings and modern skyscrapers in a mixture of architectural styles. Modern air-conditioned shopping malls can be found near colourful outdoor markets.

In the new city are the government buildings, the National Monument, which at 110 metres (360 feet) is one of the highest structures in the city, a teachers' training college, the National University, and two large museums. American-style freeways intersect this part of the city, and the traffic jams, with every type of vehicle including motorized tricycle taxis called *betjaks*, clog up the city.

Tanjungpriok has a breakwater which encloses its harbour, and can handle ships needing water 12 metres (40 feet) deep. The docks handle most of the imports and exports of Indonesia. The products of the islands—such as tea, rubber, coffee, spices, copra, and palm oil—are brought to the warehouses before they are shipped to other countries. The airport is between the port and the old city.

History

In 1619 the Dutch trader Jan Coen built a fort, called Batavia, next to the town of Jakarta. After the town was destroyed in the following year, the Dutch rebuilt it and called it Batavia. It kept that name during the more than 300 years of Dutch rule, and became an important port of call for European colonial trade in the East Indies, China, and Australia. The Dutch made it a beautiful city with large squares and wide tree-lined streets. The many canals and old Dutch buildings including the old colonial city hall, now a museum, make the old part of the city look like a part of Holland. After

ZEFA

Jakarta is a typical city of the developing world with modern roads and buildings beside village houses.

Indonesia became independent in 1949, the Indonesians once again gave Jakarta its original name. Nearly all of the Dutch people have left Jakarta. The population is 7,636,000 (1983).

JAMAICA is one of the larger islands in the Caribbean Sea, and is an independent member of the Commonwealth. It lies about 150 kilometres (93 miles) south of Cuba. Somewhat further distant to the east across the Jamaica Channel is the island of Hispaniola, now divided into two countries, Haiti and the Dominican Republic.

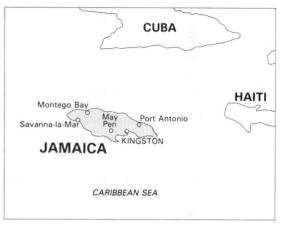

Jamaica is a very mountainous island. A ridge of high land runs along the island rising in the east to the Blue Mountains with a peak of 2,256 metres (7,400 feet), the highest in the West Indies. In the northwest the limestone hills have been worn away by tropical rains into large sink holes and pits, and this part is called the Cockpit country. In many places between the hills and the shore stretch fertile plains.

The Arawak Indians who once lived on the island called it *Xaymaca*, meaning "land of springs", and more than 100 rivers and streams fed by mountain springs find their way to the sea. Except for the Black River in the west, which can be used by small craft as it winds through the marshes, and the Rio Grande in the east where rafting is now a pastime, rivers in Jamaica are too narrow for navigation. Some of them, such as the Rio Cobre and Black River, are used for making electricity by water power. Jamaica has excellent harbours. That of Kingston in the southeast is protected by a natural breakwater formed by a narrow strip of land 12 kilometres (7 miles) long called the Palisadoes. Other harbours are Port Morant, Old Harbour, and on the north coast Montego Bay, Falmouth, St. Ann's Bay, Port Maria, and Port Antonio. New harbours such as Port Esquivel, Ocho Rios, and Port Kaiser have been developed in recent years by the bauxite companies who ship aluminium ore from Jamaica.

FACTS ABOUT JAMAICA

AREA: 10,990 square kilometres (4,244 square miles).
POPULATION: 2,365,000 (1987).
GOVERNMENT: Independent parliamentary state; member of the Commonwealth.
CAPITAL: Kingston.
GEOGRAPHICAL FEATURES: A mountainous island, the highest peak being 2,256 metres (7,400 feet); coastal plains, especially in the south; many rivers; many natural harbours.
CHIEF EXPORTS: Alumina (aluminium oxide) and bauxite, sugar, bananas, rum, pimento, fruit juices, coffee, cocoa, cigars, ginger.
IMPORTANT TOWNS: Kingston, Spanish Town, Portmore, Montego Bay.
EDUCATION: Schooling is free and compulsory. Higher education is also free.

Jamaica has a pleasantly warm climate and the rather damp heat of the coast changes in the mountains to a delightful fresh coolness. Most rain falls in the north and east, chiefly in the form of heavy showers in May and October. Like other Caribbean lands, Jamaica is occasionally swept by severe hurricanes in the late summer and these sometimes cause tremendous damage to property.

Many different kinds of trees and flowering plants grow in Jamaica. The Cockpit country is densely covered with valuable timber trees, including the immensely hard lignum vitae ("wood of life"), mahogany, ebony, cedar, and greenheart. The biggest tree is the ceiba or silk-cotton tree, from whose thick trunk canoes are sometimes made and whose seedpods contain the fluffy material called kapok (see KAPOK). In the mountain forests grow many flowering creepers and plants such as orchids; brilliant flowering shrubs such as the hibiscus and bougainvillea are widely cultivated and on the coastal plains coconut palms and cacti (see CACTUS) may often be seen. Among the food plants growing wild are cassava (tapioca), arrowroot, guava, pawpaw, and breadfruit. Jamaica has few remarkable wild animals, but crocodiles and freshwater turtles are found. Among the wild birds are parrots, hummingbirds, and tanagers, which are songbirds related to the sparrow family but with brilliant plumage.

Peoples and Industries

The Arawak Indians who once lived in Jamaica were wiped out by the Spaniards who settled there early in the 16th century, many of them being carried off to work in the gold mines of Central America. In place of the Indians the Spaniards brought black slaves from Africa to work in Jamaica. The English continued this practice when they took the island and by 1807, when the slave trade in British lands was abolished, there were more than 300,000 slaves in Jamaica. Slavery was not abolished on the island until 1833. (See SLAVERY.) The Jamaicans of today are the descendants of all the peoples who have inhabited the island since this time—blacks from Africa, the white plantation owners, servants and overseers from Britain, and Indian and Chinese servants from the east. Most Jamaicans are Christians and the island has a high density of population.

Although only a small part of the area of Jamaica can be cultivated, agriculture is important. The chief crops are sugar cane, bananas, coffee, citrus fruits (grapefruits, limes and oranges), coconuts, tobacco, cocoa, ginger, and pimento (allspice). Most of the level land is in estates or large farms but there are many smallholders who grow maize, rice, and vegetables for sale in the local markets as well as bananas and citrus fruits for export. Cattle are now kept in large quantities, providing almost enough meat to supply the island's needs. Goats and poultry are also kept.

There are a number of important industries

This modern sports stadium was built for the 1966 Commonwealth Games in Kingston, Jamaica's capital.

in Jamaica today. In addition to processing the island's agricultural products, a wide range of manufactures is now produced. These include clothing and footwear, toilet articles and textiles, cement, paint, building materials, and agricultural machinery. In addition tourism is now a major island industry.

Jamaica contains one of the largest known deposits in the world of the clay-like mineral bauxite from which aluminium is made. (See BAUXITE.) Large-scale mining of Jamaican bauxite only began in 1952 and is now the island's largest industry, with great quantities being shipped to Canada and the United States. Jamaica is the world's second largest producer after Australia, accounting for nearly a fifth of the total world production. Another mineral, gypsum, is also mined in Jamaica, and a large oil refinery is established there.

The magnificent scenery of Jamaica combined with its pleasant climate and splendid bathing beaches has brought a number of wealthy people to live there and encourages a very large and important tourist trade. Many holiday-makers from America and Britain come to stay in the luxury hotels, and ships call at the island during their cruises in the winter months.

The capital of Jamaica is Kingston, situated on the Liguanea Plain at the foot of the Blue Mountains. Most of the city is modern, because a great earthquake in January 1907 destroyed much of the old Kingston. At the tip of the Palisadoes guarding the harbour is the town of Port Royal, once the headquarters of the buccaneers. These were pirates who in the 17th century raided the Spanish Main (the Spanish settlements in Central America).

Kingston itself is surrounded by a larger suburban area stretching up into the foothills in which many families live in modern homes in pleasant surroundings. There are large residential areas of good housing in the city. However, owing to poverty and unemploy-

Spanish Town, formerly the capital of Jamaica.

ment, there are still a good many shacks and slum dwellings in Kingston. About 19 kilometres (12 miles) inland from Kingston is Spanish Town (formerly St. Jago de la Vega), the capital of the island until 1872. Montego Bay in the northwest is an important tourist centre. Several places in Jamaica have Spanish names, such as Ocho Rios ("eight rivers"), a seaside resort near which there is a magnificent waterfall. Some of the villages are oddly named—examples are Maggotty and Gimme-me-bit.

Jamaica has good roads and a government-owned railway with branches from Kingston to Montego Bay and Port Antonio. Ships from Europe, North and South America, India, Australia, and New Zealand call at Jamaica and there are large airfields at Palisadoes and Montego Bay as well as some smaller airfields which can be used by small aircraft and helicopters.

History

Jamaica was discovered on 3 May 1494, by Christopher Columbus, who landed at Dry Harbour (now Discovery Bay) about 21 kilometres (13 miles) west of St. Ann's Bay on the north coast. It was then inhabited by Arawak Indians. In 1509 a Spanish governor was appointed and until 1655 the island, although several times raided by the English, remained under Spanish rule. Then Admiral William Penn and General Venables, who had been sent out by Oliver Cromwell to attack Hispaniola, captured Jamaica and drove out the Spaniards. Some of the black slaves set free by the Spaniards escaped to the mountains and for many years strove to keep their freedom, fighting back whenever they were attacked and welcoming runaway slaves from the rest of the island. In 1783 the runaway slaves (called maroons, from the Spanish *cimarron* meaning "untamed") living in the mountains gained sovereign right to five maroon towns, which they controlled under their own leaders.

For some time Port Royal was the base of the buccaneers, some of whom went to sea as pirates when they grew bored with being planters and merchants. The leading buccaneer was the Welshman Henry Morgan (1635–88). In 1670 a treaty was signed in which Spain recognized Jamaica as an English possession. The buccaneers were put down and Morgan was sent home under arrest, but he gained the favour of King Charles II and was soon back again in Jamaica as Sir Henry Morgan and lieutenant-governor, although that did not stop his buccaneering. Much of the buccaneers' town, Port Royal, was destroyed by a great earthquake in 1692, and this led to the foundation of Kingston. Despite earthquakes and hurricanes, the island grew prosperous from the profits made from the sugar, cocoa, and coffee plantations. Bananas were introduced and became a profitable crop. Many Jamaicans found work on Central American banana plantations and later in the building of the Panama Canal.

Jamaica, which became a British crown colony in 1866, obtained an increasing degree of self-government from 1884 onwards. From 1944 the island had a House of Representatives elected by the people, and in 1953, and again in 1958, the constitution was altered to give the parliament more control over Jamaican affairs. Jamaica was one of the leading countries of the short-lived West Indian Federation set up by the British in 1958. The federation was dissolved on 31 May 1962, and on 6 August Jamaica became fully independent.

With independence Jamaica became a member of the Commonwealth with the British

Monarch as its head of state, represented by a local governor-general. A prime minister is elected in general elections held every five years. Jamaica helped to set up CARICOM, a Caribbean organization for economic development. During the 1970s development included land reforms and progress in housing. The 1980s witnessed political swings between the moderates and those who favoured more drastic changes in the country.

JAMES (Kings of Britain). There were two kings named James who ruled over both England and Scotland. Both belonged to the House of Stuart. The struggle between the Crown and parliament began in the reign of James I. It flamed into revolution under Charles I and was kept under control by the diplomacy of Charles II. The struggle ended with the triumph of parliament and the expulsion of James II in 1688.

James I (1566–1625), the son of Mary, Queen of Scots, and Henry Stuart, Lord Darnley, her second husband, was born in Edinburgh Castle. He came to the throne of Scotland as James VI in 1567 after his mother had been deposed.

Mary sought refuge in England, but was executed there in 1587. James was still a child when he became king of Scotland and was therefore completely in the power of the Scottish barons. His education, though excellent, was largely from books and little from practical experience. His narrow scholarship led to his being called "the wisest fool in Christendom". In 1582, when he was 16, he was captured and held as a prisoner in the interests of the Protestant party. The next year he escaped and began to govern the country as an absolute monarch.

James did in Scotland what had been done by the Tudors in England. He broke the feudal power of the Scottish barons and established a strong royal government. The Church, too, which in the hands of the Presbyterians was as powerful as the Church of Rome had ever been, was forced to obey him. James did a great deal of good in Scotland. He developed Scottish industries and enforced peace among the unruly barons.

In 1603 James was called to England to succeed Elizabeth I. He was a Protestant, and the chance of uniting the two kingdoms under a Protestant rule was too good to be missed. But James himself was unpopular. He was physically feeble and undignified in his personal appearance. His Scottish accent, his talkativeness, and his desire to show off his learning made him appear ridiculous in England.

James boasted of his "king-craft", and treated the English parliament with lies, bluff, and bullying. These methods had worked well enough with the feudal barons of Scotland but were not acceptable to the experienced politicians of England. His mild

National Portrait Gallery, London

Two kings named James have ruled England, both in the 17th century and both from the Stuart family. **Left:** James I (ruled 1603–25); **Right:** James II (ruled 1685–88).

and frequently changed foreign policy offended the mass of the people, who were proud of victory over Spain and the exploits of their daring sea captains. Jamestown, Virginia, and Plymouth, Massachusetts, were founded as English colonies during his reign, and England dreamed of expansion.

James, however, was too undecided when action was called for and placed too great faith in his own political schemes. He married his daughter Elizabeth to the Protestant elector of the Palatinate and tried to marry his son Charles to the daughter of the Catholic Spanish king Philip III. He alternately favoured the Catholics and Protestants in his kingdom, and succeeded only in angering both.

In resentment against the persecution of Catholics, which James permitted, a small group of Catholic noblemen sought to blow up the House of Lords (see FAWKES, GUY). The Protestants, on the other hand, continually suspected him of favouring Catholicism. They resented his theory of the divine right of kings, that kings were appointed by God and so their subjects had a holy duty to obey them. At one time he sought an alliance with Spain, yet later he allowed himself to be drawn into a useless and unprofitable war with that country. His whole reign was a series of contradictory and untimely acts.

James was a writer of some ability, though his works often aroused the amusement of his subjects. His *Daemonology* was a denouncement of "witches", who were hunted and burned during his reign. His *Counterblaste to Tobacco* stormed without effect against the new habit of smoking. Only one of James's literary commissions met with the full approval of his Protestant subjects. This was the new translation of the Bible, known as the "King James Version". It was James's idea but was the work of the most learned linguists and scholars that could be brought together. It is a masterpiece of beautiful and accurate English. On his death James I was succeeded by Charles I.

James II (1633–1701) was the grandson of James I and the brother of Charles II. After the restoration of Charles II, James, as duke of York and lord high admiral, proved himself courageous and hardworking. He beat the Dutch in 1665 and fought a drawn battle with Admiral Michel Adriaanszoon de Ruyter in 1672. When James became a Catholic and married a Catholic princess, however, indignation swept the country. Parliament had earlier passed the Test Act, which forbade Catholics to hold office. James resigned all his offices and left England.

He was called to the English throne in 1685. Two Protestant rebellions broke out against him—those of the Duke of Monmouth in the west and the Earl of Argyll in Scotland. Most of the people supported James, and he was able to crush the revolts. The trial of Monmouth's followers was called "the Bloody Assizes". It was a stain on James's character because of its cruelty.

James never quite understood that England, while it was loyal to its constitutional king, would not submit to unconstitutional acts. He entered on a pro-Catholic policy and filled the army with Catholic officers. In 1687 he published the Declaration of Indulgence, granting freedom of religion to his subjects. Unfortunately England was then too much afraid of the Catholics to appreciate this wise and generous act. He ordered all bishops and clergymen to read his declaration from the pulpit. Seven bishops refused and were put on trial. James was determined to obtain a conviction, but the fury of the people was so great that the jury was forced to acquit the bishops.

Parliament invited the Protestant William of Orange, the husband of James's daughter Mary, to come to England, depose James II, and take the throne. William landed on 15 November 1688, and James was left without a single supporter. William allowed him to escape to France.

JAMES, Henry (1843–1916). Henry James was a great writer who showed how the thoughts of his characters affected the way they behaved. His novels, short stories, travel pieces, and literary criticism were popular in his own day, and have been a major influence on the way prose writing in the 20th century has developed.

Born in New York City, the son of a rich and highly respected writer on religious subjects, Henry James spent an unusual childhood travelling between Europe and the United States. This early knowledge of how people lived on both sides of the Atlantic became a central theme of his writing, which explored the differences between the American and European people of his day, and showed what happened to them when they met and their customs and values came into conflict.

BBC Hulton Picture Library

The American-born writer Henry James, photographed in middle life. He lived for many years in Europe.

In his novels and short stories, the people of the New World are innocent, enthusiastic, great believers in the democratic ideals of equality. Those of the Old World are wise, weary, and corrupt, upholders of aristocratic traditions. It was the interaction of these people in social situations that interested James, rather than action in the form of a lively plot.

James spent the years between 1864 and 1875 writing short stories and book reviews for American magazines. His first two books, a collection of short stories and a group of travel pieces, were both published in 1875. He continued to travel in Europe during these years, and in 1875 settled there permanently. He lived in London for more than 20 years, and then moved to the old seaport town of Rye on the English Channel, where he lived until his death.

In a writing career that spanned more than 50 years, James wrote nearly 100 short stories, 23 novels (2 were unfinished), 12 plays (only his plays were unsuccessful), literary criticism that if collected would make more than 10 volumes, 7 travel books, 3 autobiographies, 2 biographies, and more than 15,000 letters of literary importance. Among his novels are his first, *Roderick Hudson* (1876), *The American* (1877), *The Europeans* (1878), *Daisy Miller* (1878), *The Portrait of a Lady* (1881), and *What Maisie Knew* (1897). His last three finished novels – *The Wings of the Dove* (1902), *The Ambassadors* (1903), and *The Golden Bowl* (1904) – are considered his greatest.

JAPAN is an island country in the North Pacific Ocean off the coast of Asia, from which it is separated by the Sea of Japan. In the southwest, the chain of islands lies about 175 kilometres (108 miles) from Korea and about 800 kilometres (500 miles) from China. The most northerly island of Japan is less than 300 kilometres (185 miles) from Siberia in Russia.

Japan consists of a group of four large islands and hundreds of small ones. The largest and most important island is Honshu, in the southern part of which are the chief cities Tokyo, Yokohama, Nagoya, Osaka, Kyoto, and Kobe.

Across the beautiful Inland Sea from Honshu is the island of Shikoku, one of the chief rice-growing regions. Southwest of Honshu across a narrow strait lies Kyushu, the island which the Japanese first settled. North of Honshu is Hokkaido, which is much colder and is thinly populated.

Japan is a land of mountains and sea coasts. The many high mountains rise steeply from narrow valleys. The highest and most beautiful is Fujiyama, west of Tokyo, which is 3,776 metres (12,388 feet) high. On the coasts there are a number of small plains, but less than one-fifth of the land can be planted and most

The country of Japan consists of a chain of islands in the western Pacific Ocean. The four main islands (from bottom left to top right) are: Kyushu, Shikoku, Honshu, and Hokkaido.

of the mountains are too steep for anything to grow except trees. Many short but swift-flowing rivers and streams provide water power for making electricity.

The warm north-going current called the *Kuroshio*, the "black stream", flows past the coast of Honshu and prevents the winters there from becoming too cold or long. But Hokkaido is washed by a current from the Arctic and has long, bitter winters. The summers are hot and damp, being almost tropical in southern Japan. June and July are the most unpleasant months of the year, when it rains continuously for about six weeks.

Countryside and Wildlife

The country is at its most beautiful when the cherry, plum, and peach trees come into blossom in the spring. The mountain slopes are thickly wooded with pines, Japanese cypress, spruce, cedars, firs, beeches, oaks, birches, and bamboo. Evergreens and palms grow in the southern lowlands.

As the Japanese islands stretch so far from north to south, the kinds of animals and plants found there vary greatly. There are many foxes, badgers, otters, martens, ermine, and Japanese mink. In the forests live small pink-faced monkeys called macaques, and giant salamanders are to be seen in the mountain streams. Large wild animals are rare now, but there are still some bears and a few wolves. Tremendous numbers of fish come and go with the ocean currents around the coast, and the seas are also rich with shellfish. The giant crabs found on the west coast have a limb spread 3 metres (10 feet) across. Whales, seals, and walruses are also found.

Of the 450 species of birds on the four main islands, about a third are waterfowl including the rare and elegant Japanese white-necked crane (which features in many ancient Japanese paintings). Birds visit Japan all year round, coming from Russia, in the north, to enjoy the warmer winter, and from China and Asia, in the south, to spend the summer in Japan.

The insects of Japan are of many kinds.

Butterflies and beetles are abundant, fireflies are seen in summer and dragonflies in the autumn. Ticks, mantises, and crickets are also common in late summer. The calls of the *suzumushi*, or bell insect, are like the soft tones of a bell, while the *kusahibari*, or grasslark, produces a very high, clear note with a metallic ringing sound. Most insects begin their songs in the evening but one of them, a kind of grasshopper, sings in the day-time. Poisonous snakes and dangerous insects are rare.

Japan has been called the flowery kingdom, and the Japanese are known for their love of nature. They not only practise and teach *ikebana*, the art of flower arrangement, but have contributed hundreds of flowering shrubs and trees to the gardens of the world. Wistaria, azalea, iris, and peony are common in the spring. In summer, the lotus drops red and

Courtesy, Consulate General of Japan

ZEFA

Top left: Haruni Street, Tokyo, ablaze with neon lights at night. **Bottom left:** The Kodama Express, one of Japan's high-speed bullet trains, passes through Tokyo on its way to Osaka. **Above:** Mount Fuji, Japan's highest mountain and sacred shrine, is beautifully reflected behind these fishermen on Lake Yamanaka. **Below:** A Shinto shrine with its *torii*—the gateway which marks its spiritual area.

Courtesy, Consulate General of Japan

The Hutchison Library

white blossoms on the lakes, and autumn blankets the countryside with chrysanthemums, the national flower of Japan.

Japan is a volcanic country, with a number of active volcanoes and many hot springs; from time to time earthquakes cause tremendous damage. The earthquake that destroyed most of Tokyo and Yokohama in 1923 was the worst in history and more than 100,000 people were killed. Japanese houses, which are light and built mostly of wood, are well suited to a region where earthquakes can destroy sturdier structures, but they easily catch fire. Large modern buildings in the cities are specially designed in steel and concrete to withstand earth movements, but areas where old buildings are jammed together along narrow streets are very dangerous during earthquakes. In the autumn there are storms called typhoons (see HURRICANE).

The People

The Japanese are a Mongoloid race (see RACE), with straight black or dark brown hair, yellow to light brown skin, brown eyes and round faces. They most closely resemble their neighbours the Chinese and Koreans of northeast Asia. But like all modern peoples the Japanese are racially mixed.

The Japanese are believed to have come to the islands from the mainland about 3,000 years ago. They were met by the natives of the islands, a group of people called Ainu. The Ainu, who are considered Caucasian, were a hairy people with a light complexion. The men wore thick beards and the women, at marriage, inscribed a moustache-like tattoo above their mouths. The Ainu were slowly driven north to Hokkaido by the migrating Asians and most were later absorbed into the society of the new Japanese. Now only about 15,000 Ainu remain.

St. Francis Xavier, the 16th-century missionary, wrote: "These Japanese are supremely curious—eager to be instructed to the highest degree." Still curious, and skilled in grasping new methods, the Japanese have learned much of western technology but retain a love of tradition. They have a keen feeling

for beauty and art. Life is ordered by strict rules of manner and conduct, and self-discipline is considered to be very important. Duty comes first and a Japanese must put the good of his family and country before all else. In recent years, dedication to a person's employer has become as strong as national loyalty for most Japanese.

Until recently the family, including a large group of relatives, decided on the careers of the young people and arranged their marriages. More than half of Japanese marriages are still arranged in part by the parents. Children are much loved, and seldom scolded in public, but order is kept strictly at home. Since World War II, the strict codes of behaviour have been relaxed and life is now more free for women as well as for men.

FACTS ABOUT JAPAN

AREA: 377,781 square kilometres (145,862 square miles).
POPULATION: 122,265,000 (1987).
GOVERNMENT: Independent kingdom.
CAPITAL: Tokyo.
GEOGRAPHICAL FEATURES: Four main, mountainous islands (Honshu, Kyushu, Shikoku, and Hokkaido) and hundreds of small islets. The highest mountain is Fuji or Fujiyama at 3,776 m (12,388 ft). There are many active volcanoes.
CHIEF AGRICULTURAL AND MINERAL PRODUCTS: Rice, sweet potatoes, potatoes, barley, wheat, fruit; coal.
LEADING INDUSTRIES: Textiles, chemicals, shipbuilding, steel and engineering, motor, and electrical consumer goods, manufacturing.
IMPORTANT TOWNS: Tokyo, Osaka, Nagoya, Kyoto, Yokohama, Kobe, Sapporo, Fukuoka, Kawasaki, Kitakyushu (all with populations over 1 million).
EDUCATION: Compulsory between the ages of 6 and 15.

Loyalty is the virtue most prized in Japan. Both in ancient dramas and in modern plays, heroes put loyalty above everything else. Until the end of World War II, the Japanese regarded their emperor as a sort of god. No one was allowed to look down on him from a height, and the upper storeys of houses were cleared of people before the emperor went by. During World War II the Japanese were willing to die for their emperor and thus fought valiantly, until he announced Japan's surrender. Since that time, the emperor has become a constitutional monarch (see MONARCH), and lives much more like an ordinary person.

The city dwellers in Japan live modern "westernized" lives for the most part, but large areas of the countryside still cling to the traditional ways of Japanese life. Rural life has changed little for centuries. A small home is built on a wooden frame, with a narrow porch along the sunny side of the house which serves as a hall on to which the rooms open. Sliding screens made of paper-covered frames divide one room from another, and the main room always has an alcove adorned with a vase of flowers or a dwarf tree and a scroll painting drawn in flowing lines. Outer wooden doors slide shut at night to protect the house from rain and cold winds, and open in the morning to let in the fresh air and light.

There is little furniture. Cushions and large folding mattresses are used for sitting and sleeping. Bed quilts and pillows are put in cupboards in the daytime. The floors are covered with thick, soft straw mats. To protect the fine woodwork in the home and to keep the mats clean, everyone removes his shoes at the door. There are no fireplaces or chimneys since in winter the rooms are heated by oil and gas heaters that can be moved from room to room.

In the cities the Japanese wear European-style clothes when going to work in a factory or modern office building and frequently eat lunch in a western-style restaurant. Homes in the city are likely to be apartments (flats) in a tall block or in houses owned by the company. At home, some office workers may change into a *kimono*, a loose gown caught at the waist by a large decorative belt called an *obe*. This is the traditional form of clothing and is worn with flat wooden clogs, but most young people and children wear trousers, shirts, and dresses all day long. Japanese today are very Western-style conscious, particularly in clothes, and their fashion designers are among the top in the world.

Equipped with television, furniture, and modern appliances, modern Japanese living-rooms and kitchens look much like those of any Western house. But the bedroom has *tatami* flooring and there is no bed. At dinner time, Japanese families gather around an electrically-heated table. This table, the *kotatsu*, is draped with warm quilts under which the members of the family warm their feet.

Japanese-style meals include very little meat, butter, and cheese. The chief food is rice served in a bowl and eaten with chopsticks. A great deal of fish is eaten, sometimes raw, and other foods include pickled vegetables, bamboo shoots, bean-curd soup, sweet potatoes, and fruit.

Weak green tea without milk and sugar is very popular, but the Japanese drink coffee and soft drinks too. Another native drink is *sake*, a spirit made from rice which is usually drunk warm. Beer is popular, especially in the hot summers.

The Japanese enjoy a daily bath either at home in large, deep tubs, or at a public bathhouse. For farming families the public bathhouse is often the centre of their social life. They gather with neighbours to relax and talk together in the hot, steaming water. Hot sulphur spring baths are considered healthy.

Recreation and the Arts

Table tennis, lawn tennis, golf, baseball, football and swimming are popular sports, as are skiing and ten-pin bowling. *Sumo* is a form of wrestling in which very fat, strong men, specially trained, try to push each other out of the ring. Another form of wrestling called *judo* is practised by amateurs as well as by professionals (see JUDO). Fencing with two-handed swords is performed now only for show, but archery is popular and children enjoy flying kites.

As well as theatres for modern plays and many cinemas in the cities, there are two kinds of Japanese traditional theatre. The *kabuki* theatres have plays based on stories and legends of Japan's ancient warriors. The *Noh* plays date from the 14th century when they were entertainment for the aristocrats and warrior classes in the days of feudal Japan. All the parts are played by actors wearing masks. Many *Noh* plays are given at one performance since they are brief and consist of music and symbolic dancing accompanied by recitations. Puppet plays, originally imported from China, are performed with large puppets, to a background of Japanese music and the singing of dramatic ballads.

Traditional Japanese music is very different from western music. It still lingers in classical dances and theatres and in festivals. Most Japanese instruments came from China, Korea, and India. The most popular, the *samisen*, is a guitar-like instrument with three strings. Jazz, ballroom, and popular music is enjoyed and the great cities have symphony orchestras and opera companies. Still a form of entertainment among wealthy men are the tea houses where *geisha* girls, dressed in rich silk kimonos with elaborately dressed hair, dance, play the samisen, sing, recite poetry, and talk with the guests.

There are many Japanese festival days. The most important is at the New Year, when houses are decorated outside with bamboo stems and pine branches and people visit and give presents and cards. Special foods and ceremonial drinks are served. According to the old way of calculating ages, this was everyone's birthday. Children were one year old at birth, and everyone added a year at the New Year.

March 3 is the girls' festival when families of special dolls representing the emperor and his court are set out and treated with great respect. The Dolls' Festival, or Peach Blossom Festival, reminds small girls that they must be as peaceful and gentle as peach blossoms.

The boys hold their festival on May 5 when they bring out and show toy images of ancient Japanese warriors and hoist paper carp over their homes. The carp, a fish that swims upstream against the current, shows the spirit of determination with which the boys must face future difficulties. This day is known as the Feast of the Flags.

In July is the *O-bon* festival when families are supposed to be visited by the spirits of their ancestors. The spirits are given a great welcome, offerings are made to them and there is then a farewell ceremony.

The Japanese are fond of gardens and almost every home has at least a small one. Miniature evergreen trees, flowering bushes, pools, streams, and bridges are expertly arranged to look like a whole landscape of mountains and lakes. By opening a door on to the garden, it seems to become part of the house.

Religion

The chief religions of Japan are Shintoism and Buddhism, on which there are separate articles. Once the Japanese were also much influenced by the teaching of the Chinese philosopher Confucius (see CONFUCIUS). A Japanese proverb says that a young man worships before a Shinto shrine and that when older he obeys Confucius, but that when he is near the end of his life he studies Buddhist teaching. Shintoism, which is the original religion of the Japanese, teaches the people to love nature and respect their ancestors. It was established as the state religion in the Meiji era, which began in 1868. After World War II, however, state support of Shinto was abolished. Buddhism, brought in from China around the 6th century AD, is now the leading religion in Japan. In addition, there are also about 700,000 Japanese Christians. In each Japanese home, there are usually both a miniature Shinto shrine and Buddhist temple for ceremonies on holy days. The countryside abounds with beautiful Shinto shrines and famous Buddhist temples, some many hundreds of years old. People of all faiths come to visit these historic monuments.

Culture and Language

Japanese art owes much to that of China, but it is not just a copy of it. The colour woodcut (see WOODCUT), is the form of Japanese art best known in Europe. It was popular in the 18th and 19th centuries and made art available to the common people. Among the great masters of this art were Harunobo and Utamaro in the 18th century and Hokusai in the 19th. Japanese woodcuts greatly influenced western artists, especially the French Impressionist painters.

Japanese pottery, ivory carving, and bronze, brass, and lacquer work have been famous for centuries. Japanese architects have a strong love for simple, natural beauty. Traditional buildings and homes are designed in harmony with the countryside. Much of Japan's traditional architecture was influenced by Buddhists who built temples according to the Chinese plan. However, the *torii*, the traditional Japanese gateway, is seen at Shinto shrines. Modern buildings follow western styles and Japanese architects have become famous for their modern work in Japan and abroad.

The Japanese language is difficult for foreigners, for although the words are easy to pronounce, they are written in a complicated way, using characters originally taken from Chinese. The characters represent sounds or ideas and a man has to know several thousand before he can read an ordinary book. However, once it is mastered, reading Japanese is much faster than reading English. Handwriting is regarded as a form of art and the characters are often written with a brush. Scrolls displaying fine writing are hung in the alcoves of homes.

Japanese children must attend school between the ages of 6 and 15. At the free schools boys and girls attend the same classes, and all Japanese children study English. Although not free, the many high schools, technical and preparatory schools are attended by a large majority of the children. Almost 1 million Japanese students attend more than 300 colleges and universities.

Farming and Fishing

Because land is scarce, Japanese farmers have to work hard at cultivating their small plots. Most farms are very small and irrigation is widely used. The warm wet summers and mild winters allow heavy crops to be grown, and in some places four different crops are harvested in a season. Harvests have become better, thanks to widespread use of modern techniques, but Japan supplies only 80 per cent of its food needs. Workers are leaving the farms for jobs in the cities, and less than 10 per cent of Japanese now work on the land.

Rice grows on more than half the farmland and the farmers grow it more intensively than in any other Asian country. Each rice seedling is grown in a kind of nursery, carefully transplanted by hand in the early summer, and from then on tended carefully and fed with fertilizer. Wheat, barley, potatoes, millet, vegetables, and fruit are grown on the upland fields, and tea in southern Honshu. The Japanese formerly ate little meat or dairy produce, so there were few cattle and sheep except in Hokkaido. Livestock farming is now more widespread.

Some Japanese farmers raise silkworms, which are kept in trays in a special room of the farmhouse. They are fed on the leaves of the mulberry tree, which will grow on poor soil and steep slopes. When the silkworms have spun their cocoons these are collected and sold to silk-reeling mills. Raw silk was once one of Japan's most valuable products but since the invention of synthetic fabrics it has been less important.

Japan's fishing industry is one of the largest and most highly developed in the world. Canned and frozen fish and shellfish are valuable exports. From coastal waters come sardines, herring, salmon, cuttlefish, yellowtail, and other fish. Seaweed is harvested for food, fertilizer, and fodder. Deep-sea fishing fleets travel great distances for cod, bonito, shark, mackerel, and tuna. Oyster farms produce oysters for eating and for pearls.

Industry and Transport

Japan is one of the great industrial powers of the world and the chief manufacturing nation in Asia. Its industrial progress in the past century, achieved without many essential raw materials, has been amazing. In the 19th century most goods manufactured in Japan were made in small workshops or in people's homes. They included silk cloth, lacquer ware, pottery, and handicrafts. Little machinery was used.

Courtesy, National Museum, Tokyo

Woodcuts were used in Japan to produce brightly coloured portraits and landscapes, which became popular from the 17th century.
Above: One of a series of woodcuts called *Fifty-three stages on the Tokaido Highway* by Ando Hiroshige (1797–1858) shows men battling against a storm. **Right:** The actor Ichikawa Ebizo by the artist Sharaku, *c.*1794. **Below:** This woodcut by the famous artist Hokusai (1760–1849) is called *Maple Leaves on Tsutata River*.

Courtesy, National Museum, Tokyo

Trustees of the British Museum. Photo, Mansell Collection

Today, Japan's industries include the manufacture of heavy and light machinery, electrical goods, textiles, and steel. Japanese shipyards and engineering works build the largest ships and marine engines. Japan also produces railway locomotives and rolling stock, motor cars and motor bikes, sewing machines, cameras, televisions, videos, hi-fi, clocks, watches, toys, and pottery. Japanese methods of business management, which concentrate on getting workers and managers to work together with enthusiasm as a team, are highly successful and greatly admired overseas.

Electricity is produced from water power and there are supplies of copper, zinc, and gold; but Japan has to buy most of its ore for making iron and aluminium, and most of its petroleum. In addition coal, cotton, wool, and rubber have to be bought from abroad.

Japan produces most manufactured goods more cheaply than other industrialized nations, and has achieved a leading position in world trade. The metal, chemical, engineering, electronics, computer, and other high technology industries have grown very rapidly. Like other industrialized nations, Japan has suffered industrial ills such as smog, pollution, and overcrowding, so the government now places greater importance on public welfare and on cleaning up industrial waste.

The four main Japanese islands have good railways, the lines in Honshu and Kyushu being connected by a tunnel under the straits. Trains on the Tokaido line from Tokyo to Osaka are among the fastest in the world. Many lines are electrified and some have automatic control systems for safety. There is a road tunnel between Honshu and Kyushu, and a double-decked road and rail bridge is under construction between the islands of Honshu and Shikoku. When completed, it will be the world's longest suspension bridge.

There are bus, taxi, and underground railway services in the cities and the number of cars is growing steadily. Japan has the largest fleet of merchant ships in the world, and handles nearly one quarter of the world's ship cargoes. The chief seaports are Kobe, Tokyo, Yokohama, and Osaka. Air travel is also important and Tokyo International Airport is one of the world's busiest.

History

Before the 7th century AD, the Japanese lived a tribal life, in which the family of the emperor, who claimed descent from a sun goddess, was continually struggling for power with other important families. The Buddhist religion and Chinese ways of thought, together with Chinese characters for writing, were gradually introduced. The most important idea borrowed from China, then the richest and mightiest land in the world, was that of a central government under the emperor to rule the whole country. The Japanese emperors tried to follow this idea, but the laws they made were often ignored and disobeyed by the noblemen in the country districts. By the 12th century, most of the power had passed from the emperor to lords called *shogun*, who were military governors ruling in the emperor's name. The emperors remained for centuries shadowy and powerless figures living with their court noblemen at Kyoto, the second capital after Nara.

In the feudal period, the Middle Ages in Europe (see FEUDALISM), Japan was disturbed by frequent wars between the rival noblemen and their knights or *samurai*, the title of shogun passing from one family to another. It was not until the second half of the 16th century that three great leaders, coming one after another, succeeded in bringing the country together. The third of them, Ieyasu, who was of the Tokugawa family, became shogun at the beginning of the 17th century and his rule brought a long period of peace. The *daimyo*, or feudal lords, still ruled their own lands, but they all recognized the Tokugawa shogun as their leader. To make sure that they were loyal, the shogun ordered them to spend every other year at his capital Yedo (which is now Tokyo).

Early in the 17th century Japan's rulers, fearful of foreign influences, shut off their

Courtesy, The Museum of Fine Arts, Boston

This detail from a 13th-century scroll depicts the burning of the Sanjo Palace during a revolt which took place in 1159. Japanese artists prepared many such scrolls, illustrating religious and historical scenes filled with drama.

country from the outside world. No Japanese was allowed to go abroad and it was even forbidden to build ships large enough to cross the ocean. Foreigners, with the exception of the Dutch, were forbidden to settle in Japan or have any dealings with its people. Christianity, to which many Japanese had been converted in the 16th century by St. Francis Xavier (see XAVIER, SAINT FRANCIS) and other missionaries, was almost rooted out.

In 1858, Japan once again opened its gates to the world. By this time the shogun system of government was breaking down. Its final collapse came when United States warships commanded by Commodore Matthew Perry visited Japan to persuade the shogun to open trade links. Other nations quickly followed this lead.

In 1867, the emperor was restored to his position as supreme ruler of the country. Soon afterwards a new emperor came to the throne,

and his rule from 1868 to 1912 was known as the *Meiji* period. (Meiji means "enlightened government".) Swiftly the remains of the old feudal system, which had given the noble families almost complete power over their own districts, were swept away. A modern system of government took its place, and the emperor moved his court from Kyoto to Yedo. An army and navy, copied from those of western countries, were formed, and western books, industries, railways, and ships were introduced. European and American advisers were brought in, and foreign travel and trade was encouraged. The laws were revised, a new system of education adopted and political parties started.

In 1894, a dispute with China about who should rule Korea (the part of Asia nearest to Japan) led to war. The Japanese won important battles on land and at sea, forcing China to give up the valuable island of Taiwan (see

TAIWAN). Korea became for a short while independent. Then disputes between the Japanese and the Russians as to who should govern Manchuria in northern China led to a new war. Japan again won many victories and a peace treaty in 1905 recognized Japan's claims in Korea and southern Manchuria. In 1910, Korea came under Japanese rule and was renamed Chosen (see KOREA, NORTH, and KOREA, SOUTH).

During World War I, Japan was an ally of Britain against Germany and as a result obtained some groups of islands in the Pacific which had formerly been German colonies.

Up to this time the government of Japan had been mainly in the hands of a small group of officials and army and navy officers who ruled in the emperor's name. Although the emperor had granted rights to the people in 1890 and formed a parliament, the people had very little say in the decisions made by the government. After World War I, the right to vote was granted to almost all Japanese men, and the power of parliament increased.

In 1930, however, Japanese industry and agriculture suffered badly from the worldwide reduction in trade. The bad conditions made it easy to put the blame on the government, and at the same time the army leaders wanted to increase Japan's power on the mainland of Asia. In 1931, paying no heed to the government's orders, the army attacked the Chinese troops in Manchuria and swiftly took over the whole of that country. As in Taiwan and Korea, raw materials from Manchuria were sent to Japan in exchange for Japanese manufactured goods.

In 1937, Japan attacked China itself, and although the Chinese resisted bravely they were almost everywhere defeated. By the end of 1938, the Japanese had captured most of the great cities and ports of China. Before this, Japan had signed a pact by which it became an ally of Germany and Italy against its old enemy and neighbour Russia. When World War II broke out in 1939, Japan's relations with Britain and the United States grew steadily worse.

On 7 December 1941, aircraft from Japanese aircraft carriers attacked the United States naval base at Pearl Harbor, Honolulu. War had not been declared when the surprise attack took place and the American fleet suffered severe losses. Japan also attacked Hong Kong, Burma, and Malaya—all of which were then British— as well as the Philippine Islands and the Netherlands East Indies (now Indonesia). Within a year, all of these countries had been conquered, and for a short time Japan had all the oil, coal, food, and raw materials it wanted. Then the tide began to turn. By May 1945, when Germany surrendered, Japan's strength had been crippled. In August 1945, United States aircraft dropped atomic bombs on Hiroshima in southwestern Honshu and Nagasaki in Kyushu. The two cities were almost completely destroyed and more than 100,000 people were killed. As a result, the emperor ordered Japan to surrender.

For the next few years, Japan was ruled by occupation forces under General Douglas MacArthur. Votes were given to women and freedom of thought and discussion were encouraged. The form of Shintoism that encouraged worship of the emperor and his ancestors was abolished, and attempts were made to discourage the people from glorifying the warlike exploits of the Japanese national heroes. Japan lost all its overseas possessions and was restricted to the four home islands.

In 1947, the United States began to restore Japan's industries and trade and in 1951, 48 allied nations signed a peace treaty with Japan. The country regained full sovereignty less than a year later. After 1954, the Japanese steel and engineering industries grew fast, and during the next ten years Japan produced more ships than any other country. Japan was admitted to the United Nations in 1956.

Under the protection of a security treaty signed with the United States in 1960 Japan began a development programme that brought it to third place among industrialized nations, behind the United States and the USSR. After its long isolation from the rest of the world,

Japan emerged in the 1970s as the strongest trading nation in Asia. Japanese goods were sold all over the world; and this prosperity led to rapid changes in the country and the way of life of the Japanese people. In the 1980s Japan is a dominant industrial nation whose manufacturing companies are household names that not only export goods to almost every country in the world but have also set up factories in many of them.

JASMINE is the name given to about 300 species, or kinds, of shrub, some of which climb, some trail, and some grow as bushes, with beautiful fragrant blossoms, yellow, white, and sometimes reddish in colour. Jasmine belongs to the Oleaceae family and its relatives include lilac, ash, privet, and olive. The genus is called *Jasminum*.

This beautiful species of jasmine is native to China. It grows as a tender, evergreen, rambling shrub.

Jasmines have a wide distribution in the tropics and subtropics, and are native to all continents except North America. Some kinds have evergreen leaflets and others are deciduous (they shed their leaves in winter). Common jasmine, or poet's jasmine (*Jasminum officinale*), is sometimes deciduous and sometimes half evergreen. It has exquisite little five-petalled flowers, with a very sweet scent, studding its misty greenery from early summer until the frosts begin. Winter jasmine (*Jasminum nudiflorum*) is deciduous, and its golden, star-like flowers light up the plant's bare branches throughout the winter. If, while the buds are closed, the twigs are cut and are then brought into the house, the lovely flowers will open.

Some kinds of jasmine need to be grown in greenhouses, but others are hardy enough to do well in the open garden. Young plants can be grown from cuttings, which take root and grow quickly. Some, like the common jasmine, climb easily, but others need to be supported by trelliswork, walls or stakes. Some jasmine flowers are so sweet that their scent is used in soap and perfumes, and the flowers of Arabian jasmine (*Jasminum sambac*) are used to make jasmine tea.

The word jasmine comes from the Persian *yasmin*, which is also a girl's name. A poetic spelling is jessamine.

JAY. There are about 37 species of jay, medium-sized birds of the crow family.

There are four species of North American jay. The blue jay (*Cyanocitta cristata*) has bright blue plumage and is very good at imitating sounds. Stellar's jay (*Cyanocitta stelleri*) is dark blue, with a noticeable black crest, and is found in mountains from Alaska to Mexico. The Canada jay (*Perisoreus canadensis*) is also called the whiskey jay, which is probably the white man's version of an Amerindian name. It is duller in colour than the others, having soft grey and white fluffy plumage and a dark cap. It is a very tame bird and even takes bacon from the frying pans of campers. The scrub jay (*Aphelocoma coerulescens*) of western North America is locally called "blue jay" but lacks a crest.

The European jay (*Garrulus glandarius*) has pinkish feathers on its body, a pure white rump and black tail, a crest of black and white feathers and a patch of bright blue, barred with black, on its wings. It is shy and restless, and little more can usually be seen of it in woodlands than a flash of bright colour among the leaves.

NHPA/Stephen J. Krasemann

The North American blue jay is an aggressive bird that drives other birds away from garden feeders.

Jays are active, aggressive birds that feed on a great variety of animal and plant food. Some steal eggs and young of other birds and store seeds and nuts which they dig up during the harsh winter months. Their most obvious calls are harsh with screams and whistles, but all jays have softer melodious calls that they use especially in the spring. Jays are good mimics and a tame jay can copy a wide range of sounds.

JAZZ is a kind of music that began among black Americans just before the end of the 19th century and is today popular all over the world. Many people use the word "jazz" to describe only that music which is very like the music of the original jazz bands that played in New Orleans, in the United States, in the early 1900s. However, the great majority of people use the word to cover many forms of rhythmic music which developed from those beginnings.

The first jazz grew mainly from rough-and-ready brass bands that marched in the streets of New Orleans, playing at funerals, weddings, and elections. The bands started to play indoors—in saloons, restaurants, and dance halls—and began to use different instruments. Finally, someone invented the word "jazz" to describe a music that combined several different influences. These influences were: the marching bands; the Blues (work songs sung by the slaves on the cotton plantations); the syncopated black hymns known as Negro spirituals; the popular songs and dances favoured at that time by white audiences; the drum rhythms the black slaves had brought with them from Africa; and a few traces of European music.

The bands that played this music usually consisted of drums, piano, banjo, trumpet (or cornet), trombone, and clarinet. Sometimes a tuba was added to the first three instruments, which were known as the rhythm section. Later, the tuba was dropped in favour of the string bass, or double bass, and most of the banjo players switched to the guitar.

The rhythm section supplied a basic beat—the main ingredient of jazz—and the other instruments improvised; that is, they played their own version of a theme or melody in their own individual way. Sometimes the "frontline" instrumentalists (the trumpeter, trombonist, and clarinettist) would all improvise at the same time, weaving their variations of the melody into exciting and unusual patterns of sound. At other times, an instrument would play on its own, accompanied only by the rhythm section.

Today the rhythm section is still the backbone of the band, but the front-line often consists of anything up to 14 musicians. In big bands like this—and in many of the smaller ones—the musicians play to written "arrangements" or "scores". Improvisation is restricted to solos.

In these solos, the really great jazz players—old and new—can express their feelings in a most moving way. Many of them, because of their influence on other musicians, have changed the style of jazz entirely.

The Changing Styles of Jazz

The first jazz style to become popular, New Orleans jazz, was made famous by the Original Dixieland Jazz Band (1917) and the bands

Melody Maker

Four of the main instruments of jazz, as seen in a section of Louis Armstrong's band: trombone, trumpet, clarinet, and bass. Armstrong played the trumpet and was the first to make jazz widely famous.

of the pianist Ferdinand "Jelly Roll" Morton (1885–1941), the inventor of "boogy-woogy", and the cornet player Joseph "King" Oliver (1885–1938). These bands played mainly blues, marches, and "ragtime"—a popular form of piano music which had developed since the 1880s; many piano rags were composed by the pianist Scott Joplin (1868–1917).

These early bands were made up of a group of musicians who improvised among themselves. The first jazz musician to make a mark as a soloist was Louis Armstrong (1900–71), who is regarded by many people as the greatest jazz musician of all. A former member of "King" Oliver's band, Louis Armstrong went on to form his own band and to become a world-famous trumpet soloist. Other musicians such as the pianist Earl Hines (1903–83), the sax-

ophonist Sidney Bechet (1897–1959) and the trombonist Jack Teagarden (1905–64) also became well known as soloists.

At the same time larger bands began to play jazz music in orchestral arrangements. Musicians such as Fletcher Henderson (1898–1952) succeeded in turning an ordinary dance band (see BAND), with its brass, woodwind, and rhythm sections, into a jazz band. Paul Whiteman's (1890–1967) big band was known as the "concert jazz" orchestra, and featured Bing Crosby (1904–77) as a singer. The most important of the big bands was formed by the pianist Edward "Duke" Ellington (1899–1974). Ellington's bands combined superb orchestration with brilliant solo playing. Another band which became famous for its rhythmic playing was that of Count Basie

(1904–84). The big band style of jazz was taken up by Benny Goodman (1909–86), who developed "swing" music, and bandleaders such as Stan Kenton (1912–79), who called his music "progressive jazz".

Valerie Wilmer

The US alto saxophonist, Ornette Coleman, led an outstanding quartet in the 1950s. Unusually it had no piano but featured a tenor saxophone instead. Drums and a double bass completed the line-up.

During the 1930s and 1940s many great jazz musicians became famous. They included such men as vibraphonist Lionel Hampton (born 1913); saxophonists Johnny Hodges (1906–70), Coleman Hawkins (1904–69), and Lester Young (1909–59); and pianist Art Tatum (1910–56). During the 1940s some jazz musicians began playing jazz which they meant people to listen to carefully, rather than dance to or use as "atmosphere". New ideas of rhythm, at first known as "bebop", were introduced by men such as Charlie "Bird" Parker (1920–55), saxophone, and John "Dizzy" Gillespie (born 1917), trumpet.

This new style of jazz was more formal and more "cool" (relaxed) than the traditional New Orleans style, and was played mainly by small groups. Among the leading figures of "modern jazz" were trumpeter Miles Davis (born 1926), pianists Thelonious Monk (1917–82) and Dave Brubeck (born 1920), and groups such as the Modern Jazz Quartet. Jazz musicians continued to explore new styles, although basing their music on the jazz tradition. Among the most original musicians have been the saxophonists Ornette Coleman (born 1930) and John Coltrane (1926–67).

Most of the leading jazz musicians still come from the United States, although jazz is played and enjoyed all over the world. In France, for example, the outstanding jazz musicians have been violinist Stéphane Grappelli and guitarist Django Reinhardt. In Britain, leading jazz musicians have included Ken Collier, Kenny Ball, Chris Barber, Monty Sunshine, and John Dankworth. Jazz musicians often join with popular, folk, and classical musicians to play music which combines different styles, and composers such as John Dankworth have written jazz for orchestra and chorus.

Jazz Singers

Jazz is as much a vocal as an instrumental art. The first sound film, made in 1927, was in fact called *The Jazz Singer* and featured Al Jolson (1886–1950). Many of the greatest jazz vocalists were women. Bessie Smith (*c.* 1898–1937) won fame in the 1920s with her "earthy" style of singing. She became known as "the

Topham

Ella Fitzgerald, one of the greatest jazz vocalists of the 20th century, singing at Rome in 1983.

Empress of the Blues". She was followed in the 1930s and 1940s by another great blues singer, Billie Holiday (1915–59). Other outstanding singers have included Ella Fitzgerald (born 1918) and Sarah Vaughan (born 1924). Both these singers are outstanding exponents of *scat-singing*, in which the vocalist uses meaningless syllables while improvising on a given melody.

JEFFERSON, Thomas (1743–1826) was the third president of the United States and the author of the Declaration of Independence. He was one of the greatest Americans ever to hold office, a champion of freedom and human rights. Broad shouldered and tall, strong and graceful, he had a soft voice and a charming manner. He sought to free the people from the restraints of unjust government, ignorance, intolerance, and prejudice.

Jefferson was born on 13 April 1743 at Shadwell in Albermarle County, Virginia. His father was a wealthy planter and a leading member of the community who left his son a considerable plantation and many slaves. Thomas received a classical education in languages, philosophy, and mathematics, graduating from William and Mary College in Williamsburg in 1762. At 24 he started to practise law and soon became a successful lawyer. He designed his beautiful home at Monticello on his plantation. In 1772 he married Martha Wayles Skelton, daughter of a rich Williamsburg lawyer.

Jefferson became interested in politics at an early stage of his career. He was a member for six years of the Virginia House of Burgesses and joined a group working to end British rule. His support of the actions leading to the Boston Tea Party (see BOSTON TEA PARTY), and a strong attack on British tyranny read to the Williamsburg convention in 1774, made him a leader of the opposition to the king and parliament. In 1775 he was a delegate to the Second Continental Congress. When the American Revolution began, the Virginia convention instructed its delegates to the Continental Congress to declare for independence. Jefferson was named chair-

Underwood and Underwood
Thomas Jefferson, US president, 1801–09.

man of the Congress committee selected to write the declaration. The Declaration of Independence adopted by Congress on 4 July 1776 was mostly what Jefferson wrote. In clear and challenging words Jefferson said that government is established by the consent of the governed and must serve the people. He listed many unjust acts of the king which left the colonists no choice but to rebel. (See DECLARATION OF INDEPENDENCE.)

Jefferson carried through several important reforms in the Virginia legislature including the separation of Church and state. He was elected governor in 1779 and had to suffer an attack by British troops who swept through the state burning and destroying. From 1784 to 1789 Jefferson was abroad, making trade agreements with European countries. In 1790 President Washington appointed Jefferson secretary of state. He became the leader of the supporters of democratic government known as Republicans. He opposed the Federalists, led by secretary of the treasury Alexander Hamilton, who believed in government by a few men of wealth and education serving the interests of the merchants and bankers.

After a period in retirement Jefferson returned to politics, running for the presidency against Federalist John Adams. Adams narrowly won and Jefferson was elected vice-president. A split developed in the Federalist party and in the 1800 election the two Republican candidates Jefferson and Aaron Burr won a clear victory, each receiving the same number of votes. The House of Representatives eventually chose Jefferson. When he took up his duties he put on a suit of plain black cloth and went on foot to take the oath of office instead of driving in a coach drawn by six horses.

Jefferson's first administration was a great success. Government expenditure and the public debt were reduced and unpopular taxes ended. The courts were made more fair by the removal of some Federalist judges. The most important event was the purchase of Louisiana in 1803. Jefferson had some doubts but complete control of the Mississippi valley and removal of the French from the continent were so important that he believed he had no choice.

Jefferson was re-elected in 1804 by the overwhelming vote of 162 to 14 against his Federalist opponent. His second term brought great problems and many failures. His efforts to acquire Florida from Spain failed. United States ships were unable to reach European ports because of blockades by Britain and France. The Embargo Act of 1807 cutting off overseas trade was intended to damage the two offending countries, but instead it injured American farmers, shipowners, merchants, and seamen. The act was repealed in 1809. Another problem was posed by Aaron Burr's conspiracy. He apparently plotted to join the western states with Mexico in a great empire over which he would rule. Jefferson ordered his trial for treason, but Burr was acquitted because of the narrow interpretation of treason adopted by Chief Justice John Marshall, a political enemy of Jefferson.

Jefferson spent his retirement at Monticello writing, looking after his plantations, and establishing the University of Virginia.

JEFFREYS, George, 1st Baron (1645–84), better known as Judge Jeffreys, was a judge famous for his conduct of the so-called Bloody Assizes. This was a series of trials following the suppression of a rebellion against the crown led by the Duke of Monmouth. The savage sentences he imposed on the rebels have made him a byword for cruelty and injustice.

Mansell Collection

Judge Jeffreys received the highest legal appointment in England after trying plotters against the monarchy.

Jeffreys was born in North Wales, the son of a country gentleman. He studied law in London, becoming a barrister (lawyer) in 1668. He was a fine performer in court, keeping accused and witnesses ill at ease with his compelling gaze and powerful voice. He gained a reputation for his bullying and ridiculing tactics. In 1678 he was knighted and later he sat at the trials of Roman Catholics falsely accused by Titus Oates of plotting against King Charles II (see OATES, TITUS). Many were executed or imprisoned.

In 1683, while still under 40 years of age, Jeffreys was appointed lord chief justice of England. In his first cases he sentenced to execution two Whigs (members of a party opposed to the king) accused of treason against the king, even though the evidence was weak. In 1685 Jeffreys tried Titus Oates and sentenced him to a flogging and life imprisonment. Soon afterwards King James II created him Baron Jeffreys of Wem.

In June 1685 James Scott, Duke of Monmouth (see MONMOUTH, DUKE OF), sailed from the Netherlands and landed at Lyme in southwest England to claim the crown. A revolt also started in Scotland led by the Earl of Argyll. Both risings were quickly put down. King James decided that all the captured rebels should be tried for high treason (instead of merely executing the ringleaders and inflicting light punishments on the rest).

Jeffreys was sent to the scene of the uprising to conduct the court hearings known as the Bloody Assizes. Trials were short and death sentences many. Hangings were soon carried out. On the last day of the assize, of 238 people found guilty 61 were sentenced to death. Those who pleaded guilty generally escaped death and were instead transported overseas to the colonies. In all about 200 people were executed and about 800 were sold into slavery on West Indian plantations.

Jeffreys received his reward when he was appointed lord chancellor on his return to London. He presided over a commission set up to compel the Church of England to follow the king's Catholic policies. Jeffrey was himself a Protestant and was somewhat lukewarm in his support for this body.

When William of Orange landed at Torbay in 1688 and overthrew James's government. Jeffreys tried to sail to safety but he was arrested disguised as a seaman. He was imprisoned in the Tower of London and died there four months later.

JEHOVAH'S WITNESSES are a religious group founded in 1872 by an American called Charles Taze Russell. The name Jehovah's Witnesses was adopted in 1931 by Joseph Franklin Rutherford. They believe the whole Bible to be inspired and therefore give it the final say in what they do and believe. They also believe that the end of the world is near, based on their interpretation of certain books of the Bible.

Because they recognize only one kingdom, that of Jehovah (God), the Witnesses have refused to obey the law where it is believed to be in conflict with God's law, for example, they refuse to perform military service. In some countries they have been banned. They also refuse blood transfusions on religious grounds.

Jehovah's Witnesses believe that a great battle called Armageddon between God and Satan (or the Devil) will precede the setting up of the new kingdom of Jesus. During what they believe are the "last days" of the present world system, they try to tell everyone what the Bible says they should do and preach their message in hundreds of countries. They publish Bibles and also the magazines *The Watchtower* and *Awake!* in over 80 languages. Jehovah's Witnesses do not hold services of worship, as the Christian churches do, but instead meet to discuss the Bible's teachings. Each Witness is considered to be a minister and spends much time spreading to others the teachings of the group.

CEPHAS Picture Library/Mick Rock

Jehovah's Witnesses spend as much time as possible going from door to door preaching their beliefs.

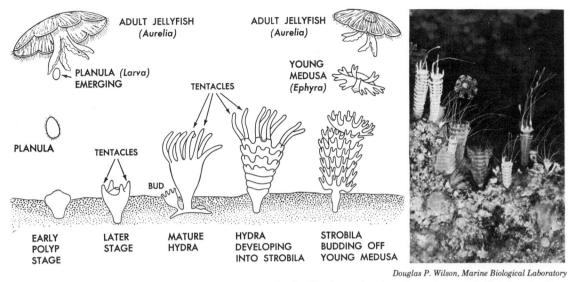

ADULT JELLYFISH
(Aurelia)

ADULT JELLYFISH
(Aurelia)

YOUNG
MEDUSA
(Ephyra)

PLANULA (Larva)
EMERGING

TENTACLES

PLANULA

TENTACLES

BUD

EARLY
POLYP
STAGE

LATER
STAGE

MATURE
HYDRA

HYDRA
DEVELOPING
INTO STROBILA

STROBILA
BUDDING OFF
YOUNG MEDUSA

Douglas P. Wilson, Marine Biological Laboratory

The development of a common jellyfish begins when the fertilized egg develops into a larva called a planula. The planula has many hair-like cilia that beat together causing the larva to swim through the water. Later the larva settles and becomes fixed on the sea bed and changes form into a hydra that looks like a small, transparent sea anemone. The hydra elongates and horizontal segments, that resemble a pile of saucers, appear and break off, and swim away as young jellyfish. The picture above right shows budding hydras.

JELLYFISH are not fish, but are soft-bodied animals that belong to a group of animals called the Coelenterates. Their bodies are made up of about 99 per cent water and they have no blood vessels or brain. When stranded on the beach in the sun they gradually dissolve.

Jellyfishes vary from tiny blobs to ones with a body of over 3.5 metres (11.5 feet) across. Some of the small ones are very attractive, being transparent or pale-coloured, and some kinds glow in the sea at night.

The body of a jellyfish is usually shaped like an umbrella or bell, and it swims by the contraction and relaxation of a ring of muscle fibres that lie near the edge of the "umbrella" or "bell". As water is driven out on contraction, the jellyfish is driven up or along in the water. Around the edge of the umbrella is a fringe of small tentacles, or feelers, and in the middle, four or more large tentacles hang down. At the point where these larger tentacles meet is a mouth leading to a large stomach, and at intervals round the edge of the umbrella are tiny pigment spots which serve as eyes. There are also other sense organs, which are probably used to balance the jellyfish.

From the jellyfish egg comes an oval larva which swims about for a while before settling down on the sea-bottom. Then a mouth appears at the upper end of the larva, surrounded by tentacles, and rings appear round the body, dividing it into sections. One by one these sections break off and float away in the form of tiny jellyfishes. When they are full grown, jellyfishes generally live near the surface of the sea, although some kinds live in the sea depths.

The tentacles of jellyfishes are armed with cells which sting tiny sea creatures to make them helpless and at the same time hold them and later pass them to the mouth. The sting of some of the smaller kinds of jellyfish of the tropics are extremely dangerous especially the sea wasps (*Chironex* and *Chiropsalmus*) that live in the seas between Queensland (Australia) and Malaysia. These jellyfish contain poison that can kill a person within a few minutes.

The Portuguese man-of-war (*Physalia physalis*) is a jellyfish-like coelenterate with a gas-filled float. Beneath the float hang tentacles up to 50 metres (165 feet) long. These are armed with stinging cells capable of paralyzing fish (as large as mackerel) which are drawn up by muscles in

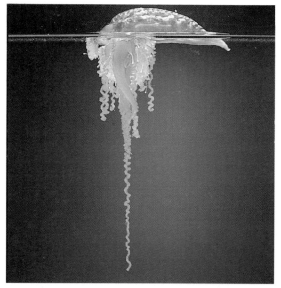

NHPA/Anthony Bannister

The Portuguese man of war is a relative of the true jellyfish. The animal is swept along with the ocean currents, buoyed up by its gas-filled float. Its long stinging tentacles may extend down several metres.

the tentacles, and digested in the stomach of the animal. Colonies of Portuguese man-of-war are often blown into coastal areas far from their native sub-tropics, where they can be dangerous to bathers.

Another name for jellyfish is medusa. In Greek legend the Gorgon Medusa, killed by Perseus, was always pictured with writhing snakes on her head instead of hair, and the confused bunch of tentacles hanging from some jellyfish reminded people of this.

JENNER, Edward (1749–1823). The painful and dangerous disease known as smallpox was eliminated worldwide in the late 1970s. Yet 2,000 people died of it every year in the 18th century in London alone. The defeat of smallpox was begun by Edward Jenner, a country doctor, who was born, lived, and died in the small village of Berkeley, in Gloucestershire, England.

When he was 21, Jenner went to London and became a pupil of the great surgeon John Hunter (see HUNTER, JOHN). The two became lifelong friends. Like Hunter, Jenner was interested in natural history as well as medicine, and in particular he studied the way in

which the female cuckoo makes other birds bring up her young.

Jenner became a doctor in Berkeley in 1773. He was intensely curious, and as he rode about the country on horseback visiting his patients he noticed that a person who had suffered from cowpox (a mild disease that human beings could catch from cattle) did not get smallpox. Jenner suspected, therefore, that having cowpox protected sufferers against smallpox, and that this protection could in some way be transmitted from a person infected with cowpox to others who were not infected. The practice of immunization, or injecting the germs of a disease into a healthy person so that he has a mild attack of it and does not get it more seriously, was already known by this time. (See IMMUNITY; VACCINATION AND INOCULATION.)

In 1796, Jenner came across a dairymaid,

Mansell Collection

Statue in Kensington Gardens, London, of Edward Jenner inoculating a boy against smallpox.

Sarah Nelmes, with fresh cowpox sores on her finger. He decided to test his theory about cowpox offering protection against smallpox. So Jenner inoculated a boy with cowpox from Sarah Nelmes. Eight weeks later he inoculated him with smallpox and the boy did not develop the disease.

Within a few years Jenner became one of the most famous doctors in the world. He received large sums of money from Parliament, and awards from the Russian Czar, Napoleon Bonaparte, and Indian chiefs in the United States. Yet, in spite of his fame, Jenner continued to practise medicine at Berkeley until his death, when he was buried there.

JERBOA is the name of about 25 species (kinds) of long-tailed, leaping rodents with large eyes, and soft, sandy-coloured fur. Jerboas live in deserts and dry plains from North Africa across Central Asia to China.

Although only mouse-sized, a jerboa can leap up to 3 metres (10 feet) on its extremely long hind legs, balanced by a slender, often tufted tail. When looking for seeds and insects to eat, jerboas hop either on all fours like rabbits or else on their hind legs, using their tail as a prop.

Jerboas avoid the heat of the day by sleeping in burrows, which may be up to 3 metres (10 feet) long. They often plug the entrance with earth, but may have an additional emergency exit. Some species live together in communal burrows. Most species hibernate in their burrows during the winter months.

Jerboas generally have two litters, with an average of three young per litter. They are born naked and crawl with their forelegs. The hindlegs do not develop until they are eight weeks old.

JERUSALEM is an ancient, holy city to Christians, Muslims, and Jews, located near the centre of modern-day Israel. It lies about 24 kilometres (15 miles) west of the Dead Sea, and 56 kilometres (35 miles) east of the Mediterranean. The city has warm, dry summers and cool, rainy winters.

The Old City

The old city of the Bible is roughly square in shape and stands on a tableland with the steep valleys of Hinnom and Kedron to the south and east. It is surrounded by a 16th-century wall which (except on the southern side) probably follows the line of the ancient Jewish walls. The gates in the northern wall are called Damascus, Herod's, and the New Gate. On the west side is the Jaffa Gate, on the south the Zion and Dung Gates, and on the east the Golden Gate (now walled up) and St. Stephen's Gate. Within the walls are narrow winding lanes hardly wider than footpaths where there is little motor traffic, as most goods are carried by camels and donkeys.

The main Christian shrine is the Church of the Holy Sepulchre, most of which dates from the time of the Crusades. The tomb where it is believed Jesus Christ was buried after he was taken down from the Cross is in a marble chapel surrounded by the Rotunda, a lofty domed building. Facing it is the Greek cathedral, around which a dark unlit passage leads first to the Place of the Scourging and then to the underground chapel where the Empress Helena discovered the True Cross in 326. Some steps lead up to Calvary and below it is the Stone of the Washing of the Body.

From the Sepulchre a narrow road leads downhill along the *Via Dolorosa* ("sorrowful way"), up which Jesus Christ reportedly carried his cross, and into the Muslim quarter. Here the whole southeast corner of the old city is taken up by a vast stone-flagged platform on which stood the great Jewish temple of Herod. After they had destroyed the Temple the Romans built another one to Jupiter, one of their gods, and later on Christian churches stood there; but for over a thousand years the platform has been occupied chiefly by the magnificent Dome of the Rock, or Mosque of Omar, which is the most sacred Muslim shrine after Mecca. Along the west side of the platform for about 25 metres (80 feet) there stand the remains of the ancient outer wall of the Jewish temple. This is called the "Wailing Wall", a

Picturepoint

The most sacred place in Jerusalem for Jewish people is the Western (or Wailing) Wall.

sacred place where Jews come to pray. Most of the Jewish part of the old city near by was destroyed during the Arab-Jewish fighting in 1948. In the southwest corner is the Armenian quarter overlooking the Zion Gate and the Valley of Hinnom, and some damage was also done in this part during the fighting.

From the eastern wall there is a steep drop into the Valley of Kedron, in which lies the Garden of Gethsemane where according to the Gospels in the Bible, Jesus Christ was seized and dragged off to be condemned to death. From the valley rises the Mount of Olives, on which stands a chapel on the spot from which Christians believe Jesus ascended into Heaven (see JESUS CHRIST). These places were occupied by Israel in the 1967 Arab-Israeli war. Far away to the east can be seen the Mountains of Moab above the Dead Sea.

Modern Jerusalem

No part of Jerusalem lay outside the walls until 1858, when some new building began on the broad ridge west of the old city along the road leading to Tel Aviv. Since then west Jerusalem has grown into a big modern city with government buildings, banks, and other buildings housing finance and insurance companies. Factories include diamond cutting, printing, furniture, chemicals, and textiles. There are also theatres, cinemas, as well as hotels for the vast number of tourists and religious pilgrims who visit the city. Nearly all the buildings are of stone. There is a Biblical Zoo containing a collection of the animals mentioned in the scriptures. The great Hebrew University occupies buildings in the west of the city. Its former site on Mount Scopus, recaptured from Jordan in the 1967 war, is being rebuilt. West of the University is Mount Herzl, on which is the tomb of Theodor Herzl, the founder of Zionism (see ZIONISM). The tomb is surrounded by a national cemetery and is a centre for Jewish pilgrimages.

Jerusalem is connected by road and rail with Tel Aviv-Yafo on the coast and has a total population of about 415,000 (1982).

History

Jerusalem has had a stormy history. It was once ruled by Egyptians. About 1000 BC, the city was captured by David, and became the Jewish capital. David's successor, Solomon, built his Temple there (see SOLOMON). In succeeding centuries, Jerusalem was invaded and destroyed again and again (see ISRAEL-ITE). In AD 70 a Roman army destroyed much of it, and after the Jewish war of freedom in AD 132 the Romans pulled down every building and on top of the ruins built a new city where no Jew might live. In 614 Jerusalem was captured and damaged by the Persians and in 637 there began a long period of Arab rule. In 1099 the Crusaders, seeking to recover the Holy Places of Christendom, took the city and held it until 1187, when it was retaken by the Saracens.

Except for a few years in the 13th century, Jerusalem remained in Muslim hands until 1917, when it was captured by British troops under General Allenby. The city then became the capital of Palestine, which was ruled by Great Britain on behalf of the League of Nations. After World War II, the United Nations wished to make Jerusalem an international city, but as soon as the British left Palestine in 1948, fierce fighting broke out between the Jews and Arabs. When this ended six months later, the Jews held the modern western part of the city, while the eastern part, including the old walled city and the remains of the Jewish quarter, was in the hands of the Arabs. In 1950 western Jerusalem became the capital of Israel and the seat of the Knesset, or Israeli parliament. In the Arab-Israeli war of 1967, the eastern part of the city, which had been part of Jordan since 1948, was captured by Israel. Israel declared the city as its capital, but this has not been recognized by the rest of the world while the Arab-Israeli conflict continues.

JESUITS. A Jesuit is a member of the Society of Jesus, which is a Roman Catholic Order of religious men well known for its educational, missionary, and charity work. The Society had its beginnings in the 1530s at the University of Paris where a small group of brilliant students gathered round Ignatius of Loyola, a Spanish soldier who had been converted to Christianity. (See IGNATIUS OF LOYOLA, SAINT.) In 1534 seven of the group vowed to live in poverty and celibacy and pledged themselves to go to Jerusalem to preach Christianity and help the sick. As war made it impossible for them to undertake the journey, they went instead to Rome and offered to do whatever work the Pope chose for them. So far they were merely a group of people who had come together because they had the same aims and ideals. They realized, however, that if they were always going to work together they ought to have a definite organization with rules to guide them and so they applied to Pope Paul III for permission to start a permanent order. On 27 September 1540, he granted their request and the Jesuit Order was founded. At first they preached in Italy and worked in hospitals; later they opened schools.

Ignatius trained the members of his Order in such a way that they were ready to undertake work of any kind in every part of the world. Francis Xavier, one of the first companions of Ignatius, was sent to India and later visited Malaya and Japan before he died on an island off the south coast of China. (See XAVIER, SAINT FRANCIS.)

Jesuits have worked in many parts of the world, and today many Jesuits live among the poor in the world's less developed areas.

A Jesuit's training is long. He spends the first two years of his training with his companions away from other people learning their new religious life. During this period, when he is known as a novice, the Jesuit spends a month quietly studying the plan drawn up by Ignatius, known as the *Spiritual Exercises*, to be sure that he is really suited to become a Jesuit. At the end of two years a Jesuit takes the three vows of poverty, celibacy, and obedience, in common with all other Roman Catholic religious orders. Afterwards, he continues in his studies, learning philosophy and theology, and is ultimately ordained a priest. Some Jesuits, chosen to be leaders, take a special vow to do any religious work ordered by the Pope.

The men of the Society of Jesus are thus highly trained and they have to be ready to do every kind of work. The motto of Ignatius was "All for the greater glory of God". Many Jesuits teach, others work in missions, some are chosen for preaching, for running church communities, writing books, newspapers and magazines. Jesuits vow not to seek high positions in the Church and if these are offered they accept only if ordered to by the Pope. Jesuits wear no special habit (clothing).

Some Jesuits are not priests. These members are called brothers and they look after the practical needs of the Order, cooking, farming, building, and nursing the sick. These days, some also work as teachers, counsellors, or artists.

With around 25,000 members, the Jesuit Order is the Roman Catholic Church's largest religious order. Unlike many other Orders, it has no female branch.

JESUS CHRIST (*c.* 6 BC-*c.* AD 30). If you had visited some of the larger towns of Asia Minor and Greece nearly 2,000 years ago you would have found, in the back streets, a number of

The Bridgeman Art Library

The Last Supper by Leonardo Da Vinci. Jesus is seated in the centre. To his left is Judas, his betrayer.

small secret societies that met late at night or early in the morning behind locked doors. If their members had been asked what they called themselves, they would have answered that they were "Christians", or "followers of Christ". The Jewish followers of Jesus called him "Messiah" which means "the anointed one". The Greeks translated this into their own language and thus called Jesus "Khristos". This is where we get our name for him, "Christ", and the word "Christian".

The teachings of Jesus Christ are the basis of the Christian religion. Nearly all we know about him comes from the four Gospels of the New Testament of the Bible. We have no record of the exact date of Jesus' birth, but it was probably around 6BC, several years earlier than historians at first thought.

Jesus Christ was born in Bethlehem on the west bank of the River Jordan to a young girl called Mary who was engaged to be married to a carpenter called Joseph. Some time before the couple were due to get married the angel Gabriel visited Mary and told her that she was going to have a very special baby: "Thou shalt bring forth a son and thou shalt call his name Jesus". This is known as the Annunciation.

Sonia Halliday Photographs

Bethany, about 3 km. (2 miles) from Jerusalem, is where Jesus stayed with sisters Mary and Martha.

According to the Gospels, Jesus was not the son of Joseph in the ordinary sense. He was miraculously conceived by Mary through God, without any human father. That is why Christians say that he was "conceived by the Holy Ghost, born of the Virgin Mary". The Bible tells us how the simple people, especially the shepherds, who lived at Bethlehem, welcomed the birth of this baby. It also describes how the wise men from the East brought presents to him in the stable where he was born. They seemed to know that something quite out of the ordinary had happened.

Jesus spent the first 30 years of his life as a carpenter and was brought up in a poor but comfortable home. Very little is known of his life as a child and young boy. The only story recorded in the Gospels is of a visit which he made to Jerusalem with his parents at the age of 12. This was during the feast of the Passover, the Jewish spring festival. St. Luke tells us how his parents suddenly discovered that he was missing. Eventually they found him in the Temple where, to their great astonishment, he was holding a serious conversation with all the learned men of the city who were astonished by his wisdom.

Jesus must have been nearly 30 years old when he met a man called John the Baptist, who had started a religious movement to prepare for the coming of the Messiah, or saviour (see JOHN THE BAPTIST, SAINT).

Jesus was baptized by John in the River Jordan. Not long afterwards he gathered a small group of followers and started preaching up and down the countryside. Sometimes Jesus preached in the Jewish places of worship (called synagogues), for he too was a Jew, but more often he chose the open air. His preaching was a challenge to his fellow-countrymen, for he told them, "The reign of God is at hand! Make a new start and believe the good news."

If we are to understand what an immense effect this message had on his listeners we must remember that, for centuries, the Jews had believed that God would send the Messiah, "the anointed one", to them. Though the Jews had been conquered, oppressed, and exiled from their own land, they had clung to the belief that God would finally rescue them and set up his reign of peace and justice. They believed that this would be brought about by the Messiah.

In his preaching, Jesus deliberately appealed to this old Jewish belief, though as we shall see, it meant to him something very different from what it meant to most other Jews of his time. He had taken part in John the Baptist's religious movement and became convinced that it was himself whom God intended to be the Messiah. He went off alone to decide how he ought to set about his task. In that time he thought of, and gave up, several possible ways in which he might win support in setting up God's reign on Earth, realizing that these were temptations by the devil. Having chosen the way in which he believed God intended him to work, he started on his mission. He devoted himself to teaching and healing.

Jesus taught everywhere—in the synagogues, in houses, by the lakeside, and on the slopes of hills. Wherever he came, "the common people heard him gladly". During the first part of his ministry he made tours from his base at Capernaum in Galilee to the neighbouring towns and villages, proving the authority of his mission by performing miraculous deeds. The Gospels describe various miracles, such as raising the dead, casting out devils, healing the sick, calming the winds and waves by command, and other wonderful deeds. Jesus often taught by using parables, or short, vivid stories that he made up about ordinary people's lives and that illustrated his message.

The crowd enjoyed the outspoken way in which Jesus attacked the religious authorities, who disapproved of him. The Jewish leaders accused him of being far too easy-going, for he broke the rule about not working on the Sabbath, the religious day of rest, and he welcomed all sorts of people, including the not very respectable, as friends. When the leaders rebuked him, he told them that God did not much care about their regulations and their respectability, and that he was looking for kindness and mercy in people.

Jesus' gift of healing the sick made an even

stronger impression than his words, but he did not use these powers very much, for he realized people might easily pay more attention to "these signs and wonders" than to his teaching about God, which he considered to be far more important.

As Jesus made no attempt to flatter them, the religious authorities began to dislike him more and more. Some of the Jewish leaders honestly thought that his teaching was wrong, and that it was leading people astray. Others feared that he might start a political movement against the Romans, who governed Palestine at that time, and that this would lead to great trouble. A good many of the leaders realized that his teaching was a direct challenge to their own leadership. For one reason or another they came to the conclusion that they must get rid of him and started to find out whether any of his friends could be persuaded to be disloyal to him.

Jesus knew what was happening, and knew that he must be ready to meet this threat to his life. He had already chosen a little group of 12 disciples, or followers, called apostles, to travel round with him and help him in his work (see APOSTLES, THE). He began to give them special teaching and shared with them some of his own deepest religious experiences so that they should understand fully who he was. All sorts of rumours were flying about. Some people said he was not the Messiah but that he had come to prepare the way for the real Messiah; others thought he must be one of the old prophets risen from the dead. When he asked his disciples who *they* thought he was, Peter, who was always impetuous, immediately replied, "Thou art the Christ". Jesus then warned the disciples that his victory would not be like that of a victorious Earthly ruler, who would overthrow his enemies and rule in power at Jerusalem.

It was not enough for Jesus' little band of disciples to acknowledge him. The real question was whether the Jewish leaders were prepared to do the same. It was in order to put that to the test that in the last year of his life he went up to Jerusalem for the great national feast of the Passover. At this time the city was crowded with pilgrims who had come to commemorate the Jews' delivery from slavery in Egypt many hundreds of years earlier.

If we really were listening to people telling this story nearly 2,000 years ago, we should find that they spent a great deal of time on the details of Jesus' last days in Jerusalem. It would be obvious that they treasured the memory of every incident and knew that each incident had its own importance. At the start things went well. The crowds hailed Jesus as the prophet from Nazareth. He knew, however, that the opposition to him was becoming stronger. Worse still, he knew that one of his own disciples was turning against him. We shall perhaps never know for certain what made Judas Iscariot betray Jesus. Whatever the reason, the danger was great and Jesus knew that he must prepare for the end.

His first concern was for his disciples. He knew that they had scarcely begun to understand what he would have to go through, and that their faith might easily break under the shock of his death. He gathered them together for a final meal, known as the Last Supper, and explained to them that his death was necessary because it would establish a new covenant (bond) between God and men. At the same time the disciples would be taken into a special new bond with God because it would be their duty to spread Jesus' teaching after he had gone. He took bread and wine, blessed it, and gave it to his disciples saying, "This is my body . . . this is my blood". Christians remember this when they celebrate Holy Communion.

After the meal Jesus and the disciples went to the Mount of Olives, a hill on the east side of Jerusalem, and to the Garden of Gethsemane at its foot. It was to this garden that Judas brought men to arrest him. They took him to the Jewish leaders, who tried him hurriedly during the night. After several questions, the High Priest asked him, "Art thou the Christ, the Son of the Blessed?" and Jesus replied, "I am". The leaders considered that it was wicked for him to make this claim and sentenced him to death.

The sentence they had passed could not be

carried out until it had been approved by the Roman governor of Judaea, Pontius Pilate. Pilate made a real effort to find Jesus innocent of the charges against him. However, the Jewish leaders insisted that Jesus' claim to be the Christ really meant that he was conspiring against the Roman Emperor. Pilate was therefore uncertain what to do, for if it became known in Rome that he had freed such a dangerous prisoner his reputation would suffer. After consulting the crowd he gave in, and sentenced Jesus to be crucified (this was the Roman method of executing criminals by nailing them to a cross). Then Pilate's soldiers mocked Jesus by making him wear a scarlet robe (this colour was often worn by a king) and by putting a crown of thorns on his head, crying out, "Hail, King of the Jews!" After this they crucified him. These things happened on what we call Good Friday. In the evening of that day the dead body of Jesus was taken down from the cross and laid in a tomb that belonged to one of his followers called Joseph of Arimathea, and a great stone was rolled across the entrance to the tomb.

Early on the Sunday morning, Easter Sunday, a group of women disciples went to the tomb and found the stone rolled back and the body gone. (These things are fully described in the article EASTER.) Soon after this discovery Jesus appeared to Mary Magdalene and to the disciples, and the news quickly spread that he had returned from the dead.

What are we to make of this? It has been suggested that somebody had stolen the body and the people who claimed that Jesus had appeared to them only *imagined* that they saw him. However, the gospel accounts make it clear that the witnesses were not expecting to see Christ after death, any more than they would have expected to see anybody else who had died. They were completely taken by surprise. On one occasion they themselves wondered whether they had seen a ghost, and it was only when Jesus showed them the wounds of the nails on his hands and feet that they were convinced it was he. It is argued that people who have merely imagined something do not behave in this way. Christians believe

the true explanation to be just as the story says: "On the third day He rose again". It is a matter of great importance, for the Christian faith is based on the resurrection of Christ.

Growth of Christianity

After Jesus was crucified, his disciples became disillusioned by the apparent failure of the ministry. His resurrection filled them with renewed enthusiasm and they travelled widely, preaching Christ's message.

Ever since, Christians have tried to live according to his teaching. They believe that God showed himself to people, as fully as he could in a life lived on Earth, through the person of Jesus. Jesus' life of selfless love and service, which ended in his crucifixion, was God's way of helping to lift people out of their sinful ways. St. Paul said, "God was in Christ, reconciling the world unto himself"; St. John remembered Jesus' own words, spoken just before the crucifixion, "He that hath seen me hath seen the Father".

Since its early beginnings in Palestine, a small country of the Roman Empire, the Christian faith has been carried across the world and been taken up by people of many races. The way in which this faith has developed is described in the article CHRISTIANITY.

JET PROPULSION is the means by which modern aircraft and space rockets are moved at high speed through the air. To understand fully how jet propulsion works we need to look first at a few general ideas on the way things travel through fluids.

When something has to be moved through a gas or liquid, the process is usually carried out by pushing some of the fluid in the opposite direction. A swimmer pushes water backwards with his arms and legs as he propels himself along; a bird forces air down and back with its wings in order to hold itself up and to move forward. The propeller of a ship or an aircraft turns the power of the engine into rearward force on the water or air. There is a basic law of physics, discovered by the 17th-century scientist Sir Isaac Newton, that for every action (force) there is an equal and opposite reaction;

A deflating balloon (right) rushes through the air by jet propulsion caused by air being forced out through the neck. The combustion chamber of a jet engine works in the same way as the balloon.

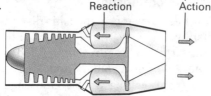

Reaction   Action

Hero's "aeolipile" (left), powered by steam, was the first jet engine. A garden sprinkler rotates by jet propulsion caused by the force with which the water leaves the sprinkler.

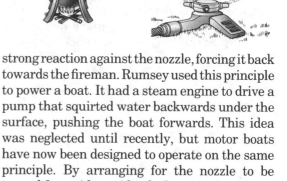

so the rearward force on the water or air is balanced by a forward force on the propeller (see FORCE AND MOTION.) This force is transferred through the engine to the ship or aircraft and moves the vehicle. You can demonstrate action and reaction by blowing up a balloon and releasing it. The *action* of the air as it is forced out of the neck of the balloon produces an equal *reaction* in the opposite direction, making the balloon fly through the air.

The size of the reaction force depends on two things – the amount of fluid forced backwards, and the acceleration that it is given (see ACCELERATION). Propellers usually act on quite large amounts of water or air, and only force them backwards at relatively low speeds. However, the same effect can be obtained by forcing back a smaller amount of fluid at a higher speed. This is known as jet propulsion.

Jet propulsion is found in nature: squids move along by taking in water and squirting it behind in a jet. Hero of Alexandria, a Greek who lived during the 1st century AD, was the first person to use jet propulsion, although his machine, known as an aeolipile, was no more than a toy. He connected a steam boiler to a wheel with four hollow spokes, each of which had a small opening at the end, bent at right angles. As the steam squirted out of the jets, the wheel was driven round in the opposite direction. (See STEAM ENGINE.) The rotating water sprinklers used on lawns today work in the same way.

The first practical use of jet propulsion came in 1787 with the work of the United States inventor James Rumsey. He observed that when a fire hose squirted water at high pressure there was a strong reaction against the nozzle, forcing it back towards the fireman. Rumsey used this principle to power a boat. It had a steam engine to drive a pump that squirted water backwards under the surface, pushing the boat forwards. This idea was neglected until recently, but motor boats have now been designed to operate on the same principle. By arranging for the nozzle to be turned from side to side, the boat can be steered as well as propelled by the jet.

Jet Propulsion in Aircraft

Jet propulsion came into widespread use in aircraft in the 1940s. During World War II, the conventional piston engine reached the limit of its development. By 1945, engines that produced over 2,000 kilowatts of power were available, but they weighed 3 tonnes (3.3 US tons) and were extremely large and complicated. It was clear that aircraft needed a smaller, lighter type of engine which would work efficiently at high speeds and great altitudes, and which could produce very high power.

Compressors   Combustion   Turbines
                   chamber

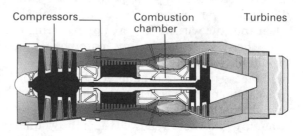

Jet engines consist of three parts: a compressor, to pressurize the air; a combustion chamber, where the air–fuel mixture is ignited; and a turbine, which provides power.

The gas turbine was found to meet this need. Since the early 1930s, designers in Great Britain and in Germany had been working independently on this type of engine. The British inventor Frank Whittle (see WHITTLE, SIR FRANK) patented his ideas in 1930, but his first engine did not fly until 1941; a German designer, Hans von Ohain, started work a little later, but he received immediate financial support for his design, and his engine first flew in August 1939. (See AVIATION, HISTORY OF.)

The Jet Engine

Both Whittle's and Ohain's engines worked on the same principle (described under INTERNAL COMBUSTION ENGINE). In simple terms, the *turbojet* consists of a rotating shaft with a compressor at the front and a turbine wheel at the back. When the shaft is turning, air is drawn into the front of the engine and compressed; the air is then led to a combustion chamber where liquid fuel, such as paraffin, is injected to form an inflammable mixture which burns continuously. The hot gases thus produced are allowed to escape from the back of the combustion chamber, and as they do so, they blow on the blades of the turbine. Some of the force of the gas is taken up by the turbine, which turns the shaft to drive the compressor at the front, but the gas is still travelling at very high speed when it leaves the jet pipe at the back of the engine. This fast jet of gas produces a forward reaction in the engine, in the direction of flight.

The jet engine operates efficiently at high altitudes; indeed, it is at its best in very cold air. It can also be made to work at speeds two or three times that of sound. By clever design of the air intake, the air can be slowed down as it enters the engine so that, regardless of the speed of the aircraft, it is travelling at the design speed of the engine, which must be less than the speed of sound when it reaches the front of the compressor. (Higher speeds result in a disruptive airflow.) Once the air has been heated up in the combustion chamber, its speed can be increased because the speed of sound in hot air is much higher. The jet engine

Types of jet engine

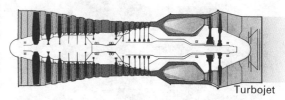

Turbojet

The *turbojet* is the simplest jet engine. Air is compressed then burned with fuel in the combustion chamber. The gases produced drive a turbine that powers the compressor.

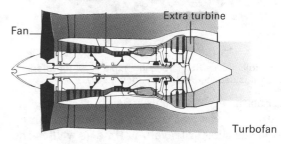

Turbofan

In the *turbofan* some of the air drawn into the engine bypasses the turbine. This engine gives lower aircraft speeds but better fuel efficiency than the turbojet.

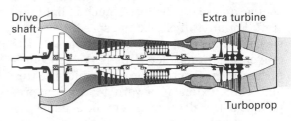

Turboprop

The *turboprop* engine is a turbojet with an extra turbine that drives a propeller, which is usually located at the front of the engine.

is a basically simple piece of machinery, although it has to be accurately made from special heat-resistant metal that can withstand temperatures of up to 1,300°C (2,370°F). Its one large moving part rotates steadily rather than continually reversing like the pistons of earlier engines, so there is less wear and tear, less wasted energy, and very little vibration.

At first, the jet engine was used for military aircraft, especially fighters, bombers, and reconnaissance aircraft, in which high speed is very important. Within a few years, however, it was being used for airliners as well, because it enabled them to fly faster and more

Rolls Royce

The Rolls Royce RB211-535 jet engine is of turbofan type. It is used to power the Boeing 757.

economically at greater heights, where the thin air gives less drag. Passengers appreciated the shorter travelling time as well as the smooth, quiet journey.

At low speeds and altitudes, the turbojet burns more fuel than a comparable piston engine, and so it is not used much in light aircraft. For aircraft of medium speed, there is a way of linking the simple gas turbine with the conventional propeller. This is the propeller-turbine engine, or *turboprop*, in which the turbine shaft extends forward to drive a propeller. Nearly all the energy of the exhaust gas is absorbed by the turbine, and transferred to the propeller, so that fuel consumption and noise are reduced.

The turbojet itself has been developed considerably. The first British and German engines used a centrifugal compressor, in which the incoming air was forced out across the rim of a single large compressor wheel; this type of engine has largely been replaced by a piece of equipment called an axial compressor, in which the air flows straight back between rows of small static and rotating blades. Twin-spool engines have two shafts, one inside the other, each carrying compressor and turbine blades: some of the air may be allowed to by-pass the combustion chamber and turbine to reduce noise and cool the casing. Extra thrust can be gained by *reheat* or *afterburning*. Unlike a piston engine, in which an exact

amount of air is introduced to burn the fuel, a jet engine operates with an excess of air, so a certain amount of oxygen remains in the exhaust gases. Fuel injected into the jet pipe will burn in these exhaust gases (afterburning) and therefore increase their velocity, producing extra thrust. This is made use of when short bursts of extra power are required, such as during take-off.

The *turbofan* is virtually a combination of the turbojet and the turbo-prop, in which some of the compressed air from the front of the compressor is allowed to flow out into the slipstream, without passing through the combustion chamber and turbine. Thrust increases of up to 100 per cent can be achieved by reheat in turbofans. Efforts are being made to produce quieter jet engines, so that airliners can continue to fly from airports near to large cities without causing hardship to the people who have to live close by. The latest turbofans have almost eliminated noise as a problem.

Because the thrust on the engine is always in the opposite direction to the line of the gas jet, the direction of thrust can be varied by deflecting the jet. The first application of this was "thrust reversal", in which special scoops were placed in or behind the jet pipe so that the exhaust gas was deflected diagonally forwards. The effect of this was a rearward thrust on the engine, which was used to help slow the aircraft down after landing. More recently, "vectored thrust" engines have been used for vertical/short take-off and landing (V/STOL); rotating nozzles on the engine can be moved so as to give a rearward jet for normal flight, or a downward jet to give vertical thrust for

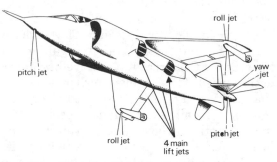

The vectored thrust engines of a Harrier jump-jet use small air jets to control the angle of flight.

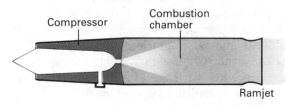

Compressor   Combustion
chamber

Ramjet

The ramjet has no moving parts. It can only function when the aircraft is already flying at high speed.

hovering. Other V/STOL aircraft have a battery of special engines, known as lift jets, which give only a downward thrust and are switched off during forward flight.

Some jet engines do not use gas turbines to compress the air. The *pulse jet,* for example, is a simplified jet engine that has no moving parts except for spring-loaded shutters across the front of the air intake. It runs by burning fuel in a series of very rapid explosions in the combustion chamber. When the fuel is burning, the increased pressure closes the shutters so that the exhaust gas can escape only from the back of the engine; when combustion is complete, the pressure falls and the shutters open to allow air in for the next cycle.

An even simpler form of engine is the *ramjet*, which has no moving parts at all. It looks like a turbojet with no compressor or turbine, and it is shaped so that the incoming air is compressed (or "rammed") into the combustion chamber by the forward speed of the aircraft. After fuel has been injected and burnt, the hot exhaust gas is allowed to expand and escape backwards at high speed through the jet pipe. The difficulty is that the ramjet will not work when the aircraft is standing still, and does not run efficiently until a high forward speed is reached. Therefore an aircraft using a ramjet must be launched by other means, and cannot easily be flown slowly. Such engines are used only for such things as missiles.

Jet Propulsion in Rockets

It is a mistake to think that the thrust of a jet engine is in any way due to the exhaust gas pushing against the surrounding air. The principle of jet reaction works even better

in a vacuum, but the jets already described cannot be used outside the Earth's atmosphere because they require oxygen from the air in order to burn their fuel. The rocket, which employs a form of jet propulsion, carries oxygen in liquid form or uses solid fuel that already contains oxygen. The fuel is burned in a combustion chamber and the resulting gas allowed to escape from an expanding nozzle. The rocket gives high thrust for a low motor weight, but as it has to carry all its oxygen it cannot run for long. In aircraft, rocket motors are suitable only for increasing speed or rate of climb for a short period. In space exploration the rocket is essential. The solid fuel rocket has no moving parts, and because of its lightness and simplicity, it is used for missiles. The liquid fuel rocket is used where variable thrust or precise control is needed. (See ROCKET.)

One further use of the reaction principle is in controlling the direction in which an aircraft or spacecraft is to be pointed. This is known as the craft's *attitude*. When a V/STOL aircraft is hovering, no air is flowing over its control surfaces, and they cease to work. At this stage of flight, air is bled from the engine compressor, and led through pipes to small jets in the wing tips, nose, and tail. As the pilot moves the control column, one or other of these jets is opened, causing the aircraft to bank, pitch, or turn as required. Similarly, when it is necessary to change the attitude of a spacecraft – for example, to fire a retro rocket or to complete a docking manoeuvre – the force is obtained by firing small, controllable jets of gas from one side or the other. In space, the slightest force will start the spacecraft turning, and an opposite force of the same size, or total impulse, will be necessary to stop it when the desired attitude is obtained.

See also AERONAUTICS; SPACE FLIGHT.

JEWEL AND JEWELLERY. Jewels (which are also often called gems) are valued because they are beautiful, they last a long time, and they are very rare. Some jewellers call diamond, ruby, sapphire, and emerald "precious" stones, and all others "semi-precious". In earlier times jewels were named according to their colour—for example, the name ruby was given to all jewels that were red—but as more scientific interest was taken in them a branch of mineralogy (the science of minerals) came into being. This is known as gemmology.

One of the earliest writings in which jewels are mentioned is the Bible. Chapter 28 of the Book of Exodus speaks of a rich breastplate made for the high priest Aaron which had 12 different jewels set in it to represent the 12 tribes of Israel. An ancient Hebrew legend tells how God gave King Solomon four jewels, and of how these stones gave him power to rule over the whole world. Some jewels were supposed to give their owners the power of seeing into the future. Jewels were even thought to have the power of distinguishing between good and evil, and so they were sometimes placed on a person who had been accused of a crime. If he was innocent the jewel was said to shine brightly; if he was guilty it was said to lose its colour and become dull and lifeless.

Diamond has always been known as the "king of gems" because it is about the hardest known substance, and also because, when properly cut and polished, it is brilliant and beautiful. It is of simple chemical composition, being almost pure carbon (see DIAMOND). The red ruby and blue sapphire belong to the same mineral group, corundum, and large stones of fine quality are rare. Corundum is a crystallized form of aluminium oxide, and although the red variety is called ruby, the range of colour in sapphire may be from white to almost black.

Emerald is a beautiful velvety-green variety of the mineral beryl, which also includes the lovely blue and blue-green gem called aquamarine. Emerald owes its colour to traces of chromium oxide. (See CHROMIUM; EMERALD.) Among other beautiful jewels are opal, jade, spinel, chrysoberyl, topaz, and amethyst. The range in colour is often remarkable. Jade, usually thought of as being green, may be white, brown, yellow, grey, or mauve, and this is true of many other jewels. Some of them are heated to cause a change of colour, such as yellow topaz which becomes a delicate pink. It

is wrong to call quartz of a yellow colour "topaz-quartz". The proper name is citrine. The lovely mauve amethyst is a variety of the mineral quartz. Colourless quartz is called rock-crystal. Chalcedony, agate, cornelian, and prase are varieties of a mixture of silica (quartz) and hydrated silica (opal).

The minerals of which jewels are composed are inorganic, but some organic substances are classed as gems. The most important of these is pearl. (The words "inorganic" and "organic" are explained in the article CHEMISTRY.) Natural pearl is found in the pearl oyster living in warm seas. Cultured pearls are formed by placing a mother-of-pearl bead in the body of a living pearl oyster. Other organic substances which are used as gems include coral and amber. (See AMBER; CORAL REEF; PEARL AND PEARL FISHING.)

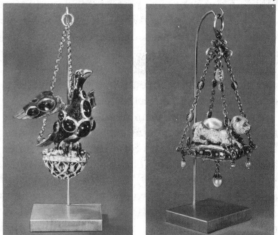

The gold and emerald bird pendant (above left) is from 16th-century Germany. The cat pendant of gold and pearl (above right) is 16th-century French.

Some jewels, such as ruby, sapphire, and emerald, are produced synthetically (artificially). These stones are made by heating and slowly cooling mixtures of the chemicals of which the natural stones are composed and adding various metallic oxides to give the colour. In 1955 artificial diamonds were produced in the United States and by the 1960s, both the United States and South Africa were producing many of them for use in industry.

The craftsman who cuts and polishes

coloured jewels is called a lapidary, while in the diamond industry he is called a diamond cutter. Jewels are fashioned by using small discs, soaked with an abrasive (a substance suitable for rubbing or grinding down), which turn quickly. Various abrasives are used according to the stone, but because of its extreme hardness diamond is usually cut with diamond powder. Faceted stones are those which have had flat surfaces cut upon them. Cabochon stones are domed; this is the oldest style of cutting or shaping. Opaque (non-transparent) stones, which depend entirely on a colour effect, such as turquoise and opal, are cut in this style or shaped into beads.

Jewellery

The term "jewellery" is generally used to refer to decorations made from metals, ivory, gems, plastics, or enamels that are worn by people. The earliest jewellery that has been found dates back thousands of years to the time when people used shells, stones, teeth, and other items for decoration. Early jewellery, which often tells us a good deal about the men who made it, is sometimes found in tombs and sometimes by accident.

Although jewellery is usually meant to be ornamental, it has often been used for other purposes. For instance, certain American Indians used necklaces made of pierced shell instead of money. Even nowadays, especially in times of war or unrest, people sometimes prefer to keep their wealth in jewels, which can easily be carried about. For, unlike money, jewels are less likely to lose their value as the years go by. Kings used to take their treasures with them when they went into battle; this explains why King John of England, who reigned from 1199 to 1216, lost his jewels as well as his baggage in the sea! After Napoleon's defeat at Waterloo in 1815 a quantity of valuable jewellery was discovered in a secret drawer in his travelling carriage. The jewels which belonged to the kings and noblemen of ancient countries such as Egypt were often buried with them.

Jewellery also used to be taken into battle because people believed that precious stones

Courtesy, Cleveland Museum of Art

Above: Gem-studded gold crosses and an altar of 11th-century Germany. **Below:** The diamond basket pin, the diamond tulip pin, and the diamond buckle pin date from the 18th century, and all are part of the Russian crown jewels. **Below centre:** An English diamond link bracelet of the 18th century. **Bottom:** The tiara of the Empress Josephine, first wife of Napoleon.

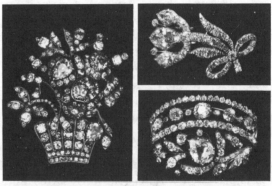

Courtesy, A La Vieille Russie, New York City (above and below)

Courtesy, Gemological Institute of America

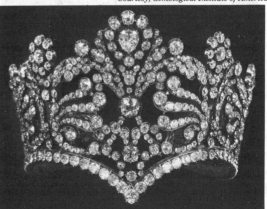

had magical power and would bring the wearer good luck and keep off evil. In ancient Egypt, for instance, lucky stones with magic words inscribed on them, called amulets or talismans, were worn by everyone, and the same word was used for *bead* and *luck*. Certain stones were meant to cure illness. For example, sapphire was thought to relieve insanity, and topaz to ease asthma. Even now corals are often given as a present for a baby. This comes from an old Roman belief that coral was supposed to ward off evil. Other stones became associated with particular months of the year: garnet with January, ruby with July, topaz with November.

In ancient times jewellery was usually more splendid and extravagant than it is now. The Mesopotamians were famed for their silver and gold jewels. Five thousand years ago, for instance, wealthy Egyptians wore wigs made entirely of jewels, and they carried on their breasts small jewelled shrines, or caskets, which were called pectorals. They often gave lucky rings to their guests at banquets. The Egyptians made great use of stones, and of mother of pearl. The Greeks learned from the Egyptians the art of working in gold, and they became perfect in using gold to make delicate twisted wires, called filigree. Later, the Etruscans perfected various gold-work styles, and they in turn influenced Roman jewellery. When the Roman Empire rose to power, wealthy Romans loved to show off their wealth in extravagant jewellery, which they forced captured Greek goldsmiths to make for them. Some Roman senators wore six rings on each finger, and had different sets of rings for summer and winter.

In the Middle Ages, jewels often had a religious meaning, for the art of making jewellery was carefully kept up in the monasteries. Jewels were used to adorn shrines, the vestments of the priest, and the vessels used in Church services. These were often made of gold and decorated with precious stones. Gradually, however, the making of jewellery became a trade as well as an art, and jewels grew to be looked on as a part of costume. During the Renaissance, many great artists, such

Courtesy, Victoria and Albert Museum, London (above)

Courtesy, A La Vieille Russie,
New York City

Courtesy, Trustees of the Wallace
Collection, London

Top: This 19th-century English set of necklace and earrings is made of gold and amethysts. **Above left**: A gold and emerald Spanish cross of the 17th century. **Above right**: A 16th-century German pendant adorned with rubies, sapphires, pearls, and emeralds.

as Dürer, Botticelli, and Cellini, designed jewellery. In fact, many artists of the time first trained as goldsmiths. Sometimes whole dresses were covered with jewels. Gold and silver were worked into elaborate shapes, to represent things such as ships and dragons, in which precious stones such as pearls and rubies were set. Queen Elizabeth I and her courtiers often wore wonderful jewels, some of which were brought to England from South America.

One example of the use of jewellery which was not simply for ornament was the pomander. This was a metal ball pierced with holes, containing perfumes which were supposed to keep off infection. Pomanders were often very beautiful and made of gold and precious stones.

After the Industrial Revolution, jewellery was produced commercially, and more people than ever before could afford to wear it. Cheaper materials were used, for example gold plate, cultured pearls, and imitation gems.

Modern jewellery is usually simpler in design than the ornate brooches and necklaces made in the earlier centuries, but it often contains more precious stones. These are grouped into delicate designs which are often exceedingly beautiful. The most popular metals are gold, silver, and platinum, while the stones most often used are diamonds, sapphires, emeralds, and rubies. Pearl necklaces are very popular, too. A number of what are called semi-precious stones are also often used, such as opals, garnets, or amethysts. Much of the jewellery worn today is "costume jewellery", but although this is often attractive to look at, it is not usually valuable.

This article has been mainly about European jewellery; but some of the most magnificent jewellery comes from the East, from China, India, and Persia. In these countries ornaments of every kind, from jewelled headdresses to gold hair pins, and toilet implements, are made in wonderful settings and very valuable gems are used.

Courtesy, D. A. Thomas and Co.I.D.

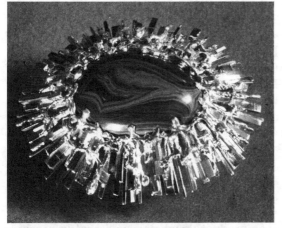

This example of a modern brooch is in yellow and red gold set with malachite.

JEWS AND JUDAISM

JEWS AND JUDAISM. The Jews were originally a nomadic people of the Middle East. They trace their history back to Abraham who, some time after 2000 BC, led a migration of Hebrews from Mesopotamia in southwest Asia, to the land of Canaan, later called Palestine. Abraham was the first man to preach that there is only one God (monotheism). According to the Hebrew scriptures he made a pact of mutual loyalty with God, known as the Covenant. Abraham, his son Isaac, and his grandson Jacob are known as the Three Patriarchs. Jacob was also named Israel; therefore the twelve tribes descended from him are referred to as the Children of Israel, or Israelites. (See ABRAHAM; ISRAELITES.)

Towards the end of Jacob's life, a famine drove the Israelites to seek food in Egypt. There they prospered until the 13th century BC, when a new Pharaoh, Ramses II, enslaved and oppressed them. Then one of the Israelites called Moses, resolved to free them, feeling himself commanded to do so by the God of the Patriarchs, now called *Yahveh*. (This name may mean "He-Who-Is", the Eternal One, or "He-Who-Causes-To-Be", the Creator. *Jehova* or *Jehovah* are incorrect versions of the same name.) Under the leadership of Moses the Israelites escaped from Egypt, crossed the Red Sea, and made their way to Mount Sinai. There God revealed himself to them and, through Moses, gave them the *Torah* (the word is usually translated "Law" but really means "Teaching") comprising the Ten Commandments and many other rules. (See MOSES.)

Moses warned the Jews that the future of their race would depend on how they lived and behaved, promising that if they followed God's commandments they would live in peace. If they disobeyed him, they would be exiled. Moses' successor Joshua led the Israelites across the River Jordan to conquer the "Promised Land" of Canaan. There they faced the hostility of the tribes that were already living in and around Canaan, especially the Philistines (after whom the country was later called Palestine.) This prompted them first to unite under tribal leaders known as Judges and later to establish a monarchy. Their first king was Saul of the tribe of Benjamin. The second, who made Jerusalem his capital, was David of the tribe of Judah. The third, who built the Temple in Jerusalem, was his son Solomon. (See DAVID; SAUL; SOLOMON.)

The danger was that the Israelites might be lured away from their own religion to a belief in many gods, and the worship of images. For a while they resisted this danger largely due to the influence of a succession of prophets (spokesmen of God). (See PROPHET.)

After Solomon's death the ten northern tribes broke away and set up their own kingdom, called Israel, which lasted until 722 BC, when it was conquered by Assyria. The survivors were exiled and so became the "Ten Lost Tribes". Now there remained only the southern kingdom, and since this was called Judah after the name of the Hebrew patriarch and of the tribe descended from him, we may from this time refer to the Israelites as Jews ("Judeans").

In 586 BC Judah was conquered by the Chaldeans, who destroyed the Temple and deported much of the population to Babylon; hence the "Babylonian Exile". This time, however, the Jews remained faithful to their belief that one God ruled all people, so that when, half a century later, the Persians, having conquered Babylonia, allowed them to return to their homeland, many of them did so, and rebuilt the Temple in 516 BC.

Thereafter the effective ruler of the restored Jewish community was the High Priest, who presided over the Temple. In 167 BC, the king of Palestine tried to force the Jews to adopt the culture, including the religion, of the Greeks. At this they rebelled and established an independent Jewish kingdom, ruled by descendants of Mattathias called Hasmoneans, which lasted until it was swept away by the might of Rome.

During the centuries after the Babylonian exile, three important developments took place. First, the Jews assembled their sacred writings (the Torah, the speeches of the Prophets, the Temple hymns called Psalms, and various other books) into what Christians call the Old Testament but what to Jews is simply the Bible (see BIBLE). Secondly, a growing number of Jews left Palestine and settled in other countries such as Babylonia and Egypt; these communities became known as the Diaspora (Dispersion). Thirdly, they evolved a new institution, the Synagogue (the Greek for "meeting place"). This differed from the Temple in that its worship consisted, not in sacrifices offered by priests, but in congregational prayer and Bible readings, conducted by learned laymen. Soon synagogues sprang up wherever Jews lived, both in Palestine and in the Diaspora. (See SYNAGOGUE.)

Closely associated with the synagogues were the Pharisees, who emerged in Palestine in the 2nd century BC and whose teachers later became known as Rabbis (Masters). Their aim was to make Judaism a "people's religion" by bringing it from the Jerusalem Temple into the local synagogue and the people's homes, and by starting a programme of religious education for all. They also stressed the so-called Oral (spoken) Torah teachings handed down by word of mouth. This theory enabled them to develop Judaism in many new ways, including a belief in life after death, domestic rituals such as the kindling of Sabbath lights, and new ways of referring to God. (The Jews had already ceased to use the name Yahveh, which was considered too sacred to be pronounced, and substituted for it the word *Adonai*, usually translated "The Lord".)

In 63 BC Palestine came under Roman rule. The Jews sought comfort in the hope that one day they would be liberated by a descendant of David, known as the Messiah ("The Anointed One"). This hope gave rise to a number of freedom movements, all of which were crushed by the Romans. The Jews did not accept Jesus as the Messiah. Their traditionalists still await the coming of the Messiah to bring about a new world order.

Finally the Jews launched an all-out war against Rome which ended in their total defeat and the destruction of their second Temple in AD 70. Nevertheless, Judaism survived. It even produced a whole new literature, including a compendium of the Oral Torah, known

Jews in Jerusalem pray at the Wailing Wall (far left) the only remaining part of the Temple, destroyed by the Romans in AD 70. A Jewish family (above) holds a Passover service, which celebrates the Jews' escape from captivity in Egypt. A Jewish boy lights the first of eight Hanukkah candles (left).

Photos Owen Franken—Stock, Boston (above);
Ronald Sheridan (top right);
Ellis Herwig—Stock, Boston (bottom right)

as the Talmud. (See TALMUD.) The Jews came to realize that God could be worshipped through prayer and through the Jewish way of life, anywhere.

For several more centuries the main centre of Jewish life remained in the East. Around AD 1000, following the rise of new kingdoms upon the ruins of the Roman Empire, Jews migrated to Europe and began to make important contributions to intellectual and economic life. From the 9th to the 12th century they enjoyed a golden age of Jewish learning and literary achievement, particularly in Moorish Spain (see MOORS).

Other Jewish communities found themselves in Christian lands, where the Church tried to convert them; they were gradually deprived of the ownership of land, and most occupations other than petty trading and moneylending. In the end they were confined to ghettos, and they were frequently persecuted. In 1290 the Jews were expelled from England; in 1392 from France; in 1492 from Spain; and in 1497 from Portugal. (See CRUSADES; GHETTO.)

Only in the 18th and 19th centuries were the Jews gradually freed from the restrictions imposed on them in the Middle Ages and admitted to equal citizenship with others, a process known as emancipation. But the emancipation did not reach Russia, where millions of Jews lived and where, from 1880 onwards, they were subjected to vicious mob attacks called pogroms. In western Europe the old anti-Semitism (hatred of Jews) flared up afresh. This produced a massive emigration of Jews to the United States, and gave rise to the Zionist movement. (See ZIONISM.)

The Jews had always maintained a deep love for their ancient homeland, and especially for Jerusalem, also known as Zion. Towards the end of the 19th century the Zionists, whose greatest leader was Theodore Herzl, resolved to make this dream come true. In 1917, the British government issued the Balfour Declaration, promising to help set up a national home for the Jews in Palestine. This would take place after the anticipated defeat of the Turks, who had ruled the country for four centuries. But when Britain received the mandate (trusteeship) over Palestine from the League of Nations in 1920, it faced a dilemma. On the one hand, the Arabs increasingly opposed Jewish mass-immigration to Palestine. On the other hand, the Jews' need for a refuge grew more and more urgent, especially after Adolf Hitler came to power in Germany and subjected the Jews to the most barbarous persecution in history. By the end of World War II, in 1945, 6 million Jews had been murdered in Germany and the German-occupied territories. (See NAZISM; WORLD WAR II.)

In 1947 Britain handed the problem over to the United Nations, which decided to partition (divide) Palestine, and in 1948 the independent republic of Israel was proclaimed. The Arab challenge to Israeli territory led to wars in 1956, 1967, and 1973, and resulted in the expansion of Israel's boundaries and continuing Arab hostility.

The Jewish population of Israel is about 4.4 million. Large numbers of Jews also live in the United States (about 6 million), France (about 600,000), Russia (about 550,000), Ukraine (about 480,000), Great Britain (about 350,000), and Canada (about 320,000), with smaller numbers in other countries. The total number of Jews is about 14 million. (See also ISRAEL; PALESTINIANS.)

The Religion of the Jews

The Jews are not a race, for they include many racial types and have accepted many converts. Nor are they exactly, except in Israel, a nation, since Jews are citizens of many countries. They are best described as a people with a distinctive culture and, above all, a distinctive religion. But nowadays there are many non-religious Jews who nevertheless feel a strong bond with their people.

Religious Jews, too, are not all of one kind. A large number (except in the United States) are Orthodox. This means that they try to carry on their religious life more or less exactly as it was in the past. A smaller number describe themselves as Progressive. This means that they belong to one or another of the "modernizing" movements which began to affect Judaism in the 19th century. But the main beliefs and practices of Judaism, as described here, are held to by all religious Jews.

The fundamental belief of Judaism is that there is one God, and that he alone is to be worshipped. This is proclaimed twice daily in the so-called *Shema*, a passage from the Book of Deuteronomy which begins: "Hear, O Israel, the Lord is our God, the Lord is One."

Jews believe God created man "in his own image", that is to say, with powers that raise him above other animals and make him more "God-like" than they are. These powers include the ability to think and create; to choose between right and wrong; and to communicate with God himself through prayer. They also include an immortal soul. Man has both a "good inclination" and an "evil inclination"; but when he sins, it is always possible for him to repent, and if he does, God forgives and the result is atonement (reconciliation).

As God rules nature, so he guides human history. He guides it towards a perfect age, when all men and women will acknowledge him and obey his will, and therefore live together in justice, brotherhood, and peace. Orthodox Judaism teaches that this will happen through the coming of the Messiah and the return of the Jewish people to their homeland. Progressive Jews do not generally take that view; nevertheless, they too look forward to the end-result and commonly refer to it as the "Messianic Age".

The Jewish people have a special responsibility in helping to bring about the coming of the Messianic Age. It is for this purpose that God "chose" them, made a "Covenant" with them and, in the Torah, revealed his will to them. Orthodox Judaism maintains that the Torah, as contained in the Bible and interpreted in Rabbinic literature, is a true and unchangeable account of what God requires, and must therefore be obeyed in every detail. Progressive Jews believe that it was written by human beings who, though inspired by God, were nevertheless fallible, and that change is therefore permissible in the light of contemporary knowledge and circumstances.

The duties involved, called *Mitzvot*, are of two main kinds: ethical and devotional. On the ethical side, the Jew is required to be truthful, just, kind, and generous, and so to fulfil the commandment, "You shall love your neighbour as yourself". Judaism defines right conduct in great detail, not only between people in general, but between husband and wife, parent and child, teacher and pupil, merchant and customer, employer and employee, and so on.

Judaism is rich in devotional observances, some of which affect everyday life. They include daily prayer; grace before and after meals; dietary laws; and "reminders" such as the *Mezuzah*—a miniature scroll inscribed with the *Shema* which is housed in a tube and affixed to the doorpost. Many Jews will not eat food that is not *Kasher* (or *Kosher*); that is, has not been prepared according to certain special regulations.

The Sabbath is observed on the seventh day of the week, from Friday evening till Saturday evening. It is a day of bodily rest and spiritual recreation, including worship and study, which begins with the lighting of candles and a ceremony called *Kiddush*, involving wine and bread, and ends with a "farewell" ceremony called *Havdalah*. (See SABBATH.)

The yearly calendar is studded with festivals. The most solemn of these, which occur in the autumn, are *Rosh Hashanah* (New Year), when a ram's horn is blown as a call to repentance, and, ten days later, *Yom Kippur* (the Day of Atonement), which is entirely devoted to prayers of confession and contrition, and to fasting. More joyful are the three seasonal festivals of *Pesach* (Passover, in the spring), *Shavuot* (Pentecost, seven weeks later), and *Sukkot* (Tabernacles, beginning five days after *Yom Kippur*). Of these, the first commemorates the Exodus from Egypt, the second recalls the Revelation at Mount Sinai, and the third is a thanksgiving for the harvest. There are also minor feasts such as Purim (*Lots*), based on the Biblical book of Esther, and *Chanukkah* (Dedication), which celebrates the rededication of the Temple after the Maccabean Rebellion, as well as days of mourning

for the tragedies of Jewish history. (See PASSOVER.)

Some Jews pray in their synagogue every day; most do so only on the Sabbath, or even less frequently. The main feature of a synagogue is the Ark containing parchment scrolls inscribed with the Torah (the Five Books of Moses.) Each Sabbath morning one lesson is read from the Torah and another from the books of the Prophets, and the Rabbi's sermon is usually based on these readings. Otherwise the service consists of prayers and songs in which all participate. In Orthodox synagogues it is conducted entirely in Hebrew, and the men and women sit separately from each other; in Progressive synagogues it is conducted partly in Hebrew and partly in the language of the country, and men and women sit together. In most synagogues the men are required to cover their heads and, on certain occasions, to wear a prayer-shawl with fringes.

Jewish boys are circumcised when eight days old; this is regarded as a symbol of their entry into the "Covenant". Religious education begins at the age of five or six and continues a least until 13, when boys are confirmed in a ceremony called "*Bar Mitzvah*" ("Son of Duty"). Relatively recent and not yet generally accepted is a similar ceremony for girls. Most Progressive synagogues also hold a group confirmation ceremony for boys and girls at the age of 16. The Jewish marriage service is a colourful one which takes place under a canopy called *Chuppah*. The main feature of the funeral service is the recital of a prayer called *Kaddish* which expresses the principle that one should praise God, and look forward to the coming of his Kingdom in times of sorrow as well as of joy.

See also HEBREW LANGUAGE AND LITERATURE.

JINNAH

JINNAH (1876–1948). Muhammad Ali Jinnah was the founder and first governor-general of Pakistan. Largely as a result of his efforts Britain agreed to the partitioning of the Indian subcontinent to make the two great countries of India and Pakistan.

Jinnah was born in Karachi, the son of a wealthy merchant. He studied in London to become a lawyer. After ten years practising law in Bombay he became active in Indian politics. At first he supported the Indian National Congress but later joined the All-India Muslim League. He strove for the political unity of the Hindu and Muslim peoples as the means of obtaining independence from British rule. He opposed the strictly Hindu approach of Gandhi (see GANDHI, MOHANDAS), but continued to work for co-operation between the two sides in spite of a number of religious riots. Eventually, disillusioned, he returned to England, remaining in London from 1930 to 1935.

Popperfoto

Muhammad Ali Jinnah was Pakistan's first head of state after its partition from India in 1947.

In the 1937 elections Congress overwhelmingly defeated the Muslim League and excluded Muslims from places in the provincial governments. Jinnah felt betrayed and took up the cause of Muslim nationalism. Under his leadership the League demanded a separate Muslim state. The Hindu leaders, Gandhi and Nehru (see NEHRU, JAWAHARLAL), and the British government were against partition. But the new Muslim state of Pakistan was formed in 1947 and Jinnah became its first head of state. He strenuously urged Pakistan's case in the dispute with India over Kashmir (see KASHMIR).

See also INDIA, REPUBLIC OF; PAKISTAN.

JOAN OF ARC (1412–31) is the greatest national heroine of France and, for reasons that will be explained, is often called the Maid of Orléans.

Joan came to the help of France at a time when help was sorely needed. Although the Hundred Years' War against England was still going on, the French were divided and were fighting amongst themselves. (See HUNDRED YEARS' WAR.) King Henry V of England had won the Battle of Agincourt in 1415, married the French King's daughter and controlled a great deal of France. It is true that, after Henry's death in 1422, the English were less successful, but it was Joan of Arc who really roused the French.

Joan was born at Domrémy, a village on the River Meuse in eastern France. (It is almost certain that she was born on 6 January 1412.) She was the daughter of a prosperous farmer, but never learned to read or write. When she was 12 she began to hear voices. The voices continued and, she said, were those of St. Catherine, St. Margaret, and St. Michael who, as well as speaking to her, also appeared to her in visions. They told her that she must go to the French court and help the Dauphin (the heir to the throne) to be crowned King of France. Charles, the Dauphin, was rather a weak man. Although his father had been dead for some years, the war had prevented the Dauphin from being crowned.

In May 1428, when she was 16, Joan went to Robert de Baudricourt, the governor of Vaucouleurs, a fortified town near Domrémy, telling him that she came from God and asking him to send her to the Dauphin. De Baudricourt did not take her seriously at first and sent her back home, but she went to him again early the following year and at last persuaded him to give her permission to go to the Dauphin. The people of Vaucouleurs bought her a horse, de Baudricourt gave her a sword and she dressed herself in boy's clothing as a page. With a few companions she set out for Chinon, in the west of France, where the Dauphin was living. It was a long journey and they had to travel by night in order to escape capture by the English soldiers and the Burgundians (the army of the Duke of Burgundy, a great nobleman of eastern France who was fighting on the English side against the French). At last she was brought before the Dauphin. He stood among his nobles to test whether Joan could pick him out, for she had never seen him. However, she approached him immediately and said, "Most noble Dauphin, I have come from God to help you and your Kingdom."

Rescue of Orleans

Joan was now sent to the city of Tours, where the army was preparing to go to the help of Orléans, on the River Loire, which was being besieged by the English. She put on full armour and rode at the head of the army of

Giraudon

Joan of Arc leading the French into battle. A miniature picture from a 16th-century French manuscript.

4,000 men. At last the troops had a leader who inspired them, and they followed her with trust and enthusiasm. She had the power of making them believe in victory even though, apart from her leadership, they had little reason to believe in it.

On the night of 28 April 1429 Joan entered Orléans. On 5 May she and her companions stormed one of the forts held by the English and two days later captured another. Joan was wounded in the shoulder by an arrow, but Orléans was saved from the English. After this she led the French to victory after victory. She persuaded the Dauphin to march on Reims in northeastern France, so that he could be crowned in the cathedral there. On 17 July 1429, he was crowned King Charles VII of France and Joan knelt before him and said, "Gentle King, now is fulfilled the will of God that I should raise the siege of Orléans and lead you to the city of Reims to receive the holy coronation, to show that you are indeed the King and the rightful lord of the realm of France."

The King was now satisfied, but Joan was determined to take Paris. She led the army against one of the gateways to the city, and was wounded and forced to stop fighting. She returned to the court where, in gratitude for what she had done, the King gave her the rank of a noblewoman and said that the people of her village need not pay taxes. However, Joan did not want rewards; she wanted to drive the English out of France and end the war.

In May 1430 Joan rode to Compiègne in northeast France to help defend it against the Burgundians. On 23 May she led a small body of troops out of the town and was taken prisoner by the Burgundians. The King, who owed his crown to her, did nothing to save her. In November the Burgundians sold her to the English who imprisoned her in Rouen, the town that was their military headquarters, near the mouth of the River Seine. The University of Paris declared that Joan was a witch. The English wished to destroy her influence, to blacken her reputation, and to prove that she had merely imagined her visions and voices. If they could prove this it would make the French people forget her and what she stood for, which was the freedom of France. The English therefore had her tried by a religious court, known as the Inquisition, which was presided over by the Bishop of Beauvais. (See INQUISITION.) Joan was accused of having committed 12 sins. One was that she had imagined her visions and voices; others were that she had worn men's clothing, disobeyed her parents, and disobeyed the teaching of the Church. The account of her trial still exists. It was not a fair trial, for the members of the court were hostile to her and determined to please the English.

After a long trial the court found Joan guilty of heresy (that is, of holding beliefs considered wrong by the Church) and condemned her to be burned. It is said that Joan broke down (she had been questioned for weeks, and was terrified of death by burning) and that she confessed to having behaved wrongly. However, if in a moment of weakness she did make such a confession, she took it back and, with great courage, insisted that she was innocent. On 30 May 1431, at the age of 19, she was burned to death in the Old Market at Rouen.

Twenty-five years later an examination of her career and her trial was held, and the Pope declared that she had not been guilty of heresy.

Joan, the Maid of Orléans, has become a symbol of patriotism to the French. In 1920 Pope Benedict XV made her a saint. May 8, the day in 1429 on which the main fort at Orléans was captured, is a national holiday in France.

JOHANNESBURG is the largest city in South Africa and the centre of the world's wealthiest gold-mining industry. It is sometimes called the "city of gold"; its African name is *egoli*, the place of gold. It lies in the Transvaal province of the Republic of South Africa on the southern slopes of the Witwatersrand range of hills (see TRANSVAAL). In 1886 gold was found there, and a mining camp of tents and shanties sprang up under the guidance of the surveyor Johannes Rissik, after whom the city is named. From that beginning has grown a modern city which is often called Jo'burg.

The city is 1,740 metres (5,709 feet) above sea-level. For such a large African city, it is unusual in not being sited near a river, lake, or by the sea. The nights are always cool—in winter very cold—and even the summer days are seldom too hot.

Georg Gerster—Rapho/Photo Researchers
High-rise offices and mining headquarters cluster together in downtown Johannesburg.

Johannesburg is the biggest industrial centre of South Africa and the head office of most businesses are in the city, although it is not the capital of the Republic. It is also a financial centre, and the South African Stock Exchange is located there. There are factories making engineering products, clothes, chemicals, and food. Johannesburg has two of the largest universities in South Africa, and a number of modern hospitals. Other important buildings are the art gallery in Joubert Park, designed by the English architect Edwin Lutyens, the public library, and the Gubbins Africana Museum, which is devoted to South African history.

The most important occupation in Johannesburg is gold and uranium mining. In the city are the offices of the big mining companies but there are only two large mines in Johannesburg itself. The rest are along the Reef which stretches east and west of the city for more than 45 kilometres (28 miles) in each direction. Together with Johannesburg, the "Reef towns" form an almost continuous built-up area. The Witwatersrand reef, often called the Rand, has since 1910 produced between one-third and one-half of all the gold mined in the world each year. After the gold has been removed, the crushed rock is dumped on to great white mountainous heaps, the Dumps, which are landmarks all over the Rand. Some of the mines near Johannesburg are the deepest in the world, reaching nearly 3,000 metres (9,800 feet) below the surface. In recent years valuable uranium has been obtained from the waste material of the mines.

As in all other South African cities, whites and blacks are segregated (kept apart) by the political system called apartheid. In the 1950s, Soweto (South Western Townships) was established for blacks, and it is home today for close on 2 million people. There are other townships for "coloureds" and for Asians. Soweto has its own municipal administration, sports fields, schools, and community halls, but is mostly a vast collection of small, cheaply constructed and overcrowded houses on unsurfaced roads with poor amenities. It was the scene of rioting in 1976, and, again, from 1985. Many black mine workers are migrants living in special groups of buildings called mine compounds. They are temporary workers who come from all over South Africa and neighbouring territories to the north. They may not remain permanently in Johannesburg, and they cannot bring their families with them.

Johannesburg has little natural beauty but contains more than 100 parks. In Hermann Eckstein park there is a zoo and a lake and large wooded grounds which are a favourite resort at weekends. The Wilds park is a botanical garden where flowers and plants from all parts of South Africa grow on a rocky hillside.

Johannesburg has good rail and road links with the rest of South Africa and the Jan Smuts international airport is 22 kilometres (14 miles) east of the city centre. The population of Johannesburg, excluding Soweto, is about 712,000

JOHN (King of England; 1167–1216). The power and freedom of the English barons were nearly crushed by John during his reign as king of England. His attempts to suppress the barons met with final failure at Runnymede. Not until the reign of the Tudors 300 years later were English barons brought under the supreme authority of the crown. King John

was clever in his political judgements and wise to try to control the barons. His failure was caused by failings in character and a disagreeable personality, which made the nation deny him the support he needed.

Mansell Collection

King John (ruled 1199–1216).

John was the youngest son of Henry II and Eleanor of Aquitaine. He was born at Oxford. His brothers gave him the nickname of "Lackland" because his father gave him no territory in the continental provinces. At that time, the English king also ruled large areas of France. Each royal prince would expect a territory to govern. However, despite being landless, John was his father's favourite.

In 1185 Henry sent him to govern Ireland. John treated the Irish chieftains with such arrogance that they revolted and drove him out of the country. Four years later he sided with his brother Richard Coeur de Lion (The Lion Heart), who stirred up a revolt of the French provinces against the king. Henry is said to have died of a broken heart when he saw John's name at the head of the list of conspirators.

Richard came to the throne in 1189 and was kind to his younger brother. When he went on the Third Crusade in 1190, he provided John with funds to keep him from causing trouble. But knowing how unreliable John was, he put William Longchamp, a loyal and sensible man, in charge of the kingdom. Instead of naming John as heir, Richard declared Arthur of Brittany heir to the throne. John was furious and joined with the barons and other leaders to force the expulsion of William Longchamp.

When Richard was on his way home from Palestine he was captured by Leopold of Austria. John did his best to persuade Leopold to keep him imprisoned. Yet Richard, when released, forgave his brother. On his deathbed Richard reversed his earlier decision and made the barons swear to accept John as king.

John came to the throne in 1199. He started his reign by dissolving his marriage to Isabella of Gloucester. He forced Isabella of Angoulême, who was betrothed to another man, to marry him. Hugh of Lusignan, her betrothed, stirred up Poitou against the king. He brought about a war in which John lost all English possessions in France with the exception of Aquitaine.

In 1207 John refused to accept Stephen Langton, the pope's candidate for archbishop of Canterbury. Pope Innocent III prohibited all Church functions such as baptism, confirmation, and Christian burial in England. John boldly replied by taking the property of those clergymen who obeyed the command of the pope. He strengthened his position by compelling the king of Scotland to submit. Pope Innocent III declared him deposed, and Philip Augustus of France threatened to invade England. Before these threats John had to give way. He accepted Langton and made his peace with the Church. In 1214 he destroyed a French fleet but was beaten at Bouvines.

The English barons took advantage of the weakness of their king. They marched on London in 1215 and compelled the king to meet them at Runnymede. The barons forced John to sign Magna Carta (the Great Charter). The charter established the privileges claimed by the barons, and ensured certain civil rights. (See MAGNA CARTA.)

The pope, having reduced John to obedience, did not want to see him overthrown by the barons. He freed John of his oath to observe Magna Carta. The barons replied by declaring war on the king and inviting Louis, ruler of France, to come to their aid. He came with an army in May 1216. John retired to the north, was taken ill, and died shortly after. He was succeeded by his son Henry III.

JOHN, Saint. St. John was one of the Twelve Apostles, or chief disciples of Jesus Christ. He and his elder brother James were sons of a fisherman called Zebedee, and Jesus called them to follow him almost as soon as he started preaching (see APOSTLES, THE). John must have been a very young man at the time and probably was the youngest of the apostles. Three of the Twelve—James, Peter, and John—seem to have been especially loved by Jesus, who permitted them to be present on special occasions when the others were not so privileged. For example, it was these three alone who were with him on the mountain when Jesus "was transfigured [changed] before them: and his face did shine as the sun, and his raiment was white as the light". (This story is told in chapter 17 of St. Matthew's Gospel in the Bible.) Again, it was these three who were with Jesus while he prayed in the Garden of Gethsemane just before he was arrested and crucified. As he was dying, Jesus left his mother and John in each other's care, saying, "Woman, behold thy son!" and then to John, "Behold thy mother!" This seems to show that Jesus had a very special affection for the youngest of his followers. In the Gospel of St. John, John is described as the "disciple whom Jesus loved", and he was the only one of the Twelve Apostles who stood by Jesus on the day of his crucifixion, when the others all ran away in fear. John took a leading part in preaching Christianity. It is believed that he alone of the Twelve was saved from a martyr's death (see MARTYR) and that he lived to be a very old man.

The Gospel According to St. John

Scholars are not sure whether the Gospel of St. John, as we know it, was written by John himself. It is more likely that it was written by one of his followers who had the same name. However, most scholars agree that St. John supplied the details of the story, whether or not he actually wrote it down himself.

It was the latest of the four Gospels to be written and is quite different from the other three. When John either wrote the book or gave the details for it, he was a very old man. He seems to have remembered many sayings of Jesus Christ which, during his lifetime, had seemed unimportant and which the three earlier writers (Mathew, Mark, and Luke) had not bothered to include in their books. Therefore in the fourth Gospel we find many sermons of Jesus that are not found in the other Gospels, which give as much space to the things that Jesus did as to the things that he said. Though John's is the hardest of the four Gospels to understand, many people believe that it is the greatest book in the Bible. In ancient times it was called the "Spiritual Gospel" and it has had a powerful influence on the development of Christianity.

JOHN XXIII, Pope (1881–1963). Angelo Roncalli, who became Pope John XXIII, was born in a poor peasant family in the village of Sotto il Monte, near Bergamo in northern Italy. By calling together the second Vatican Council he introduced many changes in the Roman Catholic Church.

Aged 77 at the time of his election, and regarded as being a "compromise candidate" (nobody's first choice), Pope John might have been expected to have a short and uneventful reign. He was in fact pope for only four and a half years, but in that time he completely altered people's ideas about how popes behaved. He ended the tradition by which the

Camera Press

Pope John XXIII started a new era in the Roman Catholic Church by his openness to change.

popes, in protest against the loss of their lands in the 19th century, rarely left the Vatican City. Pope John went all over Rome, visiting prisoners and patients in hospitals. In 1962 he went on a pilgrimage to Loretto (a shrine of the Virgin Mary) and Assisi, thus beginning the series of papal journeys continued by his successors.

The decision to call a general council—the first held by the Roman Catholic Church for nearly 100 years—was entirely Pope John's, and some of its most important pronouncements—on the relation of the Church with the world, and on reunion among Christians—reflected his own deepest interests. He began the practice of meeting leaders from other Christian Churches.

His encyclical letter *Pacem in terris* (Peace on Earth) showed Pope John's desire for international co-operation. But above all it was the simplicity of his character and his friendliness that stirred the imagination of people everywhere. He died in 1963 and was succeeded as pope by Paul VI.

JOHN DORY (*Zeus faber*) is a fish with a high, narrow body and flattened sides. The front dorsal fin has very long rays which extend almost to the tip of the tail. There are rows of strong, bony, thorn-like spines along the base of the dorsal and anal fins. The pelvic fins, which are far forward on the body, also have long rays in them. The fish is olive or brown in colour and on each side of the body

The John Dory's unusual mouth shoots forwards to seize its prey.

is a black spot surrounded by a yellow ring. Legend says that these black spots were left by St. Peter's forefinger and thumb, when he caught the fish that had a coin in its mouth. (See St. Matthew's Gospel, chapter 17, verse 27.)

The John Dory is a fish eater, usually feeding on herring, pilchards, and sand eels. It has a peculiar mouth in which the bones are arranged so that the mouth can be shot forward when the fish sees its food. The flesh of the John Dory is white, firm, and very good to eat. It lives in the Mediterranean, and in the east Atlantic, and in the seas around Australia. It is one of Australia's prime restaurant fish.

JOHN OF GAUNT (1340–99) was the fourth son of King Edward III of England and Queen Philippa. He is known as "John of Gaunt" because he was born at Ghent (now in Belgium), which the English pronounced as "Gaunt". During his lifetime he was rarely called by this name and it only became popular because William Shakespeare used it when he made Gaunt a character in the play *Richard II*.

When he was only 15 years old John accompanied his father in a raid on northern France. When he was 19 he married Blanche, daughter of the Duke of Lancaster. She brought him great estates, mostly in northern England, and when her father died in 1361 John became Earl of Lancaster and the next year was created Duke of Lancaster. In 1367 John went with his eldest brother, Edward the Black Prince, to fight in Spain. This was the beginning of a long connection with Spain for, his wife Blanche having died, he married Constance of Castile (a kingdom in Spain) in 1371 and through her claimed the throne of Castile.

Much of John's fighting was done in France, for England and France were engaged in the Hundred Years' War. (See HUNDRED YEARS' WAR.) John failed, on the whole, as a soldier. His armies were defeated by the French several times and this made him unpopular with many English people. John's enemies said that he plotted to become king of England. There is no proof that this was true, and he was loyal to Richard II when Richard became king in 1377 at the early age of ten.

John set out on his last campaign in 1386 when he went to Spain to fight for his kingdom of Castile. Although at first his armies were successful, they were beaten later and the territory they had conquered was lost. However, the king of Castile suggested that his son should marry Catherine, John's daughter by his second wife, Constance of Castile. John agreed and, as his daughter would one day be queen of Castile, he gave up his own claim to the throne. In 1394 his wife Constance died and two years later he married Catherine Swynford.

John of Gaunt had eight children, and many of his descendants became kings and queens. His eldest son Henry became Henry IV of England and was followed by two more kings of the family of Lancaster. The later royal family of Tudor was also descended from John of Gaunt through his son John, Earl of Somerset. (See KINGS AND QUEENS.)

JOHN OF THE CROSS, Saint (1542–91). St. John of the Cross belonged to a poor but noble Spanish family who lived near Avila in central Spain. When he was 21 he entered a monastery belonging to the Carmelite Order of Friars (see MONK AND FRIAR) and became a priest four years later.

At that time the Carmelite Order was going through bad days, for both the friars and the nuns had become slack and lazy in their duties. They were disobeying the rule that said they must sleep on straw, wear rope sandals, and eat no meat. St. Teresa of Avila was just starting to bring back the old strictness among the nuns at Avila in Spain, and with her aid John started to do the same thing among the friars. She sent him to found a new monastery at Duruelo, some distance away and it was then that he took the name John of the Cross. At Duruelo he lived very strictly and found deep spiritual happiness.

In 1577 friars who objected to John's reforms kidnapped him and kept him shut up in a tiny, dark cell for nine months. He managed to escape and rose to a high position in the Order, but again became involved in disputes and lost his high position. When he died at the early age of 49 he was only a simple friar.

Although he took part in such violent struggles about how the friars should live and work, St. John of the Cross is remembered chiefly as a mystic (see MYSTICISM). Like all mystics he spent much of his time in religious meditation. In his writings, he explained how he had been able to unite himself with God. One of his best-known poems was called *The Dark Night of the Soul*.

Saint John of the Cross was canonized (declared a saint) in 1726.

JOHN PAUL II, Pope (born 1920).

Karol Wojtyla, who became Pope John Paul II, was born on 18 May 1920, in Wadowice, Poland. He studied literature and drama at the University of Krakow in the 1930s and worked in a factory during World War II. Wojtyla was ordained a priest in 1946 and began his ministry as a teacher and parish priest during a period of Communist persecution of the Catholic church. In 1958 he became Poland's youngest bishop, and in 1964 he was named archbishop of the important diocese of Krakow. In his speech to the second Vatican Council (1962–65) he encouraged discussion between Catholics and other church leaders. He became a cardinal in 1967.

When Pope John Paul I died in 1978, after only 34 days in office, Wojtyla was elected pope and took the name John Paul II as a mark of respect. He was the first non-Italian pope in over 450 years, and the first Pole ever to hold this office. A scholar, poet, and sportsman, John Paul II had a friendly manner that made him popular. He spoke several languages and travelled widely.

Popperfoto

Pope John Paul II visited Ireland in 1979, where an estimated 400,000 people came to see him.

In 1979 he drew huge crowds during a visit to the United States. He addressed the United Nations and became the first pope ever to visit a US president in the White House. During the trip he made speeches about human rights and world peace. The same year he became the first pope to visit a communist country, when he made a seven-day tour of his native Poland. In 1981 John Paul II was shot in an assassination attempt at St. Peter's Square, in Rome. He was struck by two bullets and rushed to the hospital where successful surgery was performed.

Pope John Paul II has made efforts to bring together Christians from churches all over the world and to establish friendly relations with people of all faiths. Within the Catholic Church, he has reaffirmed many traditional teachings.

JOHNSON, Amy (1903–41) was the first woman to fly alone from England to Australia. She was born at Hull (now in the English county of Humberside). After completing her education at Sheffield University she took up flying in 1928 and soon qualified as a pilot and as a ground engineer.

BBC Hulton Picture Library

Amy Johnson, British aviation pioneer of the 1930s.

She made her historic flight in 1930. Piloting a de Haviland Moth, she set out from Croydon, in Surrey, on 5 May. After making several stops *en route* for repairs, she landed in Port Darwin, Australia, on 24 May. The flight made her a national heroine. The *Daily Mail* awarded her £10,000 and she was made a Commander of the Order of the British Empire (CBE). In 1931 she flew from England to Tokyo (Japan) and back, and in the following year to Cape Town (South Africa) and back. On both these flights she beat the record in each direction.

In 1932 Amy Johnson married J. A. Mollison (1905–59), also a well-known aviator, and with him in 1933 flew across the Atlantic from east to west in 39 hours. In 1936 she again made flights by herself in record time from London to Cape Town and back. She and Mollison were divorced in 1938.

When World War II began she joined the Air Transport Auxiliary, a group of civilian pilots who flew new or repaired RAF aircraft from the works to the airfields. She was killed when the plane she was flying crashed in the Thames estuary on 5 January 1941. Amy Johnson was a brave and determined woman whose exploits helped to make flying popular.

JOHNSON, Samuel (1709–84). Samuel Johnson was a writer who became the most famous literary personality of his day in England. Among his writings were poems, essays for magazines, biographies (life stories) of other English writers, and a dictionary of the English language. But he is perhaps best known to most people today because of the biography of him written by James Boswell. Boswell knew Johnson for the 21 years from 1763 to his death, and made notes of what he did and said during that time, so that in Boswell's book the reader can enjoy the company of the great man just as his friends did when he was alive.

Everyone who knew him loved to listen to Johnson's conversation, for it was in talking that his genius came out most of all. Sometimes in the heat of argument he could make the most crushing and rude remarks to people—many of them very amusing to read now—but beneath his crustiness he was known to be extremely kind hearted and generous. His favourite "talking-place" was among the members of the Literary Club, which was founded in London in 1764 by Sir Joshua Reynolds. (See REYNOLDS, SIR JOSHUA.) If Johnson were alive today, he would undoubtedly find a popular place on a television talk-show.

Samuel Johnson was born in Lichfield, Staffordshire, on 18 September 1709. His father was a bookseller and a magistrate. He went to Lichfield Grammar School, and later a wealthy neighbour promised to help pay for him to study at Oxford University. Samuel only stayed at Oxford for just over two years, however, for the money never came, and he could not afford to finish his course. He had been despised by some of his fellow students for his ragged clothes and laughed at because of his strange appearance. He was a big, clumsy young man, and his face, scarred by the disease known as scrofula, twitched uncontrollably.

Samuel Johnson (right) talking to James Boswell, his biographer, in a drawing by Samuel Collings.

After unsuccessfully trying teaching, first in someone else's school and then, after his marriage in 1735, in one he set up himself, Johnson went to London in 1737, hoping to earn his living by literary work. He was accompanied on the trip from Lichfield by a former pupil of his, David Garrick, who later became an outstanding actor (see GARRICK, DAVID). Johnson began his literary career writing articles for *The Gentleman's Magazine*. He also wrote poetry. Though his first book, a long poem called *London*, was fairly successful, he was not paid very much for it and for about ten years he was miserably poor. In 1747, however, he was engaged by a group of booksellers to prepare a really good dictionary of the English language. The work on the dictionary, which aimed at providing a complete list of English words with their correct spelling and meaning (the meaning was shown in many cases by quotations from English authors), took Johnson and his eight assistants seven years to complete. Johnson's fame, which had been increasing through his other writings, was at last assured with the publication of the *Dictionary* in 1755. (See DICTIONARY.)

He was still poor, however, and continued to support himself by journalism and literary criticism. He founded two magazines in the 1750s, *The Rambler* and its successor, *The Idler*. When his mother died in 1759 Johnson had no money to pay for her funeral. In order to make some quickly he wrote a long philosophical story called *Rasselas* in a single week and sent it to the publishers who paid him the sum of £100.

Johnson once told Boswell that no one but a fool would write unless he had to for money, and so it is not surprising that the happiest time of Johnson's life came after 1762, when he was given a pension from the government of £300 a year. It was in the years after this, during which he did not write very much, that Johnson's talk became so well known and, because of this, that his company was welcome wherever he went. In particular he made friends with some people called the Thrales, and in their house he was able to be at ease and to talk happily in the way he liked best. He continued to live in London, which he loved, except when in 1773 he went with Boswell on a tour in Scotland and visited several islands of the Hebrides. His most important literary efforts during this closing period of his life were his edition of Shakespeare, finished in 1765, and his book, *The Lives of the Most Eminent English Poets*, published in 1777, a work still valued for its literary insight. Trinity College, Dublin, conferred on him the honorary degree of Doctor of Laws, and he is still often referred to as Dr. Johnson.

Johnson died on 13 December 1784, in his 76th year, and was buried in Westminster Abbey. The house at Lichfield where he was born and the London house (17 Gough Square) where he lived from 1748 to 1759, are now museums, containing many interesting things that belonged to him.

JOHN THE BAPTIST, Saint. The story of the life and work of John the Baptist is told in the four Gospels and the Acts of the Apostles in the New Testament of the Bible. He was born in a mountain village in Judaea six months before Jesus Christ was born in the city of Bethlehem, also in Judaea.

This was not the only link between them, for John's mother was Elisabeth, a relation of the Virgin Mary, mother of Jesus. His father was Zacharias, a priest of the Temple at Jerusalem.

When he was about 28 years old, John began to preach on the banks of the River Jordan, telling the people that the Messiah (see JESUS CHRIST) would soon come. Because of this, John is often known as the "forerunner" of Jesus. He urged them to prepare for the Messiah's coming by asking forgiveness for their sins and setting themselves to lead better lives. When they repented he baptized them in the waters of the River Jordan, and thus came to be called John the Baptist. Wearing only a garment of camel hair tied with a leather girdle, and living on locusts and wild honey, John probably reminded people of the great prophets of Old Testament times, for they had lived and dressed in this way. Many Gentiles (people who were not Jews), as well as many Jews, came to listen to his preaching and were baptized. Chapter 3 of the Gospel according to St. Matthew tells how Jesus himself asked to be baptized. Realizing that Jesus was far greater than he was, John felt himself unworthy to do this, saying, "I have need to be baptized of thee, and comest thou to me?" However, Jesus insisted that John should baptize him, and afterwards received signs from God that he should begin his own preaching.

John continued to preach to the people until he was thrown into prison by Herod Antipas (see HEROD), the ruler of Galilee. Herod had married Herodias, the wife of his half-brother Philip, and John publicly criticized him for marrying his brother's wife. Herod himself feared and respected John as a holy man, but Herodias hated him. She persuaded Herod to imprison him, and wanted to have him killed. This Herod refused to do. However, one day at a feast, Herodias' daughter, Salome, danced so beautifully that Herod promised to give her anything she should ask. Herodias told her to ask for the head of John the Baptist. Having given his promise, and being afraid of the sneers of his guests if he broke it, Herod unwillingly ordered John to be executed. This was done and John's head was brought to Salome on a great dish, which she carried to her mother. John's disciples took his body away and buried it and then went to tell Jesus of what had happened.

Herod later believed that Jesus was John the Baptist come to life again.

JOLLIET, Louis (1645–1700) was a French Canadian who explored and made maps of much of the unknown wilderness of the Great Lakes and the Mississippi River.

Jolliet, whose name is sometimes spelled Joliet, was born in Canada. He was educated in the Jesuit college at Quebec, where he was a bright student. He was sent to France for a year of scientific study. On his return he made a trip to the west, where he made friends and traded with the Indians. In 1672, Jean Talon, intendant (governor) of Canada, sent Jolliet to find out whether the Mississippi River flowed into the Gulf of Mexico or the Pacific Ocean. Father Jacques Marquette was to go with him. Marquette was a missionary who had spent several years in the wilderness and knew several Indian languages. Jolliet was an expert map maker. He paddled up the St. Lawrence River and through the Great Lakes to St. Ignace, Michigan, where he met Father Marquette. The following year, Jolliet, Marquette, and five companions left St. Ignace in two birchbark canoes. They went into Green Bay and up the Fox River to central Wisconsin. There they got Indian guides to lead them through the forests to the Wisconsin River. They floated down the Wisconsin to the Mississippi, and down the Mississippi to the mouth of the Arkansas River. At night they anchored in midstream and slept in their canoes. Finally, what they saw and what they heard from friendly Indians convinced them that the Mississippi flowed into the Gulf of Mexico.

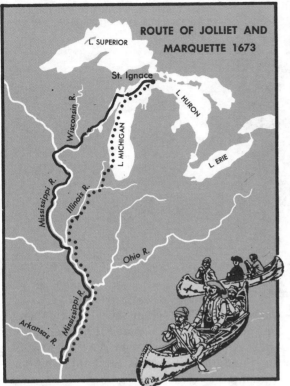

Jolliet was the first European to travel down the Mississippi between the Wisconsin and the Arkansas.

Fearing capture by the Spaniards, they turned around and headed home. This time they went up the Illinois River and passed the present site of the city of Chicago.

In the Lachine Rapids, near Montreal, Jolliet's canoe overturned. His maps and notes were lost. Fortunately he was able to draw many of them from memory. Jolliet was later given the island of Anticosti in the Gulf of St. Lawrence as a reward for this trip and one he made to Hudson Bay.

In his later years, Jolliet made more explorations in Hudson Bay, the Gulf of St. Lawrence, and along the coast of Labrador. In 1697 he was made royal hydrographer; he made maps of the rivers and the coast of Canada.

JONES, Inigo (1573–1652), was an English architect, artist, and designer of costumes and scenery for court masques, or plays (see MASQUE). He visited Italy as a young man, where he saw for himself the wonderful classi-

cal buildings of the Renaissance period as well as the ancient ruins, and returned to England to create the English classical school of architecture during the reign of King James I (1605–25) and his son, King Charles I (1625–49). His were the first Renaissance-style buildings in England.

We know little about Jones's early life. He grew up in London, in an ordinary family. His father was a clothmaker. He probably first visited Italy around 1600, and on his return to England (via Denmark, where he did some work for King Christian IV) he started to design costumes and scenery for court masques at the invitation of Queen Anne, the Danish wife of King James I.

Jones was an attractive and forceful personality. His stage designs established his reputation, and in 1611 he was appointed Surveyor to Prince Henry, and in 1613 became Surveyor of the King's Works. At this time he started to design buildings. He visited Italy for a second time in 1613 and was re-enthused with the architecture that he saw.

Jones built, rebuilt, and added to many existing royal buildings. Unfortunately, few of these buildings have survived. One that still stands is the Queen's House at Greenwich (now the National Maritime Museum) commissioned by Queen Anne in 1616. This was

A. F. Kersting

The Banqueting House at Whitehall, London, rebuilt by Jones in 1622, is one of his surviving buildings.

Inigo Jones' skill as an architect was also employed in designing stage sets for royal entertainments.

Devonshire Collection, Chatsworth

an Italian-type villa, heavily influenced by the Italian Renaissance architect, Andrea Palladio. It was followed by the Banqueting House at Whitehall. The original Banqueting House had been destroyed in a fire, and Jones rebuilt it in 1622. The third surviving building is the Queen's Chapel at St. James's Palace in London.

In the 1640s, King Charles I, son of King James, invited Jones to submit a design for the total rebuilding of Whitehall Palace. While the work was never carried out, the designs still exist.

Inigo Jones also designed London's first square, Covent Garden, in 1630. But little of it survives. His restoration of St. Paul's

This doorway and window are in the classical style. Inigo Jones was among the first to use it in England.

Cathedral, which took nine years to complete, was destroyed in the Great Fire of London in 1666. When Sir Christopher Wren (see WREN, SIR CHRISTOPHER) rebuilt St. Paul's, he was influenced by Jones's style.

The classical style of Inigo Jones was not widely copied, either in his day or later. The more popular English style of architecture was Gothic, with a few classical influences. (See also ARCHITECTURE.)

JONSON, Ben (1572–1637). Ben Jonson became one of England's greatest dramatists. Most experts consider that Jonson was the best playwright of his day, after Shakespeare.

Jonson was born in London soon after his father's death. His stepfather was a bricklayer, and the family were fortunate enough to send Ben to Westminster School, where he received a basic education. His schooling was cut short, however, and he took up his stepfather's trade. But he soon gave up bricklaying to serve as a soldier in the Netherlands, and later turned to acting.

A brilliant but quarrelsome man, Jonson narrowly escaped hanging in 1598 after killing a fellow actor in a duel. That year his first successful comedy, *Every Man in His Humour*, was performed by the Lord Chamberlain's Men, with William Shakespeare probably among the cast. Despite his lack of a full education, Jonson read widely among Greek and Latin writers and introduced to the English drama the "comedy of humours" ("humours" here means types of characters), which the Latin writers Plautus and Terence had employed.

Two of his surviving plays are tragedies in the classical manner, *Sejanus* (1603) and *Catiline* (1611), but he is best remembered for his witty, biting satirical comedies. These include *Every Man out of His Humour* (1599), *Volpone* (1606), *The Alchemist* (1610), and *Bartholomew Fair* (1614). Jonson wrote vividly about London life, and the characters in his plays are often dominated by a ruling passion. For example, Volpone—"the Fox"—is truly fox-like in his cunning, and other characters are given similar animal natures.

Jonson also developed the masque in England (see MASQUE), often working with Inigo Jones, who designed the settings and

BBC Hulton Picture Library

The English dramatist Ben Jonson in an engraving by H. Robinson, after the Dutch artist Gerrit van Honthost.

costumes. Among these entertainments were such works as *The Masque of Blackness* (1603), *Love Restored* (1612), and *Neptune's Triumph for the Return of Albion* (1624). Many of these masques were performed at court and Jonson received a pension from the king. He had a wide circle of important friends, sometimes known as "the tribe of Ben". He also wrote poetry and compiled an English grammar. He died in 1637 and was buried in Westminster Abbey.

JORDAN is a small country in the Middle East. Its official name is the Hashemite kingdom of Jordan. It is bounded on the north by Syria, on the east by Iraq, on the south by Saudi Arabia, and on the west by Israel. In the western part are the bare hills of Judaea and Samaria and then comes the deep valley of the Jordan River flowing southwards into the Dead Sea. East of the Jordan Valley the Mountains of Moab overhang the Dead Sea and stretch south as far as the city of Petra. In the north a fertile highland plateau, or tableland, slopes down eastwards into the desert. Jordan is an almost treeless country because the forests have been destroyed by centuries of overcutting, and the rather scarce natural vegetation is mostly of shrub-like plants. In the southern mountains wolves, jackals, and wild goats known as ibexes are common. The upland parts have hot summers and cold rainy winters. The Jordan Valley itself is almost unbearably hot in summer and often flooded in winter (see JORDAN RIVER), but the desert regions have little rain. Since the Six-Day War of 1967, the land west of the Jordan River, called the West Bank, has been occupied by Israel.

Most of the people are Arabs and belong to the Muslim religion. About 5 per cent are Christian. Arabic is the official language. Slightly less than half of Jordan's people live by farming. The chief crops are wheat and barley, but fruit, vines, olives, and vegetables are cultivated in the valleys. Goats, sheep, cattle, and camels are reared, although the pastures are mostly poor. Industry is developing, and minerals found in the country include phosphates (used for making fertilizers), iron, phosphorus, manganese, and copper. Chemicals are obtained from the very salty waters of the Dead Sea. Tourism is also a major source of income, for many visitors come to see Jordan's historic sites, including places associated with early Christianity.

Amman, the capital city, has about 770,500 people (1984). Of the six other large towns, Jordanian Jerusalem, Nablus, Hebron, and Jenin are on the West Bank. Bethlehem and Jericho, also on the West Bank, are little more than villages. Near the southern end of the Hejaz railway are the remains of the ancient city of Petra whose houses, shrines, and tombs were carved out of the solid rock. From the southern end of the Hejaz railway a road connects with the port of Aquaba on an arm of the Red Sea. Roads join Amman with Jerusalem and with Damascus in Syria.

Graphic House/EB Inc.

Two minarets of a Muslim mosque overlook hilly Amman, the capital and largest city of Jordan.

History

Jordan is a 20th-century country on an ancient site. The Jordan River Valley is one of the earliest settled areas in history. It was an important area in biblical times. In the 1st century BC the area that is now Jordan became a part of the Roman Empire. Arabs overran the land in the 7th century AD, and Turks took control in the 16th century. The Jordan area remained a part of the Ottoman Empire until

the end of World War I. As a Turkish possession it was neglected, although the Turks built the Hejaz railway early in the 20th century to improve their control of the country. In 1916 the Arabs were encouraged to rebel against the Turks (with whom Great Britain was then at war) by a British army officer, T. E. Lawrence (on whom there is a separate article). After the war Transjordan (as the country east of the Jordan River was then called) came under British rule. In 1921 Abdullah, a son of King Husain of the Hejaz who had led the Arab revolt, became the ruler of Transjordan with British advisers, and in 1946 he was proclaimed king. This new, independent country was named Jordan.

FACTS ABOUT JORDAN

AREA: 94,946 square kilometres (36,659 square miles).
POPULATION: 2,859,000 (1987).
GOVERNMENT: Constitutional monarchy.
CAPITAL: Amman.
GEOGRAPHICAL FEATURES: Jordan is mainly a plateau with an average height of 900 metres (2,950 feet), sloping down to the east. In the west is a steep slope overlooking the Jordan river valley. In the south are mountains and sandstone canyons. There is a short coastline on the Gulf of Aqaba (Red Sea).
CHIEF PRODUCTS: Phosphates, wheat, vegetables, fruits, olive oil.
IMPORTANT TOWNS: Amman, Zarqa, Irbid, Aqaba; (in Israeli-occupied West Bank) Jordanian Jerusalem, Nablus, Hebron, Jenin.
EDUCATION: Children must attend school between the ages of 6 and 14, but a great many people can neither read nor write.

In 1947, when war broke out between the Arab states and the Jews in Palestine, the Jordanian army—known as the Arab Legion—occupied and held the old part of Jerusalem and the Judaean and Samarian hills. Many Arab refugees fled across the frontier from Israel and settled in Jordan, and there was border fighting between the two countries. King Husain succeeded his father, Talal, in 1953. In 1958 Jordan joined Iraq in a union called the "Arab Federation", but this ended when Iraq became a republic soon afterwards. In 1967 Jordan fought with Egypt and Syria against Israel. After fierce fighting, especially in Jerusalem, Jordanian forces were defeated and Israel held the whole of Jordan's West Bank territory. The occupied West Bank makes up about 6 per cent of Jordan's land, one half of its farm land, and about one-third of its people.

The Jordanian government later took strong measures against Palestinian guerillas who used Jordan as a base against Israel, but took little part in the Arab-Israeli war of 1973. More than 1 million refugees live in Jordan, mostly in special camps. Their presence and the continuing occupation of the West Bank by Israel are two of Jordan's greatest problems as a country.

To learn more about the history of Jordan, see MIDDLE EAST.

JORDAN RIVER. Few rivers appear so often in history as the Jordan. It has played a central role in the cultures of Muslims, Jews, and Christians in the Middle East. It was the boundary of the Promised Land into which Joshua led the Israelites after the death of Moses. Jesus Christ was baptized in its waters by St. John the Baptist. Egyptians, Assyrians, Greeks, Romans, Crusaders, Saracens, Turks, and Britons, as well as Arabs and Jews, have made their camps or built their castles near its crossings. In the 20th century it was used to mark the division between the newly-created countries of Jordan and Israel.

Most rivers flow in valleys which they carve in the soil. Not so the Jordan. It wanders south from Mount Hermon in Syria at the bottom of a deep trench created by the sinking of a long strip of the Earth's crust. This rift valley, as it is called, runs southwards to the Dead Sea and just beyond it. The steep slopes on each side of the valley are about 15 to 25 kilometres (9 to 15 miles) apart, and its floor is far below sea-level when it enters the clear blue Sea of Galilee. On leaving the Sea of Galilee the Jordan becomes muddy with the clay and dirt it washes from its banks. The valley is almost unbearably hot and stuffy in the summer and is often flooded in the rainy season, which comes in January and February. For the last 110 kilometres (68 miles) the river flows through desert. Finally it flows into the Dead Sea at 400 metres (1,315 feet) below sea-level. It is the lowest river in the world, and about 360 kilometres (225 miles) long. It is too swift-moving and dangerous for navigation but, in the 20th century, has become an important source of water for irrigating crops in Jordan and Israel.

JOULE, James Prescott (1818–89), was a British physicist who discovered by experiment that heat, mechanical energy, electrical energy, and so on, are all different forms of the same thing and are all interchangeable. He also established the relationship between work and energy. The joule, the unit of both energy and work in the *Système Internationale*, is named in his honour. (For an explanation of the physical concepts see ENERGY; WEIGHTS AND MEASURES.)

BBC Hulton Picture Library

James Prescott Joule, the English physicist who did pioneering research into heat and electricity.

Joule was born in Salford, in the industrial heartland of northern England. He did not have a university education but in 1835 he studied briefly with the famous chemist John Dalton. Joule's father, a wealthy brewer, provided the money and facilities for him to devote himself to scientific research, and in 1838 the 20-year-old James published the first of a large number of academic papers.

During his youth Joule had invented a so-called "electromagnetic engine". From this he turned to the study of how work and the energy needed for it are related. Through a series of careful experiments Joule measured the amount of heat produced by friction caused by a paddle rotating in water, by falling weights, by the forcing of water through narrow tubes, and by the compression of air. Joule's measurements were so accurate that he was able to show that a fixed amount of work of any kind always produced a fixed amount of heat. In other words, the amount of work needed to produce a single unit of heat was always the same and could be expressed by a formula using a mathematical constant. In 1843 Joule published a paper in which he announced a value for this constant, which he called the "mechanical equivalent of heat".

By proving that any kind of work could be converted into heat Joule showed that heat was a form of energy and was independent of the substance being heated. His theory opposed the scientific opinion of the time, which was that heat was itself a substance. His researches showed that mechanical energy could be changed into heat. Indeed, given suitable means, any form of energy could be changed into any other form. This fact is known as the principle of the interconvertibility of energy. It leads on to one of the most important laws of physics, the Law of Conservation of Energy (sometimes called the First Law of Thermodynamics). This states that energy cannot be created or destroyed but can only be changed from one form into another.

In 1852 Joule and his fellow scientist William Thomson (later Lord Kelvin) discovered that when a gas is allowed to expand without doing any external work, the temperature of the gas becomes cooler. This is known as the "Joule-Thomson effect" (or the "Joule-Kelvin effect") and has proved of great significance for the refrigeration industry. It is also employed in the design of air conditioning systems. (See REFRIGERATION.)

Joule's lack of academic training led initially to the failure of British scientists to appreciate the importance of his findings. The Royal Society refused to publish his early researches. But by 1850 Joule's contribution to physics could not be overlooked. He was elected a Fellow of the Royal Society and went on to win its highest awards, the Gold Medal and the Copley Medal. In 1885–87 he edited all his scientific papers, which were published in two volumes by the Physical Society of London.

JOURNALISM is the profession of gathering, writing, and telling the news to the public. People who are journalists do this through newspapers, television, radio, news agencies, magazines, and other means of communication. Together, these are called "the media", shortened from "the news media". (Printed forms of journalism may still be called "the press"—a reference to printing presses—but this term is falling out of use.)

Sometimes called "current events", news is what is happening around us every day. Journalists report on disasters such as air and car crashes, earthquakes, fires, and floods; politics, elections, and world affairs; social issues such as schooling, housing, and poverty; wars; kidnappings, murders and other crimes; economics and banking; and things of popular interest such as sport, fashion, leisure pastimes, and the doings of important or interesting people.

The Work of a Journalist

The first duty of a journalist is to be accurate. He or she must give correctly all of the facts in a news story. A journalist must also be fair, and report all the different sides or points of view in a news story. This is called being impartial.

In gathering and writing a news story, a journalist should always try to answer the questions Who? Where? When? What? Why? and How? This is not always easy. Sometimes information is difficult to get. Sometimes people do not want the truth to be known about something. A journalist must be careful when a story about a person or group of people might be harmful to their reputation (see LIBEL AND SLANDER). Governments, especially in times of war or difficult political situations, may not want all of the facts to be known. They may also not allow journalists to report all the information the journalists have gathered (see CENSORSHIP).

Journalists must work quickly, for they compete with other journalists covering the same story for other employers. A journalist is always looking for a big item of news or information that others do not have. If he, or she, succeeds, this is called a "scoop" or a "beat". Exclusive interviews with people who are newsmakers or newsworthy are also highly sought after.

Journalists gather information from many sources. An editor or, in the case of radio and television, a producer, is in charge of organizing their work. That person assigns stories to be covered. The reporter, a journalist who goes out from the office and reports back, travels to the scene of disasters, listens in on political debates, attends news conferences, talks to the police, the fire department, witnesses, or anyone involved in a news story, and spends whatever time is necessary collecting and checking information before a story is written.

A journalist who is sent to live and work abroad, reporting on events in another country, is called a foreign correspondent. That journalist will make a special study of the foreign country, and will usually speak its language.

Journalists may be experts on special topics, from politics, to fashion, to chess, and may travel all over the world reporting on only that topic.

Journalists who are self-employed and work for a number of different media are independent journalists and are called freelancers. News photography is called photojournalism. It plays a major role in television news coverage, and in the acquiring of photographs used in newspapers and magazines. It demands technical skills and "news sense" for what will make a good picture.

The Role of Journalism

Countries that respect their citizens' right to freedom of speech also usually respect the freedom of the media. Historically this has been called the "freedom of the press". It is not allowed everywhere in the world.

The democratic, Western idea of journalism is that it acts as a mirror to the world, honestly reflecting its nature and reporting on events, however good or bad those might be. In dictatorships, where the freedom of the people is restricted, journalism is looked on as a tool of the state, to be used to control and "educate". In such countries the government tries to make the people adopt the government's views without question, and be unaware or scornful of the nature and doings of the outside world. In many of these countries, the media are owned or controlled by the state, and journalists are government employees. This type of journalism is often called propaganda (see PROPAGANDA). In other countries, journalists' work is censored by the government (see CENSORSHIP).

In influencing public opinion and thus affecting the way people act, the power of the media is great. The reporters on the American newspaper *The Washington Post* who investigated and revealed the truth about President Richard Nixon's role in the Watergate Scandal of the 1970s, brought about his resignation. The journalists who sent back pictures and stories of the starving people of the African famine of the 1980s shocked the world, and there began a huge outpouring of money and aid by governments and people everywhere.

Journalism as a Career

Young people thinking about becoming journalists need to be curious. They must want to ask questions, and must ask them in a way that will get answers. They must get on well with other people and be able to develop the contacts and inside sources that will help them to get at the facts.

Would-be journalists must enjoy writing, and be able to meet the demands of accuracy and speed. They must not mind having to

A typical scene of journalists with microphones, cameras, tape recorders, and notebooks surrounding someone in the news, trying to find out what has happened. This photograph, taken by a photo-journalist, shows South Africa's Bishop Desmond Tutu outside the White House in Washington, DC, after a meeting with President Ronald Reagan.

Popperfoto

write to a set length, and must be willing to have their material questioned and changed by editors. They must not mind working at any time of day or night.

The education of a journalist should be as broad as possible. It is a mistake to specialize in any subject too early. Editors are looking for people who can write about many different things.

Valuable experience can be gained by working on school or university newspapers, magazines, radio and television stations, not only in reporting and writing, but in the technical skills required by the latest electronic methods and equipment. In many countries university courses are offered in journalism or communication studies, and some of the different media offer training schemes.

Most journalists start their careers as reporters on a local newspaper, or with a local radio or television station.

Brief History

The first collection and distribution of news that we know of was made by members of the Roman senate, who put together the *Acta Diurna* (Daily Business) from 59 BC onwards. Scribes wrote out more than 2,000 copies, which were sent everywhere in the Roman Empire and hung up in public places. People who could read called out the news to people who could not.

For centuries news spread only by word of mouth or in handwritten forms. It therefore travelled very slowly, and reached few people. The development of the printing press in the 15th century quickly led to the publication of newspapers and magazines. Newspapers were first published on a regular basis in German cities and in Antwerp, Belgium, in the early 17th century.

In those days journalism was strictly regulated by governments, who were often keen to stop the reporting of their doings. Strict libel laws, the need to have a license to print, and censorship made journalism difficult.

As more and more people learned to read, the number and influence of newspapers and magazines grew. Faster methods of printing and distribution led to more and more competition among newspaper and magazine owners to win the widest audience for their products. The growth in communication technology, with inventions such as telegraph, telephone, radio, film, and television, brought more speed, coverage, and competition.

In the latter half of the 20th century, electronic journalism, with the use of computers, satellites, laser printing, and photography, led to a dramatic change in the nature of news gathering and distribution.

See also the article NEWSPAPER.

JOUSTING was a form of mock combat practised in medieval times. To keep themselves in training for real battles, armoured knights would gather at meetings known as tournaments, and large crowds would watch the jousting and other mock fights that then took place. Strictly speaking, a *joust* was a fight with lances only between two knights on horseback. The knights rode at one another within long wooden enclosures called *lists*. A *tourney* was a fight between groups of knights using swords, while a *mêlée* was a kind of free-for-all, or pitched battle.

Topham

A "knight" in armour jousts with a rubber lance in a modern tournament in England in 1964.

Jousting could be dangerous, and knights were sometimes seriously wounded or even killed. As a result, tournaments were often forbidden, although they were also popular entertainments, particularly at the marriage of a king or noble. From the 13th century jousting was made safer by the introduction of special lances and swords without points, and padded armour for both men and horses.

A great deal of pageantry was added to tournaments which, by the 15th century, consisted entirely of jousting. The contestants wore handsomely decorated armour, and in fact armour was worn for jousting for some time after it had ceased to be practical for real warfare. By the 16th century, a tournament had become little more than an excuse for dressing up, and with the disappearance of the mounted knight from the battlefield, jousting too came to an end.

However, medieval-style jousting is still occasionally to be seen today, at country shows and festivals in Britain.

JOYCE, James (1882–1941). The work of the Irish writer James Joyce ranks among the most complicated, experimental literature ever produced. His most famous books were two long fictional works, *Ulysses* (1922) and *Finnegans Wake* (1939), both landmarks in the development of the 20th-century novel. Meant to be read in several different ways, these books are among the most difficult in any language and must be re-read several times for all their many levels of meaning to become clear. Joyce also wrote poems, short stories, and a play.

James Augustine Aloysius Joyce was born in Dublin. He was educated at two Jesuit boarding schools and attended University College, Dublin, where he studied languages. Joyce was academically gifted, although his

BBC Hulton Picture Library

The great Irish novelist James Joyce, author of *Ulysses* and *Finnegans Wake*.

father's drinking and debt had reduced the family to poverty. At university Joyce read widely and taught himself enough Norwegian to read the plays of Ibsen. He wrote a review of one of Ibsen's plays, and this review convinced Joyce that he wanted to be a writer.

At school Joyce had begun to lose his faith in Roman Catholicism and he became dissatisfied with life in Catholic-dominated Ireland. In 1904, after brief visits to Paris, France, he left Ireland for ever, to teach English abroad. From 1905 until his death, Joyce and his family lived at Trieste, Zurich, and Paris. After the fall of France in World War II, he returned to Zurich, Switzerland, where he died in 1941.

Joyce's Writings

Joyce's most important work before *Ulysses* was *A Portrait of the Artist as a Young Man*, an autobiographical novel first published in a magazine called *The Egoist* in 1914–15. Joyce identified himself with the central character Stephen Daedalus, a character also in *Ulysses*. Among other early works were a collection of short stories, *Dubliners* (1914), and his only play *The Exiles* (1918).

Ulysses was published in Paris in 1922, although many extracts of it had appeared in a magazine and it was already famous. Like *Portrait of the Artist as a Young Man*, parts of *Ulysses* are concerned with sex, and the book was banned in many countries soon after its appearance.

The novel deals with the events of one day in Dublin, 16 June 1904. The central figures of the novel are Leopold Bloom, a Jewish advertising man, his wife Molly, and Stephen Daedalus. The story follows Bloom and Daedalus around Dublin and covers their eventual meeting. The parts of the book correspond to the episodes of Homer's *Odyssey* (see HOMER; ODYSSEY), and the story is full of obscure literary and cultural references. In *Ulysses* Joyce uses the "stream of consciousness" technique, in which the writer relates the unspoken thoughts of his characters. *Ulysses* ends with a famous "monologue" expressing Molly Bloom's thoughts.

Joyce's other great novel *Finnegans Wake* (1939) is even more obscure than *Ulysses*. On the surface it is the story of a dream dreamed by a Dublin tavern-keeper, Mr Humphrey Chimpden Earwicker. But there are many layers of meaning, and Joyce carries his experiments in language – puns, made-up words, and allusions – to the very limits of communication.

JUÁREZ, Benito (1806–72). Juárez was a great Mexican statesman who devoted his life to helping his countrymen. He was a Zapotec Indian. His parents died when he was three years old and he spent the next few years in his native village Guelatao under an uncle's care. When he was 12, he ran away to Oaxaca, the capital of his state.

BBC Hulton Picture Library

Benito Juarez, president of Mexico 1861–72.

In Oaxaca a kind priest befriended Juárez and encouraged him to study. He became a lawyer in 1831, was elected to the state legislature in 1845, and to the national legislature in 1846. From 1847 to 1852, he was governor of the state of Oaxaca. Because of his liberal ideas he was exiled in 1853 by the Mexican dictator Santa Anna. He spent two years in New Orleans working as a printer and cigar maker. After Santa Anna was overthrown in 1855, Juárez returned to Mexico. He became a cabinet minister, and in 1857 he was appointed provisional president of the country.

The conservatives would not accept him as president. The civil war that resulted is known as the War of the Reform (1858–61). Juárez was forced to leave Mexico City and set up his government in Veracruz. The liberals defeated the conservatives in 1860. Juárez returned to Mexico City in January 1861 and shortly thereafter he was elected president.

He found that the government was deeply in debt to Spain, France, and England. Unable to collect their debts, these nations sent troops to Mexico. Spain and England soon withdrew, but in 1862 France invaded Mexico. In 1864 the Archduke Maximilian of Austria became the emperor of Mexico, although Juárez refused to resign as president. He was forced to flee the capital and soon became the leader of the liberation movement against the French. When the French finally withdrew their troops in 1867, the Mexicans executed Maximilian and re-elected Juárez as president. His reforms set up state schools and brought about the separation of church and state. Juárez died in Mexico City at the age of 66.

See also MEXICO.

JUDAISM see JEWS AND JUDAISM.

JUDAS TREE (*Cercis silquastrum*) is an attractive member of the pea family, native to the Mediterranean and the Near East. Before the leaves appear in the spring, the tree blooms with purplish-pink blossoms. The legend of the tree is that it blushes each spring because Judas Iscariot, the betrayer of Christ, hanged himself from it. The Judas tree is commonly planted as an ornamental tree along the streets of Mediterranean towns.

Several other species are known as redbuds including the eastern redbud of North America (*Cercis canadensis*), a hardy tree that grows to 14 metres (45 feet). It has reddish-brown scaly bark, and a broad, rounded crown with pinkish flowers. The smaller California redbud (*Cercis occidentalis*) has flowers that

J. Horace McFarland Company

The small, rosy-purple blossoms of the Judas tree appear well before the leaves in the spring.

are more purple-lavender coloured. The Chinese redbud (*Cercis chinensis*) is often cultivated as a shrub.

JUDGE. A judge is the person who presides over a court of law (see COURT). There are many different types of judges, varying from justices of the peace, who sit in court in ordinary clothes, to the robed justices of the Supreme Court of the United States or the English Court of Appeal who decide questions of national importance. Yet they are all judges.

In some countries judges at all levels are professionally trained in the law. In others, including Britain and the United States, only a proportion are professional lawyers.

Lay Judges

A judge who is not trained in the law is known as a "lay" judge. He or she is an ordinary person, chosen as being reliable and trustworthy.

In England lay judges are called magistrates or justices of the peace. They do the job part-time and are unpaid. Over 90 per cent of criminal cases in English courts are heard by magistrates. Professional judges deal only with the most serious crimes. Like all judges in England they are appointed by the Lord

English High Court judges take part in a ceremony in the autumn of each year to mark the beginning of the legal term. The judges have breakfast with the Lord Chancellor at the House of Lords and then attend a service at Westminster Abbey.

Universal Pictorial Press Agency

Chancellor, who is the highest judge in the land and also a member of the government.

In the United States, and also in Russia, lay judges are used to a lesser extent. They are elected by local people and serve for a limited time. In the United States lay judges preside alone over the court and work full-time. In Russia they are called "assessors" and sit with a legally qualified judge.

Professional Judges

Legal systems can be divided into those based on the common law tradition, such as in England, most of North America, Australia, and New Zealand, and those based on the civil law tradition, such as Quebec, and most of Europe. (See LAW.)

Professional judges in these two different systems are trained and chosen in different ways. In the common law countries, after training at a college or school of law, a person goes into private practice as a lawyer (see LAWYER). After years of legal experience, usually at about the age of 45 or 50, he or she may be appointed a judge. Judges do not have to pass any special examination or go through further training.

In England, as with the lay judges, appointments are made by the lord chancellor without political considerations – that is, whether or not someone is appointed does not depend on whether they support the political party that

is in office at the time. In the United States, judges are appointed on a political basis. Appointments are often made by the president or a state governor.

In many US states judges are elected by the people. In some states there is a system known as the Missouri Plan whereby a committee assesses candidates and puts forward a list of names to the appointing authority. The person appointed serves as a judge for a limited period and then stands for election for a longer term.

A person does not necessarily become a judge first at a low level and then work his way up. He or she may be appointed to a low or intermediate court and stay there, or he or she may be appointed directly to a higher court. In England, High Court judges are usually appointed from senior barristers and then may go on to become Appeal Court judges. Some English judges in the intermediate courts work part of the time as practising barristers or solicitors (see LAWYER) and may never become full-time judges.

In the United States judges are sometimes appointed from academic lawyers or from lawyers in government service. All judges are appointed for a limited term and then must be re-elected or re-appointed if they want to continue serving.

In common-law systems judges are not subject to supervision in the way that judges in civil-law countries are. Of course their judgments may be overruled by a higher court, but a judge has to misbehave very badly before he can be removed from office. The procedure is long and complicated and rarely used. In parts of the United States, however, new systems are being developed which allow a senior judge to reprimand junior colleagues or even remove them from office.

In civil law systems, after legal training, a person decides whether to practise as a lawyer or become a judge. If he or she wants to become a judge the next step is to take a further examination leading to appointment to a low-level court. Progress up the judicial ladder is dependent on continual assessment by a council of senior judges. A civil-law judge is really a form of civil servant. Civil-law judges are appointed by a minister of justice who is a politician.

JUDO is a combat sport, in some ways similar to wrestling. It was developed from a form of unarmed combat known as jujitsu which was practised in Japan. Other martial art sports, such as karate (see KARATE), are also based on the original jujitsu method of fighting.

Keystone

Striving to gain advantage, by unbalancing the opponent.

Jujitsu was probably introduced to Japan from China in the 12th century by monks who had developed the art to protect themselves against armed brigands. The *Samurai*, or warrior class, used it if they became unarmed during battle.

Jujitsu consists of many dangerous blows and throws, and also locks, or holds, on bones and joints and even various methods of strangulation which can render a person unconscious in seconds. The original idea of jujitsu – and it is this that makes it different from wrestling – is that it is "non-resistant". If two men are pushing against one another the stronger man will probably win. If, however, one man suddenly gives way by moving backwards or sideways, his opponent will continue to move forward and can easily be thrown by his own impetus.

The possibilities of jujitsu as a sport were seen by Jigoro Kano, who improved many of the grips and throws and got rid of the dangerous ones. He thus developed a sport which he called judo, and in 1886 founded the Kodokan Judo Institute in Tokyo.

Judo has been an Olympic Games sport since 1964 and is now popular in many countries. It is also taught as a means of self-defence. Girls can become as expert as boys at judo. The aim is to throw the opponent cleanly, to pin him to the floor, or to master him by applying pressure to arm joints or the neck.

BBC Hulton Picture Library

A shoulder throw. Moves like this should only be practised with an instructor.

The word judo comes from a Chinese word meaning "gentle way", and judo opponents observe a ritual of courtesy. The usual clothing for judo is a loose jacket and trousers of strong white cloth. Beginners or novices wear a white belt.

There is nothing mysterious about judo. A strong man would probably defeat a weaker man of the same skill, but if the weaker man is the more skilful he may well win. Skill is developed only through constant training and practice.

The first thing learned in judo is how to fall. This is called "breakfall". It is done by striking the mat with the inside of the arm from fingertips to armpit, a fraction of a second before the body hits the mat, so that the shock of the fall is absorbed painlessly in the arm. With practice a person can be thrown really hard without harm but the basic breakfall is taught without actually being thrown.

There are three stages of judo training. The first, called *uchikomi*, consists of repeating and improving the technique of a throw without actually throwing an opponent. The second phase, *randori*, consists of practice in which the opponents attempt to defeat one another using the knowledge of the various throws, holds, and locks they have been taught, but without actual contest. The third way is by means of actual contest. Points are scored by throwing an opponent with skill, intention, and impetus on to his back and holding him down for 30 seconds, or by him submitting (giving in) when held in a lock or strangle hold.

The standard reached in judo is shown by the colour of the belt worn. There are six *kyus*, or student grades. The colours of the belts in ascending order of skill are white, yellow, orange, green, blue, and brown. Then follows the hardest step in judo—entry into the *Dan* or master grades which are shown by a black belt.

JULIUS CAESAR (*c*.100–44 BC). Gaius Julius Caesar was a great Roman soldier and statesman. There is some doubt about the date of Caesar's birth but it was almost certainly 12 July 100 BC. A date two years earlier is sometimes given. Although he belonged to one of the noble families of Rome, when he grew up he supported the people's party in politics. This was probably due to his admiration for Marius, the husband of his aunt Julia. Marius was not of noble origin but had risen to a great position in the army and in the government, and thus won the young Caesar's admiration. As Caesar was growing up a civil war was being fought between Marius, representing the people, and Sulla, representing the nobles. Caesar was involved in this conflict on the side of Marius, and when that side was defeated he escaped death only because powerful friends pleaded for him with Sulla. After this he went abroad to serve with the army in the province of Asia and in Cilicia. In 78 BC Sulla died and Caesar returned to Rome.

Mansell Collection

Julius Caesar was assassinated in 44 BC when he became too powerful in Rome.

The leader of the nobles was now the brilliant young general Pompey, who soon left Rome to take up military duties abroad (see POMPEY). While Pompey was out of the way Caesar set himself to win the favour of the people of Rome. He achieved his aim and they appointed him *aedile*, or magistrate in charge of public buildings and public festivals. He spent a great deal of money giving entertainments and fell heavily into debt. In 63 BC he became pontifex maximus, or head of the state religion. Two years later he went to rule the province of Further Spain, but soon returned to Rome because Pompey had returned, and Caesar wanted to have a hand in the politics of the day. He supported Pompey and made a secret alliance with him and the wealthy Crassus. This alliance became known as the first triumvirate. "Triumvirate" comes from a Latin word that means "a group of three men", and this one is called the "first" to distinguish it from another grouping of three leaders which was formed later. Soon after making the agreement with Crassus and Pompey, Caesar became a consul; that is, one of the two men who were elected each year to rule the Roman state for the next year. He was thus able to carry out his own plans and those of his two friends.

Caesar realized that the political struggles that were going on in Rome would one day break out into actual fighting and that it would be useful to have an army ready. He therefore obtained for himself the post of governor of Cisalpine Gaul (northern Italy) and later that of Transalpine Gaul (Gaul north of the Alps) as well (see GAUL). Cisalpine Gaul had been conquered long before but much of Transalpine Gaul remained unconquered and Caesar was to spend the next nine years of his life bringing it under Roman rule.

He had already fought a successful campaign in Spain, but so far had done little to show that he would become one of the greatest generals the world has ever known. He had chosen to go to Transalpine Gaul because the almost unknown country beyond the Alps offered him a chance to rival the exploits of the great Greek general Alexander (see ALEXANDER THE GREAT). Caesar was by now a bald-headed man of 42 of unimpressive physique, but with remarkable energy and a passion for doing everything thoroughly, whether it was building a road, planning a

campaign, or leading an attack. His troops adored him. They were amazed that he could turn so easily from the luxurious life of Rome to the discomfort of a hard campaign and still joke about it.

Setting out on his conquests in 58 BC, in less than ten years Caesar subdued what is now France and Belgium, together with parts of the Netherlands, Germany, and Switzerland. He did not merely conquer these countries but changed the way of life of their tough and unruly inhabitants. He stopped them fighting amongst themselves and founded cities like those of Italy, encouraging the people to follow more civilized habits and customs. He built a bridge over the River Rhine and frightened the German tribes into remaining peaceful. In 55 and 54 BC he invaded Britain but did not bring enough troops to conquer the island. Throughout his campaigns Caesar wrote an account of all that he did. To this account is due much of our knowledge of how the Gauls, Germans, and Britons lived, of their religions, their countries, and even the animals in their forests.

Meanwhile Crassus had been killed fighting in Asia, leaving Pompey and Caesar as rivals for power. In 49 BC Pompey persuaded the senate to order Caesar to give up his command and return to Rome. Caesar realized that to give up his command would mean giving up his troops and he had no intention of doing this. He therefore marched back towards Italy at the head of his army. On the banks of the River Rubicon, which divided his province of Cisalpine Gaul from the rest of Italy, he hesitated before crossing the river, for he knew that to cross it with his troops would begin a civil war in Italy. At last he crossed the boundary. (It is from this event that we have obtained the expression "to cross the Rubicon", which means to do something that cannot be undone, however much one may regret it.)

Rome was on Caesar's side, so Pompey and his friends fled to Greece and raised an army there. Caesar pursued them and defeated them at Pharsalus in 48 BC. Pompey himself escaped to Egypt, where he was murdered.

Caesar had followed him to Egypt and remained there a year, under the spell of the beautiful Cleopatra, whom he restored to the throne of Egypt (see CLEOPATRA). During the next three years Caesar fought many battles in order to gain the complete mastery that he desired. After one victory in Asia he sent back to Rome the haughty message: *veni, vidi, vici*—"I came, I saw, I conquered."

In 45 BC Caesar settled in Rome, determined to give order and peace to the city and to the empire, and pardoned all those who had sided with Pompey. He was made permanent head of the government and given many other powers and honours. He was treated as though he was a god and seems to have claimed to be divine. His statue was put up in one of the Roman temples, and written underneath it were the words, "To the Unconquerable God". All this was hateful to the noble families of Rome, who believed firmly that the empire should be governed, as it had been earlier, by a group of people and not by one man alone. It may be, also, that some of them were jealous of his success. A group of the nobles plotted together to bring about his downfall. They chose Marcus Brutus as their leader, for he was well known as an upright, honourable man, and at a meeting of the senate on 15 March 44 BC, they stabbed Caesar to death. Thus died one of the greatest rulers of all time. (You can read the drama of Caesar's death in the play *Julius Caesar* by William Shakespeare.)

Caesar was married four times. His first wife was Cossutia, about whom very little is known. His second wife Cornelia, the mother of his daughter Julia, died in 68 BC. After divorcing his third wife Pompeia, he married Calpurnia in 59 BC, and she survived him.

JUNE BEETLE. There are over 5,000 different species of chafer beetle, including the June beetles (*Phyllophaga*). The beetles are about in early summer, flying at night and often entering open windows attracted by the light.

The female lays between 50 and 200 small, pearl-like eggs in the soil. The eggs hatch into curved, white grubs which feed on the roots of

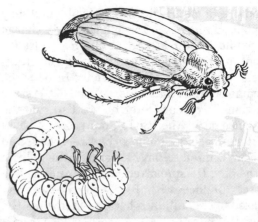

The fat white grub of the June beetle spends two or three years in the soil eating the roots of plants before emerging as the adult beetle. The adult feeds on the flowers and foliage of trees and shrubs.

many plants, though the roots of grasses are their favourite food. The grub grows very slowly and does not become a pupa for two or three years. (A pupa is rather like a butterfly chrysalis.) The adult beetle crawls out of the pupa a few weeks later but stays beneath the ground throughout the winter. The following May or June it digs its way out and flies away.

The beetle grub is often dug up in gardens. It is creamy white with a shiny brown head armed with strong jaws like a pair of pincers. Although it has six legs, it lies helplessly on its side if placed on a flat surface because its fleshy body, which is thick and swollen at the tail end, is curiously bent in a half circle. Moles devour the grubs in great quantities and birds, especially crows, dig them out with their beaks and regard them as tasty morsels. They are serious pests in many parts of the world because they feed on the roots of crops, such as strawberries, buckwheat, and corn.

Adult beetles are almost as much a nuisance as the grubs because they feed greedily upon the leaves of many kinds of trees, including fruit trees. Every few years the beetles appear in vast numbers and then become a serious pest.

JUNG, Carl (1875–1961) was a Swiss psychiatrist and psychologist, and one of the great figures of modern psychiatry. The son of a Lutheran minister, Carl Gustav Jung was born in Kesswil, Switzerland. He spent a lonely childhood, and thought about all sorts of questions raised by his dreams. He was fascinated by science, in particular by the study of ancient man, and by religion. Thus he was interested in both observable and spiritual matters.

Jung studied medicine at the University of Basel and graduated in 1900. At first he was not drawn to psychiatry (the study of diseases of the mind), which was very unfashionable at the time. But after reading a textbook on the subject, he was immediately interested and excited. He took a position at a mental hospital near Zurich, and tried constantly to unravel the causes of mental illness and to understand what was happening in the mind of a mentally ill person.

In 1907, Jung met the Austrian psychiatrist Sigmund Freud (see FREUD, SIGMUND).

BBC Hulton Picture Library

Carl Gustav Jung (1875–1961), Swiss psychiatrist and founder of the analytical school of psychoanalysis.

They had much in common and immediately became close friends. Jung became a follower of Freud's school of psychoanalysis (the investigation and treatment of mental illness). But they did not entirely agree about the causes of mental illness. Freud traced everything back to early childhood, while Jung was more concerned with understanding a person's mental illness by studying problems and events that he or she was experiencing at the time of his illness. What Freud and Jung had in common was a concern with the "unconscious". This can be described as a region of the mind which consists of hidden memories and desires, and which is inside every person. The aim of psychoanalysis was to bring all unconscious thoughts into the conscious. Only when the patient was made aware of all these hidden thoughts could he begin to recover.

Freud and Jung eventually parted company, and Jung started his own school of psychology, which is called the Analytical, or Jungian, school.

Jung introduced various terms into psychology, for example, "complex", "extravert", "introvert". He travelled, read widely, and wrote many books and papers. He influenced many people outside the field of psychology, including writers, artists and art historians, and musicians. His autobiography, *Memories, Dreams, and Reflections*, was published after his death.

JUNGLE see RAIN FOREST.

JUNIPER is the name of 60 to 70 species of aromatic evergreen trees or shrubs (*Juniperus*) of the cypress family. They can be distinguished from members of Pinaceae, the pine family, by the fact that the cones look like berries and consist of three fleshy scales. They are black when ripe and covered with a bluish, waxy bloom.

Junipers are sometimes small trees, occasionally growing 12 metres (39 feet) high, but more often they are erect or sprawling shrubs. The leaves are evergreen and usually needle-like in shape, although some junipers

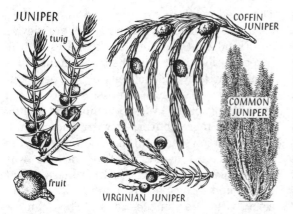

JUNIPER
twig
fruit
COFFIN JUNIPER
COMMON JUNIPER
VIRGINIAN JUNIPER

have tiny, scale-like leaves which grow close to the branches.

The common juniper (*Juniperus communis*) has needle-like leaves growing in whorls, or rings, round the branches, but the Virginian juniper (*Juniperus virginiana*), also called the red cedar, has small scale-like leaves in opposite pairs. Many varieties of the Virginian juniper are grown in gardens for the beauty of their leaves and blue berries. In the United States this tree reaches a height of 30 metres (98 feet). The East African juniper (*Juniperus procera*) has spiny leaves and may be 27 metres (88.5 feet) tall. Its trunk is over 1 metre (3.3 feet) across, and the bark hangs from it in shreds.

Junipers are made use of in many ways. The berries of the common juniper contain a strongly flavoured oil, which is used in medicine and in making gin. In Lapland ropes are made from the stringy bark.

From the Virginian juniper comes a sweet-smelling red timber. Because of its straight grain and the ease with which it can be whittled (trimmed to shape by cutting), this has long been used for the casings of lead pencils. As the Virginian juniper is becoming scarce, other timbers are replacing it for pencil manufacture, one of the best being the East African juniper.

On the mountains of Burma and in the Himalayas grows another fine juniper, which has fragrant timber used by the Chinese for making coffins. After being felled and cut into planks, it is carried for hundreds of miles over steep mountains to China, where it is sold at very high prices.

JUNO was the name the Romans gave to the queen of the gods and goddesses, the wife of the supreme god Jupiter. (The Greeks called the queen of the gods Hera, and her husband Zeus.) Iris, goddess of the rainbow, was Juno's messenger, and she was attended by the peacock who was said to have 100 eyes in his tail. She was queen of earth as well as heaven and especially protected women who called upon her for help in their troubles. June, the month of marriages, was named after her.

Juno was very jealous of her husband Jupiter. Without pity she persecuted the mortal women whom he loved and her anger followed even their children. She struck one of them, Bacchus, with madness and another, the hero Hercules, she pursued with misfortune all his life. She had three children: Mars, the god of war; Juventas, or Hebe, the goddess of youth; and Vulcan, the blacksmith of the gods.

According to Greek stories, their goddess Hera had sworn undying hatred to the whole race of Trojans because the Trojan prince called Paris had once been asked to judge which of three goddesses, one of whom was Hera, was the most beautiful. He chose Aphrodite (Venus) the goddess of love and beauty, and not Hera. She therefore helped the Greeks in the Trojan War and was the bitter enemy of the Trojan Aeneas in his voyage from Troy to Italy. (See PARIS; TROJAN WAR.)

In Greece Hera's chief temples were at Argos, Sparta, and Mycenae.

Among the Romans Juno was worshipped on 1 March, the Roman New Year's day, at a festival called the Matronalia. Later she was thought to have something to do with the moon, since it was supposed to direct the fortunes of women, and she was worshipped each month at the rising of the new moon. The Romans also regarded her as the guardian of anything to do with money. The cow, the cuckoo, the peacock, and the goose were all held sacred to her.

JUPITER see ZEUS.

JUPITER is the largest of the nine planets that travel around the Sun. Its orbit lies out beyond those of Mars and the asteroid belt, at an average distance from the Sun of 777 million kilometres (483 million miles). It takes 11.86 Earth years to complete one orbit and rotates on its axis once every 9 hours 55 minutes 29 seconds.

NASA

Jupiter is the largest planet in the Solar System. The Great Red Spot can be seen (bottom of the photograph) and also the characteristic belts.

From Earth, Jupiter appears as a bright disc second only to Venus in brightness. Ancient astronomers called it Jupiter in honour of the ruler of the gods worshipped in the Greco-Roman world, known in Greek as Zeus (see ZEUS). But at the time they had no idea how suitable this name was. In fact, Jupiter is larger than all the other planets put together. Its mass is 318 times as great as that of the Earth, and its diameter is 142,800 kilometres (88,730 miles), 11 times that of the Earth. Jupiter's surface gravity is nearly three times that experienced on Earth. It would take more than 1,500 Earths to fill up the space occupied by Jupiter. But Jupiter is, comparatively speaking, a remarkably light planet; its density is 1.33 grams per cubic centimetre, only just above that of water, which is 1 g/cm³.

A Hostile Planet

Jupiter is actually a very different and much more unfriendly world from the inner, so-called terrestrial, planets (Mercury, Venus, Earth, and Mars). Unlike these solid, rocky bodies, it is a mostly fluid planet. Scientists think that Jupiter has a solid core about the size of the Earth, around which there is thought to be a region of liquid hydrogen. This is in turn surrounded by an immense, deep atmosphere.

The outer layers of this atmosphere are the only parts of Jupiter that we can see from outside. The atmosphere consists mostly of hydrogen, together with small amounts of helium, methane, ammonia, ethane, and water. Among the other compounds present are carbon monoxide, acetylene, and hydrogen cyanide. The outermost regions of Jupiter's atmosphere present a beautifully coloured display of dark belts alternating with bright zones. You can easily see these markings through even a simple telescope. They are caused by clouds and the tops of vast weather systems. The clouds are composed of ammonia crystals or compounds of ammonia, hydrogen, and sulphur. The weather systems are huge storms or anticyclones circulating in the atmosphere like weather systems on Earth, but much more violent and extreme. (See also METEOROLOGY.)

Most of Jupiter's weather systems are in constant motion, lasting only a few days. But some are more permanent. The Great Red Spot, an oval marking in Jupiter's southern hemisphere, has been visible since detailed observations of the planet began in the 17th century. The Great Red Spot is so enormous that the Earth could fit comfortably into it. Scientists believe that it is an anticyclone, or high-pressure centre, an area of calm surrounded by circling winds that reach speeds of 290 kilometres (180 miles) per hour.

Deep beneath Jupiter's turbulent outer atmosphere, there is a build-up of heat. The outer layers may be as cold as –130°C (–202°F), but near the planet's centre the temperature may be well above 25,000°C (45,000°F). This intense heat combined with

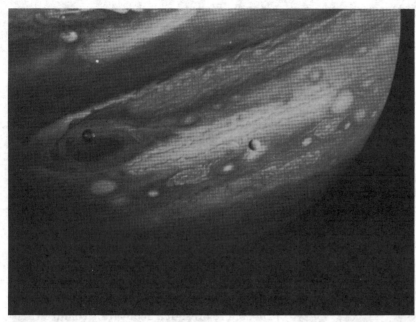

Jupiter as seen from the US spaceprobe Voyager 1 at about 20 million km (12 million miles) from the planet. The huge and turbulent weather systems in Jupiter's outer atmosphere are clearly visible, including the enormous Great Red Spot, a feature that has persisted for at least 300 years. The picture also shows two of Jupiter's satellites, Io and Europa. Io (left) is directly above the Great Red Spot. Io's rocky surface has an orange-red appearance, owing to the presence of sulphur. Europa is also composed of rock but has a smooth surface.

NASA

the enormous atmospheric pressure is thought to make hydrogen behave like a metal, a very good conductor of electricity. Electric currents in this region are believed to be the cause of immense bolts of thunder and lightning in Jupiter's atmosphere, and the planet's fast rotation gives rise to a very strong magnetic field that surrounds Jupiter to form what scientists call the *magnetosphere*. It extends well beyond the planet for over 7 million kilometres (4.4 million miles) on either side.

Signals from Jupiter

Jupiter gives out nearly twice as much energy as it receives from the Sun. Much of this is thought to be due to heat from the planet's interior being carried by convection currents through the atmosphere. But Jupiter also gives out radio waves. These are caused by electrically charged particles (protons, electrons, and ions) trapped in Jupiter's magnetic field. The particles also cause radiation belts around the planet similar to the Van Allen Belts around the Earth (see VAN ALLEN BELTS), as well as auroral displays and electrical storms at Jupiter's poles. (For an explanation of an aurora, see NORTHERN AND SOUTHERN LIGHTS.)

Space Probes to Jupiter

With its dense, unbreathable, poisonous atmosphere, its frequent and ferocious storms, its crippling gravity, and its outbursts of lethal radiation, Jupiter is not a place where life as we know it can survive at all. But people have sought to find out more about this hostile world in order to help piece together the origins and present workings of the Solar System.

In the 1970s our knowledge grew considerably when US spacecraft passed close to Jupiter, sending their valuable data about it back to Earth. Pioneer 10 in 1973 and Pioneer 11 in 1974 flew past Jupiter and discovered its magnetic field. Voyagers 1 and 2 flew past in 1979 and sent back images of a previously unknown ring system surrounding the planet. The rings are less than 1 kilometre (0.6 mile) thick and consist of microscopic particles of matter.

The Satellites of Jupiter

Scientists have so far discovered 16 moons circling Jupiter. The four largest, named Ganymede, Callisto, Io, and Europa, were discovered by the Italian astronomer Galileo in 1610 and are thus known as the Galilean satellites. Ganymede, the largest, with a diameter of 5,276 kilometres (3,279 miles), is larger than the planet Mercury (see MERCURY).

The Galilean satellites were photographed by the Voyager spacecraft. The two largest, Ganymede and Callisto, seem to be made mainly of water ice. Callisto shows a deeply cratered surface like that of the Earth's Moon, but unlike the Moon it has no dark plains. Ganymede is also cratered, but has light-coloured plains in which the craters form lines called rays that fan out from them. The craters on Ganymede and Callisto have been caused by meteorites and bits of asteroids and comets crashing into them. Europa and Io, though smaller than Ganymede and Callisto, are heavier and denser. They are probably made of rock. The surface of Europa appears very smooth; scientists believe that water has flowed out from the interior to form a frozen sea of ice on the outer surface of the satellite. Io is very different. Reddish-orange in colour, it is a little world of active volcanoes, which erupt frequently, pouring out debris (including ions) into space. These are among the particles trapped in Jupiter's magnetic field. Io's redness is due to the presence of volcanic sulphur.

The Pull of Jupiter

Because of its position as the largest planet in the Solar System, Jupiter's gravitational effect on other bodies is very strong. Some of its moons may well be asteroids captured from their orbits round the Sun. The asteroids of the two Trojan Groups are kept where they are by Jupiter's gravity. (See ASTEROID.) Jupiter also has the power to deflect comets out of their orbits and send them close to the Sun. When US scientists sent their first Voyager spacecraft on a tour visiting the outer planets of the Solar System, they used the power of Jupiter's gravitational influence to boost it on its course.

JURA MOUNTAINS. The Jura is a mountain range in Europe that forms the boundary between France and Switzerland. It is about 360 kilometres (225 miles) long and 19 to 29 kilometres (12 to 18 miles) wide. It covers the western and northwestern portion of Switzerland between Geneva and Schaffhausen and extends nearly to Zurich. The western part of the Jura is a plateau that slopes gently toward the rich fields of France. The word *jura* means "forest".

High mountains make up the eastern part of the range with the parallel ridges separated by valleys and wide basins. The highest peak is Mount Crêt de la Neige, 1,718 metres (5,636 feet) above sea-level.

Since the mountains lie across the main road of commerce between northwest Europe

Greg Evans

The town of Laufenburg sits on either side of the Rhine, partly in Switzerland and partly in Germany, at the northernmost end of the Jura Mountains.

and Italy, they are a barrier to travel. Rivers have cut gaps through them in only three places. The most famous of these is the Belfort Gap, which lies in hilly country between the Jura and Vosges Mountains. The gap is an important highway between France and central Europe.

People on both sides of the border are French speaking and live the same kind of life. About the only difference between them is their loyalty to different countries.

Flower-covered meadows scattered through the mountains flourish during the spring and summer rainy season. Cattle are pastured in the summer on these meadows, which are reached by steep, rocky slopes up the mountain sides.

Winter in the Jura Mountains is long and severe and many of the people work in their homes. The region is the centre of the Swiss watchmaking industry. In some years as many as 20 million watches have been made there, besides thousands of watch parts. Clocks, tobacco pipes, and music boxes are also made. Boxwood trees that grow on the mountains' higher slopes furnish wood for toymaking. Timber cutting is an important occupation. Increased amounts of water power are being developed for use in industry. (See WATER POWER.)

The natural beauty of the mountain scenery has made them a popular area with tourists in summer. Modern ski resorts have been built that attract visitors in winter as well.

JURY A jury is a group of people whose task is to decide the facts at issue in a trial (see TRIAL). A jury normally has 12 members, and is under the supervision of a judge.

Exactly what a jury can decide depends on the laws and customs of the country. But its central purpose is to allow ordinary people who are not professional lawyers to consider a case in secrecy, to reach a decision on it, and then to announce the decision in court.

The idea of juries is an ancient one going back to the Middle Ages or earlier in England. Before that, the guilt or innocence of a person was decided by a variety of methods, usually involving some sort of ordeal or torture. If the defendant survived the ordeal he was considered innocent. Juries were introduced to provide a fairer way of deciding guilt or innocence. It then became a tradition that everyone had a right to be tried by his "peers" (equals).

Today, juries are used in the common-law system as practised in England, the United States, Canada, Australia, and New Zealand, and some other countries which were once colonies of the United Kingdom. They are not used in countries with a civil-law system such as France and most of Europe, but they are used in Scotland. (See LAW.) In some countries where juries are not used there are lay assessors to help the judge hear cases. These are ordinary people with no legal qualifications who serve a similar purpose to that of a jury.

In the United States trial by jury is a right provided for in the constitution. This does not mean, however, that every case is tried by a jury. In 1968 the Supreme Court decided that a jury trial is a constitutional right only in criminal cases in which the penalty might exceed six months' imprisonment. Nevertheless, jury trials are very common in the United States and 90 per cent of all jury trials occurring worldwide each year take place there. In England, the use of jury trial is limited by law to a small number of cases – mainly serious crimes but some civil cases also.

Serving on a Jury

Juries consist of ordinary people living in the district of the court. There is usually an age limit, and there may be a requirement that they have lived in the country for a certain amount of time and understand the language. Certain people are disqualified from jury service. These include the insane and those with a criminal record. Others are exempt, including doctors and nurses, and anyone concerned with the law (such as lawyers and police officers). Otherwise, jurors are chosen at random to represent a cross-section of the community.

The jurors for a particular trial are selected by court officials who read out names at random from the list of people summoned for that day. The lawyers involved have a right to challenge a certain number of jurors (that is, demand that they be replaced by another juror) without giving any reason. When the correct number has been chosen they are sworn in, which means they must take an oath to give a fair verdict according to the evidence.

The judge has many powers in a jury trial. He or she can decide what evidence the jury may or may not hear, summarize and discuss the evidence, and instruct the jury as to the law it should apply in reaching a verdict. If the judge decides that there is not enough evidence, he or she may direct the jury to acquit the defendant. The judge cannot however instruct the jury to declare the defendant guilty.

In criminal cases in England and in most American states, the jury only decides the guilt or innocence of the defendant. The judge decides the sentence. In some southern American states the jury also decides the sentence, within a range laid down by the law. In civil cases juries decide both the question of liability and the amount of damages to be awarded.

When the jurors have heard the case they are taken to a room away from other people and must come to a decision. Sometimes juries are required to be unanimous, which means that all the members must agree on the verdict. More often they may give a majority verdict, which means that a certain number (usually 10 out of 12) must agree. If at the end of a reasonable time the jury cannot agree, then the case must be heard again with a new jury. In Scotland a jury may return a verdict of "not proven", if it is not satisfied that the case has been decided one way or another.

JUTE (*Corchorus*) is a plant that is cultivated for the fibre of its stems, also called jute, which is used to make sacks, bags, and many other articles that contain fibre. Its Hindi name is *pat*. It is an annual plant (lives for only one year) with straight unbranched stalks varying from 2 to 5 metres (6 to 16 feet) in height, and small yellow flowers that have four petals. There are two species: white jute (*Corchorus olitorius*), and tossee and daisie varieties of *Corchorus capsularis*. The leaves are slender and saw-toothed along the edges. Although so much smaller than a lime tree, jute belongs to the same family. It is believed that the plant originally came from India.

Most of the world's jute comes from Bangladesh, northeastern India, and China. (Brazil produces quite large amounts, but does not sell any to other countries, for all that is grown in Brazil is used there.) Two slightly different kinds are grown; one kind has seed pods that are long and brown, while in the other they are fat and blue. The seed is sown in spring and while the plants are growing they are thinned out so as to give the plants more room to develop fully. The crop is harvested when the flowers begin to fade, which is in late summer or early autumn. The plants are pulled up by the roots and then soaked in pools or streams for ten days to a month in order to loosen the valuable fibres from the rest of the plant. This soaking is known as *retting*. It is very important to know exactly when to take the plants out of the water, for if they are taken out too soon the fibre is difficult to remove and cannot be properly cleaned; if they are left too long the fibre is weakened.

After retting, the fibre is stripped from the rest of the stem and from the root. The stripper usually stands in shallow water and beats the root end of the plants with a paddle. He then breaks the stems over his knee about 30 centimetres (1 foot) from the root end. He grasps the loosened fibres and jerks them free from the rest of the stem. Then they are hung to dry in the sun.

The fibre is then graded into different qualities and sent to the factories where it goes through several more processes before it is ready to be woven. It may be woven into material for sacks, other coarse wrapping

Hutchison Library

Left: Jute growing in Bangladesh. When fully mature, a plant may stand more than twice the height of a man. **Right:** Jute fabric being produced in a jute mill in Calcutta, India.

cloth, rough carpets, or backing for floor coverings. Root ends of the stalks and coarser fibre are used in paper making.

The main importers of raw jute fibre are Japan, Germany, Britain, Belgium, and France. The first factory producing jute yarn was already working in Dundee, Scotland, in the 1820s.

JUVENILE DELINQUENCY generally refers to a criminal act which is committed by a child or young person. The age at which a young person becomes an adult varies from country to country. Thus in one country a young person of 18 would be tried in a juvenile court; in another country he or she would be tried in an adult criminal court. Juvenile delinquency includes any action or behaviour by a child or young person that, if performed by an adult, would count as criminal.

More than half the people who are arrested for serious crimes are boys between the ages of 11 and 17. Thus juveniles commit more crimes than adults. For most of these young offenders, however, delinquency is a phase in their experience of growing up, and they eventually grow out of criminal activities and become non-criminal adults. But for a few delinquents, particularly those who start young and carry on to a later age than most youths, crime becomes a way of life. By the time they are 17 or 18, these offenders are usually committing more serious crimes than they did earlier, stealing cars, for instance, and committing other acts of theft and violence. They are on their way to becoming adult criminals.

Why Do Children Become Delinquents?
This is a difficult question to answer. Two children from similar environments may turn out quite differently, so family background is not a certain predictor of delinquency, although it may be a cause. Recent studies of delinquency, however, have indicated that most delinquents come from problem families. Relationships within a family may be excessively difficult: the parents may be divorced; they may be violent or drink too much; they may themselves be criminals.

The relationship between social class and delinquency has been much discussed. In the past it was thought that most delinquents come from deprived neighbourhoods in large cities. However, later studies have shown that juvenile crime is more widely spread among the social classes than was previously thought. A decisive factor may be educational achievement. A large proportion of delinquents have a record of bad behaviour at school and drop out at an early age. With poor job prospects and low status, a young person may seek to vent his frustration with society by taking to crime.

Treatment of Delinquents
Treatment of the delinquent begins with the police and other public authorities who handle reported cases of juvenile crime. Many cases of misconduct are handled unofficially without an arrest. In more serious cases the child appears before a juvenile court for an informal, private hearing of the case without the many rules of the adult criminal court (see COURT).

Many first offenders are sentenced to probation, which means release of the juvenile into the care of his parents or guardian (see PROBATION). He or she remains under the supervision of a probation officer.

If more strict measures are thought to be necessary, the juvenile is placed in a correction centre, or reformatory. Nowadays, this is only done when no alternative can be found. The trouble with putting juvenile delinquents together in correction centres is that they may learn each other's criminal habits. Thus courts try wherever possible to use the more lenient method of probation, and sometimes foster care. In foster care, the offender is placed in a family more stable than his own, in the hope that he will learn more constructive ways of coping with life.

See also the article CRIME.

KABUL is the capital of Afghanistan, and its largest city. About 1,800 metres (5,900 feet) above sea-level, the city lies less than 160 kilometres (100 miles) north of the border with Pakistan. Much of its importance comes from its strategic location, which commands the passes through the mountains of the Hindu Kush and the main approaches through the Khyber Pass to Pakistan. The town is an important trade centre.

The history of Kabul goes back 3,000 years. It was a principal city of the area by the 7th century AD. Babur, founder of the Mogul dynasty, captured the city in 1504 and made it the capital of the Mogul empire. (See MOGUL EMPIRE). It has been the capital of Afghanistan since 1776. The British occupied Kabul for two short periods during the 19th century.

Much of the old city has been destroyed and rebuilt on modern lines, but Kabul still has many historical monuments. Babur's garden and tomb are a popular resort. Industries include food-processing plants, rayon and wool mills, a furniture factory, and a marble works.

In 1979 the Soviet Union invaded Afghanistan and set up a military command in Kabul to prevent the Communist government from being overthrown. Fighting between Afghan guerrillas and the Soviet and Afghan army continued in the city for the next decade. The USSR withdrew its troops in 1989, but the Communist government kept control of Kabul and most of the other cities. The population is 1,297,000 (1987).

Barnaby's

Kabul, the capital of Afghanistan, lies in the eastern part of the country. The city is dominated by the Asmai and Sherdawaza mountains.

KAFKA, Franz (1883–1924), was an author who lived most of his life in Czechoslovakia but wrote in German. His works include three novels and a large number of short stories, in most of which the central figure finds himself alone and defenceless in a strange, violent world where grotesque events occur without any apparent reason. This is one recurring theme in his writings; another is his conflict with and dependence upon his father and Felice Bauer, a woman whom he loved.

Kafka was born of a Jewish family in Prague, the capital of Czechoslovakia. He studied law at Prague University, obtained his doctorate in 1906 and then took a job in an insurance company. In 1917 he was found to be suffering from tuberculosis and took early retirement in 1922. He went to Berlin to devote himself to writing, but his condition worsened and he sought treatment in Vienna, where he died.

Kafka disliked his humdrum work in an insurance office, although he did it well. But he lacked the will to give up work and take up the literary career for which he yearned. His friends in Prague found him charming and witty, and few of them had any idea of the inner conflict and frustration he felt. He found an outlet for these feelings in his writings.

Kafka published a few short stories during his lifetime. These include *"Das Urteil"* (The Judgment, 1913) and *"In der Strafkolonie"* (In the Penal Colony, 1919). Perhaps his best-known short story is *"Die Verwandlung"* (Metamorphosis, 1915). It tells of a young man who wakes up in bed one morning to find that he has turned into a monstrous insect.

Kafka's greatest works are his three novels *Der Prozess* (The Trial), *Das Schloss* (The Castle), and *Amerika*. All were published after his death by his friend Max Brod, along with his letters and diaries. English translations of Kafka's works began to appear in the 1930s.

KALAHARI DESERT. The Kalahari Desert is a dry region in Africa, covering part of Botswana and extending into the Republic of South Africa to the south and into Namibia in the west. Its southern limit is the Orange River. Its total area is over 260,000 square kilometres (100,000 square miles).

The Kalahari is not as dry as the Sahara. It is truer to say that it is a region of semi desert. On the west, however, lies the Namib Desert, which is very arid. Most of the Kalahari has some vegetation – tall, sun-bleached grass, thorny bushes, and even some forest. The rainfall varies a great deal from year to year. There is only one river, the Boteti, but water can usually be found in wells and boreholes. Animal life includes springbok, wildebeest, giraffes, zebras, and elephants.

In times of great drought people and animals in the Kalahari quench their thirst with bushman "melons". These look like toy balloons lying on the desert soil, and even on the driest days they are soft and juicy.

Most of the inhabitants are Bantu-speaking people. There are also some San (Bushmen) and a few Europeans (see AFRICA, PEOPLES OF). The Bantu-speaking people mostly live in villages situated near wells and boreholes. They keep herds of cattle to sell, and goats to provide milk and meat. Most families cultivate crops of maize, sorghum, and pumpkins. All but the smallest villages have primary schools.

The San used to live by hunting game and gathering food, but now mainly work on farms. Some still follow their ancient way of life, travelling in small groups and living off the desert, whose ways they know better than anyone.

In 1971 diamonds were discovered in the Kalahari and there are now several diamond mines. There are a few good roads connecting major settlements and the mining areas, but

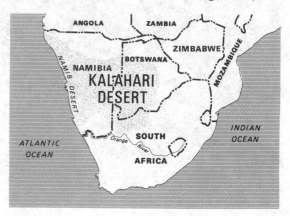

The Kalahari is the territory of the San people (Bushmen) of southern Africa. Traditionally they lived by hunting and gathering what fruit and vegetables were to be found. These have become less plentiful and many San have now abandoned this way of life.

Barnaby's Picture Library

most are dirt tracks passable only by trucks and vehicles with four-wheel drive.

See also the article BOTSWANA.

KALEIDOSCOPE. The kaleidoscope is an instrument that shows regular patterns when you look into it. It was invented by Sir David Brewster, a Scottish physicist, in 1816, and its name comes from Greek words meaning "watch beautiful forms".

The instrument is a tube 30 centimetres (about 1 foot) long or less, inside which are two or three plain mirrors running the length of the tube and fastened at an angle of 45° or 60°. One end of the tube has an eyepiece. At the other is a thin box made of two glass discs. In the box are pieces of coloured glass. If the box is turned the pieces tumble together. Shaking the tube has the same effect. When you look into the peephole, several images of each fragment are seen, because the image formed in one mirror is also reflected by the other and so on. All the images together form a regular pattern which can be completely changed by turning the box so as to move the glass fragments to new positions. Countless patterns are made in this way. The instrument is not just a toy, however. Designs for wallpapers, carpets, and printed and woven fabrics can be obtained from kaleidoscope patterns.

KAMPALA is the capital and largest city of Uganda in East Africa. Greater Kampala, including the city and its suburbs, had an estimated population of 750,000 in 1990.

The city, which lies near Lake Victoria, just north of the equator, stands about 1,190 metres (3,904 feet) above sea level. Because of its height, it is not as hot as many places on the equator. Average temperatures range from 23°C (73°F) in January to 21°C (70°F) in July. Rainfall occurs in every month of the year. The average annual rainfall totals 1,170 mm (46 inches).

Kampala stands on a group of hills separated by formerly marshy valleys. These valleys have been drained and now contain industrial areas and sports grounds. Kampala is Uganda's chief commercial city and it houses the head offices of most of the country's major companies. It is also the centre of a highly developed farming region and it exports cotton, tea, tobacco, and sugar. Kampala ranks second to Jinja as the country's leading manufacturing city and it produces goods that are sold throughout Uganda.

The city lies at the centre of the country's road network and it stands on a railway that runs from western Uganda to the Indian Ocean port of Mombasa. The city's international airport is at Entebbe, about 34 kilometres (21 miles) to the southwest.

A Hindu temple in Kampala. Uganda had a large Asian population before mass expulsions in 1972.

ZEFA

The city was founded close to Mengo, the site of the palace of the Kabaka (king) of Buganda. Buganda was the largest of the kingdoms into which Uganda was divided before the country became a British colony. The Imperial British East Africa built a fort near Mengo in 1890. This fort became the headquarters of the British colonial rulers. In 1905, the colonial headquarters were moved to Entebbe. Kampala again became the capital in 1962, when Uganda became an independent country.

Today, Kampala is the seat of Makerere University. It contains the Uganda Museum, the Namirembe Anglican Cathedral and the Rubaga and St. Peter's Roman Catholic cathedrals. It also has mosques, including the impressive white Kibuli Mosque, and several Hindu temples. Other impressive buildings include Parliament and the National Theatre.

KAMPUCHEA see CAMBODIA.

KANGAROO. Kangaroos are the best known of the marsupials (see MARSUPIAL), found in Australia, Tasmania, New Guinea, and nearby islands. There are about 47 species, ranging in size from rat kangaroos only as big as rabbits to the true kangaroo which may be almost 3 metres (10 feet) from nose to tail tip. A kangaroo appears on the Australian coat of arms.

The largest kangaroo is the grey kangaroo (*Macropus canguru*), which may stand over 2 metres (6.5 feet) tall. Like most other kangaroos it has short front legs with small paws,

Promotion Australia, London

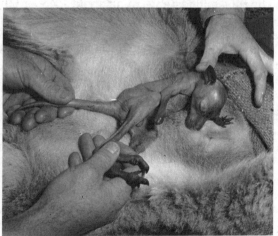

This young kangaroo looks newly born but is 18 weeks old. At birth it measured just a few centimetres.

International News Photo Inc.
The mother kangaroo carries her new-born offspring or "joey" in a pouch between her hind legs.

pink, naked creature, about 2 centimetres (0.75 inch) long and of the thickness of a pencil. Helpless as it is, it is able to claw its way to the pouch where it remains for about six months feeding on its mother's milk. At six months old, the "joey", as Australians call the young kangaroo, is able to stick its head out of the pouch as its mother hops along. When she stops to feed on tree branches it stretches out its neck and pulls off leaves for itself. The joey still returns to its mother's pouch for a time after it has learned to walk and run. When danger threatens, the mother hops over to it, picks it up in her mouth without stopping, and drops it safely into her pouch.

The grey kangaroo is hunted by the Australians, not only because it may destroy crops when present in large numbers but also because its meat is eaten and its skin makes good leather. It is not easy to catch because, besides being able to make great hops, it can also hear an enemy from a long way away. If cornered by a dog, a kangaroo may seize the dog with its forefoot and, with one swing of its hind foot, rip the dog open with its sharp toe-nails and kill it.

The red kangaroo (*Megaleia rufa*) is a graceful animal of the inland plains. Males are brick red and twice the weight of the females which are generally a blue-grey and

and very powerful hind legs which enable it to jump as far as 8 metres (26 feet). (A red kangaroo, however, has been known to clear a 2.5 metre (8 feet) fence with a leap of almost 13 metres (42.6 feet). It rests on its tail, which serves to balance the fore parts of the body when jumping. The head is small with upright ears and sharp front teeth. The grey kangaroo lives in Australia on grassy plains or in open forest country. It eats grass and grain as well as the leaves and twigs of trees.

The female kangaroo has a fur-lined pouch between her hind legs and carries her young in it. At birth the young kangaroo is a tiny,

ZEFA

Kangaroos travel over the ground by leaping on their hind legs. Their tails are used for balance. Speeds of 40 kph (25 mph) can be reached over short distances.

are known as blue fliers. The wallaroo (*Macropus robustus*) is more stockily built. Many of the medium-sized kinds of kangaroo are known as wallabies (see WALLABY). Two groups of kangaroos are very different from the others, with thinner tails and less powerful front legs.

Other Kinds of Kangaroo

There are several species of rat kangaroo, that live mostly among scrub and scattered trees. The largest is the rufous rat kangaroo (*Aepyprymnus rufescens*) up to 90 centimetres (3 feet) long including the tail. Rat kangaroos have rounded ears, a naked muzzle, and often a prehensile tail. They rest by day in nests of grass and some species use their tails to carry around bundles of nest material. Aboriginal names for these animals include bettongs, boodies, woilies, squeakers, and potaroos.

Tree kangaroos have large padded feet with cushion-like pads that prevent the animals from slipping among tree branches. The forefeet have strong nails for gripping and the long, thick tail is used as both a balancer and a brace when the animal is climbing. Tree kangaroos live in dense rain forests of Queensland and New Guinea. There are three species (*Dendrolagus*). The New Guinea species have reddish backs and bright yellow limbs and undersides.

An extinct kangaroo that lived thousands of years ago seems, from its remains, to have been nearly as heavy as a fair-sized horse, standing over 3 metres (10 feet) in height.

KANSAS.

KANSAS. The state of Kansas sits at the geographical centre of the 48 states of the United States of America that lie between the Canadian border and Mexico. This centre is marked by a limestone shaft and a flag in a field near the town of Lebanon, in Smith County. And 67 kilometres (42 miles) to the south, in Osborne County, is the geodetic centre of North America. All geodetic land surveys are controlled from this point. (Geodesy is the large-scale measurement of the Earth, and takes into account its curvature).

Kansas appears to be one vast and flat featureless plain. But appearances can be deceptive. The state is part of the high Great Plains, which rise slowly toward the Rocky Mountains. From 213 metres (700 feet) in the southeast, the Kansas plains rise gradually to 1,231 metres (4,039 feet) at Mount Sunflower. (Kansas is known as the Sunflower State.) It is in the western section that one can see some of the state's most dramatic geological formations. Castle Rock consists of chalk spires rising high above the plains. Horse Thief Canyon looks like a miniature of Arizona's Grand Canyon.

The soil of Kansas is among the most fertile in the world. It was built up millions of years ago, when this land was part of an inland sea. Today Kansas is the nation's leading wheat producer. It is also first in sorghum grains (see SORGHUM) and fourth in hay. Its western ranches provide some of the best cattle grazing land in the United States.

Although agriculture in Kansas is a major occupation, it is industry which has become the greatest contributor to the economy. The chief cities – Wichita, the largest, and Topeka, the capital – are industrialized. Wichita is the world's largest manufacturer of camping gear. Grain milling is another sizeable industry. Garvey Elevator, near Wichita, is the world's largest single-unit grain elevator.

The Land

Kansas is a nearly perfect rectangle, broken only by the Missouri River at the northeast corner. It is bordered on the north by the state of Nebraska, on the west by Colorado, on the south by Oklahoma, and on the east by Missouri.

Kansas is almost twice as long as it is wide. Its greatest length is about 660 kilometres (410 miles), and the greatest width is 336 kilometres (210 miles). The total land area of 213,063 square kilometres (82,264 square miles) includes only 1,235 square kilometres (477 square miles) of inland water.

The state consists of four different plains regions, all part of the Great Plains: the Glacial Plains, the Osage Plains, the High Plains Border, and the High Plains.

The High Plains, on the western end of the

Aircraft are built at Wichita by the state's largest manufacturer.

Courtesy, Boeing Airplane Company

state, are a rolling tableland with little rainfall and few trees. Just to the east is the High Plains Border, which covers most of west-central Kansas. This area is an intermediate zone between the High Plains and the lower prairies in the east. The Glacial Plains lie in the northeast corner. These plains get their name from the glaciers which deposited layers of soil on them millions of years ago. The Osage Plains cover most of southeastern Kansas. This is an area of gently rolling, rich farmland.

Kansas has an entirely continental climate, with hot summers and cold winters. Precipitation increases as one moves from west to east. In the west the average is only 40 centimetres (16 inches) annually, while in the east it reaches a maximum of 101 centimetres (40 inches). Kansas has been subject to seasonal crop-destroying droughts. The worst in recent history occurred during the 1930s and produced the well-known Dust Bowl; it almost destroyed the state's agriculture and drove many people to other states to seek a living.

People

Kansas was originally home to a number of tribes of Plains Indians. Among them were the Osage, Pawnee, Wichita, and Kansa (after whom the state was named). When the state was opened for settlement by the Kansas–Nebraska Act of 1854, it was settled by rival groups of whites from the Northeast and the Deep South. Those from the Northeast were determined to keep Kansas free of slavery, while the Southerners were equally determined to import slaves.

After the American Civil War of 1860–65, more settlers, including large numbers of European immigrants, were attracted to Kansas. There are still remnants of Bohemian, Russian, Amish, Mennonite, Swedish, German, and other ethnic and religious groups. During World War II many servicemen trained at one of the military bases within the state, and many returned afterwards. Other workers arrived to work at the aircraft plants, which remain a vital part of the economy.

The Economy

There are about 77,000 farms and ranches in Kansas. Land holdings in the western part of the state tend to be large, rarely covering less than one section, 260 hectares (640 acres).

Courtesy, Santa Fe Railway

Beef cattle are fattened for market in the winter feed lot near Dodge City.

Kansas ranks first among American states in wheat production. Tall grain elevators dominate the landscape.

Courtesy, Santa Fe Railway

Eastern Kansas began with small farms, many no more than 16 hectares (40 acres), but many of these have grown much larger. Besides its chief grain and hay crops, other crops are maize, popcorn, soya beans, and sugar beet. In recent years, with the help of irrigation, there has been an increase in production of market gardening crops.

Cattle and sheep are grazed in the central and western parts of the state, while in the east there is dairy farming and the raising of pigs and poultry. In beef production Kansas ranks fifth in the nation, and in pig production, eighth.

There are about 4,300 manufacturing and processing plants in Kansas. Wichita, the industrial centre, is known as the "Air Capital of the World", because it produces more aircraft than any other city. Other industries include motor vehicles, farm and transport equipment, heating and air conditioning equipment, processed foods, newspapers, periodicals, and books.

Kansas is also one of the top 15 mineral producing states. It is rich in oil and natural gas, propane, cement, clay, sand, salt, gravel, lead, zinc, chalk, limestone, and bituminous coal.

Education

The first territorial legislature provided for a system of free public schools in 1855. Compulsory school attendance has been in effect since 1874. The first high school in the state was built at Chapman in 1889.

The main state-supported institutions of higher education are the University of Kansas, at Lawrence, with its Medical Centre at Kansas City; Kansas State University, at Manhattan; and Wichita State University.

FACTS ABOUT KANSAS

AREA: 213,096 square kilometres (82,277 square miles).
POPULATION: 2,490,000 (1988).
CAPITAL: Topeka, 115,266.
CITIES: Wichita, 279,835; Kansas City, 161,148; Overland Park 81,784; Lawrence 52,738.
HIGHEST PEAKS: Mount Sunflower, 1,231 metres (4,039 feet).
PRODUCTS.
    Agriculture: Wheat, maize, sorghum, soya beans, oats, barley; dairy cows and beef cattle, sheep, lambs, pigs.
    Minerals: Petroleum, natural gas, propane, cement, sand and gravel, salt, coal, limestone, clay, shale.
    Manufacturing: Aircraft, motor vehicles, farm and transport equipment, heating and air conditioning equipment; processed food; newspapers, periodicals, books.
STATE EMBLEMS: Flower: Wild sunflower. Tree: Cottonwood. Bird: Western meadowlark.
JOINED THE UNION: Kansas became the 34th state in 1861.

History

The first European to visit Kansas was the Spanish explorer Francisco Coronado in 1541. The area was claimed for France by the explorer La Salle in 1682, and during the 18th century fur traders prospered by dealing with the Indians. The United States acquired the region in the Louisiana Purchase of 1803. The explorer Zebulon Montgomery Pike passed through Kansas in 1806 and called it the "Great American Desert".

Kansas was thoroughly explored in the fol-

A replica of Front Street as it was in Dodge City's pioneer days.

lowing decades. In 1830 it was designated Indian Territory, a place to which Indians from more settled regions were relocated. The Kansas–Nebraska Act of 1854 opened both territories to white settlement and left it up to the settlers to decide whether they wanted Kansas to become a free state or a slave state. Slavery supporters settled the towns of Atchison and Leavenworth, while anti-slavery groups founded Topeka and Lawrence. The abolitionist (opponent of slavery) John Brown and his sons took part in the violence that followed, and the territory earned the name "Bleeding Kansas".

Kansas joined the Union in 1861 as a free (anti-slavery) state. In the years after the Civil War Kansas became part of the Old West, a frontier region to which cowboys drove their cattle to such lively, and often lawless, towns as Dodge City, and Abilene. The cow-town era lasted for only a decade and brought prosperity to the state. It brought as well some of the most colourful outlaws and lawmen of the time, including Wild Bill Hickock, Bat Masterson, and Wyatt Earp.

After the cattle boom ended in the 1880s, wheat farming took over and brought a greater prosperity. By 1900 most of the farmland had been taken over by settlers. The disastrous Dust Bowl of the 1930s cost the state about 80,000 residents. This was more than made up for by World War II and the prosperity that followed, which brought in about 379,000 people. Because the economy has expanded slowly, people still leave the state in search of work elsewhere.

KANT, Immanuel (1724–1804) was a German philosopher who is most famous for his writings on the "theory of knowledge". This is the name philosophers give to the study of how the things we think we know can be proved to be true. His work is a key to understanding the writings of many 20th-century philosophers.

Kant was born in Königsberg, East Prussia and lived there almost all his life. In 1755 he received a doctor's degree from the University of Königsberg, where he later taught metaphysics and logic.

In the 17th and 18th centuries Descartes, Leibniz, and other philosophers believed that all the knowledge that we gain from "experience" – that is, through our senses – is untrustworthy because our senses can be deceived. The only sure truths, they said, were those obtained by "pure reason" – that is, logical argument independent of experience. They used such reasoning to try to prove what they felt were certain truths, such as the existence of God. In simple terms, the argument for the existence of God ran thus: "I was born with a number of clear and distinct ideas. These ideas are so clear and distinct they must be true. The idea of God is one of these ideas. Since I have the idea of God as a perfect being, God must exist, because if he did not exist he would not be perfect."

In 1781 Kant published *The Critique of Pure Reason* and proved that such arguments merely played with words. He showed that the human mind cannot by "pure reason" arrive at the truth about anything that by its very nature can never be experienced. Although we are sometimes misled in our observation of the world about us, said Kant, no real knowledge can be gained without it.

In the second part of the *Critique* Kant dealt with the problem of how scientific principles, such as the laws of physics, could be proved to be universal and true and yet be learned from observation of the outside world. The 18th century was a time of enormous scientific advance (see ENLIGHTENMENT), and for scientists and philosophers this was a vital question.

Kant's answer was as follows. The laws of physics do not exist independently of human beings. The things that exist in the outside world are real, but the human mind is needed to give them order and form, and to see the relationships that exist between them. Space and time, and the relation between cause and effect, and action and reaction, are *concepts* imposed by the human mind on the things that exist in the world. Thus, Kant believed, that these concepts can be shown to be universal and true because their reality does not depend on experience.

But, as is often the case in philosophy, Kant's positive ideas were less well received than his criticism of the work of others. His new theory of the basis of scientific knowledge was questioned by many scientists and philosophers, who said that no genuine new knowledge could be proved to be absolutely infallible in the way Kant had suggested. Another problem was that, as science became more theoretical, Kant's insistence that scientific study should be limited to the things we can actually observe did not take account of the work being undertaken in some of the more theoretical branches of mathematics and physics. But even though much of Kant's work was rejected by later philosophers, its value lies in the fact that his was the first attempt to establish a sound philosophical basis for science.

In later works, including *The Critique of Practical Reason* (1788), Kant dealt with morality and religion. His theories showed how it is possible to have a personal morality that does not depend on religion. These revolutionary ideas brought him into conflict with the Church and the Prussian authorities.

KAPOK is another name for the silk cotton tree (*Ceiba pentandra*), but it is more often used for the silky fibre that lines the fruit of this tree. The trees originally grew wild in the West Indies and in tropical parts of America but are now cultivated for their fibre in many countries in the Far East and Sri Lanka. The tree itself is large, with umbrella-like crowns. The white or pink flowers are pollinated by bats.

Kapok looks like fine, yellowish, shiny cotton. It is springy, smooth, does not absorb water, and is twice as light as wool but just as warm. Because of these qualities, it is valuable for stuffing mattresses, pillows, cushions, chairs, and lifebelts. Kapok-stuffed lifebelts support 30 times their own weight in water and last a long time without becoming waterlogged. Because it prevents the passage of heat, kapok is often used to line sleeping bags.

Courtesy, The Information Section, Indonesian Consulate, New York

Kapok is a cotton-like fibre (right) that grows in pods on the tropical kapok tree (above).

Kapok fibres cannot be spun into thread and cannot, therefore, be used to make material. The oil from the fruit is used both for food and to make soap.

The Indian silk-cotton tree (*Bombax malabaricum*) produces a brownish-yellow kapok, but the fibre is not of such high quality. There is another kapok tree (*Bombax emarginatum*) confined to the western part of Cuba.

KARACHI is the largest city, chief seaport, and industrial centre of Pakistan. It lies on the Arabian Sea a few kilometres northwest of the mouths of the Indus River and has one of the best harbours in Asia. Its airport is used by many airliners flying between Europe, Asia, and Australia.

The city stands on the north edge of the harbour. The harbour is sheltered on the west and south by a sandbar which is 16 kilometres (10 miles) long. At the end of the sandbar is a rocky point called Manora. At the east side of the harbour a small island has been joined with the mainland to give greater protection against storms and high seas. Karachi's port has more than 3 kilometres (2 miles) of wharves, docks, and other installations.

The chief products of Karachi are textiles and shoes, metal products, food, and paper and printing. Local handicrafts, such as lace, carpets, and items made of brass, are also sold for export.

Through the port of Karachi pass most of Pakistan's imports, as well as those of nearby Afghanistan, which has no seaports of its own. Petroleum, machinery, and motor vehicles are the principal items imported. The chief exports from the city are wheat and cotton, grown in the irrigated fields of the Indus River valley.

The port was founded by Hindu merchants at the beginning of the 18th century, but Karachi itself is a modern city built after the British general Sir Charles Napier had conquered the province of Sind in the 1840s. Its trade and prosperity were increased by the construction on the Indus in 1932 of the Sukkur Barrage, one of the largest irrigation works in the

Graphic House, Inc.

Karachi's municipal government building, with nearby market stalls and passing pedal-powered traffic.

world. Karachi was the capital of Pakistan from 1947 to 1959. Its population is about 5,208,132 (1981).

KARATE is a form of unarmed fighting. It was developed in China and Japan, and the word karate comes from Chinese letters meaning "empty hand". Though taught mainly in Japan, karate originated in China where bare-handed fighting was practised as early as the 6th century. It developed particularly in Okinawa, one of the Ryukyu Islands, which are now part of Japan but were for several centuries linked with China. In 1609 the Satsuma clan from Japan occupied Okinawa and all weapons were forbidden to the inhabitants. Resistance groups developed a form of martial arts known as Kung Fu. In the early 19th century it began to be called karate. The man sometimes considered the father of modern karate is Gichin Funakoshi, an Okinawan who demonstrated his ability in 1915. He stressed the philosophical and moral aspects of what was to him more an art than a sport. He taught discipline and proper etiquette. Two of his teachings were: "Karate begins and ends with courtesy" and "There are no offensive techniques in karate". Karate has become a popular sport in the West among men, women, and children.

A karate match is generally fought on a matted area 8 metres (9 yards) square. Inside there are four lines. On two of them stand the fighters, one wearing a red belt and the other a white belt. The referee and a judge stand on the other two lines. The referee is in charge of the match, awarding points and penalties. The judge assists. Both officials move around during a match so as to get a perfect view. Matches last for two or three minutes of actual fighting time. When there is an interruption the clock is stopped. Each fighter tries to score three points made up of full points and half points. A fighter scores a full point by showing perfect technique in striking a scoring area of the body. Half points are awarded for near-perfect technique.

ZEFA

Karate was developed in China and Japan and evolved from Kung Fu, a form of martial art.

Karate is not a non-contact sport as many people believe. Blows may land with considerable force, though not with full force. However, only light touches are allowed to the head and face. The feet may be used as well as the hands. Blows with the knee, elbow, and forearm are all permitted. Kicks to the head, being difficult, often score full points. But kicking to the groin is not allowed. Penalties for breaking the various rules range from a warning, through loss of a point, to disqualification.

The referee gives his verdict at the end of a match. A half-point margin is sufficient for a win. In the case of a tie the referee will decide if one fighter should win because of better technique or greater spirit, but he may award a draw.

In karate each participant tries to concentrate all his power at the point of contact. All the striking areas, such as the outer edges of the hands and heels, are toughened by constant practice on hard surfaces. An expert can break several thick planks of wood or bricks with one blow of his bare hand or foot.

KASHMIR is a mountainous region which lies in the northernmost corner of the Indian subcontinent, next to the Sinkiang region of China and Tibet. The northern part of Kashmir contains some of the highest mountains in the world, including K2, which is 8,611 metres (28,250 feet) and other mighty peaks around the Baltoro Glacier.

Kashmir is divided into two states. The larger, Jammu and Kashmir, belongs to India while Azad (Free) Kashmir is controlled by Pakistan. But parts of Jammu and Kashmir are claimed by Pakistan and China.

Most of the people live in the famous Vale of Kashmir in the Indian-controlled part. This is an oval plain about 140 kilometres (85 miles) long and 40 kilometres (25 miles) broad which is surrounded by the snowclad range of the Himalayas and is watered by the River Jhelum. It is one of the loveliest places in the world and in summer is carpeted with flowers. It was conquered by the Emperor Akbar in 1587 and the court used to go there every year to escape the heat of the Indian plains. The Mogul Emperors (see MOGUL EMPIRE) laid out many gardens, the most famous being the Shalamar gardens near the Dal Lake.

Much the largest town in the Vale of Kashmir is Srinagar. It is a quaint place of wooden houses, with picturesque bridges over the river. Here the people make Kashmir (cashmere) shawls from fine soft goats' wool, silks, carpets, and silver ornaments and wood carvings which they sell to tourists.

Much rice is grown in the Vale of Kashmir, as well as maize and other grain crops, and

Barnaby's

The River Jhelum, running through Srinagar, is crowded with *shikaras* – small river craft.

Camera Press

Two Kashmiri girls wearing traditional headdresses and ornaments.

region is famous for its fruits. It is the sole producer of the spice saffron in the Indian subcontinent. The rough country makes transport difficult.

After the decay of the Mogul Empire, Kashmir was overrun by the Sikhs from the Punjab in 1819. The Sikhs ruled it until defeated by the British in 1846. The British handed over Kashmir to a Rajput chief named Gulab Singh who was already ruler of the small state of Jammu south of Kashmir. However, the rule of Gulab Singh and his successors was unpopular because they were Hindus and about three-quarters of the people were Muslims. Also the peasants were oppressed by officials who took labour and produce from the villages without payment. This system was abolished in 1889 and the increasing popularity of Kashmir with Europeans as a holiday and health resort made it prosperous.

When British India was divided between India and Pakistan, the rulers of the princely states were allowed to choose which country they wished to join and Kashmir, having a Hindu ruler, chose India. But because of its largely Muslim population the state was claimed by Pakstan and fighting broke out. A cease-fire line was enforced in 1949, leaving India holding the east and south, and Pakistan the north and west. From 1959 Chinese troops have occupied parts of eastern and northeastern Kashmir which they claimed were theirs. In 1965 and again in 1971 there was more fighting between India and Pakistan along the cease-fire line. There has been unrest in the Indian part of Kashmir because its inhabitants are mainly Muslim.

The population of the Indian controlled portion of Jammu and Kashmir is around 6,000,000; the capital is Srinagar. Azad Kashmir has a population of about 2,800,000; its capital is Muzaffarabad.

KAUNDA, Kenneth (born 1924). Kenneth David Kaunda, African statesman, became Zambia's first president. Kaunda was born at Lubwa in what was then the British colony of Northern Rhodesia. Both his parents were teachers. After going through secondary school, Kaunda too became a teacher, first in Northern Rhodesia and then in Tanganyika (now Tanzania).

In 1949 Kaunda acted for a time as adviser to a liberal member of Northern Rhodesia's legislative council and later joined the strongly anti-colonial African National Congress (ANC). He became its secretary general and chief organizer. The ANC attempted to break the colony's social and industrial colour bar, organizing protests and boycotts. Both Kaunda and the ANC president Harry Nkumbula were imprisoned for their activities in 1955. The two leaders quarrelled over future policy and Kaunda formed a new political party known as the Zambia National Congress. He opposed a British plan to weld the three colonies of Southern Rhodesia, Northern Rhodesia, and Nyasaland into a federation. A campaign of civil disobedience led to the dropping of this plan, the banning of the Zambia African National Congress, and Kaunda's imprisonment once more.

Topham

Kenneth Kaunda became president of Zambia upon its independence in 1964.

On his release Kaunda was elected president of the newly formed United National Independence Party (UNIP). After a conference in London in 1960 the British government agreed that both Northern Rhodesia and Nyasaland should receive their independence. The white settlers refused to co-operate in creating a new national government but Kaunda succeeded in uniting the Africans behind him. He became prime minister of Northern Rhodesia which, on 24 October 1964, became an independent republic taking the name of Zambia. Kaunda was its first president.

On the whole Kaunda managed to avoid the inter-tribal conflicts that troubled other newly independent African countries. But in 1973 he imposed a single-party system on

Zambia, and three years later as civil war raged in neighbouring Angola he took on emergency powers. In spite of severe economic difficulties, Kaunda won new five-year presidential terms in 1978 and 1983. At all times he supported the anti-apartheid movement in South Africa. In spite of Zambia's reliance on its white-ruled southern neighbour for much of its economic prosperity, he urged in 1986 that the Commonwealth countries should apply severe sanctions to compel South Africa to change its racial policies.

See also ZAMBIA.

KAZAKHSTAN is an independent republic in central Asia, and a member of the Commonwealth of Independent States. It is bordered by Russia to the north and west, by Turkmenistan, Uzbekistan, and Kyrgyzstan to the south, and by China to the southeast and east. Kazakhstan covers an area of about 2,717,300 square kilometres (1,049,150 square miles). The population of the country is 16,536,000 (1989). The capital of Kazakhstan is Alma-Ata.

Most of Kazakhstan is a dry, treeless plain. There are, however, a few rugged mountain ranges along the eastern and southeastern borders. In the southeast the Dzungarian Alatau Range has elevations above 4,200 metres (14,000 feet). In east-central Kazakhstan is an extensive upland that rises in places to more than 1,500 metres (5,000 feet). The Ust-Urt Plateau, between the Caspian and Aral seas, in southwestern Kazakhstan, is a barren desert. Further east are two sandy deserts, the Kyzyl Kum and the Muyun Kum.

A few major rivers, such as the Irtysh, Syr-Darya, Ural, and Ili, flow for long distances through Kazakhstan. Some streams dry up in summer or lose themselves in sandy wastes. Few areas of the republic receive more than 30 centimetres (12 inches) of rainfall a year. Only in the north is large-scale agriculture possible. Summers are hot and winters are cold throughout Kazakhstan.

Most of the Kazakhs, the people of Kazakhstan, raise livestock. The principal crop grown

Novosti Press Agency

Alma-Ata, capital of Kazakhstan, is a well-planned city, with wide tree-lined streets and many parks.

on the northern grasslands is wheat. Cotton, rice, tobacco, sugar-beet, and fruit are grown on irrigated land in the south of the country. Principal industries include food processing and the mining and smelting of copper, lead, zinc, nickel, iron ore, manganese ore, gold, and silver.

Railways are the major means of transport. The country has more than 9,600 kilometres (6,000 miles) of track.

The land that is now Kazakhstan has long been inhabited by nomadic herders. Historically, these Turkic people were Muslims. They lived in tents called yurts and roamed on horseback in search of pastureland for their sheep, goats, and camels. Their livestock provided them with food, clothing, and the covering for their tents.

During the 19th century the nomads' lands were forcibly incorporated into the Russian tsarist empire, which was expanding into central Asia. In 1920 the new Russian communist government established Kazakhstan as an autonomous soviet republic (ASSR), and soon afterwards began to settle the nomads. Large numbers of people from Russia and Ukraine began to move into the area. In 1936 the Kazakh ASSR became the Kazakh Soviet Socialist Republic (SSR), and it remained part of the Soviet Union until 1992, when, following the break-up of the Soviet Union, it became an independent republic.

KEAN, Edmund (1789–1833), is regarded as one of the greatest English actors of tragedy. It is not certain who his parents were, and he apparently had an unusual and adventurous childhood. He was looked after by various people, including Moses Kean, a ventriloquist and mimic, from whom he took the name Kean. As a child he did some acting and broke both legs when performing as an acrobat.

Kean married the Irish actress Mary Chambers in 1808, and together they performed in various provincial theatrical groups, but they were not at all successful. In January 1814, Kean first appeared at the famous Drury Lane theatre in London as Shylock in Shakespeare's *Merchant of Venice*. This performance made him instantly famous, and by the end of the play the audience was hoarse with shouting. He went on to play all of Shakespeare's leading parts. William Hazlitt, a respected critic and essayist, saw Kean perform the death scene in *Richard III* and wrote, "He fights like one drunk with wounds; and the attitude in which he stands with his hands stretched out after his sword is wrested from him has a preternatural and terrific grandeur." The poet Samuel Coleridge wrote of how Kean revealed Shakespeare "by flashes of lightning". And the owner of a Birmingham theatre who had first seen him act in his unsuccessful provincial days said later, "How little did I know, or could guess, that under the shabby green dress was hidden one of the most extraordinary theatrical geniuses."

Kean's personal life was marred by excessive drinking, public emotional outbursts, and affairs with women. His last performance was at Covent Garden in March 1833. He played Othello, and his son Charles, also an actor, played Iago. He suddenly collapsed in the middle of the performance. He managed to whisper to his son, "Oh God, I am dying: speak to them for me." A few weeks later, he died.

KEATS, John (1795–1821). John Keats was in one way the most remarkable of all English poets, for he did not begin to write poetry seriously until he was 21 and he died when he was 26. So in only five years he wrote some of the most famous poems in the English language. Some of the loveliest are odes, among them, "To a Nightingale", "On a Grecian Urn", and "To Autumn".

John Keats had one sister and two brothers. Their father kept a riding stable in the City of London, and although he had not had much education himself he sent John to school at Enfield, Hertfordshire. His father died when John was nine, and eventually the family went to live at Edmonton, near Enfield, with their grandmother.

He left school at 15 and was apprenticed to a surgeon, and after four years went to London to become a medical student. He worked hard at medicine and passed his examinations, but already he had started writing poetry and soon he began to feel that he wanted to give up his

whole life to being a poet. Unfortunately, because he and his brothers and sisters were so young when their parents died, the money they should have had to live on was tied up in trusts controlled by their guardian. The guardian felt that John was wasting his time writing poetry, and so all his life he had a problem in finding enough money to live on as a poet.

One of his best-known poems was written after reading a translation of a poem by the ancient Greek poet Homer. He was so thrilled by it that he had to write a poem himself about his excitement:

> Then felt I like some watcher of the skies
>   When a new planet swims into his ken;
> Or like stout Cortez when with eagle eyes
>   He stared at the Pacific – and all his men
> Looked at each other with a wild surmise –
>   Silent, upon a peak in Darien.

Keats decided to give up medicine and almost immediately he set to work to write a long poem called "Endymion", which tells the story of a Greek shepherd-prince's adventures in searching for the moon-goddess who has fallen in love with him. The poem begins with a famous line:

> A thing of beauty is a joy for ever.

In 1818 his brother Tom was dying of tuberculosis (then called consumption), and while he nursed him night and day till his death, Keats developed the disease himself. His mother had also died of the same disease. At this time he fell passionately in love with Fanny Brawne, but love brought him more unhappiness than joy. Yet during these troubles Keats wrote some of his most wonderful poems, including "Hyperion", which he never finished, a story-poem called "The Eve of St. Agnes", and the beautiful odes.

In 1821 he became too ill to write, and his friends sent him to Rome hoping that he would get better, but after a few weeks there that were full of suffering he died.

The letters Keats wrote to his friends during his life have been collected together and published, and they tell much about him and about his ideas of poetry.

National Portrait Gallery, London

John Keats, painted by his friend Joseph Severn.

KELLER, Helen (1880–1968), was a United States author, educator, and lecturer, who led an active life despite being both blind and deaf.

Helen Adams Keller was born in Tuscumbia, Alabama. She was a perfectly normal and healthy baby until a severe illness at 19 months left her blind, deaf, unable to talk, and prone to violent temper tantrums.

Helen Keller, aged 17, with Anne Sullivan who helped Helen to overcome her severe disabilities.

When she was about six, her parents asked Alexander Graham Bell, the inventor of the telephone, to advise them about possible ways of educating her. As a result, in 1887, a 20-year-old partially sighted teacher called Anne Sullivan came to the Keller home to try to teach her. Sullivan had received her training at the Perkins School for the Blind at Boston, and adapted her methods to cope with Helen's additional problem, the fact that she could not hear. Miss Sullivan used a doll for the first lessons, and she spelled the word d-o-l-l into the child's palm. Helen enjoyed this new game and quickly learned many words. Within a short time, Helen came to know that everything had a name. She also learned to speak by placing her fingers on Sullivan's larynx in order to "hear" vibrations.

In 1890, Helen, accompanied by Miss Sullivan, went to the Horace Mann School for the Deaf in Boston, where she learned to read and write in Braille. She was clearly exceptionally bright and could manage the normal school curriculum without difficulty. She later attended Radcliffe College, Cambridge, Massachusetts. Anne Sullivan sat next to her in lectures and "spelled" the lectures into her hand. Helen graduated *cum laude* in 1904.

As an adult, Helen devoted herself to the problems of blind people. She published an autobiography of her early years, *The Story of My Life*, in 1902. In it she detailed many of the problems she had in learning to read, write, and speak, and described her extraordinary relationship with Anne Sullivan. In 1959, the book was turned into a play, *The Miracle Worker*, which won a Pulitzer Prize in 1960. Her other books included *The World I Live In*, *Out of the Dark*, *Helen Keller's Journal*, and *Let Us Have Faith*.

In 1913. Helen Keller made her first speaking tour. She was always willing to lecture for groups that would help the blind, but she was not easily understood and required a translator. In her latter years she lived in Connecticut, where she spent her days reading, writing, and answering her vast volume of mail. In 1964, four years before her death, she won the Presidential Medal of Freedom, the highest United States civilian award.

KELVIN, William Thomson, 1st Baron (1824–1907). The great mathematician and scientist William Thomson (later Lord Kelvin) was born in Belfast. His father was a professor of mathematics. William was so clever that he matriculated (passed the entrance examination) to Glasgow University at the age of ten. Later he had a brilliant career at Cambridge University and when only 22 was made Professor of Natural Philosophy at Glasgow, a post which he held for 53 years.

Thomson was a skilled engineer and designer and a brilliant mathematician. He had the rare gift of being able not only to work out scientific theories of his own but also to pull together ideas from different branches of physics and combine them to produce theories that were truly original.

Heat was one of the subjects that he studied. It was not very well understood even as late as the mid-19th century, and Thomson's observations about it were of very great significance. Firstly, in 1851 he concluded that heat can only flow from a hot object to a colder object and not the other way round. (This is often called the Second Law of Thermodynamics.) Then, in 1852, together with J. P. Joule, he discovered that a gas cools when allowed to expand, an effect that has come to form the basis of refrigeration (see JOULE, JAMES PRESCOTT; REFRIGERATION).

Mary Evans Picture Library

Lord Kelvin, one of the 19th century's great men of science, photographed in 1892 at the age of 68.

Another subject in which Thomson was very interested was electricity. In the 1830s his researches suggested a way of making electric waves that was later used by the German, Heinrich Hertz, and others to produce radio signals. The first transatlantic telegraph cable failed because of the big electric currents that were passed through it in order to obtain a readable signal at the other end. However, Thomson invented and patented telegraph instruments that would work on weak currents, and he also designed more efficient cables. For this work he was knighted in 1866.

In 1873 he undertook to write for a magazine a set of articles about ships' compasses. He wrote the first article, but then so many doubts occurred to him about the way the compass was made that he redesigned the whole instrument and it was five years before the second magazine article appeared. He also invented a sounding machine; that is, a machine by which sailors can tell what depth of water their ship is in. He was one of the first people to suggest that the rushing waters of Niagara Falls should be used to make electric power.

In 1892 Thomson was made a peer and chose as his title Baron Kelvin of Largs. He retired in 1899 but continued to write scientific papers. He was buried in Westminster Abbey.

William Thomson was one of the most enquiring scientists of his time. Apart from heat, electricity, telegraphy, and naval matters, he speculated about the age and shape of the Earth and opposed the evolutionary theories of Charles Darwin.

Kelvin, Thomson's title as a peer, has lived on in scientific usage as the name of a unit of temperature. In two papers delivered in 1848 and 1849 Thomson described a scale for measuring temperatures based on *absolute zero*, the theoretical point at which all molecular movement stops. This temperature equals about –273°C (–459°F). Thomson's so-called *absolute scale of thermodynamic temperature* has been adopted by scientists all over the world, and has in the 20th century been redefined and made more accurate for all sorts of uses. On this scale temperature is measured in units called kelvins (written as °K, or more usually just K). The size of a kelvin is equal to the size of a degree on the Celsius (Centigrade) scale, but the zero point, signified by 0 K, is equal to –273°C. Therefore to convert from the absolute (kelvin) scale to the Celsius scale, we just subtract 273. To convert from Celsius to absolute we add 273. Thus water freezes at 0°C, which is 273 K.

KENNEDY, John F. (1917–63). John Fitzgerald Kennedy, the 35th president of the United States, occupies a unique place in American history. In 1960, at the age of 43, he became the youngest man ever elected to the presidency. He was the first president born in the 20th century and the first Roman Catholic elected to that office. Although many of his aims were not achieved during his brief administration, much of the legislation he desired became law after his death.

Early Life

John F. Kennedy was born on 29 May 1917 in Brookline, Massachusetts. He was the second of nine children born to Joseph and Rose Kennedy. Politics was a part of John Kennedy's heritage. Both his grandfathers had been prominent in local and state politics. His father, a wealthy businessman, held three government posts under President Franklin D. Roosevelt's administration, including that of United States ambassador to Britain.

Popperfoto

John Kennedy was a leader at ease in front of microphones and television cameras.

Kennedy was educated at private schools and studied political science at Harvard University, graduating in 1940. In 1941 he was rejected by the army because of an old injury to his back. But he was determined to fight in World War II and after strengthening his back by exercises he was accepted by the Navy. In 1943 the torpedo boat PT109, which he was commanding, was sunk by a Japanese destroyer and Kennedy showed courage in leading his men to safety.

Political Career

After the war Kennedy worked briefly as a newspaper correspondent, but then he decided to follow the family tradition of public service. In 1946 he won the Democratic nomination for the congressional seat of the Massachusetts eleventh district and easily defeated his Republican opponent. He served three terms in the House of Representatives. His chance for a seat in the Senate arrived when the Republican Henry Cabot Lodge, Jr., came up for re-election. Lodge was popular and apparently unbeatable, but Kennedy enlisted the help of his family to help him win a narrow victory.

In 1953 Kennedy married Jacqueline Lee Bouvier and they later had two children, Caroline and John. In the Senate, Kennedy sponsored several bills to help New England industries. However, he also took a broader position on issues affecting the whole country. He was a member of the committee headed by Joseph McCarthy which investigated Communist activities in government. He was later criticized for not taking a stand against McCarthy who made many wild accusations.

In 1956 Kennedy just failed to win the nomination for vice-president, but he worked tirelessly for the Democratic presidential candidate Adlai Stevenson. He campaigned vigorously to win the nomination in 1960, succeeding on the first ballot. In the election he beat his Republican opponent Richard M. Nixon by only 119,000 popular votes, though he obtained 303 electoral votes compared to only 219 for Nixon. In his inaugural address Kennedy said, "Ask not what your country can do for you—ask what you can do for your country."

United States President

President Kennedy called his programme for the nation "The New Frontier". He sought an end to poverty and ignorance at home and a re-establishment of United States prestige abroad. However, some proposals were blocked by Congress, including a plan for medical care for the aged. He tried to help the black civil rights campaign and started the Peace Corps, a volunteer service to help poorer countries.

In 1961 an invasion of Cuba by Cuban exiles attempting to overthrow Fidel Castro's Communist government failed disastrously. Kennedy had supported this Bay of Pigs invasion, and had to take the blame for its failure. In 1962 he ordered United States warships to blockade Cuba in a successful attempt to make the USSR remove missiles it had placed there. In space exploration, Kennedy strongly advocated the United States plan to send astronauts to the Moon.

On Friday 22 November 1963 Kennedy and his wife visited Dallas, Texas. As the presidential motorcade passed through the city shots rang out. The president was hit in the neck and the back of the head. He died soon after and Lyndon B. Johnson, his vice-president, was sworn in as president. The alleged murderer, Lee Harvey Oswald, was himself shot dead two days after his arrest.

KENT is a large county in the southeast corner of England. It is often called "the Gateway of England", being the nearest county to the mainland of Europe, and "the Garden of England" because of its many fruit and vegetable crops.

The Kent coastline runs from the mouth of the River Thames to the River Medway, around North Foreland, Pegwell Bay, and Dover to the shingle promontory of Dungeness on the English Channel. To the southwest of the county lies East Sussex, with Surrey and Greater London to the northwest. Across the River Thames to the north lies Essex. A large part of northwest Kent, including the towns of Bromley, Orpington, and Bexley, was absorbed into Greater London in 1965. The county now has an area of 3,731 square kilometres (1,441 square miles) and a population of 1,491,700 (1984 estimate).

The North Downs, a range of chalky hills, stretch through Kent from the Surrey border to meet the coast at the famous white cliffs of Dover and the city of Folkestone. North of this ridge the land falls to the marshy, low-lying shore of the Thames Estuary. To the south is part of the rolling, wooded area called the Weald. The county's areas of marshland include the Minster marshes of Thanet, parts of the Isle of Sheppey, and the open land of Romney Marsh, which has been reclaimed from the sea since Roman times. The low Thames coast is bordered by islands, including Grain and Sheppey, although the former island of Thanet is no longer separate from the mainland. The chief river of Kent is the Medway; others are the Darent and Stour.

Towns and Industries

Kent is still a major farming county, producing crops of barley, wheat, oats, and potatoes. It is also famous for fruit growing, particularly in the Medway valley and north Kent. Many of the country's apples and cherries are grown in Kent, as are most of its hops, used for brewing beer. When gathered, the hops are dried by hot air in kilns or oast houses, which are a familiar feature of the county. There are many market gardens, and much soft fruit is produced. Livestock are raised and sheep are reared in the Romney Marsh area. Whitstable has oyster fisheries.

The Medway valley and north Kent are also home to industries such as paper and cement making. Engineering and chemical works are found along the Thames, while plastics, bricks, and tiles are produced on the lower Medway and Swale. At the mouth of the Medway is the Isle of Grain, with its oil refineries. At Dungeness there is a nuclear power plant.

Tourism is an industry which has been important in Kent since the Middle Ages, when pilgrims travelled to visit the tomb of Thomas Becket at the cathedral at Canterbury. This city has been the seat of the Archbishop of Canterbury since St. Augustine, the first Archbishop, established himself there around AD 597. Canterbury is also the site of the University of Kent. The city of Rochester has both a cathedral and a ruined castle, as

S. & O. Matthews

A hop field and old oast house in Kent. The oast house has storage space, a kiln for drying, and a cooling floor.

well as many places associated with the writer Charles Dickens, who lived in Chatham as a child and at Rochester near the end of his life. Kent seaside holiday resorts include Whitstable and Herne Bay in the north, Margate and the smaller towns of Birchington and Westgate-on-Sea further east, and Broadstairs and Ramsgate beyond the North Foreland. Inland, the town of Tunbridge Wells near the Sussex border has been a popular spa resort since the 18th century.

The busy Channel ports of Dover and Folkestone are important for road and rail travellers to the Continent, and for trade between Britain and its partners in the European Community. Other coastal towns are Deal and Hythe, and Gravesend on the River Thames.

History

Scattered flint flakes and tools left by Stone Age people are quite commonly found in Kent. Because of its position opposite the mainland of Europe, Kent has experienced landings by invaders and settlers from the Continent since prehistoric times. Julius Caesar arrived on the Kent coast in 55 BC and Roman settlement began in AD 43. In the 5th century came Saxons and Jutes, and it was on a mission to bring Christianity to England that St. Augustine landed at Thanet in 597 to preach to Ethelbert, king of Kent. Later, the Normans rebuilt Rochester and Canterbury cathedrals and built a number of castles. In 1170, Thomas Becket, the Archbishop, was murdered in his cathedral at Canterbury, which then became a focus of pilgrimage. The Pilgrims' Way extends almost continuously across the county, along the lower slopes of the North Downs. The poet Geoffrey Chaucer wrote of the Canterbury pilgrims in his *Canterbury Tales*.

The Cinque Ports, which include Dover, Hythe, New Romney, Sandwich, and Hastings in East Sussex, provided ships, sailors, and soldiers for the wars of the Middle Ages. In the 16th century coastal forts were built as protection against invasion, and naval dockyards were established at Chatham and Sheerness. At the time of the Napoleonic Wars, the Royal Military Canal was built as a defence across Romney Marsh. During World War II the coast was again fortified, and the local people were moved to safer areas.

Famous Kent buildings include the great house at Knole, near Sevenoaks, the moated Leeds Castle near Maidstone, and the castles of Dover, Deal and Walmer. Apart from Chaucer and Dickens, famous people connected with Kent include William Caxton, the first English printer, who was born in the Weald, and Christopher Marlowe, the playwright, who was born at Canterbury.

KENTUCKY is the oldest state in the United States of America west of the Appalachian mountain chain. During the late 18th and early 19th centuries, it was America's Wild West, a frontier land to which thousands of settlers came through the Cumberland Gap in the Appalachian Mountains.When the first settlers arrived, the land was part of Virginia.

Kentucky is called the Bluegrass State, after the native grass that grows in the region around the city of Lexington. Here, on land that is unmatched for grazing livestock, is the world's greatest concentration of farms for breeding thoroughbred horses. From some of these farms come horses that run in one of the most famous races in the world, the Kentucky Derby, at Churchill Downs in Louisville.

The Land

Kentucky is in the south central part of the United States. In the north the Ohio River separates it from Ohio, Indiana, and Illinois. To the northeast the Big Sandy River separates it from West Virginia. To the southeast is Virginia, to the south Tennessee, and to the east the Mississippi River, which separates it from Missouri. East to west the state's greatest length is 685 kilometres (425 miles), and its greatest width is 293 kilometres (182 miles). There are 1,930 square kilometres (745 square miles) of inland water surface.

Kentucky has three natural regions: the Appalachian Plateau, the Interior Low Plateaus, and the Coastal Plain. The Appalachian Plateau, covering about a quarter of the state, has the highest elevation. Big Black Mountain, at the Virginia border, is the highest point, at 1,263 metres (4,145 feet) Within this high plateau area are the Cumberland and Pine Mountain ranges. The Appalachian Plateau is also called the Eastern Coal Field.

The Interior Low Plateaus cover most of the state and contain four areas. The Bluegrass region around Lexington is also called the Lexington Plain. Around the edge of the Bluegrass is a semi-circle of rounded hills called the Knobs. To the south and west is the Pennyrile (or Pennyroyal) plateau, named for a variety of mint plant found there. Another low plateau, the Western Coal Field, lies on both sides of the Green River.

The Coastal Plain, in the westernmost part of Kentucky, is part of the huge Gulf Coast Plain that stretches north from the Gulf of Mexico.

Kentucky has a continental climate, with cool winters and warm summers. The growing season varies from 176 days in the eastern highlands to 197 days in the western region. Average rainfall ranges from 101 centimetres (40 inches) in the north to 132 centimetres (50 inches) in the south central region.

The People

The original inhabitants of Kentucky were members of the Shawnee, Cherokee, Chickasaw, and other tribes. The first pioneers who settled the territory were mostly of English and Scottish origin. Many of their descendants still live in eastern Kentucky, in the area known as Appalachia, relatively isolated by the mountains from the rest of the state. The people in this area are among the poorest in the nation, but they have developed one of the most interesting cultures in the United States. They have preserved songs, dances, and folk arts and crafts, handed down from their British forebears.

Early in the 19th century, French immigrants arrived from New Orleans, settling mostly around Louisville. Germans and others came from Pennsylvania and New England. There was once a large black population in Kentucky, but the proportion began to decrease after 1833. In the 1980s only seven per cent of the population was black.

Kentucky has remained a largely rural state. Only Louisville and Lexington had populations over 100,000 in the 1980s.

The Economy

During the first half of the 19th century Kentucky was one of the nation's leading producers of hemp, maize, hogs, oats, rye, wheat, cattle, and tobacco. Today the major crops are tobacco, maize, hay, soya beans, and wheat. Lexington is the heart of the light Burley tobacco country, while dark tobacco is grown in the west. Louisville was once the nation's largest tobacco market, and it still has several cigarette factories. Kentucky ranks first in the breeding of thoroughbred horses.

Coal is the chief mineral. Kentucky and West Virginia are the country's chief coal-producing states. The major coal mining counties are Hopkins, Union, and Webster in the west, and Pike, Harlan, Martin, and Perry in the east. Strip mining, controlled by law since 1962, has damaged much of the land in the east.

Other mineral resources are petroleum, natural gas, and crushed stone. Although the forests have been greatly reduced, lumbering,

The Cumberland Gap National Historical Park in Kentucky. The gap through a range of the Appalachian Highlands provided a westward passage for early settlers.

Kentucky Department of the Arts

and woodworking, still thrive. The product for which the state has become known world wide is bourbon whiskey, which is made from maize. Legend has it that the first bourbon was distilled in what is now Bourbon County in 1790.

The major industries in Kentucky are the production of both electrical and non-electrical machinery, and transport equipment. Louisville, on the Ohio River, is the chief industrial centre. Lexington is a major centre for industry, medical services, and the retail trade. Bowling Green and Hopkinsville are farm centres. The southeast is noted for mountain resorts.

Although roads and railways were slow to come to Kentucky, the state has one of the most extensive natural inland waterway systems in the nation. In the 19th century thousands of flat-boats, rafts, and steamboats plied the Ohio and Mississippi rivers.

The first road in the territory was the Wilderness Road blazed by the pioneer Daniel Boone in 1775. It led through the Cumberland Gap to Boonesboro, Harrodsburg, and, later, to Louisville. Today there are good highways throughout the state.

Railway transport began in 1832 with the opening of a line between Lexington and Frankfort. Today the state is served by about 3,000 miles of rail.

Several dams have been built to control floods and supply power. Kentucky Dam, on the Tennessee River, is part of the extensive Tennessee Valley Authority. Barkley Dam is on the Cumberland River. The lakes formed by these and other dams offer boating, fishing, and swimming, and there are camp sites along their shores.

Kentucky Department of the Arts

The production of bourbon whiskey, in distilleries such as this, is a major industry in Kentucky.

Fort Knox in northern Kentucky has been the gold bullion depository of the United States since 1936.

FACTS ABOUT KENTUCKY

AREA: 104,659 square kilometres (40,409 square miles).
POPULATION 3,742,000 (1989)
CAPITAL: Frankfort, 27,350.
CITIES: Louisville, 281,880; Lexington-Fayette, 225,660; Owensboro, 57,340; Covington, 45,320; Bowling Green, 41,970; Hopkinsville, 29,680; Paducah, 28,870; Ashland, 25,960; Henderson, 25,640; Richmond, 25,050.
HIGHEST PEAK: Black Mountain, 1,263 metres (4,145 feet).
PRODUCTS
    Agriculture: Tobacco, maize, soya beans, hay, wheat barley, potatoes, sorghum; horses, beef and dairy cattle, hogs, chickens, sheep.
    Minerals: Coal, petroleum, natural gas, stone, sand and gravel, clay.
    Manufacturing: Construction and transport equipment, conveyors, farm and garden machinery, plastics and synthetics, chemicals and paint, electrical appliances.
STATE EMBLEMS
    Flower: Golden rod. Tree: Kentucky coffee tree. Bird: Cardinal.
JOINED THE UNION: Kentucky became the 15th State in 1792.

Education

The first public (state) school law was passed in 1838. By 1853 a public school had been established in every county.

Transylvania Seminary, which was founded in Danville in 1780 and moved to Lexington in 1788, was the first school of higher learning west of the Appalachian Mountains. It had the first library, medical school, football team, and law school in the West. The largest state-supported institutions of higher education are the University of Louisville at Louisville and the University of Kentucky at Lexington.

History

The first permanent settlement in Kentucky was founded by James Harrod in 1774 at what is now Harrodsburg. In 1775 Daniel Boone's party founded what is now Boonesboro. Resistance from the Indians was overcome by George Rogers Clark during the American Revolution.

Kentucky Department of the Arts
The Kentucky Derby, one of the classic American horse races, is held at Churchill Downs, Louisville.

Before the American Revolution, both Virginia and North Carolina claimed the Kentucky territory. During the War of Independence the population increased from about 100 to more than 30,000. By 1784 a movement to separate Kentucky from Virginia had begun. Success finally came in 1792, when Kentucky became the 15th state to join the Union.

Kentucky took the lead in promoting the War of 1812, under the leadership of congressman Henry Clay. Both Abraham Lincoln, president of the United States during the Civil War, and Jefferson Davis, president of the Confederacy, were born in Kentucky within a year of each other. During the Civil War Kentucky was considered a border state. It did not secede, but many of its people preferred the Confederacy. About 26,000 of its men fought for the South, while more than 75,000 were in the Union forces. The only major battle of the war fought in Kentucky was at Perryville. Confederate forces under General Braxton Bragg were defeated by a Union army on 8 October 1862.

After the Civil War the introduction of tobacco greatly advanced the state's prosperity. Coal mining on a large scale was started in the 1870s. The first Kentucky Derby was run in 1875. Mammoth Cave, another tourist attraction, became a national park in 1936.

For the first 50 years of the 20th century the state's economy languished. Few companies moved into Kentucky, and people tended to leave the state to look for jobs in large, industrialized cities. In the 1970s and 1980s manufacturing plants moved into the state. Kentucky is now one of the nation's leading producers of motor vehicles.

KENYA is an independent republic in East Africa and a member of the Commonwealth. It is bounded on the north by Sudan and Ethiopia, on the east by the Somali

Barnaby's

Agricultural development, with small farms, in western Kenya.

Republic and the Indian Ocean, on the south by Tanzania, and on the west by Uganda. The southwestern border runs through Lake Victoria. The country is divided into seven provinces and the Nairobi Area.

Land, Climate, and Wildlife

The sea coast of Kenya is a low-lying strip, in places broken into islands by bays and branching creeks. The northern part of Kenya, making up about three-fifths of the country, is an arid area. There are scattered dwarf shrubs and bushes, and many species of wild animals. Here live pastoral people, who move around the area with herds of cattle and camels.

Inland from the coastal belt the country

rises through a land of thorn scrub to the foothills of the highlands. Stretching roughly north and south is the Aberdare Range, whose highest peaks are Sattimma, 3,999 metres (13,120 feet) and Kinangop, 3,906 metres (12,815 feet). East of the Aberdares is the extinct volcano Mount Kenya, 5,199 metres (17,058 feet), the second highest mountain in Africa. West of the Aberdares is the rift valley, an extraordinary split in the Earth's surface stretching from the Jordan Valley in the Middle East for more than 6,400 kilometres (about 4,000 miles) southwards. To the west of the rift valley the land rises in high tablelands and mountains, the tallest being Mount Elgon 4,321 metres (14,177 feet) on the Uganda border. The Tana, flowing from the eastern highlands into the Indian Ocean, is Kenya's most important river, but there is a network of small, shallow rivers which sometimes dry up.

The equator runs across the middle of Kenya. The northern part of the country has a hot, dry climate, and in the area around Lake Turkana (formerly Lake Rudolph) years pass without rain. In the highlands there is a plentiful rainfall and the air is generally bracing with cool breezes. The shores of Lake Victoria have a tropical climate, and the sea coast is hot and rather damp.

Great importance is attached to the Kenya forests which cover approximately 3 per cent of the total area of the country and are found mostly in the highlands. Being in the rainiest districts, the forest trees help to keep the land moist and their roots bind the soil together. Yellow-wood and great camphor trees, African cedars (a kind of juniper), and giant bamboos grow in these natural forests. Kenya is noted for its wildlife. Vast areas of land that are not suitable for agriculture have been turned into game reserves. The largest one is Tsavo National Park. Tourists from all over the world are attracted to Kenya by its wildlife, ranging in size from the lion and rhinoceros to the tiny antelope called the dik-dik, which when fully grown stands only about 30 centimetres (12 inches) high at the shoulder. Tourism is one of Kenya's fastest-growing industries.

People and Towns

Most of Kenya's people are black Africans, but there are small numbers of Europeans, Asians and Arabs. The largest single African group is the Kikuyu, followed by the Luhya, the Luo, and the Kamba. There are just over a million herders such as the Masai and Somali living in the semi-desert areas. Many languages are spoken, but the most common are English and Swahili, a Bantu language which contains many Arabic words. Three-quarters of the people are Christians; others follow local religions or are Muslims or Hindus.

The capital is the modern city of Nairobi (see NAIROBI), site of the national university. In the south-east is Mombasa, situated on an island sheltering the deep-water port of Kilindini, the best harbour in East Africa. Further north along the coast is Malindi, a pleasant holiday resort where there is a pillar set up by the Portuguese navigator Vasco da Gama in 1498. Kisumu in the west is the port on Lake Victoria served by the railway.

Agriculture and Industry

Agriculture provides the bulk of Kenya's income. But most of the land is unsuitable for cultivation, and farming is largely restricted to the highland region. Many of the farms are "co-operatives" in which small farmers work

together so that modern farming methods can be used. The crops include coffee, tea, maize, wheat, fruit, vegetables, and cotton. Among the livestock raised are cattle, goats, poultry, and sheep. Dairying is most important near the towns of the highlands. Dairy products, such as fresh milk and canned butter, are exported.

FACTS ABOUT KENYA

AREA: 582,646 square kilometres (224,961 square miles).
POPULATION: 23,883,000 (1989).
GOVERNMENT: Independent republic. Member of the Commonwealth.
CAPITAL: Nairobi, 1,429,000
GEOGRAPHY: The northern part is mostly dry bush country, with Lake Turkana, 248 kilometres (154 miles) long and some high mountains in the west. In the southeast is a low-lying coastal strip from which the land rises through a region of scrub to rolling, fertile plains at between 1,500 and 2,700 metres (4,920 and 8,850 feet) in the southwest. From the plains rise the Aberdare Mountains and Mounts Kenya and Elgon. The highlands fall away to the shores of Lake Victoria, 1,134 metres (3,720 feet) above sea-level.
CITIES: Mombasa, 425,600; Kisumu, 167,100; Nakuru 101,700; Machakos, 92,300.
ECONOMY. Products and exports.
  Agriculture: Sugar-cane, maize, wheat, millet, barley, potatoes, cassava, pulses, plantains, pineapples, bananas, tea, coffee, sorghum, tomatoes, cashew nuts; cattle, goats, sheep; timber; fish.
  Minerals: Coal, limestone, soda ash, salt, fluorspar, rubies.
  Manufacturing: Cement, food processing, sugar refining, flour milling, soap, fabrics, beverages, paint.
  Exports: Coffee, tea, petroleum products, vegetables and fruit, maize, hides and skins.
EDUCATION: Nearly all children go to primary school, which is free.

Coffee is the principal export crop. The coffee grown in Kenya is noted for its fine flavour. Next in value among exports are tea, grown in the western highlands, and fresh vegetables and fruit, especially pineapples, which are transported by air to European countries. Pyrethrum (a chrysanthemum whose leaves are used in the manufacture of insecticides) is also exported. Wattle, a bark used for tanning hides, is produced in the highlands.

Large amounts of soda are produced from the Magadi soda lake in southern Kenya.

Young men from a Masai tribal group take part in a special ceremony. The nomadic Masai live along the Kenya-Tanzania border.

Norman Myers/Photo Researchers Inc.

Other minerals are coal, limestone, copper, salt, rubies, and gold. Factories in the main towns produce canned foods, beer, soft drinks, flour, soap, and paint. There are large cement factories. The Tana River hydroelectric scheme provides electricity. Kenya's main fuel resource is hydroelectric power. Imported oil is refined at Mombasa.

The railway from Mombasa to Kisumu was built between 1895 and 1903. Later a line was taken from Nakuru through Eldoret westwards right across Uganda. This now carries most of the goods to and from both Kenya and Uganda. There are a number of branch lines in the highlands. The main highway is the Great North military road, joining Nairobi with Uganda in the west and with Tanzania in the south. New roads are being built and old ones improved. Regular air services connect Nairobi with other African countries and Europe.

History

At the end of the 19th century the great powers of Europe: Britain, France, and Germany, sought to take possession of areas of Africa valuable for their fertile land, mineral wealth, and cheap labour. In 1890 the British government took over part of East Africa as a "protectorate". This meant that it refused to allow other European countries to interfere in the area, and Britain itself began to manage the protectorate, encouraging the establishment of British companies and of a rich European farming community in the cool, fertile highlands. In 1920 the protectorate became a British colony and was named Kenya, after the highest mountain in the country. In World War II, Kenya was the centre for operations against Italy in Ethiopia and Somaliland, and Kilindini became an important naval base.

After the war, Kenya continued to develop and many new British settlers came there. Then, in 1952, the Kikuyu, who lived mostly in the central part of Kenya, rebelled against the Europeans: they objected to their presence in the country and their ownership of land. The rebels formed a movement which became known as Mau Mau (what the name means is uncertain). The rebellion was brought to an end in 1960.

In 1963 Kenya was granted internal self-government and later that year it became a

ZEFA

The Jamai Mosque in Nairobi. Only 6 per cent of Kenyans are Muslim; the majority are Christian.

fully independent country. Jomo Kenyatta, one of the leaders of the Mau Mau movement whom the British had imprisoned for several years during the 1950s, became its first prime minister (see KENYATTA, JOMO). One year later Kenyatta became president of the new republic of Kenya. When he died in 1978, he was succeeded by Daniel arap Moi. Kenya has an elected national assembly, or parliament. It has close trade links with Britain, West Germany, and Uganda.

KENYATTA, Jomo (1894–1978) was an
African statesman who became the first prime minister and later the president of independent Kenya.

Kenyatta was born at Ichaweri to parents of the Kikuyu tribe and was named Kamau, son of Ngengi. He went to a school run by Church of Scotland missionaries, and in 1914 was baptized as Johnstone Kamau. In the capital, Nairobi, he worked as a clerk in the public works department and adopted the name Kenyatta (the Kikuyu word for a fancy belt, which he liked to wear). He became interested in African nationalist movements and worked on behalf of the East Africa Association. This became the Kikuyu Central

Association, of which Kenyatta became the general secretary in 1928.

In 1929 Kenyatta went to Europe to argue against British plans to unify Kenya with Uganda and Tanganyika. He remained in Europe for 17 years, spending two years at Moscow University and then reading anthropology at the London School of Economics. His thesis on the Kikuyu way of life was published in 1938 under the title *Facing Mount Kenya*. He now adopted a new first name, Jomo (Burning Spear). Kenyatta was strongly influenced at this time by socialist ideas and by his contacts in Britain with other leaders of the African nationalist movements.

In 1946 Kenyatta returned to Kenya to take up the presidency of the newly formed Kenya African Union. He was also principal of the Kenya African Teachers' College and head of the Independent Schools Association. He became enormously popular among the Kenyan people.

Kenyatta had long forecast violence against

Topham

Jomo Kenyatta became president of Kenya in 1964, a year after it became independent.

the colonial government and it broke out in the form of the Mau Mau rebellion in 1952. The rising was in protest against the privileges of the white settlers and the lack of proper African representation in the legislative council. In the ensuing fighting terrible atrocities were carried out by both sides. Kenyatta was convicted of managing the Mau Mau terrorist organization, though it is uncertain to what extent he had in fact been involved in terrorism. While in prison Kenyatta was elected president of the Kenya African National Union.

On his release in 1961, he negotiated Kenya's independence in 1963 and became its first prime minister. A year later he became president, presiding over Kenya's development into one of Africa's most prosperous and peaceful nations. He was acknowledged as among Africa's most respected leaders. He died at Mombasa.

See also KENYA.

KEPLER, Johannes (1571–1630).

Johannes Kepler, one of the founders of modern astronomy, was born at Weil in southwestern Germany. He suffered an attack of smallpox when he was three that left him with crippled hands and poor eyesight. However, in spite of these handicaps he attended the University of Tübingen and proved himself a brilliant scholar. It was at Tübingen that he learned of the astronomical theories of the Polish astronomer Nicolaus Copernicus, whose work was just then becoming known, nearly 50 years after his death. (See ASTRONOMY; COPERNICUS, NICOLAUS.)

In 1594 Kepler was made professor of mathematics at the University of Graz, Austria. Much of his work was connected with astronomy and through it he got to know Tycho Brahe, the great Danish astronomer. (See BRAHE, TYCHO.) After only four years at Graz, Kepler was invited by Tycho to join his research staff. Tycho, who was then working as imperial mathematician to the emperor Rudolf II, ran an observatory near Prague, which is now the capital of Czechoslovakia. After Tycho's death in

Mansell Collection

German astronomer Johannes Kepler worked out the laws of planetary motion in the early 17th century.

1601, Kepler took his place as imperial mathematician.

At Prague Kepler used Tycho's remarkably accurate observations to prepare astronomical tables (published in 1627 under the title *Tabulae Rudolphinae* in honour of the emperor) and a star catalogue, which appeared in 1628. He also undertook research into optics (the study of light), designed a refracting telescope (see TELESCOPE), and studied a *supernova*, an exploding star, that appeared in 1604 (see STAR). In 1629 Kepler moved to Silesia, where he continued his astronomical work for a short while. He died in Regensburg in 1630.

Kepler's Laws

Kepler's outstanding achievement as an astronomer was the development of his three laws of planetary motion. Copernicus had taught that the Earth and the other planets travel around the Sun in paths called orbits. The orbits were thought to be circular, but the planets' motions in the sky were too complicated for this to be so. Kepler worked out from Tycho's observations that the planets' orbits were slightly oval or elliptical in shape. This important fact formed the basis of Kepler's first two laws, published in 1609. His third law, concerning planetary distances and orbital times, appeared in 1618.

In simple terms, these laws explain the shape of a planet's path around the Sun, the varying speed of a planet at different points in its orbit, and the general length of time an orbit takes in relation to a planet's distance from the Sun. Thus, for example, the third law shows why Mercury, the planet closest to the Sun, completes its journey in only 88 Earth days, while Pluto, the most distant planet, takes nearly 250 years to make one orbit. For an illustration of Kepler's laws, see ASTRONOMY.

Kepler's laws can be used for any body revolving around another body in space. They can, for instance, be used to describe the motion of artificial satellites around the Earth. The English scientist Sir Isaac Newton relied on Kepler's laws for his discovery of the laws of motion and the theory of gravitation (see FORCE AND MOTION; GRAVITY).

KEPLER'S LAWS

(1) the orbits of all planets are elliptical with the Sun at one of the two foci;
(2) a line joining the Sun and any planet sweeps out equal areas in equal time spans; and
(3) the square of the time a planet takes to complete an orbit is directly proportional to the cube of the planet's average distance from the Sun.

KHARTOUM is the capital of the Republic of the Sudan. It is on the spit of land where the Blue Nile joins the White Nile River. The shape of this spit of land gave Khartoum its name, which is Arabic for "elephant's trunk".

Khartoum was founded in 1821 as an Egyptian army camp. They made it a centre of trade and administration. In 1885, the British soldier General Charles Gordon, who had been sent to Khartoum to arrange the

safe return of the Egyptians during a Sudanese rebellion, was killed on the steps of the palace by the Mahdist rebels. (See GORDON, CHARLES GEORGE.) After the defeat of the Egyptian forces, the Mahdi, the leader of the rebels, formed a government and made Omdurman his capital. (Omdurman lies on the west bank of the Nile.) In 1898 the Mahdists were defeated at Omdurman by an Anglo-Egyptian army under Sir Herbert Kitchener (later Lord Kitchener of Khartoum). During the rebellion Khartoum had declined in importance, but Kitchener had it rebuilt in the pattern of the Union Flag. Thus Khartoum again became the capital and centre of trade.

The buildings in Khartoum are of stone or brick, surrounded by green gardens and with palms and shady trees along the streets. Beside the Blue Nile is a drive 3 kilometres (1.8 miles) long, flanked by tall buildings. Khartoum has a university, which was formed from the Gordon Memorial College and the Kitchener School of Medicine.

Khartoum is joined by a rail and road bridge across the Blue Nile to the industrial town of Khartoum North and by road bridge across the White Nile to Omdurman. Its large airport deals with air lines across Africa. Sudan's trade passes through Khartoum, which is linked with Egypt by rail and river and with Port Sudan on the Red Sea.

Khartoum, together with Khartoum North and Omdurman, is the largest city area in the Sudan, with a population of 1,344,000 (1988). In 1988 the Nile overflowed its banks and flooded much of Khartoum.

KHOMEINI, RUHOLLAH (1900(?)–89) was the leader of the revolution that in 1979 overthrew the shah, Iran's hereditary ruler. From 1979 until his death ten years later, Khomeini was the political and religious leader of Iran and of the "Islamic revolution".

Khomeini was born around 1900 into an Iranian clerical family. His father and grandfather were both *mullahs*, that is, religious leaders belonging to the Shiite sect of Islam (see ISLAM). He was educated at various religious schools and when he was about 20 settled in the city of Qom, Iran's most important religious centre. As a Shiite scholar and teacher, he produced many writings on Islamic philosophy and law, but became most famous for his outspoken opposition to the shah. Many strict Muslims sympathized with Khomeini's view that the shah's Western-style economic reforms were an attack on the purity of Islam.

In 1950 Khomeini became an ayatollah, the title given to major Shiite religious leaders. In the early 1960s he was promoted to grand ayatollah, making him one of Iran's supreme religious leaders. By 1963 his criticism of the shah had become so outspoken that he was arrested and in 1964 exiled from Iran. He settled in Iraq from where he continued to call for the shah's overthrow. Later he moved to Paris.

In the late 1970s, civil unrest caused the Iranian government to collapse. In 1979 the shah left the country and Khomeini returned amidst popular acclaim. An "Islamic republic" was proclaimed with Khomeini as its leader.

The country was now run by its religious leaders according to the strict rules of Islam. New industrial projects were halted, Iranian women were made to wear the veil, Western music and alcohol were banned, and Islamic law was restored. Khomeini called his reforms the "Islamic revolution" and urged his followers to help spread them to all corners of the Muslim world.

In foreign affairs Khomeini's anti-Western attitudes led him to agree to the seizure in 1979 of the United States embassy in Tehran and the holding of American diplomats as hostages. He supported anti-Western terrorist groups including Palestinian organizations based in Lebanon. His attempts to spread the Islamic revolution caused unrest in the Shiite communities of other Middle Eastern countries, including Saudi Arabia and Egypt. Between 1980 and 1988 he pursued a futile war against Iraq. The war cost Iran dear. Its economy was ruined and perhaps a million of its people were killed. Khomeini died in 1989, shortly after calling upon his followers to carry out a sentence of death on the British author

Salman Rushdie for publishing a book critical of Islam.

The ten years of Khomeini's rule impoverished Iran and isolated it from the outside world at a time when it needed help. It is said that tens of thousands of Khomeini's political opponents were imprisoned or executed. Nevertheless, he enjoyed unswerving support from the mass of the Iranian people for raising Islam to a supreme place in the country's affairs. As the leader of the Islamic revolution he will long be regarded as a major figure in Middle Eastern history.

KHRUSHCHEV, Nikita (1894–1971). Nikita Khrushchev was leader of the Soviet Union from 1953 until he was "relieved" of his duties in October 1964. He became first secretary of the Communist Party at the time of Joseph

Nikita Khruschev led the USSR as premier and first secretary of the Communist Party from 1958–64.

Stalin's death in 1953. He succeeded Nikolai Bulganin as premier in 1958. As first secretary and premier he controlled both the Soviet government and the ruling Communist Party. (See UNION OF SOVIET SOCIALIST REPUBLICS.) Khrushchev was replaced by Leonid Brezhnev (see BREZHNEV, LEONID) as first secretary and by Aleksei Kosygin as premier.

Khrushchev was born in Kalinovka, a

village in the Ukraine. His father was a coal miner. During his youth, Khrushchev is reported to have worked as a shepherd, farm hand, miner, and factory worker. When the Russian Revolution broke out in 1917, he joined the Communist party. During the civil war that followed he served in the Red Army. When he was released from military service Khrushchev returned to Yuzovka (present-day Donetsk), where he had worked in the coal mines as a boy. His new job was to organize the Communist party. While there he also attended a workers' school. He later went to Kiev and, in 1929, to Moscow, where he continued his studies at the Industrial Academy.

In Moscow, Khrushchev began his rapid rise through the ranks of the party. He was a strong supporter of Joseph Stalin. In 1939 he was appointed a member of the ruling body of the Communist party. He had become one of the most important political leaders in the Soviet Union by the time of Stalin's death.

Khrushchev overcame the challenge of Stalin's most likely successor, Georgy Malenkov, to win the leadership for himself. Later, he criticized Stalin's rule as brutal and misguided. But he himself ordered the Soviet occupation of Hungary (1956).

In 1959 he visited the United States. In 1962 Khrushchev and US President John F. Kennedy had a tense confrontation over the Cuban missile crisis, the USSR finally agreeing to remove its missiles from the Caribbean island so close to the United States. Another feature of Khruschev's time in power was the Soviet Union's quarrel with China.

Khrushchev declared himself in favour of peaceful "coexistence" with the West, but failures of policy at home, especially in agriculture led to his removal (officially "retirement because of age and poor health") in 1964. Thereafter he lived quietly until his death in 1971.

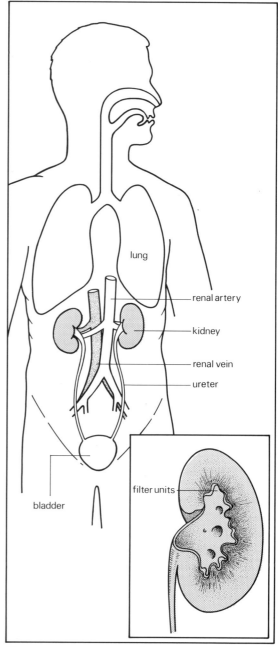

The excretory system: renal arteries carry blood to each kidney; the blood is then purified, and the renal veins take it away. Urine is taken from the kidneys to the bladder through the ureters. **Inset:** Cross-section through a kidney, showing its structure.

KIDNEY. The kidneys are two bean-shaped organs, about 10 centimetres (4 inches) long, which are found in the middle of the abdomen, at the back near the spine. The job of the kidneys is to get rid of unwanted and impure water from the body in the form of urine.

The outer part of each kidney is called the

cortex. In the cortex are about a million tiny spaces each containing a mass of capillary (very small) blood vessels called a glomerulus. Each glomerulus is surrounded by what is called a capsule. There are so many glomeruli that the amount of blood passing through them at any one time is enormous. The kidneys filter all the blood in the body in about five minutes.

As it is pumped through the kidneys the blood gives off some of its water, containing dissolved waste and other body chemicals, and this goes through the capillary wall and into the capsule. A long, twisting tube runs from the capsule and carries the water down into the inner part of the kidney, the medulla, and then in a loop back to the cortex again. One filtering "unit" of a glomerulus, its capsule, the long tube and the capillaries that surround the tube, is called a *nephron*.

As the water flows slowly along the microscopic tube, the kidney absorbs from it useful salts and other chemicals (such as glucose) back into the blood. In this tube, too, some of the water itself may be reabsorbed. The kidneys regulate the amount of water in the body, under control of various hormones. If you have not had a drink for some time, your kidneys will start to save water by reabsorbing it from the long tubes. Since what is left in the tubes becomes urine, the amount of urine you make will be less. If you drink a lot, the amount of urine increases.

About 170 litres (360 US pints) of water pass from the glomeruli to the tubes each day. Of course not all this becomes urine. So much water is reabsorbed that the average person produces around 1.5 litres (3 US pints) of urine daily.

After returning to the cortex, each of the million or so long tubes begins to join up with others, becoming bigger and bigger. Eventually all the tubes run into a still larger tube called the ureter. This ureter is about 30 centimetres (12 inches) long in an adult, and it runs from the kidney to the bladder.

The bladder is a kind of sack with walls of muscular and fibrous tissues. As water passes into it from the two ureters, it expands, and when full it holds about half a litre (roughly a US pint). The urine leaves the bladder through another tube called the urethra, and is passed out of the body. This whole system, from kidneys and ureters to bladder and urethra, is called the urinary or excretory system.

Disorders of the Kidneys

The kidneys may be infected or damaged in some way yet continue to work well. However, as soon as a problem becomes too severe for them to cope with they virtually stop working and the person becomes gravely ill within a few days.

Rarely, the tubes inside the kidney become blocked by minerals that solidify to form kidney stones. The stones can be very painful, especially if they go into the ureter and get stuck there. They cause waves of terrible pain in the side, called renal colic. There are several ways of removing the stones, including drugs that dissolve them, ultrasonic sounds that shatter them, and operations to remove them.

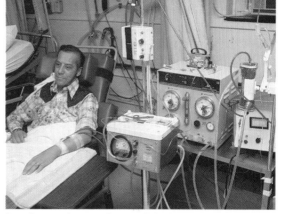

Russ Kinne/Science Photo Library

A patient undergoes haemodialysis. He spends about 20 hours per week linked to the kidney machine.

Infections of the kidneys go under the general term of *nephritis*. The symptoms depend on which parts of the kidneys are infected, but generally they include fever, headache, and a change in the colour and amount of urine produced. Puffy swellings come up on the body, caused by excess water not being removed by the kidneys. Antibiotic drugs cure mild cases. The kidneys can be helped to remove excess body fluids and salts by *diuretic* drugs.

In more serious infections when the kidneys stop working – *renal failure* – the person becomes unconscious and may die if not treated. This can also happen as a result of other, rare, kidney diseases.

There are two main treatments for kidney failure. One is *dialysis*. In haemodialysis the person's blood is fed along a tube into an "artificial kidney machine" (*renal dialysis machine*). This filters out wastes and poisons, and then returns the blood to the body. These machines are expensive and there is always a shortage of them. Also the patient has to stay linked to the machine for 20 hours or more a week (perhaps two or three sessions).

A different form of dialysis is called peritoneal dialysis. A special fluid is injected into the abdomen, where it absorbs the wastes. It is drained away and replaced a few hours later. The person does not have to be linked to a machine as with haemodialysis.

If kidney failure becomes long-term, dialysis places many limits on the person's life. Usually a better alternative is the second treatment, kidney transplant. Such operations are highly successful and most patients can return to a normal life. However, as with the machines, there is always a shortage of suitable kidneys from donors.

KIEV is the capital and oldest city of Ukraine. It is also the largest Ukrainian city, with a population of about 2,587,000 (1989). It stands on the steep west bank of the River Dnieper and owes much of its importance to this great waterway.

Although much damaged in the fighting after the Russian Revolution of 1917, and also during World War II (1939–45), Kiev remains a beautiful city, having wide streets planted with poplars and chestnuts and with gardens looking out over the river. The golden dome on the bell tower of the 11th-century cathedral of St. Sophia can be seen from afar across the steppes (plains). In the Pechersky hill, in the south of the city, many saints and monks of the Russian Orthodox Church were buried in catacombs (caves and underground passages) cut in the rock. The Monastery of the Caves, which dates from the 11th century, was the earliest centre of Christianity in old Russia.

ZEFA

The cloisters of the Monastery of the Caves, in Kiev, are a popular meeting place for residents of the city.

Kiev has always been an important trading town and is the centre of the rich grain and sugar-beet growing lands of Ukraine. It has a large electric power station and its factories make motor cars, machinery, textiles, clothing, and leather goods. Other factories produce foods, chemicals, and furniture. Besides being a busy river port, Kiev is an important railway junction and has an airport.

See also UKRAINE.

KILIMANJARO. In the northeast of Tanzania, near the frontier that separates it from Kenya, is Mount Kilimanjaro, at 5,895 metres (19,340 feet) the highest mountain in Africa. It is also known as Uhuru ("Freedom") Peak, while local people call its top the "House of God". Although Kilimanjaro is near the equator, the whole mountain area is cooler and wetter than the lower lands near by.

Kilimanjaro is an extinct volcano. The Peak, known as Kibo, is made of solidified lava and

Snow-capped Kilimanjaro, the highest mountain in Africa, rises majestically from a plain in Tanzania. The mountain and the land around it form a game reserve.

Richard Keane

is always covered with snow and ice. There is another, smaller peak, Mawenzi, which has no snow. Mawenzi has stupendous walls of rock; on its eastern side there is a fall of about 1,980 metres (6,500 feet) to a vast ravine.

On the slopes of Kilimanjaro, below about 2,000 metres (6,500 feet) above sea-level, there are many villages where bananas, coffee, and maize are cultivated.

Higher up, where the rainfall is heavier, there is a belt of thick forest, in which many wild animals live. In the cool upper forests the lobelia, whose tiny blue flowers may be seen in European and American gardens, heather, and groundsel grow to giant size. Few people live in the forest.

Above another belt of country, similar to moorland, come the snowfields. From these, glaciers (moving rivers of ice) flow down, some of them melting fast as they descend.

KINDERGARTEN see NURSERY SCHOOL AND KINDERGARTEN.

KING, Mackenzie (1874–1950). William Lyon Mackenzie King was a Canadian statesman who became prime minister three times, serving for a record total of 21 years. He was the Liberal Party leader for 29 years.

King was born in Berlin (now Kitchener), Ontario, and was educated at the University of Toronto. His knowledge and experience of labour problems led to his appointment in 1900 as first deputy minister of labour by the federal government. In 1908 he was elected to parliament as a Liberal. A year later he was made federal minister of labour. After six years out of parliament he was re-elected, in 1917, and in 1919 he became leader of the Liberal party.

In 1921 King became prime minister, an office he held until 1930 (except for an interval in 1926) and again from 1935 to 1948. As prime minister King promoted national unity and supported moderate welfare legislation. He successfully urged that all members of the Commonwealth should have equal status. He guided Canada through World War II. King resigned as prime minister in 1948, because of illness. He died at Kingsmere, Quebec.

KING, Martin Luther, Jr. (1929–68) was a black clergyman and leader of the struggle for racial equality and civil rights in the United States.

Martin Luther King, Jr., leading the Selma-to-Montgomery march in Alabama at the height of the civil rights campaign, in 1965.

Popperfoto

King was born in Atlanta, Georgia, on 15 January 1929, the son of a Baptist minister. He became a pastor in 1947 and after studying at Boston University took up his first ministry in Montgomery, Alabama. In 1956 he led a campaign to end the separation of blacks from white people on public transport. He travelled throughout the United States and abroad, lecturing and meeting many civil and religious leaders.

An inspiring speaker, he was influenced by the example of Gandhi (see GANDHI, MOHANDAS). Although often arrested and threatened (once he was stabbed and his home was bombed), he always urged his followers not to use violence. In 1963 he was one of the leaders of a great civil rights march to Washington, DC, and encouraged blacks to secure their full voting rights. In 1964 he received the Nobel Peace Prize and gave the civil rights movement the prize money, saying that he regarded the award as a tribute to all who worked with him.

On 4 April 1968 King's life ended tragically when he was shot during a civil rights campaign in Memphis, Tennessee.

See also CIVIL RIGHTS, UNITED STATES.

KINGBIRD. Any member of the tyrant flycatcher family (Tyrannidae). Kingbirds are about 20 centimetres (8 inches) long with white undersides, generally, and grey backs with a red or orange crown tipped with grey. The bright colour is hidden by overlapping feathers and the dark wing-tips. There are nine species (kinds) ranging from Canada to Argentina, with four North American species. The eastern kingbird (*Tyrannus tyrannus*) is the most common. It nests from southern Canada to the central United States and spends the winter in Central America and northern South America. In summer it is a common sight perched on wires and poles along roadsides. It makes short, swift flights after the insects on which it lives.

Kingbirds attack and drive off hawks, owls, crows, and jays that come close to their nests. The size of the enemy makes no difference. Their nests are neatly made of weed stalks,

NHPA/Haroldo Palo

A tropical kingbird from Central America. It feeds by darting from a perch to catch insects.

grasses, and moss and are lined with fine grasses. They are built on the limbs of trees, about 6 to 7.5 metres (20 to 25 feet) above the ground. The female looks almost exactly like the male. She lays five or six brown-spotted pinkish-coloured eggs. The eggs hatch in about 20 days.

Some beekeepers call kingbirds bee-martins because they eat bees. The harm they do to bee colonies is far outweighed, however, by the good they perform in destroying harmful insects.

KINGCUP see MARSH MARIGOLD.

KINGFISHER. The name kingfisher is used for any of about 85 species (kinds) of compact, large-billed birds, up to about 45 centimetres (18 inches) in length. Many are brilliantly coloured and have head crests. They catch fish and other animals by waiting on a perch such as a tree branch and then pouncing on them. Large prey are beaten against the perch to kill them, and may be tossed up into the air so that they can be swallowed more easily.

The most widespread species, the common kingfisher (*Alcedo atthis*) of Europe, Asia, and Africa, feeds mainly on fish, which it captures by hovering over water, then plunging in head first. The belted kingfisher (*Megaceryle*

alcyon) of North America hunts in a similar manner. The female of this species is more brightly coloured than the male, with a band of chestnut on her lower chest and flanks.

Despite their name, most kingfishers eat mainly land animals, rather than fish. For example, the common paradise kingfisher (*Tanysiptera galatea*) of the East Indies and northeast Australia hunts lizards, centipedes, and insects in the leaf litter of tropical forests. The stork-billed kingfisher (*Pelargopsis capensis*) of India catches fish, frogs, lizards, and crabs, and will also take the young of other birds, including hole-nesting species. The shovel-billed kingfisher (*Clytoceyx rex*) of New Guinea is unusual in that it digs for earthworms with its flattened bill.

Australia has eight species of forest kingfishers, the best-known being the kookaburra (*Dacelo gigas*).

Kingfishers nest in holes in river banks or in trees or termite mounds. They usually lay six to eight white eggs.

The kingfisher has been the subject of many legends. According to the Greeks, Ceyx, the son of the morning star, was drowned and his wife Alcyone, seeing his body drifting towards the shore, sprang into the waves, moving the gods to pity so that they changed both of them into kingfishers. Alcyone was said to build a

NHPA

A common kingfisher returning to its nest hole in a river bank with a small fish firmly gripped in its beak. The actual nest hole is dug out by the kingfishers repeatedly flying at one spot on the bank, loosening a bit of soil at each time. Once a ledge is formed, digging is made easier.

NHPA/A.N.T.

A male white-tailed kingfisher in front of its nest hole in a termite mound, in Queensland, Australia.

nest on the surface of the sea. In order that she could rear her young in peace, the sea grew calm for 14 days each December, and these days were called halcyon days.

KINGLET. Kinglets are round-bodied, short-billed little birds that live mainly in coniferous woodlands (woodlands with mostly cone-bearing trees).

The golden-crowned kinglet (*Regulus satrapa*) of North America and the goldcrest (*Regulus regulus*) of Europe and Asia both have a similar crown patch. It is red in males, and yellow in females, strikingly bordered with black. Only the male ruby-crowned kinglet (*Regulus calendula*) has a crown mark, just a tick of red that is usually hidden by other feathers.

They are active birds with thin, shrill calls.

Their high-hanging nest, of moss bound together with cobwebs, is so small that the five to ten eggs may be arranged in two layers.

Outside the breeding season kinglets live in small groups, often mixing with titmice and creepers. They continually flit from tree to tree to pick off aphids, flies, and other insects, as well as insect eggs and larvae. In their search for food, they can hover like hummingbirds, and will hang upside down from small branches.

KINGS AND QUEENS. This is the title given to male and female rulers of nations and territories. Often the term sovereign or monarch is used to describe the ruler, whether king or queen. A separate article MONARCH explains how kings and queens developed in history, and what their role is today in the countries where they still exist.

Kings and queens once ruled in many parts of the world and had real power in their lands. They passed on this power through the family line, sometimes directly from father (or mother) to the eldest son, or to another of their children by agreement with the council of state or the government, or even to a distant branch of the same family.

Kings and queens were in many ways responsible for the main events of their reigns and were praised for good achievements or useful reforms, but were blamed for injustices and disasters. Sometimes the praise was undeserved, or the blame misplaced. For example, George III of Britain (who ruled from 1760 to 1820) was blamed unjustly for Britain losing its American colonies in the 1780s; it was George III's government headed by Lord North that was responsible. Macbeth, king of Scotland (ruled 1040–57), has been accused of murdering his cousin Duncan I (ruled 1034–40) while he slept at Macbeth's castle. He did kill Duncan, but in battle.

Today there are far fewer reigning royal families, and their role is largely titular. This means that they are heads of state in name only, with little or no real power. So they no longer get praise or blame, unless it is for personal behaviour. It is the government of the day that runs the country – and receives the criticism, good or bad (see GOVERNMENT). There are, however, recent examples of a monarch influencing events, for instance, Juan Carlos, king of Spain since 1975, personally put an end to a revolt by a gang of discontented army officers who broke into the Spanish parliament building.

In earlier times, many kings and queens who had real power still had to rule in accordance with the constitution of their country (see CONSTITUTION), which they swore to uphold when they were crowned. The constitution usually placed restrictions on the king or queen to ensure that he or she did not rule as a tyrant. If the monarch was a despot it was generally because there were enough people in the government who supported him or her personally. Those same people could always change their mind and say "We've had enough". This has happened several times in British history. In 1215, for example, a sizeable group of barons compelled King John (ruled 1199–1216) to agree to a collection of rights and promises of better government, the Magna Carta. In the 1640s a serious revolt against the arbitrary rule of Charles I (ruled 1625–49) led to civil war and defeat for the king, who was later tried and executed.

The idea of kingship goes back almost to the beginnings of recorded history, to the time of ancient Egypt, whose rulers from about 3100 BC had kingly power. Most of the other early civilizations had kings – and sometimes reigning queens – among them the Sumerians and, later, the Babylonians in Mesopotamia; the Hittites in Asia Minor; and the Assyrians in northern Mesopotamia. Ancient Rome had kings for the first two-and-a-half centuries, but the last was expelled in about 500 BC and a republic was created. Ancient India had kings from about 500 BC, some of whom ruled a large part of the sub-continent. In China, there were kingly rulers from at least 1500 BC right up to AD 1911, but they were usually emperors. In Europe, the idea of kingship took hold in the 8th century AD and by AD 900 there were kings of France, England, Scotland, Denmark, Norway, and Bulgaria. By 1500, there were kings also of Spain, Portugal, Bohemia, Poland, Hungary, and Sweden, and Russia had its first tsar in the 1540s. Some of these countries, for example Britain, Denmark, Sweden, and Spain, still have monarchs.

In the English-speaking world, the best-known kings and queens are those of Britain, and their names are in the lists that follow at the end of this article. Wales and Ireland also had independent rulers for a time. Wales had ruling princes, and occasionally one of them was accepted by everyone else as prince of all Wales. The greatest of these was Llywelyn Fawr (Llywelyn the Great, ruled *c.* 1196–1240). Wales was absorbed into England in 1284. Ireland had a number of kingdoms from about AD 400 to 1170, and for most of this period one or other of the kings claimed to be *ard ri*, or high king, and occasionally was recognized as such by other kings. The greatest of these was Brian Boru, king of Munster from 976 to 1014, who in about 1002 got all the other Irish kings to accept him as *ard ri* and to pay him tribute. There were no kings of Ireland after the Normans conquered the country in the 1170s.

Over the 6000 or so years that civilization has existed, there have been many kings and queens who have left their mark upon the history of their realms and on world history. Among these, the following are more important:

> Alexander the Great of Macedon (ruled 336–323 BC)
> Charlemagne, King of the Franks (ruled 768–814)
> Canute of England, Denmark and Norway (ruled 1016–35)
> Robert I (Bruce) of Scotland (ruled 1306–29)
> Casimir the Great of Poland (ruled 1333–70)
> Philip II of Spain (ruled 1556–98)
> Elizabeth I of England (ruled 1558–1603)
> Gustavus Adolphus of Sweden (ruled 1611–32)
> Louis XIV of France (ruled 1643–1715)
> Peter the Great of Russia (ruled 1682–1725)

There are separate articles on many of the kings and queens of England and Scotland, and on some of the monarchs of other countries. Please refer to the Index.

The French royal family was overthrown by the revolution of 1789. Earlier, it dominated French life. This painting by Nicolas de Lagilliere shows four generations of French royalty: King Louis XIV (seated); his eldest son, the Grand Dauphin (behind him); his eldest grandson, the Duc de Bourgogne (right); and the third son of the Duc de Bourgogne, the infant Duc d'Anjou, who succeeded Louis XIV in 1715 as Louis XV.

Reproduced by permission of the Trustees, the Wallace Collection, London

KINGS AND QUEENS OF ENGLAND 1066–1603

Name and House	Birth	Year of Accession	Death
House of Normandy			
William I	*c.*1027	1066	1087
William II	*c.*1056	1087	1100
Henry I	1069	1100	1135
Stephen	*c.*1097	1135	1154
House of Plantagenet			
Henry II	1133	1154	1189
Richard I	1157	1189	1199
John	1167	1199	1216
Henry III	1207	1216	1272
Edward I	1239	1272	1307
Edward II	1284	1307	1327
Edward III	1312	1327	1377
Richard II	1367	1377 (deposed 1399)	1400
House of Lancaster			
Henry IV	1367	1399	1413
Henry V	1387	1413	1422
Henry VI	1421	1422 (deposed 1461)	1471
House of York			
Edward IV	1442	1461	1483
Edward V	1470	1483	1483
Richard III	1452	1483	1485
House of Tudor			
Henry VII	1457	1485	1509
Henry VIII	1491	1509	1547
Edward VI	1537	1547	1553
Jane	1537	1553 (reigned for 9 days – never crowned)	1554
Mary I	1516	1553	1558
Elizabeth I	1533	1558	1603

KINGS AND QUEENS OF GREAT BRITAIN, FROM 1603

Name and House	Birth	Year of Accession	Death
House of Stuart			
James I	1566	1603	1625
Charles I	1600	1625	1649
Charles II	1630	1660	1685
James II	1633	1685 (deposed 1688)	1701
William III	1650	1689	1702
Mary II	1662	1689	1694
Anne	1665	1702	1714
House of Hanover			
George I	1660	1714	1727
George II	1683	1727	1760
George III	1738	1760	1820
George IV	1762	1820	1830
William IV	1765	1830	1837
Victoria	1819	1837	1901
House of Saxe-Coburg-Gotha			
Edward VII	1841	1901	1910
House of Windsor			
George V	1865	1910	1936
Edward VIII	1894	1936 (abdicated 1936)	1972
George VI	1895	1936	1952
Elizabeth II	1926	1952	

KINGS AND QUEENS OF SCOTLAND FROM MALCOLM CANMORE

Name	Birth	Year of Accession	Death
Malcolm III (Canmore)	c.1031	1057	1093
Donald Bane	c.1033	First reign 1093–94	
		Second reign 1094–97	?
Duncan II	c.1060	1094	1094
Edgar	c.1074	1097	1107
Alexander I	c.1077	1107	1124
David I	c.1080	1124	1153
Malcolm IV	1142	1153	1165
William (the Lion)	1143	1165	1214
Alexander II	1198	1214	1249
Alexander III	1241	1249	1286
Margaret (Maid of Norway)	1283	1286	1290
John Balliol	c.1250	1292 (deposed 1296)	1315
Robert I (Bruce)	1274	1306	1329
David II	1324	1329	1371
House of Stewart			
Robert II	1316	1371	1390
Robert III	c.1337	1390	1406
James I	1394	1406	1437
James II	1430	1437	1460
James III	1451	1460	1488
James IV	1473	1488	1513
James V	1512	1513	1542
Mary (Queen of Scots)	1542	1542 (deposed 1567)	1587
James VI	1566	1567	1625

KINGSFORD SMITH, Sir Charles see SMITH, SIR CHARLES KINGSFORD.

KINGSLEY, Charles (1819–75), an English clergyman and novelist, is known mainly as the author of a book for children called *The Water-Babies*. He also wrote many works promoting social reform in 19th-century England.

National Portrait Gallery, London

The writer Charles Kingsley, in a portrait by the minor Victorian artist Lowes Cato Dickinson.

Kingsley was born at Holne Vicarage, near Dartmoor, in Devon, England. He was educated at King's College, London, and at Cambridge University. In 1842 he became curate of the church at Eversley, Hampshire, and was later appointed rector, a position he held until his death. From 1860 to 1869 he was professor of history at Cambridge University. He wrote novels, a poetic drama, children's and travel books, and several collections of sermons.

Alton Locke (1850), one of Kingsley's best and earliest novels, dealt with some of the social problems of his day and showed his sympathy for the English working class. The works for which Kingsley is best known are his historical novels and his books for children. *Westward Ho!* (1855) is a famous historical novel. It is a tale of naval adventure set in the days of Queen Elizabeth I. His children's books are *The Heroes* (1856), a retelling of Greek myths, and *The Water-Babies* (1863), the tale of a chimney sweep named Tom who falls into a river and is turned into a water-baby.

KINGSLEY, Mary (1862–1900). Mary Henrietta Kingsley was one of the few white women to travel in Africa during the 19th century. Born in London, she was a niece of the writer Charles Kingsley. At the age of 30, she decided to go to West Africa to study African religion and law, partly because she wanted to finish a book begun by her father.

She visited Cabinda (now part of Angola), Nigeria, the Cameroon coast, the Congo, and was the first European to enter Gabon. She travelled up the Ogooué River by canoe from the Gabon coast. These journeys were full of

Mansell Collection

Mary Kingsley's canoe trip on the Ogooué River. It was on this part of her journey that she was forced to jump at a rock wall and hang on to it "in a manner more befitting an insect than an insect-hunter"!

dangers. In her book about her adventures, *Travels in West Africa,* she describes her encounter with a crocodile: "he chose to get his front paws over the stern of my canoe and endeavour to improve our acquaintance. I had to retire to the bows to keep the balance right, and fetch him a clip on the snout with a paddle when he withdrew, and I paddled into the very middle of the lagoon, hoping the water there was too deep for him . . . to repeat the performance." Returning to England with a valuable collection of West African beetles and freshwater fish for the British Museum, she lectured and wrote about her adventures, always with great sympathy for the people of Africa. She was insistent that African customs should be respected, and argued in favour of the use of local African rulers to run the colonies.

Mary Kingsley died at Simonstown, near Cape Town, while nursing sick prisoners during the Boer War.

KING SNAKE is the name for several species (kinds) of medium-sized snakes that kill their prey by constriction – by squeezing them to death. They kill and eat many other snakes, including venomous types, and appear to be immune to their poison. King snakes range from southeastern Canada to Ecuador. There are very many differently marked subspecies.

The common king snake (*Lampropeltis getulus*) of the United States and northern Mexico is usually black or brown, blotched, ringed, or speckled with yellow or white. It grows to over 2 metres (6.5 feet). It is found in a variety of habitats but most often in woods, meadows, and near farm buildings. The black subspecies is more fond of rocky places.

The milk snake (*Lampropeltis doliata*) has attractive markings of black-bordered brownish rings or saddles on a white or yellow background. It is a slender snake that grows to 1.3 metres (4.3 feet) long. It often enters barns and cellars to catch mice.

Several species of king snake are known as false coral snakes because of their red, yellow, and black rings. One example is the Arizona mountain kingsnake (*Lampropeltis pyromelana*) (see also CORAL SNAKE).

NHPA/K. H. Switak

A harmless Californian king snake gains protection by having a similar warning colour pattern to the poisonous coral snake.

KINGSTON is the capital and chief port of the Caribbean island of Jamaica. It is also a major commercial city of the West Indies. The city is on the southern coast of the island. Beyond it rise the Red Hills and the foothills of the Blue Mountains. The climate is hot, with an average annual temperature of 26°C (79°F). Throughout its history, the city has suffered from hurricanes and earthquakes. Kingston's fine harbour, however, is protected by the Palisadoes sandbank, which has been developed as a tourist resort.

Jamaica's trading, banking, shipping, and industry are centred in Kingston. The industries include food-processing, cement manufacturing, the making of clothes and shoes, tobacco processing, brewing, and tourism.

Victoria Park, in the heart of the city, is cut by King Street. Along this street are government buildings and fine stores. The Institute of Jamaica, which maintains a library, museum, and art gallery, is near by.

Kingston was founded in 1692, after an earthquake destroyed most of the town of Port Royal. The survivors of the disaster moved across the harbour to the site that became Kingston. During the 18th century the city became the island's commercial centre. But it was not until 1872 that Kingston was made the political capital.

The population is 104,041 (1982).

KINSHASA is the capital and chief city of Zaire. It stretches along the south bank of the Zaire River downstream from Malebo Pool (formerly Stanley Pool). The climate is hot and humid. Brazzaville, capital of the Republic of the Congo, is directly across the river. Kinshasa was known as Léopoldville until 1966.

The city developed from two villages, Kinshasa and Kintambo. In 1881 Henry M. Stanley established a trading depot at Kintambo and named it Léopoldville. It became the capital of the Belgian Congo in 1923. Today it is a modern city with wide, tree-lined avenues, and skyscrapers. An important industrial centre, its principal industries include food processing, the making of clothes and shoes, and woodworking. Most of the city's small European population left when the territory became independent in 1960.

Since the Zaire (Congo) River is the main route into the interior, Kinshasa's location is very important as a "portage" point. Above the city the river is navigable to Kisangani, 1,600 kilometres (1,000 miles) upstream. However, just below the city, there is a long series of waterfalls, known as Livingstone Falls. These make it impossible for ocean ships to sail directly to Kinshasa. Cargoes are unloaded at Matadi and then "portaged" by rail for 370 kilometres (230 miles) to Kinshasa. There the cargoes are transferred to river steamers.

The population is 3,562,122 (1990).

KIPLING, Rudyard (1865–1936), was a writer and poet, who wrote books for readers of all ages. The *Just-So Stories* are tales of how all sorts of things began, such as "How the Leopard got his Spots" and "The Beginning of the Armadilloes". For older children there are *Stalky and Co.*, a series of stories about the exploits of a gang of boys in a boarding school; *Puck of Pook's Hill*, a book of short stories presenting English history in a simple, dramatic way; and the *Jungle Books*, about the jungle boy Mowgli and the wild animals who were his companions. Kipling was a wonderful storyteller, and his books are full of excitement. He was also a poet whose verse was strong and manly, if a little unimaginative. His poem "If"

remains one of the most stirring and popular pieces of verse in the English language.

Joseph Rudyard Kipling was born in Bombay, the son of an English artist and scholar who was working in India. At the age of six Rudyard was brought back to England and spent an unhappy childhood firstly in a foster home and later at the United Services College at Westward Ho, Devon, the school that he wrote about later in *Stalky and Co.* When he was 17, he returned to India and began working as a journalist. Before long his poems and stories began to be published and were successful, especially the stories about soldiers.

Rudyard Kipling, painted by Sir Philip Burne-Jones.

After travelling through India, China, Japan, and America, Kipling eventually came back to England, where he continued to write. He worked on stories of India, and also on a new book of poems which he called *Barrack Room Ballads*. These lively energetic verses, written in rough soldier slang, were published in 1892. Kipling was very patriotic and his great love of Britain and of Britain's empire throughout the world came out in these and other poems. *Barrack Room Ballads* made Kipling's reputation. The book was soon followed by others: *The Jungle Books* (1894–95); *Stalky and Co.* (1899); and the *Just-So Stories* (1902).

In 1892 Kipling married an American named Caroline Balestier. For a time they lived in Vermont in the United States but later returned to England and settled in Sussex. Kipling was very fond of the English countryside and wrote about it in *Puck of Pook's Hill* (1906) and *Rewards and Fairies* (1910).

Kipling also wrote several novels, though they are thought to be not as good as his short stories. The best-known of them was *Kim* (1901), the story of Kimball O'Hara, the son of a sergeant. It gives a vivid picture of life in India.

Much of Kipling's writing is marked by a certain brutality and an aggressive English patriotism and dislike of foreigners. This has led to a decline in his reputation in recent years. But his gifts as a story-teller still make him popular with ordinary readers who enjoy a good yarn. In 1907 Kipling's merits as a writer were recognized when he was awarded the Nobel Prize for Literature.

KIRIBATI. In the Pacific Ocean, northeast of Australia, lies a string of islands, the chief of which were formerly called the Gilbert Islands. Now they are part of the Republic of Kiribati (pronounced "kiri-bas"), one of the smallest countries in the Commonwealth. Kiribati's other islands include Banaba (Ocean Island), the Line Islands, and the Phoenix Islands.

None of the islands is large. Indeed, the total land area of Kiribati is only a little over 849 square kilometres (328 square miles). But if you were to draw a line round them on the map you would enclose an area roughly a quarter the size of Australia. The islands stretch for a distance of more than 4,500 kilometres (2,800 miles) from Banaba in the west to Christmas Island (one of the Line Islands) in the east. Most of the islands are atolls: circles formed of long, narrow coral islands linked by reefs, with each circle enclosing a lagoon. Some of the islands are so narrow that they consist of little more than a road lined by palm trees, with palm-thatched villages at intervals along the road.

Most of the people of Kiribati are Micronesians, a racial group that lives in the Pacific islands. They speak Gilbertese or English. The islanders live simply, and are renowned for their skills as sailors. Fish is their chief food, for the island soil is poor and little can be grown apart from the coconut palm and the pandanus tree (which gives edible fruit). It is on these two trees that the people mostly depend for their living.

The island of Banaba is simply a large lump of phosphate rising from the sea. Phosphate used to be exported, but now almost all of it has been used up. Phosphate mining on Banaba stopped in 1979. Without other natural resources, Kiribati depends on aid from many countries, including China, Japan, New Zealand, the United Kingdom, the United States, and the European Economic Community. In 1985 Kiribati signed a fishing agreement with the former Soviet Union for a yearly payment. Kiribati also has a fishing agreement with South Korea.

FACTS ABOUT KIRIBATI

AREA: 849 square kilometres (328 square miles).
POPULATION: 71,100 (1990).
GOVERNMENT: Republic.
CAPITAL: Bairiki.
GEOGRAPHY: A group of small Pacific islands made up of coral atolls.
CITIES: Bairiki, 22,833.
CHIEF PRODUCTS: Copra, fish, and fish products.
EDUCATION: Children must attend school between the ages of 6 and 13.

History of the Islands

Most of the islands were discovered in the 18th and early 19th centuries, and from 1888 Britain took them over, mostly at the request of the islanders. The Gilberts were joined as a single colony with the nine Ellice Islands, which lie to the southeast. Also included in the colony were the eight Phoenix Islands and the three Line Islands. Two of the Phoenix group – Canton and Enderbury atolls – are now administered jointly by Britain and the United States. Christmas Island was discovered by Captain Cook on Christmas Eve, 1777.

The Gilbert and Ellice Islands remained a British colony until 1975, when the Ellice Islands became self-governing and took a new name, Tuvalu (see TUVALU). Kiribati gained its independence in 1979.

Lord Kitchener's portrait appears on this famous recruiting poster of World War I.

KITCHENER, Horatio, 1st Earl (1850–1916).

Horatio Herbert Kitchener, better known as Lord Kitchener, was a famous British soldier. He fought in the Boer War and was secretary of state for war during the early part of World War I. He was born in Ireland and, after studying at the Royal Military Academy at Woolwich, joined the Royal Engineers.

Kitchener made his name in the Sudan, where he led the British forces at the battle of Omdurman (1898) and recaptured Khartoum from the Mahdists who had slain General Gordon (see GORDON, CHARLES GEORGE). In 1900, during the Boer War, he became commander-in-chief of the British army. In 1902 he was sent out to command the army in India and later served in Egypt and the Sudan.

When World War I broke out in 1914, Kitchener became a member of the government and was promoted to field marshal. Realizing that the war would be a long one, he began a huge programme to train volunteers for the army. His picture appeared on a famous recruiting poster. He met his death at sea in 1916 when the cruiser *Hampshire*, carrying him on a mission to Russia, was sunk by a German mine.

KITE is a hawk-like, flesh-eating bird, a member of the family Accipitridae. Kites are usually from 45 to 61 centimetres (18 to 24 inches) in length, although some are much larger. Their tails are long and forked. Like their relatives the hawks and eagles, kites have hooked bills that curve downward. Their feet are especially adapted to seizing and holding their prey. Each foot has three long toes pointing forward and one pointing backward. These are armed with sharp, curved claws.

Kites are excellent fliers. Their narrow, pointed wings allow them to hover like gulls or to swoop quickly in pursuit of their prey. Most kites live on small rodents, insects, frogs, snakes, lizards, and small birds. The buzzard kite (*Hamirostra melanosternon*) of Australia lives mainly on rabbits and lizards, but it also eats emu eggs, reportedly dropping rocks on the eggs to break the thick shells. Some species, such as the Brahminy kite (*Haliastur indus*), are scavengers.

There are many species of kite, ranging in colour from pale reddish-brown to black, with various white, orange, and black markings.

An Australian square-tailed kite with its chick.

The graceful swallow-tailed kite (*Elanoides forficatus*) is found in the extreme southern United States. It is noted for its long wings and long scissor-like tail. The Everglade, or snail, kite (*Rostrhamus sociabilis*) lives deep in the Florida Everglades. It has an extremely narrow, curving bill, which it uses to spear and pluck snails from their shells. Other members include the common, or red, kite (*Milvus milvus*) of Europe, northern Africa, and Asia Minor; and the black kite (*Milvus migrans*) of Europe, Asia, northern Africa, and Australia.

Kites nest in high trees. The nests are usually loosely built of sticks, moss, or other vegetation. Most kites lay from two to five white or spotted eggs that take four weeks or more to hatch. Many species of kite are becoming rare.

KITE FLYING. Kite flying is popular with young and old alike. A simple flat kite can be made by taking two light sticks and fastening them together in the form of a cross. One stick can be longer than the other; the long stick is fastened at the point of balance of the short stick. A strand of thin cord is stretched around the ends of the sticks to make a frame, and the frame is then covered with fabric. The fabric can be thin, strong paper, plastic, or silk, cut slightly larger than the frame so that the edges can be folded over and gummed. A "bridle" is then made of string somewhat longer than the long stick and fixed to it near the ends. At the point of balance of the bridle, the flying cord is fastened. Another piece of string with strips of paper tied along its length is fixed to the bottom end of the long stick to act as a tail. The tail stabilizes the kite, keeping the tailed end pointing towards the ground.

To fly the kite, pay out (unwind) a few metres of the flying cord from the winder and run into the wind until the kite is carried into the air. Then, standing with your back to the wind and on a height if possible, pay out cord whenever the kite is taken up by a gust and pull in cord as soon as the kite droops.

The Dutch, eddy, or bow kite needs no tail. After the cross has been made and the paper or silk covering fixed to it, a string is stretched across the crosspiece and carefully pulled tighter until the crosspiece is bent like a bow. This makes the surface of the kite curved. The bridle and flying cord are fixed in the same way as for the tailed kite.

There are other shapes, such as the tetrahedral kite and the box kite. Box kites are more difficult to make but fly better than flat kites. They are stronger because of their box-

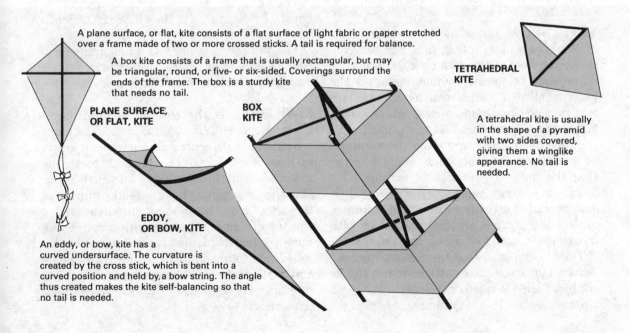

A plane surface, or flat, kite consists of a flat surface of light fabric or paper stretched over a frame made of two or more crossed sticks. A tail is required for balance.

A box kite consists of a frame that is usually rectangular, but may be triangular, round, or five- or six-sided. Coverings surround the ends of the frame. The box is a sturdy kite that needs no tail.

TETRAHEDRAL KITE

PLANE SURFACE, OR FLAT, KITE

BOX KITE

A tetrahedral kite is usually in the shape of a pyramid with two sides covered, giving them a winglike appearance. No tail is needed.

EDDY, OR BOW, KITE

An eddy, or bow, kite has a curved undersurface. The curvature is created by the cross stick, which is bent into a curved position and held by a bow string. The angle thus created makes the kite self-balancing so that no tail is needed.

like frame of wooden struts. An inexpensive kite, made at home or bought from a toy shop, can fly well and be made to perform "stunts". Large kites, which can lift a person, are used in the sport of hang gliding (see HANG GLIDING).

Kite-flying is very popular in the countries of the East. In China the ninth day of the ninth month is a festival called "Climbing the Heights" when grown-ups as well as children go out to fly kites. Some of the kites are made to look like men and women, others like birds, butterflies, dragons, fishes, and serpents. Musical kites are used to frighten away evil spirits. They carry either reeds with holes in them so as to make a flute-like wailing note in the wind, or a string stretched on a bow so as to vibrate like that of a stringed instrument.

Fighting between kites is an exciting sport in Japan and other parts of eastern Asia. The object is to cut the flying cord of the opponent's kite. The upper part of the cord of each kite is painted with glue and dipped in powdered glass so as to form a sharp cutting edge. Each flyer tries to get his kite to drift down with the wind so that its cord touches that of the opponent's kite. As soon as this happens, he jerks his cord sharply so that it cuts that of the other kite, which falls to the ground and may be kept by the first person to reach it.

KIWI. The kiwi, one of the national emblems of New Zealand, is a bird that has survived unaltered from the distant past. Its scientific name *Apteryx* means "without wings". The Maoris called it kiwi (from the cry the bird makes) and this became its popular name. Kiwis are not common and are protected by the government. They are about the same size as chickens, the female being slightly larger than the male. They cannot fly, for they have hardly any wings, and have no tails either. The thread-like feathers are reddish-brown and the legs and feet are thick and heavy, with a back toe to each foot. Kiwis can run fast.

The kiwi finds its food by means of its long curved bill, which has nostrils at the tip, so the bird is able to smell out the earthworms on which it feeds. The kiwi usually feeds at night

Courtesy, High Commission for New Zealand
Kiwis live in forests and are generally active at night, when they probe the leaf litter for insects.

and remains hidden during the day. When cornered it lashes out with its sharp claws.

The female kiwi generally lays only one egg—occasionally two—a year. The egg is very large in comparison with the bird that laid it, being about 7 centimetres (2.7 inches) wide by 12 centimetres (4.7 inches) long, and it is hatched by the male. The newly hatched kiwi is covered with down and is able to run about and take care of itself.

There are three kiwi species. The common kiwi (*Apteryx australis*) is found throughout New Zealand. The little spotted kiwi (*Apteryx oweni*), and the great spotted kiwi (*Apteryx haasti*) are restricted to the west coast of South Island.

The word *kiwi* is used as a nickname for a New Zealander or (in the United States) for a grounded member of the Air Force.

KIWI FRUIT is the fruit of a sub-tropical grapelike vine (*Actinidia chinensis*). The plant is native to south central China where it grows up trees to a height of 10 metres (30 feet). The roundish fruit has a fuzzy, brownish-green skin that resembles the bristle-like plumes of the kiwi bird. The flesh is succulent and a translucent emerald green with a refreshing lime-like flavour. It has become very popular worldwide, often used in mixed fruit salads and to decorate cakes and desserts. Its juice can also be used like papaya, as a meat tenderizer.

Courtesy, New Zealand Kiwifruit

A kiwi fruit is an egg-shaped furry fruit with a tasty green pulp and tiny reddish seeds.

It was introduced into New Zealand in 1906 and since the mid-1970s has been exported from there on a large scale. The industry is centred on the North Island town of Te Puke, known as "The Kiwifruit Capital of the World". Kiwi fruit is also grown on a commercial scale in California.

KLONDIKE. In Yukon Territory in the northwest of Canada is a small river called the Klondike which gave its name to the gold-bearing district that lies in its basin and in the basin of the Indian River.

On 17 August 1896, a rich find of gold was made on Bonanza Creek, one of the tributaries, or branches, of the Klondike River. The news swiftly spread and people rushed to Yukon in the hope of making fortunes overnight. This kind of happening is what is known as a "gold rush". (See GOLD RUSH.)

Within two or three years, between 30,000 and 40,000 people from all parts of the world had collected in and around Dawson City on the bank of the Yukon River, searching in the gravels of the creeks, which were the spots richest in gold. As the Klondike is so far north, the ground was frozen hard and it had to be melted, first with fires and afterwards with steam. Later dredges and hydraulic machinery were used to make the work easier.

Some people did make their fortune in the Klondike, but thousands were unlucky. Many suffered great hardship in the bitter cold and the rough conditions in which they had to live, and some died.

The rush was at its height in 1899. After that it steadily grew less and people left the Yukon to return to their own homes. All mining finally stopped in 1966. In the 1980s the population of Dawson City had shrunk to less than 700.

KNIFE see SILVERWARE.

KNIGHT AND KNIGHTHOOD. The first knights were fighting men who wore armour and fought on horseback. These men were needed in western Christian Europe after the death of Charlemagne in 814. At that time there was no government strong enough to keep order and protect the people. Europe was being attacked by Muslim Moors and by Slavs, Magyars, and Norsemen. There was no law, and invaders, robbers, and bandits were everywhere. Anyone who wanted to earn his living in peace had to seek the protection of the owner of a large castle. These lords became leaders not only of the serfs but also of their fighting men or knights. The overlord let the knight use a piece of land and often a castle. In return the knight had to fight for his lord a certain number of days a year. He had to appear on the battlefield properly equipped at his own expense. He also paid the usual feudal dues. (See FEUDALISM.)

Life was rough and brutal. The knights of the 9th and 10th centuries who beat back the invasions were not men of culture and refinement, but bullies, full of strength and courage, and ready to swing a battle-axe. Stories and poems about knights usually make knighthood seem far more romantic than it really was. (See ARTHUR, KING.)

The early medieval knight was a paid fighter, and he fought well. By about the year 1000 the work of driving back Europe's invaders was done. But the knights remained, warring and plundering among themselves. The Church tried to stop the fighting. The Church laws, called the Peace of God in the 10th century, declared that certain classes of persons—including clergy, women, and merchants—should not be molested. The Truce of God, in the early 11th century, prohibited fighting on Sundays and on many Church holidays during the year.

The idea that the poor, the helpless, and the Church itself ought to be protected rather than robbed was slow in spreading. If it was to be accepted, the knights would need a new purpose. The preaching of the First Crusade by Pope Urban II at Clermont in 1095 gave the knights this purpose. They were asked not to give up war but to make war in the service of the Church. (See CRUSADES.) They were expected to set an example of Christian behaviour to their fellow men.

The ideal of the perfect knight from the 11th century to the 15th was probably too high for anyone to reach, but by trying to reach it people at least began to think about their fellow men. The new ideals of chivalry (how a knight should behave) changed the knight from a fighting vassal of an overlord; in the early days, every man in the feudal society could hope to become a knight. But knighthood ceased to be given to anyone who had a horse, a suit of armour, a sword, and a good fighting arm. It was a profession involving many years of training and service, as well as the taking of certain very sacred and rigid vows. In this way knighthood came to have a religious meaning as well as a military one.

From Squire to Knight

A boy who was to be trained for knighthood was sent away from home at about the age of seven. He went to the castle of a friendly noble where there were perhaps 200 or 300 in the household, including other boys like himself.

The first stage of the young knight in training was service as a page. He was attached to the service of one of the ladies of the castle. When he was about 14 years old the page became a squire, in the service of one of the knights.

At the age of 21 the squire was ready for knighthood. He could be dubbed a knight very simply, but he usually went through a long, solemn ceremony. First he bathed and put on a white tunic symbolizing purity. Over this he wore a red garment and a black coat, to show his willingness to shed blood and face death. He then kept the "vigil of arms". This meant fasting for 24 hours, passing the night in church, kneeling by his armour, and praying.

At sunrise he confessed to the priest and received the Holy Sacrament. Then, with the whole household assembled in the church, he handed his sword to the priest. The priest placed it on the altar, praying that God might bless it for the defence of the Church and of widows and orphans. The squire then knelt and took the vows that would rule the rest of his life. He swore, among other things, to fear God and keep the Christian religion; to serve the king bravely; to protect the weak; to fight

Knights in full armour jousting. Jousts gave knights fighting practice and an opportunity to show their valour.

for good; to obey his lord; to be fair, kind, and truthful; to finish anything he started; to respect women; to accept challenges of other knights; and never to run away from an enemy. The lord then struck the squire on the shoulder with the flat of the newly blessed sword (this was the *accolade*), saying, "In the name of the Father, the Son, and Holy Ghost, I dub thee knight." The knight could then put on his armour, his sword, and his golden spurs.

The duties of the knight were a noble ideal, and even if they were only partly fulfilled they helped to civilize society. Still, the chief business of a knight was to fight. When there were no wars to keep the knights in practice, they carried on mock fights with one another. In these jousts or tournaments, each knight fought for the honour of his lady.

But war itself was changing. The hand-to-hand combat for which the knight was trained and equipped was giving way to other forms of battle. At the battle of Crécy (1346) and again at Poitiers (1356) the French knights in heavy armour were no match for the English foot soldiers armed with longbows. When gunpowder came into use, the knight was useless. (See ARMOUR; WAR AND WARFARE.)

Knightly Orders

During the period of the Crusades, when knighthood reached its greatest importance, the famous religious knightly orders grew from the general order of knighthood. The Knights Templars, Knights Hospitallers, and Teutonic Knights owed allegiance to the Church rather than to a king or baron. They swore to recover the Holy Sepulchre in Jerusalem and to wage war against the Saracens. They supplied the power which drove armies forward to gain the Holy Land for Christendom. (See CRUSADES.)

When Jerusalem was finally lost in the middle of the 13th century, these religious orders of knights were left without a real purpose. They slowly died out. The Hospitallers occupied the island of Malta until 1798. The order still exists as the Knights of Malta, a social and charitable group. (See HOSPITALLERS.)

Popperfoto

Knighthood today honours service such as the singer Bob Geldof's work for famine relief.

A number of religious knightly orders also arose in the 12th century in Spain and Portugal to fight the Moors. Important among them were the order of Santiago de Compostella, Calatrava, and Alcantara.

Even though military need for knights had come to an end, knighthood, as a social ideal, a way of conduct, and a position of honour continued. Other orders of knighthood have been started in recent times. There are today nine orders in the United Kingdom alone. The Royal Victorian Order was started in 1896 and the Order of the British Empire in 1917. There are similar orders on the continent of Europe such as the Legion of Honour of France.

Knighthood today does not have the same meaning that it had in the Middle Ages. Modern knights are men who have given service. They may be distinguished writers, artists, statesmen, scientists, or military men.

The order of knighthood is given to honour them. In the United Kingdom knights can use the title "Sir" before their names. The dubbing service is now very simple. The knight-elect usually kneels while the monarch touches his shoulder with a sword and pronounces the ceremony. The insignia of the order are usually given at the same time. A woman honoured in a similar way is known as a Dame.

KNITTING AND CROCHET. Knitting is a way of making fabric by joining together loops of yarn. Because the yarn is looped rather than stretched tight, as in weaving, knitted garments stretch more easily and so fit the body more closely. They are warm for their weight because the loops help to hold a layer of insulating air near the body, and because they absorb moisture, and they let the body breath. Therefore knitting is good for use in underwear, stockings, and sweaters.

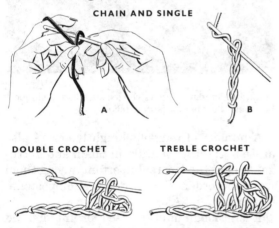

Crochet stitches. **A:** How to hold the yarn and hook; **B:** A chain of single stitches; **Below:** Double and treble stitches being built up.

Crochet also produces a fabric made of loops of yarn, but the loops are made in a continuous chain which is then doubled back on itself again and again to produce the fabric. A single needle with a hook at the end is used in hand crochet. The fabric is not as stretchy as knitted fabric and cannot be shaped so accurately. For this reason it has never been used in the same way as knitting to make useful, everyday garments, but more as a form of decoration, like lace.

Any soft yarn, such as cotton, silk, wool, nylon, and other man-made fibres, can be used for knitting and crochet. Linen is not often used as it is stiff and does not stretch. Yarns are often combined, such as wool and nylon for socks. Wool is warm and soft, but the addition of nylon makes the fabric more hard-wearing.

Hand Knitting

A series of loops is formed (cast on) on a needle. A second needle, slipping through these loops, pulls through the strand of yarn to form a second row of loops. This transfers the piece of work to the second needle. The whole process is repeated row by row. Very fine yarn and thin needles produce a tight fabric; thicker wool and larger needles produce a looser, more openly worked fabric. There are only two basic stitches—plain and purl. All the others are combinations of these two, worked in different ways to form patterns. When each piece is finished it is "cast off" by looping the stitches over the yarn to produce a neat edge.

Knitting where the yarn goes across the fabric is known as "weft knitting". A broken or dropped stitch will cause a run all the way down the fabric. It stretches more crosswise than lengthwise. It is possible to add or take out stitches to make the fabric narrower or wider. "Flat" knitting like this on two needles produces a piece of fabric which must then be joined together with other pieces to make a garment. Socks or other tubular garments can be knitted in one piece by using four or more needles and knitting round and round in a circle. There are also circular needles which are like a wire with a needle point at each end. Garments can be shaped in the same way as in flat knitting.

Machine Knitting

In a knitting machine there is one needle for each loop of yarn. Each needle ends in a hook which pulls the yarn through the preceding loop. A circular machine which knits the fabric in a tube is thought to have been invented in France in 1789. Needles may be left out or added to shape the garment. Hosiery or sweaters knitted in this way are called "fully fashioned".

Another type of machine, first used in 1775, holds a separate yarn for each needle and is called a "warp knitting" machine. The yarns cross each other and loop together diagonally across the fabric. It is really a form of crochet. Garments are always knitted flat and cannot be shaped by machine. The fabric is strong and practically runproof, but does not stretch as much as weft-knit fabric. Silk, and nylon and other man-made fibres, can be used in warp knitting, and lacy designs can be made. This fabric is used for dresses, underwear, and gloves.

Machines are available for home knitters, and with them garments can be made much more quickly than by hand. However, hand knitting is still popular as a hobby. A much greater variety of yarns can be used than with machines and more complicated designs can be produced.

History of Knitting

Knitting has probably been practised as long as sheep have been kept, because wool is the ideal fabric for knitting. Knitted socks have been found in Egyptian tombs dating from the 4th century BC. The British Isles have long been famous for their knitwear and many of the names for knitted garments and their patterns originate from Britain. The word "jersey", meaning a sweater, comes from the island of that name in the Channel Islands. Men from Jersey emigrated to Newfoundland in about 1600 to work in the shipbuilding industry and they took their knitted garments with them. It was fishermen who traditionally knitted garments, perhaps because they had to make their nets in a similar way. Guernsey, another of the Channel Islands, gave its name to a sweater traditionally worn by fishermen. It is usually made of thick, dark blue wool, and is square-shaped, rather like a smock. Guernseys were knitted all round the British coast, each fishing port having its own patterns.

Shetland wool has been used for knitting for many hundreds of years. It is a specially soft, fine wool, and is used for knitting both patterned jerseys and beautiful lacy shawls, some

Courtesy, The Sutcliffe Gallery

A fisherman in Whitby, Yorkshire, wearing a guernsey patterned with cable stitch and rows of garter stitch.

of which are so fine that they can be passed through a wedding ring. Fair Isle is one of the Shetland Islands and has given its name to a particular type of patterned jersey. It is thought that the people of Fair Isle learned to knit these patterns from Spanish sailors who were shipwrecked after the Spanish Armada in 1588 for similar patterns have been used in Spain. They are not so closely related to the Scandinavian patterns which some people believe were brought to the island by the Norsemen.

The Aran islands (off the west coast of Ireland) have also given their name to knitted garments. They are made in cream-coloured, thick wool and are richly patterned with diamond shapes, cables, ridges, and sometimes bobbles. Each pattern has a name, such as "Tree of Life", "Marriage Lines", "Fern Stitch" and "Trinity Stitch".

In 15th-century England knitting was an important home industry. The first machine was invented in 1589 by William Lee, an English clergyman. He presented a pair of silk stockings to Queen Elizabeth I, but she refused to grant him a patent since she was afraid of putting hand knitters out of work. Lee then presented his machines to King Henry IV of France and they soon became widely used. By 1657 the machines were in use in England, too. In 1816 Marc Brunel, an English inventor, built the first circular knitting machine.

J. R. Karrach

Crochet began as an imitation of lace, but may be used to make useful articles such as table mats.

History of Crochet

The word crochet comes from the French word *croche* meaning a hook. It seems to have developed as an imitation of lace and was used by nuns for decorating plain fabric. From the 16th century onwards they taught it to girls in much the same way as they taught music or drawing, and so, unlike knitting, it has always been a purely feminine pastime. Irish crochet was well known by 1743, and after the potato famine of 1846–7 many Irish people emigrated to the United States and took the art with them.

KNOT (bird) see WADING BIRDS.

KNOTS are used for fastening or joining ropes, cords, and string. Most of the words we use for ropes and knots came from sailors. A rope is considered to be in three parts—the fixed part, the intermediate part, and the end. Sometimes, of course, there may not be a fixed part in which case there are two ends. The fixed part is called the *standing part*. The portion of the rope between the end and the standing part (also any slack part of the rope particularly in the form of a loop) is called the *bight*, while the working part of the rope to the end is called the *running end*. A *bend* is a knot for joining together two ropes. A *hitch* is used for fastening a rope to a spar, a post, or a ring.

To prevent the ends of a rope from fraying or unlaying (untwisting), the end is bound with twine by putting on a *whipping* of which there are several versions, the simplest being the *common whipping*. To prevent the end of a rope from running through a hole or out of a pulley-block, either an *overhand knot* (sometimes called a *thumb knot*) or a *figure-of-eight* is tied in it.

For tying together the two ends of the same cord or string—as when tying up a parcel—a *reef knot* is used. This is made by tying two overhand knots one after the other. The right-hand end is first crossed over the left-hand end and next the left-hand end is crossed over the right-hand end. If made wrongly, the result is a "granny knot" which will either slip or jam. A *sheet bend* is the knot most often used at sea for tying two ropes, or "sheets", together. If the two ropes differ in thickness, a *double sheet bend* (in which an extra turn is taken round the knot) should be used. This knot is also used for fastening a rope to an eye in which case it is known as a *becket hitch*. For tying slippery cordage, nylon cord or gut used for fishing, a *fisherman's knot* is used.

It is often necessary to be able to make a fixed loop in the end of a rope and for this a *bowline* should be used. One way of making it is to form a loop in the standing part and bring the running end up through the loop, round the back of the standing part and down through the loop again. To make a *noose*, or an eye that will tighten when pulled, use a *running bowline*. It should never be put round a person's body, because his weight on the rope will tighten the noose and may injure him. To lower a person from a height a *bowline-on-a-bight* can be used. The person sits in one loop with the other under his arms.

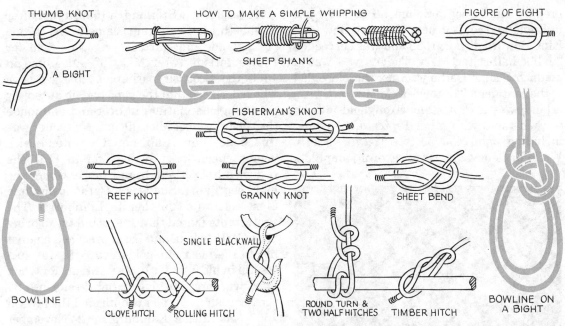

THUMB KNOT — HOW TO MAKE A SIMPLE WHIPPING — SHEEP SHANK — FIGURE OF EIGHT — A BIGHT — FISHERMAN'S KNOT — REEF KNOT — GRANNY KNOT — SHEET BEND — BOWLINE — SINGLE BLACKWALL — CLOVE HITCH — ROLLING HITCH — ROUND TURN & TWO HALF HITCHES — TIMBER HITCH — BOWLINE ON A BIGHT

To fasten any part of a rope other than the end to a pole or a railing, a *clove hitch* should be used. This will slide along a pole if pulled sideways, but the *rolling hitch* will not. Note that the clove hitch can be made in the bight of the rope without using the ends by forming two loops in it. The *round turn and two half hitches* is used for securing a rope to a pole or ring; useful for making fast a boat by its painter, or securing rope. The *timber hitch* for lifting or hauling logs or poles, can also be used for lifting bales or bundles. For shortening a rope whose ends are already fastened or out of reach, the *sheepshank* is used. It is also useful for strengthening a weak section of rope.

KNOX, John (1514–72). John Knox was a leader of the Protestant Reformation in Scotland. By the end of Knox's life many people were talking about him because of the great religious changes he had brought about in Scotland, but very little is known of his early life. He was the son of William Knox, who is thought to have been a farmer living at or near Haddington in East Lothian, Scotland. As a young man Knox attended either the University of Glasgow or that of St. Andrews, perhaps even both.

During his youth a religious movement known as the Reformation was taking place in several countries of western Europe. It was a revolt, or protest, against the Roman Catholic Church, and because of this its supporters were called Protestants. (See REFORMATION.) Although Knox had been brought up as a Roman Catholic and possibly entered the priesthood, it is clear that by 1546 he had become a Protestant.

Scotland, like other countries where the Reformation was going on, was divided over questions of religion. It had close links with France which strengthened the old Catholic faith, but in spite of this many people supported Knox's demands that the authority of the pope should no longer be recognized and that some of the old beliefs and ceremonies should be either changed or abolished.

Several times in his life Knox had to seek refuge in Protestant strongholds, sometimes on the continent of Europe. Soon after he had started preaching Protestantism he was captured by the French, who forced him to serve as a galley slave for nearly two years. It appears that the young Protestant king of England, Edward VI, asked the French to release Knox and invited him to England. In 1551 Knox became one of Edward's chaplains and therefore helped Archbishop Cranmer to prepare a new Book of Common Prayer for use in England (see CRANMER, THOMAS). However, King Edward died in 1553 and was succeeded by his half-sister Mary Tudor, who was a staunch Roman Catholic. Knox therefore fled to the continent. The town of Geneva, in Switzerland, was a Protestant stronghold and he worked there with other Protestant leaders, including John Calvin (see CALVIN, JOHN). While in Geneva he wrote several pamphlets

BBC Hulton Picture Library

John Knox arguing with Mary, Queen of Scots. Knox tried without success to convert the young queen to Protestantism.

on Scottish affairs, including one called "The First Blast of the Trumpet against the Monstrous Regiment of Women". In this title the word "regiment" means "rule of", and the pamphlet was written against Mary of Guise who was then ruling Scotland for her young daughter Mary, Queen of Scots (see MARY, QUEEN OF SCOTS). Knox did not approve of government by women, for he believed it was against God's law, and he did not hesitate to say so. Apart from his dislike of women in government he also disliked Mary and her family because they were Catholics and were trying to keep Scotland a Catholic country.

He returned to Scotland in 1559, a year after Elizabeth I (a Protestant) came to the throne of England, and started a vigorous fight for Protestantism. After Mary of Guise died in 1560 the Scottish parliament passed laws which declared that the pope had no authority over religious matters in Scotland and made the celebration of Mass illegal. No sooner was this done than Knox had to contend with young Queen Mary herself, for in 1561 she returned to Scotland from France, where she had been living. She was a Catholic and had Mass celebrated for her in Edinburgh. The Protestants feared that she would try to bring back Catholicism, and Knox preached against her in the most outspoken way. He was successful in his fight for Protestantism, for when Mary was forced to give up her throne in 1567 the Scottish parliament confirmed the laws of 1560. Knox died in Edinburgh on 24 November 1572.

KOALA. The koala (*Phascolarctos cinereus*) looks like a live teddy bear. But it is really a marsupial; that is, the female has a pouch in which to carry her young. (See MARSUPIAL.) The koala is a native of Australia and is an attractive-looking animal, with soft woolly fur (brownish above and yellow below) and a large black nose. With its powerful limbs and stout, sharp claws it can climb up trees with smooth bark, for it is arboreal, or tree-living. Often the koala goes up a tree trunk in a series of jumps, with its legs held straight down and its arms forward.

When full grown the koala is about 60 centimetres (24 inches) long. It has an unmistakable voice, which has been compared to the noise made by a saw cutting a thin board. Only one young koala is born at a time, every other year, and is carried in its mother's pouch and then rides on its mother's back until it is about one year old.

The koala feeds only on the leaves of certain species of eucalyptus tree, such as the forest red gum, grey gum, and manna gum. It therefore has to move from place to place, according to the season, in search of the right leaves.

NHPA/Michael Morcombe

The koala only eats leaves of a few eucalyptus trees and has a long digestive system to deal with them.

An adult koala eats about 1.3 kilograms (3 pounds) of leaves a day, and has a very long digestive system. Its liver is able to break down the poisonous oils in the leaves into harmless substances.

For a time large numbers of koalas were killed for their fur and the animal became rare. After 1936, however, laws were made forbidding people to kill koalas, and special reserves were made for them to live in, so that they should no longer be in danger of dying out. Although the koala population is now flourishing, these slow-moving animals are still vulnerable to the sudden fires that sweep through the dry forest areas in which they live.

KOMODO DRAGON. This reptile is not really a dragon, but a very large member of the family of lizards called monitors. For many years local people living near the small island of Komodo in what is now Indonesia and was then the Dutch East Indies told stories about the "dragons" of that island, and in 1912 a naturalist sent collectors to investigate. They brought back reports of giant lizards as long as 7 metres (23 feet), and returned with five, the largest of which was just under 3 metres (9.8 feet) in length. Evidently the early reports were exaggerated, and it is believed that Komodo dragons are seldom more than 3.5 metres (11.5 feet) in length.

These giant lizards were called *Varanus komodoensis*, after the name of their island home. The Dutch government in the islands protected the lizards to prevent them from dying out, but allowed a small number to be collected for museums and zoos. These were easily caught in box traps that had been baited with wild pig.

The Komodo dragon is the largest lizard. It can grow up to 3.5 metres (11.5 feet) long.

Like all monitor lizards, komodo dragons are entirely carnivorous, or flesh-eating, and eat any mammals or birds which they are able to catch, up to the size of deer and bush pigs. Animals too bulky to be swallowed whole are torn to pieces with the lizards' large and powerful claws. During the night they are said to lie in caves which they dig for themselves under the roots of trees, coming out by day to bask in the sun and hunt for their food.

KOOKABURRA see KINGFISHER.

KORAN. The Koran (which is also spelled Qur'an) is the holy book of Muslims, whose religion is explained in the article ISLAM. The word "Koran" comes from an Arabic word which means "recitation". Muslims believe that the Koran was recited to Muhammad, the great prophet of Islam, by the archangel Gabriel, who read from the original book which is in heaven. The recitation started while Muhammad was at Mecca (in present day Saudi Arabia), in AD 610 and continued from time to time until he died at Medina in 632. (See MUHAMMAD.)

The Koran is about the same length as the New Testament of the Bible, and consists of 114 chapters, called *suras*, which are written in verses. Each *sura* except the ninth is headed by the words "In the name of Allah, the Merciful, the Compassionate". ("Allah" is the Muslim name for God.) The first *sura* is a prayer to Allah; all the rest, apart from a few small sections, are written in what Muslims believe to be the direct words of Allah.

The Koran occupies a very important place in the life of a Muslim, for it contains rules on how to behave in ordinary worldly affairs as well as religious rules. One section contains the laws of marriage and divorce, and says how possessions are to be divided when the owner dies. Other sections set out the duties of parents to their children, of masters to their servants, and of the rich to the poor. Islamic law and punishment is largely based on the writings of the Koran. The five main *spiritual* duties which the Koran lays down are explained in the article ISLAM.

Many of the stories in the Koran are like those of the Bible, because some of the Jewish and Christian prophets are also prophets of Islam.

KOREA, NORTH. The independent republic of North Korea is located on the northern part of the Korean peninsula, in northeast Asia. It is officially called the Democratic People's Republic of Korea.

North Korea is separated from South Korea at the 38th parallel of latitude. It is about 716 kilometres (445 miles) long and 360 kilometres (225 miles) wide. It is separated from China and the USSR to the north by the Yalu and Tuman rivers. The Yellow

Sea lies to the south, and the Korean Bay is to the southwest. The Sea of Japan lies to the east.

Mountains cover more than 80 per cent of North Korea. The highest peak is an old volcano in the far north, Mount Paek-tu, which is 2,744 metres (9,003 feet). The climate, vegetation, and wildlife are the same as in South Korea, and are described in the following article, KOREA, SOUTH. North Korea has coal, magnesite, iron ore, and other valuable minerals including lead, zinc, copper, and tungsten. The Yalu and Tuman rivers provide hydroelectric power.

Several religious faiths and philosophies especially Buddhism and Confucianism, are traditionally strong in North Korea, and Christianity was brought by missionaries between the 17th and 19th centuries. Since 1945, however, with the introduction of a Communist form of government, North Korea has officially been an atheist country.

The Korean alphabet, Hangul, is now the only form of writing used in North Korea. It has replaced the traditional alphabet of most Korean literature, which has many Chinese characters.

Charles Paynter/Camera Press

North Korean children march past a statue of the president of their country, Kim Il-Sung.

Economy

North Korea has a centrally planned economy. The government decides what people will be paid. Farming is organized on the commune system. Food is rationed, and there are sometimes shortages of food and consumer goods. Generally the standard of living is lower than it is in South Korea. There is a great shortage of workers. Although North Korea is larger than South Korea, it has fewer people.

Rice is the major crop. Maize and wheat, vegetables and fruit are also grown. People also rear poultry and pigs.

Heavy industry is the backbone of the present-day economy. Farm and industrial machinery, steel, chemicals, and fertilizer, are produced. The country's many valuable mineral deposits are mined on a large scale. Coal, iron ore, and magnesite are the most important.

FACTS ABOUT NORTH KOREA

AREA: 122,370 square kilometres (47,250 square miles).
POPULATION: 21,390,000 (1987).
GOVERNMENT: Republic.
CAPITAL: Pyongyang.
GEOGRAPHICAL FEATURES: The northern part of a large peninsula notable for its many mountains.
LEADING INDUSTRIES: Cement, steel, pig iron, fertilizers, machine tools, tractors, textiles.
IMPORTANT TOWNS: Pyongyang, Hamhung-Hungnam, Chongjin, Kaesong, Wonsan.
EDUCATION: Children must attend school between the ages of 7 and 16.

The capital of North Korea is Pyongyang, near the northwest coast. It has a population of about 1,283,000 (1981 estimate). Most of the country's trade is with the USSR, China, Japan, Saudi Arabia, and India.

Government

North Korea is a socialist republic, which is controlled by the Communist ideals of the Korean Workers Party. The government is led by the president, who has great personal power.

Since 1948 North Korea has been led by Marshal Kim Il-Sung, whose son, Kim Chong Il, is being trained to take his place. The Communist government has been trying to transform what was an agricultural country into a modern, self-sufficient industrial nation.

The history of all the Korean peninsula, including the events of the Korean war, is given in the article KOREA, SOUTH.

A map of North and South Korea showing their positions relative to China, Japan, and the USSR.

KOREA, SOUTH. The independent republic of South Korea is located on the southern part of the Korean peninsula, in northeast Asia. For most of its history, the whole Korean peninsula was one country, and was once called Choson. But at the end of World War II, in 1945, the country was split in two. The two separate countries of North and South Korea were formed in 1948. In the Korean War which followed, neither country was able to gain control of the other, and the division of the peninsula continued.

South Korea is separated from North Korea at the 38th parallel of latitude. It is about 965 kilometres (600 miles) long and 216 kilometres (135 miles) wide. To the east is the Sea of Japan; to the west, the Yellow Sea. South Korea includes many small, off-shore islands, and is separated from Japan by a 193-kilometre (120-mile) stretch of water called the Korea Strait.

Land and Resources

Some of the earliest Western travellers to the Korean Peninsula likened its landscape to "a sea in a heavy gale", for most of it is rugged mountain country. About 85 per cent of South

Korea is mountainous. Only about a fifth of the land is suitable for farming, chiefly along the coasts and in the river valleys. Throughout Korea the summers are hot and rainy and the winters are cold, except in the southern part. The autumn season is long, with fair, mild weather often extending far into November.

Much of the forest that once covered Korea has been destroyed by cutting and burning, though in recent years both North and South Korea have begun to replant the forests. Pine, oak, and fir are the most common kinds of trees found on the peninsula. Wild animals native to Korea include tigers, snow leopards, bears, wolves, and wild boars. But the spread of industry has destroyed much of their habitat and the larger animals are now rare and found only in very remote areas.

Most of the many mineral deposits of the peninsula are located in North Korea.

Culture

The Koreans are a Mongoloid people, like the Chinese and the Japanese. Their language is more like Japanese than Chinese, but China has had a strong cultural influence on Korea. Much of Korea's traditional literature is written in Chinese. Many Chinese characters are still used together with the native Korean alphabet, known as Hangul. This alphabet was devised in the 15th century by a committee of scholars at the suggestion of King Sejong, Korea's greatest ruler. It is the only alphabet in use today to have been deliberately made up rather than developing gradually. In South Korea, the Hangul alphabet is gradually replacing Chinese characters.

Most South Koreans are either Buddhists or Confucians, although almost 30 per cent are Christians.

The Economy

In South Korea most farmers own their own land. A law strictly limits the amount of land that any one person may own. The chief crop is rice, the country's main food. Barley is planted on many of the rice fields after the autumn rice harvest, and reaped in the spring. Wheat and cotton are also grown, and silk-

Keystone

A Korean family hang up a supply of noodles (a type of pasta) to dry.

worms are reared to supply the silk spinning and weaving industry (see SILK). Cattle, pigs, and poultry are raised.

South Korean industries produce textiles, clothing, electrical and electronic goods, iron and steel products, and machinery. Its modern shipbuilding industry supplies ships and offshore oil equipment to many parts of the world.

The chief towns are connected by road and rail. Seoul, the capital and largest city, has spread far beyond its ancient walls with their eight gateways and now has a population of about 9,204,300 (1983 estimate). Its port is Inchon, about 48 kilometres (30 miles) to the west on the Yellow Sea. The largest and most important seaport, however, is Pusan on the southeast coast.

South Korea has made great efforts to outdo its rival, North Korea. In addition to its traditional textiles, South Korea now sells other products to many countries. Industry and transport have been modernized and welfare services improved.

History

The Korean peninsula has for centuries been a target of invasion for countries trying to control north China and Manchuria. These invaders have included the Chinese themselves, the Mongols and, in more recent times, the Japanese. The Chinese, whose power lasted longest, were generally content to rule in name only and let the Koreans govern themselves, though the Chinese language, religion, and customs took root in Korea. After the establishment of the Manchu (Ching) dynasty in the 17th century, the Chinese interfered little in Korean affairs.

After treaties had been signed with the Western powers towards the end of the 19th century, Christian missionaries began coming to Korea. Many of them were Americans, and so began a link with the United States.

However, at about the same time, Japan was becoming a modern country with an ambition to establish an Asian empire. Japan won wars against China (1894) and Russia (1905). As a result, Japan gained control of Korea which in 1910 became part of the Japanese Empire.

Courtesy, Consulate General of Korea, Chicago

Seoul is the capital of South Korea. Namsan Hill overlooks the modern, bustling business centre.

The Japanese built railways, harbours, roads, and factories on the Korean peninsula. But they did this chiefly in order to turn Korea into a source of supply for rice and metals, and to make it an advance base for attacking China. The Koreans were not allowed to teach their own language in schools and were forced to adopt Japanese personal names.

The Koreans rebelled in 1919 through nationwide peaceful demonstrations. The Japanese put down the protests with ferocity, killing and injuring thousands of people and imprisoning thousands more.

Japan lost its overseas conquests (including Korea) in 1945 after World War II. Russian and American troops entered Korea to receive the surrender of the Japanese troops stationed there. For convenience in doing this, the country was divided into two by a line along the 38th parallel of North latitude. The plan was that the United States and the USSR should, after the departure of the Japanese, consult with the Koreans to set up an independent Korean government.

However, the Russians and the Americans could not agree. The United Nations called for elections in 1948 to choose representatives from all parts of Korea to decide on the form of government. But United Nations observers were not even allowed to enter the northern part of the country, so the government that was elected represented the southern half of Korea only. Meanwhile, the Russians set up a Communist state north of the 38th parallel and trained a North Korean army.

The Korean War

In June 1950, the North Korean army suddenly invaded South Korea. United States troops were rushed to help the South Koreans and were joined soon after by troops from other countries under United Nations (UN) command. The UN blamed the North Koreans for starting the war. The North Koreans were joined by Chinese troops and got most of their arms from the USSR.

The war raged across the peninsula for three years, causing the deaths of about 5 million people and devastating Korea's cities and countryside. Finally, in 1953, a truce was signed. This is still in force, but as no peace treaty was signed, the two sides are technically still at war.

Suspicion and bad feeling between North and South Korea prevented any improvement in relations between them for years. Both countries have made economic progress and both have strict forms of government. In the 1970s and 1980s talks were held on various occasions to try to reach agreement on unifying the country, but these failed.

Government

The government of South Korea is a constitutional republic led by a president who has strong powers. It has one representative body, the National Assembly.

FACTS ABOUT SOUTH KOREA

AREA: 99,091 square kilometres (38,259 square miles).
POPULATION: 42,148,000 (1987).
GOVERNMENT: Republic.
CAPITAL: Seoul.
GEOGRAPHICAL FEATURES: The southern part of a large peninsula with many mountains, sloping down to a southern and western coast of coastal plain, river estuaries, and many small islands.
MAIN EXPORTS: Chemicals, textiles, footwear, food products, machinery.
IMPORTANT TOWNS: Seoul, Pusan, Taegu, Inchon, Kwangju.
EDUCATION: Children must attend school between the ages of 6 and 13.

KRAIT. Asked which are the most poisonous and dangerous snakes in the world, many people would list cobras and mambas. Few people would mention their smaller, less aggressive cousins, which are just as poisonous and kill dozens of people each year. These snakes are the kraits.

There are about 12 species of kraits (*Bungarus*). With their bigger relatives they belong to the group Elapidae or front-fanged snakes. Kraits live in southern Asia, from India across to Indonesia. They are generally colourful reptiles, with light and dark bands of shiny scales along their bodies. The banded krait (*Bungarus fasciatus*) has bright yellow and dark

greeny-brown bands, and grows to just over 1 metre (3.3 feet). This is average for kraits—the longest barely reach 2 metres (6.6 feet). The red-headed krait (*Bungarus flaviceps*), as its name suggests, has a bright red head and tail, with an almost black body.

NHPA

A poisonous banded krait from Indo-China.

In their body build, breeding habits and hunting behaviour, kraits are much like the cobras and mambas (see COBRA; MAMBA). They hunt mainly other snakes, some of which are also poisonous. Like most snakes, kraits swim well and some species will eat fish. In fact one genus of kraits (*Laticauda*) has taken to life in the ocean. Most sea snakes do not lay eggs, but give birth to fully-formed baby snakes; the five species of sea krait still lay eggs, usually in a cave on the shore.

Although kraits are common, they are not very aggressive. They hunt at night and lie up during the day in a hole somewhere, so people do not often come across them. When disturbed, they are sluggish and prefer to slither away or lie quietly, perhaps flicking their bodies. But if they do strike, they can easily kill with a potent venom injected through long fangs. A person bitten by a krait has only a 50-50 chance of living—even if the correct antiserum (medicine) is available.

KRILL. In the vast oceans of the southern hemisphere, and especially in the cold waters around Antarctica, live krill, swarms of shrimp-like creatures that filter-feed on tiny plants and animals. Krill are among the most numerous animals on Earth, and they are the food of the biggest animals on Earth, the great whales.

The world "krill" comes from the Norwegian sailor's term *kril*, meaning a young fish. Krill are not fish but crustaceans of the group Euphausiacea, related to shrimps and prawns (see CRUSTACEAN). There are about 90 species, which live in all the oceans. The common krill (*Euphausia superba*) of the southern hemisphere is around 5 centimetres (2 inches) long. It feeds by filtering tiny floating plants and animals from the sea water with its hairy legs. It has three pairs of long feelers, a hard casing on the front of its body, and a segmented cover on the rear part, as does a shrimp. Larger species reach 15 centimetres (6 inches) in length. The northern krill (*Meganyctiphanes norvegica*) abounds in oceans around the Arctic.

An Abundance of Krill

Not just swarms but super-swarms of krill live in the Southern Ocean. Such swarms can be tens of kilometres (several miles) long, with over 50,000 krill in one cubic metre of water. The total numbers of krill are almost countless. In a good summer the total weight of common krill in the seas might reach 650 million tonnes (715 million US tons)—just for this one species.

These super-abundant crustaceans are strained from sea water by several species of baleen (whalebone) whales (see WHALE). One blue whale can eat 4 tonnes of krill in a day. Krill are also the main food of penguins and other sea birds such as albatrosses, as well as of some seals and of over 30 species of large fish. So krill are a central link in the *food web* of the oceans. The Sun's energy is captured by microscopic floating plants, which are eaten by tiny floating animals—and both are eaten by krill, which in turn provide food for many larger creatures (see FOOD WEB.)

Krill can swim, but they tend to drift with the ocean currents. The biggest swarms live near the water's surface, although some species have been captured at depths of 2,000 metres (6,500 feet). Many species glow in the dark. They have a row of tiny light organs at the bases of their feelers and two of the pairs of front legs, and along the body. Swarms of krill make an amazing sight. Seen from the air, during the day, they turn the sea dusty red. This is because the blood shows through their almost-transparent bodies. At night the whole ocean glitters with waves of eerie blue-green light. This glow could help the krill to

Above: C. J. Gilbert; right: I. Everson (BAS)

Above: Krill are small crustaceans eaten by many fish, seabirds, and marine mammals of Antarctic waters. **Right:** Biologists count krill which have been caught on the mesh of a plankton counter.

collect in swarms during the breeding season, around November and December. One female krill can cast into the water more than 10,000 eggs, and these grow to adults in one or two years.

Some people have said that krill could solve the world's food problems. At present, trawlers catch only 1 per cent of the krill available, mainly to be ground up as fertilizer or used as animal feed. But if these animals are caught in huge numbers, it would certainly have a great effect on the creatures that rely on them for food. The great whales, for example, are already very rare, and competing for their food supply could reduce their numbers even further.

KRUGER, Paul (1825–1904).

Paul Kruger, known to his people as Oom Paul (Uncle Paul), was a great leader of the Boers, the descendants of the Dutch settlers in South Africa. He was born in the Gradock district of the British Cape Colony, and originally named Stephanus Johannes Paulus Kruger. As a boy of ten he went with his parents on the Great Trek from Cape Colony (see GREAT TREK) and the family was among the first to settle in the Transvaal.

Kruger organized resistance to the British following their annexation of the republic of Transvaal. He persuaded the British to restore independence and in 1883 he became president of the Transvaal Republic. When in 1886 gold was found in the Transvaal at Johannesburg, thousands of British and other *Uitlanders* (foreigners) flocked there. Kruger would not allow them to vote for fear they would spoil the character of the Boers' republic. This refusal led to the Jameson Raid and later to the Boer War (see BOER WAR). During the Boer War, Kruger visited Europe vainly seeking the help of other nations. He died in 1904 in Switzerland, but his body was returned to South Africa for burial in Pretoria.

KUALA LUMPUR

is the capital of Malaysia, its largest city, and the centre of the Federal Territory of Kuala Lumpur, which is under the direct control of the central government. It lies on the Kelang (formerly Klang) River, about 40 kilometres (25 miles) inland from the swampy coast of the Strait of Malacca. The city is the centre of an important rubber- and tin-producing area and has become a transport hub. Its name means Muddy Confluence.

The city was founded in 1857 by Chinese tin miners. It remained a small, quiet town until it was named capital of the Federated Malay States in 1895. Since World War II the population has more than doubled. Kuala Lumpur became capital of newly independent Malaya in 1957 and of Malaysia in 1963.

The growing city has become a blend of old and new. Gleaming new government buildings tower above the Chinese shops of the congested old city centre. Modern banks, hotels, office and apartment buildings, and sports facilities contrast sharply with old Moorish-style architecture. Kuala Lumpur is the site of the University of Malaysia, and of several important rubber and medical research centres. Its international airport has one of the longest runways in southeast Asia. Kuala Lumpur is linked to its seaport, Port Kelang, by road and rail.

More than half of the city's residents are Chinese, and about a quarter are Malays. The population of Kuala Lumpur is 958,851 (1982).

KUBLAI KHAN

(1215–94) was the grandson of Genghis Khan and in 1259 himself became the chief khan (ruler) of the Mongols. (See GENGHIS KHAN; MONGOLS.) He thus inherited an enormous empire which stretched from China to Europe. The Mongols at that time had conquered only northern China, but Kublai Khan conquered the south as well and became the emperor of China, starting the Yuan dynasty of emperors. (A dynasty is a line of rulers belonging to the same family.) He had a fine new capital built, parts of which still survive in the modern city of Peking.

As well as being a mighty and splendid ruler, Kublai Khan was an intelligent and tolerant man, and he was popular among the Chinese even though he was their conqueror. He did not try to make them change their customs or religion and was himself converted to Buddhism (see BUDDHA AND BUDDHISM). He made Buddhism the state religion of his empire and set up a priest as king in Tibet. (This priest-king was the forerunner of the line of Dalai Lamas.)

A fascinating account of the magnificent court of Kublai Khan, and of China as it was in his day was given by Marco Polo, a Venetian who served as one of Kublai's officials for many years (see POLO, MARCO).

KURDS. The Kurds are a tribal people of western Asia who live mostly in a mountainous region surrounding the upper reaches of the Tigris River. This area is traditionally called *Kurdistan*, "Land of the Kurds", but has never been an independent state. It occupies neighbouring parts of eastern Turkey, northern Syria and Iraq, and northwestern Iran. There are also Kurds living in Armenia and in the northeast Iranian province of Khorasan. Estimates of the number of Kurds vary widely, from about 12 million to 28 million.

The Kurds are a rugged mountain people who until the 20th century followed a nomadic way of life, keeping sheep and goats, and moving from place to place throughout the highlands and plains of Iraq, Iran, and Turkey. During the 20th century, many Kurds adopted a modern city lifestyle. However, outside the main towns of Kurdistan – Diyarbakir, Van, and Bitlis in Turkey; Mosul and Kirkuk in Iraq; and Kermanshah and Hamadan in Iran – the Kurds continue to live in small villages of tents or simple houses, where tribal chiefs, or sheikhs, exercise firm rule over the communities.

The ancient Sumerians, who lived in the area before about 2000 BC, wrote of a tribal people called the *Kutie*, who may have been the ancestors of the Kurds. Kurdish tribes may also be descended from the Medes, who ruled Persia (ancient Iran) from the 8th to the 6th centuries BC. The Greek general Xenophon, who led a military expedition through Kurdistan in the early 4th century BC, described a warlike people of the region called the *Kardouchoi*, who could also have been the ancestors of the Kurds.

In the 7th century AD Arabs conquered Kurdistan and converted the Kurds to Islam. Today most Kurds are Sunni Muslims, following one of the two main sects, or branches, of the Islamic faith (see ISLAM). The Kurdish language shares its origins with Persian, Armenian, and Greek. Except for a number of borrowed words and phrases, Kurdish has almost no links with Arabic or Turkish.

In the 11th century, the Turks invaded Kurdistan and the region came under Mongol rule in the 13th century. In the 12th century the Kurdish leader Saladin united the Muslim lands of Syria, Palestine, and Egypt against the Christian armies of the Third Crusade (see CRUSADE).

From the 15th century until the end of World War I, in 1918, the Kurdish lands were under Turkish rule and part of the Ottoman Empire. In the 19th century, a few educated, city-dwelling Kurds began to press for an independent Kurdish state. Following World War I, in which the Ottoman Turks were defeated by Allied forces, this hope almost came about. In 1920, the victorious Allies and Turkish representatives drew up the Treaty of Sèvres, in France. The treaty said that a self-governing Kurdish state, called Kurdistan, should be set up. But the Turks refused to agree to the treaty and it was never put into practice. The Treaty of Lausanne, which in 1923 replaced the Treaty of Sèvres, left out any mention of Kurdistan.

During the 20th century, the Kurds suffered persecution and the suppression of their language and culture. In Turkey their language and culture has been outlawed for decades.

In 1946, the Kurds set up in Iran an independent state called the "Mahabad Republic". But the Iranian authorities sent troops to destroy the fledgling state. Many Kurds were executed, and thousands more fled to Iraq.

In the early 1970s, the Shah of Iran encouraged the Kurds to fight against his rival, the Iraqi leader Saddam Hussein. But when the Shah and Saddam Hussein came to a political agreement, Iran's support for the Kurds disappeared. In 1979 a Kurdish uprising in Iran was put down by the Islamic revolutionary forces of Ayatollah Khomeini.

In Iraq, Kurdish civilians in the town of Kirkuk were massacred by Iraqi soldiers in 1963. In 1970 the Iraqi government promised the Kurds self-government, but the promises came to nothing. The Kurds also suffered during the 1980s, when a great many Kurdish villages were destroyed by the Iraqi government, and during Iraq's war with Iran (1980–88), when the Kurds were seen to be sympathizing with the Iranians. In the aftermath of the 1991 Gulf War, a Kurdish revolt was put down by Iraqi soldiers and many Kurds fled to the mountains to escape persecution.

KUWAIT. Kuwait lies between Saudi Arabia and Iraq at the head of the Persian Gulf. It covers about 18,000 square kilometres (about 7,000 square miles) of nearly flat desert. Although some Bedouin tribesmen still rear camels, sheep, and goats, hardly any of the land is suitable for agriculture. There is practically no rain, it is extremely hot, and food and drinking water have to be imported. The people are Muslims and speak Arabic.

Kuwait has large resources of oil and natural gas, and the country's industrial development has been centred around the extraction and refining of crude petroleum. Almost all of Kuwait's national income comes from the export of oil products.

Other industries include natural gas, flour milling, building, and fishing for prawns. Kuwait depends heavily on immigrant workers and recent developments have been towards industries needing less labour.

The capital is Kuwait City. There is an international airport and a modern harbour. Kuwait has a population of over 2,000,000.

There was an ancient civilization in Kuwait about 4,000 years ago and evidence has been found suggesting that Greek colonists arrived there in about 323 BC.

At the beginning of the 18th century nomadic people from the Arabian desert began to arrive. They were ruled in turn by the Caliphs of Baghdad, the Mongols, and the Ottoman Turks (see ARABIA). In 1899 the ruler of Kuwait agreed to let Great Britain

protect his country. This lasted until 1971 when British forces left the Persian Gulf.

In 1936 drilling for oil began. With the money from the large quantities of oil found, Kuwait grew into a modern state with one of the highest standards of living in the world. The oil revenues were used to develop welfare, schools, and hospitals. Education, including books and uniforms, and medical services are free in Kuwait.

Kuwait became independent in 1961. Its wealth has given it an important place in Middle East affairs. Kuwait supported the Arab cause against Israel. Many immigrants, especially from Palestine, have settled in the country. In August 1990 Iraq invaded Kuwait, declaring it to be part of Iraq. In response, the United Nations banned trade with Iraq and demanded that Iraq withdraw from Kuwait. A large UN force drawn from 28 countries, under United States leadership, was assembled. The Iraqi army did not withdraw and on 16 January war began. Iraq was driven out of Kuwait six weeks later. Great damage was done to Kuwait during its occupation and liberation, particularly to its 1,300 oil wells, more than half of which were set on fire and were still burning months later. The cost of reconstructing Kuwait was estimated at between 25 and 50 billion US dollars.

FACTS ABOUT KUWAIT

AREA: 17,812 square kilometres (6,880 square miles).
POPULATION: 2,142,600 (1990).
GOVERNMENT: Constitutional monarchy (emirate).
CAPITAL: Kuwait City, 44,224.
GEOGRAPHY: Largely desert, with a few fertile patches and oases. The highest point is 290 m (951 ft).
CITIES: as Salimiyah, 153,220; Hawalli, 145,215; al-Jahra, 111,165.
EXPORTS: Crude petroleum and petroleum products.
EDUCATION: Children must go to school between the ages of 6 and 14.

KYOTO, one of the chief cities of Japan, is a centre of ancient Japanese culture. It is located in western Honshu, 47 kilometres (29 miles) inland from Osaka. For almost 11 centuries, Kyoto was the imperial capital of Japan.

JO Graphic Room

Katsura Imperial Villa in Kyoto, built in the 17th century. The city has many fine buildings.

Kyoto differs from most other large Japanese cities, which are heavily industrial. As Japan's cultural and religious centre, Kyoto has retained traditional handicraft industries that make use of ancient arts and crafts. Skilled artisans produce fine lacquerware, porcelain ware, bronzes, dolls, and silk textiles. Weaving and dyeing have long been important. Notable heavier industries include copper rolling, food processing, and the manufacture of electrical equipment, spinning and dyeing machinery, precision tools, cameras, and chemicals. Electricity generated at nearby Lake Biwa provides power for the city.

The main port for Kyoto is on the Yodo River, to the south of the city. Kyoto is also one of the rail centres of Japan, and railways lead out in all directions from the city.

Kyoto is a traditional centre of education. Among its important schools are Doshisha University, founded in 1875, and Kyoto University, founded in 1897. The city has a world-famous collection of silk textiles at Nishijin Textile Museum. Civic buildings house the *Kabuki* and *Noh* theatres, where classical drama is staged.

Kyoto has wide streets, laid out in a rectangular pattern around its many ancient temples and palaces. The old imperial palace is within the city, as is Nijo Castle, built in 1603. Kyoto escapes bombing during World War II (1939–45), as it did not have industries important to the Japanese war effort.

Kyoto was founded in the 8th century as the village of Uda. In 794 it became the official residence of the emperor and the capital of Japan. At first, Kyoto was known by the poetic name Heian-Kyo, which means "capital of peace and tranquillity", but the people soon began calling the city by its present name, which means simply "capital city". For most of the period from the 12th century to the middle of the 19th century when the imperial court was maintained at Kyoto, it actually held little power. During this time the ruling power of Japan was in the hands of military dictators known as shoguns, who in the 16th century established their headquarters at Edo, now Tokyo. In 1867 Emperor Meiji overthrew the shoguns, and the following year he transferred his official residence from Kyoto to Tokyo, which had taken on the functions of a capital city. In Japanese, *Tokyo* means "eastern capital". Kyoto was given the name *Saikyo*, meaning "western capital", but it is still popularly called Kyoto. The city has a population of 1,470,564 (1989).

KYRGYZSTAN is an independent republic in central Asia, and a member of the Commonwealth of Independent States. It is bordered by Kazakhstan to the north, China to the east, Tajikistan to the south, and Uzbekistan to the west.

The country is located in the Tien Shan Mountains, which diverge as they extend westward from Khan-Tengri, a 6,995-metre (22,949-foot) peak at the eastern end of Kyrgyzstan. The nearby Pik Pobedy (Victory Peak), at 7,439 metres (24,406 feet), is the highest peak in the country. The southernmost range, the Alai, is sometimes considered a separate mountain chain. Between the mountains are numerous valleys, plateaus, and depressions. The largest depression is occupied by Lake Issyk-Kul. The major rivers are the Naryn, Chu, and Talas.

The high mountains are covered by snowfields and glaciers. From higher to lower elevations, there is arctic-like tundra, forest, grassland, and desert.

The Kirgiz people, the original inhabitants of Kyrgyzstan, are Muslims. They are traditionally herdsmen, and livestock raising remains a basic occupation for many of them, who live in felt tents throughout much of the year and roam in search of pasture for their sheep, goats, horses, and cattle. Other large groups living in Kyrgyzstan include Russians, Uzbeks, and Ukrainians.

The mountainous terrain of Kyrgyzstan leaves little space for farmland. Irrigated agriculture is carried on in the Chu, Talas, and Fergana valleys. Sugar-beet, cotton, tobacco, and fibres are the chief industrial crops. The poppy, raised for opium, is a distinctive crop near Lake Issyk-Kul. Wheat is the chief grain, followed by barley and oats. On the foothills are vineyards and orchards.

FACTS ABOUT KYRGYZSTAN

AREA: 198,500 square kilometres (76,600 square miles).
POPULATION: 4,290,000 (1989).
GOVERNMENT: Independent republic.
CAPITAL: Bishkek.
GEOGRAPHY: The Tien Shan Mountain range, with peaks of 7,000 metres (23,000 feet), crosses the country, with most ridges running east to west. Lake Issyk-Kul, which covers 6,236 square kilometres (2,408 square miles) lies in northeastern Kyrgyzstan.
CITIES: Osh, 188,000; Tokmak, 66,000; Przhevalsk, 56,000; Kyzyl-Kiya, 31,545.
CHIEF PRODUCTS: Sugar, cotton, tobacco, wheat; sheep, goats, cattle; mercury, antimony, sulphur, coal, petroleum; processed foods, machinery.
EDUCATION: Children must attend school between the ages of 6 and 16.

Most of the cities are located along the northern and western borders. The capital and largest city, Bishkek, is the country's major industrial and educational centre. It contains a meat-packing plant, a canning factory, and factories for processing leather, soap, and tobacco. It also produces machinery. Sugar refineries and textiles plants are located in the nearby Chu Valley. There is another concentration of industrial and mining towns in the Fergana Valley. Close by are

mineral resources, such as mercury, antimony, sulphur, coal, and petroleum.

The main railway line runs from Bishkek to the western tip of Lake Issyk-Kul. There it connects with a shipping service across the length of the lake. Bishkek has two airports.

LABOUR PARTY see POLITICAL PARTIES.

LABRADOR lies on the eastern coast of Canada and is the mainland portion of the province of Newfoundland (see NEWFOUNDLAND). It stretches from the Torngrat Mountains in the north to the Strait of Belle Isle in the south. Although Norsemen visited Labrador in AD 986, the interior remained largely unexplored until the 20th century.

Labrador has an area of about 300,000 square kilometres (115,000 square miles). The Torngrat Mountains are the highest mountains east of the Rockies. Farther south the country is a hilly plateau or tableland. The coast is rugged and deeply indented with fiords and a number of fair-sized rivers. The chief river is the Churchill, which, 335 kilometres (200 miles) from its mouth, plunges over Churchill Falls, 86 metres (282 feet) high.

The coast is washed by a current from the Arctic, so Labrador, though not very far north, is very cold. In winter the rivers and lakes freeze and the whole coastline is blocked by ice; snow usually covers the ground from October until the following May.

Much of northern Labrador is subarctic or *tundra* (carpeted with mosses and lichens), while the central portion is heavily forested and the south coast has forests broken by patches of bog or grassy marsh. The chief animals are the beaver, lynx, muskrat, otter, bear, marten (a kind of weasel), caribou

Battle Harbour, an important fishing village in Labrador. Except for coastal villages, the peninsula was an unbroken wilderness until 1941.

Ewing Galloway

(North American reindeer), snowshoe hare, porcupine, moose, and several varieties of fox. Some of the smaller animals grow thick winter coats, which make them valuable to fur trappers. The birds include grouse, ptarmigans, snipe, geese, and ducks.

The Labrador coast is populated mainly by Eskimos (Inuit) and descendants of European settlers (mostly Scottish or English). Inland there are other people of European descent and a small group of Montagnais–Nascopie Indians, who once lived as wandering hunters but are now settled.

Fishing is Labrador's oldest industry. Fine cod are caught off the coast between May and October, and herring, halibut, and salmon are taken during a shorter season. Seals are hunted in Labrador waters, but this is a declining industry. Fur-trapping, much of it carried on by the Montagnais–Nascopie and Eskimos (Inuit), was once an important industry but declined in the 20th century.

Between the headwaters of the Churchill and Kaniapiskau rivers there lie huge beds of iron. The chief iron-ore mines are at Labrador City and Wabush, in Labrador, and at Fermont, just over the border, in Quebec. All three communities are located on the iron-rich trough of the Labrador/Quebec border. Other minerals include copper, in the southwest, and nickel, west of Ungava bay. Gold and uranium-bearing ores have also been discovered. Almost unlimited water power can be obtained from the rivers, especially at Churchill Falls, on the Churchill River.

Labrador has no large towns. Labrador City and Wabush in the interior near the Quebec border, and Happy Valley-Goose Bay near the coast are the largest settlements. The airport at Goose Bay is a major refuelling point for transatlantic air flights.

In the 16th and 17th centuries fishermen from France, the Channel Islands, and Britain made settlements in Labrador and later trappers from various trading companies, including the Hudson's Bay Company, traded furs in the area. In 1821, John McLean, one of the Hudson's Bay Company's men, journeyed overland from Fort Chimo on Ungava Bay to the Hamilton Inlet.

Newfoundland had better harbours than Labrador and was nearer the new cod-fishing grounds on the Grand Banks, so Labrador was for many years neglected. In 1892, a British medical missionary Sir Wilfred Grenfell (1865–1940) went to Labrador to set up missions, hospitals, and schools, and his work and writings did much to bring the area to the attention of the world.

Labrador is today a part of Newfoundland and came under the Canadian flag in 1949, when Newfoundland became Canada's tenth province. The population of Labrador is about 33,000.

See also NEWFOUNDLAND.

LABURNUM is the name of small trees and bushes with butterfly-like flowers. The most common one, which is often planted to brighten gardens, parks, and roadsides, is *Laburnum anagyroides*, which has beautiful golden flowers that hang in graceful festoons in the early summer. Another name for the tree is golden rain.

The laburnum has a smooth bark, greenish-grey in colour. In the winter the buds are silvery-grey, covered with silky hairs, and in the spring they open to unfold leaves that are trefoil (made up of three leaflets), smooth on top and silky underneath. Each flower is the same shape as the pea flower, for the laburnum belongs to the pea family, Fabaceae.

Bees searching for nectar (which they use for honey) have to pierce a swelling at the base of the laburnum flower to get it. Both the stamens and the stigma go back inside the flower after the visit of a bee, and so an insect may come again, not knowing that the nectar has already been taken. In this way the flower is more likely to be cross-pollinated, as the stamens may shed their pollen on one visiting bee, while another bee may bring pollen from a different laburnum flower to the stigma (see POLLINATION). The seed-pods are flattened, and when ripe they explode and about six seeds fall out.

The home of the laburnum is the south of Europe and western Asia. The dark brown heart-wood in the centre of the tree is used to make tools and musical instruments, and can be polished.

All parts of laburnums are poisonous, especially the seeds. Cattle have been killed by eating the plant.

LACE is an openwork fabric made up of intertwined threads, usually with a figured design. The most common materials used in lace-making are fine linen, cotton, and silk, although nowadays many synthetic fibres are also used.

There are two basic types of lace: *bobbin lace* or *pillow lace,* in which the thread is worked with bobbins, or spools; and *needle lace, needlepoint lace,* or *point lace,* in which a needle is used. Laces may be made using both these techniques. Most modern lace is made using machines, which are able to imitate the techniques of making lace by hand.

Traditional Lace Making

True lacemaking dates back to 16th-century Venice. It is possible that it was brought there from the East. Both needlepoint and bobbin lace were made in Venice.

In needlepoint lace, the worker began by drawing threads from a linen cloth and worked over these threads to form openwork designs, called *drawn work*. Other workers made larger spaces by cutting out the material between the embroidered patterns, forming *cutwork*. The next step was to draw out threads in both directions so that only a skeleton of the cloth remained. The patterns were worked across the spaces with looped stitches. This was called *reticella*, from the Italian *rete*, meaning "net". Finally, the cloth foundation was left out entirely, and the lace was made with the needle over a pattern on paper or parchment. This was called *punto in aco*, meaning "stitches in the air".

Bobbin lace is like a very elaborate type of braiding, in which the threads are wound on bobbins. The bobbins look like small spools with handles. The wider and more elaborate the design, the more bobbins must be used.

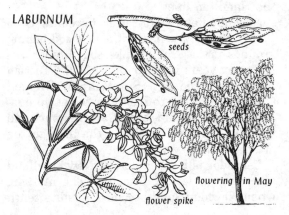

LABURNUM

seeds

flowering in May

flower spike

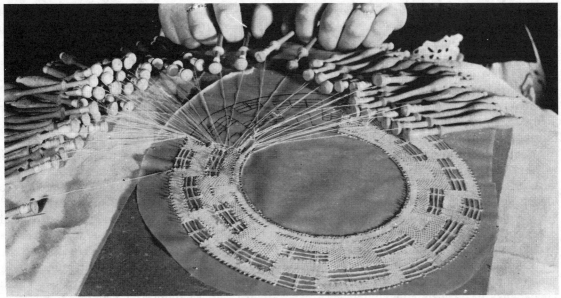

Making lace by hand: threads are wound onto bobbins and tossed back and forth to produce fine designs.

The work is done on a padded pillow or cylinder, which is why it is often called pillow lace. Lace makers draw the design on a piece of parchment or heavy paper and stretch it over the pillow. Small pins are inserted along the outlines of the design, and the intricate braiding or weaving is started. The bobbins are tossed back and forth, forming the mesh as outlined on the parchment pattern.

Machine-made Lace

The Industrial Revolution in the late 18th and early 19th centuries revolutionized the lace industry. The first machines for making lace were based on the knitting machine. By 1780 several of these machines were in use in France and England. In 1809 John Heathcoat, an Englishman, invented a bobbin lace machine which copied the mesh of handmade bobbin lace. The machine-made net was often used by the hand weaver as a background for laces. The weaver embroidered designs on it, or appliquéd designs in fine muslin cloth over it, or sewed fine handmade tapes or needlepoint motifs to it.

In 1813, the Levers machine was invented. This made it possible to make wide laces with elaborate patterns like those of the finest handmade laces. Bobbin laces can be copied so skilfully that only an expert can tell handmade from machine-made. Needlepoint laces cannot

A sampler panel of English needle lace from the first half of the 17th century.

be imitated so perfectly, but the general effect of these laces can be obtained.

The finest machine-made laces today are made in Europe, especially in England and France. Most of the lace machines and many of the yarns used are imported.

The modern Levers lace machine weighs about 15 tonnes (16.5 US tons), and can weave fabrics 2.5 metres (3 yards) or more in width. As many as 600 widths of narrow laces may be woven at one time on this loom. These narrow laces are separated into single widths after bleaching, dyeing, and finishing, by pulling out a single thread that joins the strips.

Another type of lace-like material is made by the Schiffli embroidery machine. Designs are embroidered on net, or on sheer fabrics such as organdie. Sometimes the fabric is cut away beneath the design, leaving a lacy effect. *Burnt-out* laces are made by embroidering the lace design with one type of thread, such as cotton, on a background of another material, such as silk or acetate. Chemicals are then used to destroy the background material, leaving the lace design intact.

LACROSSE is a field game which began in Canada, and is also played in Great Britain, Australia, New Zealand, South Africa, and the United States. It involves catching and throwing a ball with a netted stick.

A primitive game of this kind was played by North American Indians centuries ago. There were no rules and sometimes whole tribes took part. They called it the "ball game" or "baggataway". A Jesuit priest referred to the game in his reports as early as 1636. Another French Jesuit who went to Quebec in 1705 called it *le jeu de la Crosse* (the game of the crozier), because the stick reminded him of a bishop's crozier.

Canadian settlers took up the game in about 1840 and it spread to Britain, the United States, and Australia. In England some Canadian schoolboys played lacrosse at a Reading school in 1865, before Canadian and Indian teams first demonstrated the sport in Britain in 1867. By 1896 the game was popular in a number of British schools.

The game is played on a field about 100 metres (110 yards) long and 55 metres (60 yards) wide. The stick, called the *crosse*, is made of hickory and has a net at the end made of leather thongs interlaced with cord. Players wear light rubber-soled boots or shoes, and sometimes padded gloves. Goalkeepers wear body pads, and men may wear a helmet, women goalkeepers wear pads on their legs. The ball is made of solid india-rubber and is about 20 centimetres (8 inches) in circumference. The opening in the netted goal is 2 metres (6 feet) high and 2 metres wide, and around each goal is a circle called the goal crease. Players must be outside this crease when shooting at goal. The goal creases and the centre circle are the only ground markings.

In most countries there are ten players in a men's lacrosse team. In a women's team there are twelve players. Instead of beginning with one team in each half of the field, as in football, lacrosse players are paired off over the field, except for the goalkeepers.

The object of the game is to score goals; a goal counts one point. Under most rules for men, the team is divided into a goalkeeper, three defenders, three midfielders, and three attackers. During play, each team must have at least four defenders in its own half, and no fewer than three attackers in the opponents' half of the field. There are two officials, a referee (called umpire in women's lacrosse) and a judge, and the game is divided into four periods of 15 minutes each, with a one-minute break between each quarter and a ten-minute break at half time.

At the start, the ball is placed between the backs of the crosses of the two centres, and on the word being given they draw their crosses sharply and try to make the ball fly out to the wing players waiting on the edge of the circle. The aim is then to get the ball up the field and through the other team's goal. The players carry the ball in their crosses and pass it from one to another, trying to keep away from the defence opponents. The players of the other team try to knock the ball out of the attackers' crosses with their own or to intercept the passes by catching

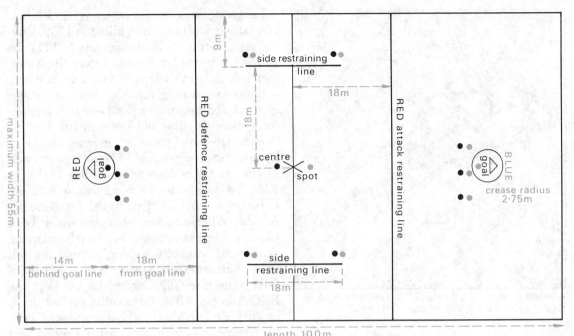

This diagram of a lacrosse field shows how players mark each other at the start of a game. There are ten players in a men's team, twelve in a women's team.

the ball in their crosses.

Good play depends on fast sprinting and on being able to catch and throw the ball accurately whilst running at full speed. An attack player has to be quick and active to escape from the defence player who is marking him. The game moves very fast, the ball passing rapidly from one end of the field to the other, and for this reason lacrosse is exciting to watch. In a good game the ball is off the ground most of the time. Rough play, such as charging, barging with the body, elbowing, or tripping, grasping, or hitting an opponent, is forbidden. However, body-checking is allowed in men's lacrosse. In women's lacrosse the ball may not be intentionally kicked or moved with the foot or leg. The men's game allows this except in shooting at goal. The ball may not be intentionally touched with the hands except by the goalkeeper who may use a hand to block it. Play is allowed behind the goals.

As the game is so fast, it often happens that 20 or more goals are scored in a game. Although lacrosse gives plenty of scope for individual players, it is chiefly a team game in which combined movements are most effective.

LADYBIRD. In spite of its name, the ladybird is an insect belonging to the beetle family. It is also called the *ladybug*. There are about 5,000 species (kinds), all less than 15 millimetres (0.5 inches) long, oval in shape and with six very short legs. They have a pair of transparent wings which are visible only when the ladybird is flying. When it is crawling, the wings are covered by a pair of smooth, hard wing covers, generally brightly coloured and as shiny as if they were varnished.

Most ladybirds have red wing covers with black spots, but some have red spots on a black background. The number of spots differs according to the species; some have only two spots, one on each wing, some 3, some 4, some 6, some 7 and some 10, as well as one with 22.

Ladybirds are often found on plants in the garden, where they are very useful, for both the grub and the full-grown insect feed on greenfly and scale insects, which are harmful to plants. Rather than spray rose-bushes with chemicals, which kill both useful and harmful insects, it is better to put a few ladybirds on them. Ladybirds are often taken to countries where insect pests are attacking the orchards.

A lunate ladybird lays a batch of up to 50 eggs at a time. It lives in the South African high veld.

For example, the Australian ladybird beetle (*Rodolia cardinalis*) was taken to western North America to help combat an outbreak of cushiony-scale insect. Some ladybirds are leaf eaters, however, and can do damage to vegetable crops.

The yellow eggs of ladybirds are laid in batches on leaves. When the grubs hatch they are very active. Usually they are grey or purplish in colour with indistinct spots. In about a month each grub fastens itself to a leaf and becomes a chrysalis. The full-grown insects hibernate, or sleep during the winter, often in large groups.

The bright colours of ladybirds protect them from being eaten by birds. When attacked, ladybirds release small drops of a fluid with an unpleasant taste. Birds soon learn to associate the bright colours of the insects with their unpleasant taste and leave them alone.

LAFAYETTE, Marquis de (1757–1834). Marie-Joseph-Paul-Yves-Roch-Gilbert du Motier, Marquis de Lafayette, was a French nobleman and soldier. He fought with the colonists in the American Revolution and took part in two French revolutions.

Lafayette was born in Auvergne, France. His father, a soldier, was killed in 1759, leaving great estates to his infant son. In 1777 the young Lafayette left France to join the American colonists in their fight for independence.

Lafayette was given the rank of major general and became one of George Washington's most popular officers and his lifelong friend. He was wounded in the Battle of Brandywine (September 1777) and fought well in the Battle of Monmouth (June 1778). In 1781 he was sent to Virginia to stop an invasion by British troops led by Benedict Arnold. When the British commander Lord Charles Cornwallis marched north from the Carolinas, Lafayette suddenly found himself against an army much larger than his. He skilfully refused to fight Cornwallis, but kept the British busy. When Cornwallis settled down at Yorktown, in Virginia, Lafayette sent word to Washington who came with French and colonial troops. The surrender of Cornwallis in October 1781 ended the war. (See AMERICAN REVOLUTION; CORNWALLIS, CHARLES.)

Lafayette wanted France also to have freedom of speech and of the press, trial by jury, and government by the people. He wanted to help the common people who suffered under unfair laws and taxes. But he wanted all of this done under the monarchy. When the French Revolution began in 1789 Lafayette was in favour of it and was one of its leaders. He became head of the National Guard, the militia organized to help the revolution. (See FRENCH REVOLUTION.)

When new leaders appeared, Lafayette feared that the monarchy was in danger. He tried to march his troops to Paris to save King Louis XVI, but his troops turned against him and he fled to Austria. There he was placed in prison because Austria was then at war with France. In 1797 he was freed at the request of Napoleon Bonaparte. But when Napoleon made himself dictator of France, Lafayette refused to follow him.

Lafayette stayed out of public life until the fall of Napoleon and return of the monarchy in 1814. Then, once again he became a liberal leader, and in 1818 he was elected to the

National Assembly. In 1830 he was a leader of the revolution against King Charles X. Lafayette helped to bring it to a quick and peaceful end when Louis Philippe was chosen as the new king.

On Lafayette's visit to the United States in 1824 he was greeted as a popular hero. He was given land and money as a reward for his help in the American Revolution.

LA FONTAINE, Jean de (1621–95). One of the best-loved of French poets, whose name is famous in many other countries besides France, is Jean de la Fontaine. Among his works were plays and stories, but his best writing is to be found in his *Fables*—short stories told in the form of amusing poems about animals, each with a hidden moral.

La Fontaine was born at Château-Thierry. In 1664 he went to live in Paris, where everyone was delighted with his poems, and his charm as a person made him a favourite both among noblemen and men of letters. His great friends included the dramatists Jean Racine and Molière (on whom there are separate articles), and even King Louis XIV tolerated his sometimes strange behaviour and outspoken frankness. As a poet, La Fontaine based much of his writing on Greek mythology. He also wrote comedies and the *libretti* (words) for operas. At the end of his life he became deeply religious.

La Fontaine's odd behaviour sprang from his absent-mindedness, and all kinds of stories grew up about it. One was that he one day met his own son and had to be told by someone else who he was, at which he remarked, "Ah, yes, I thought I had seen him somewhere!"

In 1668 La Fontaine published the first of 12 books containing 230 verse-fables. The subjects for many of his fables were taken from fables written in ancient times, but the ones he made up himself are the best of all. The stories are told very simply, with delightful descriptions of animals and nature. The way he shows the characters of human beings, while seeming to be writing about animals, is wise as well as amusing and is similar to the writing in the fables of Aesop (see AESOP'S

BBC Hulton Picture Library

One of La Fontaine's fables is about a fox and a goat who were so thirsty that they went down a well to drink. Only the fox got out of the well again.

FABLES). Among the best fables are "The Grasshopper and the Ant", "The Town Rat and the Country Rat", and "The Raven and the Fox". In this last-mentioned tale, a fox sees a raven perched on a tree, with a piece of cheese in his beak. The fox, hungry and crafty, persuades the raven to sing to show his beautiful voice: the raven opens his beak to croak and down falls the cheese to be snapped up by the waiting fox.

LAGOS is the capital city and chief port of Nigeria. It is one of the fastest-growing cities of West Africa. It consists of the marshy islands of Lagos, Iddo, Ikoyi, and Victoria and the mainland areas on the coast of the Bight of Benin, an inlet of the Gulf of Guinea. The islands and mainland are linked by road bridges. Apapa, on the mainland, is the chief port area and the most important outlet for Nigeria's exports. It contains a naval base and is a busy commercial centre.

The Portuguese first visited the area, where Lagos now stands, in the late 15th century. They later set up a slave-trading centre there. During the 19th century, the British took control of Lagos, which became the capital of Nigeria in 1914.

Industries of Lagos include brewing, printing, motor car assembly, ship repairing, and the making of soap, tyres, furniture, and metal containers. There is also a busy fishing industry.

The University of Lagos, opened in 1962, includes a law school and teaching hospital. Part of Lagos Island is laid out with houses in pleasant gardens, in other areas, housing estates are being built, but there are still many slums. However, Lagos is a sweltering place, low-lying, and not very healthy. The population has grown rapidly, and the available facilities are inadequate. Electricity and water supplies often break down, an increasing number of factories have caused serious pollution. The population is about 1,097,000 (1983 estimate). A new capital city, situated in the centre of Nigeria, is being built to replace Lagos.

LAHORE is the second-largest city in Pakistan and the capital of the Punjab province. It is located in the fertile upper Indus plain, on the Ravi River in the northeast of the country, roughly 25 kilometres (15 miles) from the Indian border. Lahore was probably founded in the 1st or 2nd century AD and reached its golden age under the Mogul Empire (see MOGUL EMPIRE). It was the favourite residence of the Emperor Jahangir, who is buried in a fine tomb at Shahdara beyond the river. His son Shah Jahan laid out the Shalimar gardens in 1641, 9 kilometres (5.5 miles) east of the city. These gardens are among the loveliest in the world and are arranged in three terraces, one above the other, with more than 400 fountains. Within the old fort in the north of the city are a number of fine palaces, decorated with the coloured tiles for which Lahore is famous.

The city is an important business and banking centre and is the centre of an industrial region making cotton, silk, shoes, rubber, and many other goods. The University of the Punjab at Lahore, established in 1882, is Pakistan's oldest university. There is also a university specifically for engineers and technologists.

The population is about 2,950,000 (1982).

LAKE. A large sheet of water surrounded by land is a lake. The water occupies a basin in the Earth's surface and is prevented from

Christine Osborne

A busy street in central Lahore. It is a city diverse in its landscape, street patterns, and architecture.

The moraine lake (formed from rocks deposited by glaciers) and Valley of the Ten Peaks in Banff National Park, Alberta, Canada.

ARDEA

escaping by the rim of the basin. Rain, inflowing streams and, sometimes, springs in the bed of the lake supply its water. When the lake is full the water overflows at the lowest point on the rim, usually into a river. Water is also lost by evaporation (see EVAPORATION) and often by soaking away underground.

Where the evaporation is so great that there is no overflow the lake becomes salt, as in the Dead Sea, the Caspian Sea, and many Australian lakes. The Dead Sea, which is between Israel and Jordan, is so salty that a person cannot sink in it. (See DEAD SEA.)

Many lake basins were formed during the great Ice Age hundreds of thousands of years ago (see ICE AGE). Finland, called by its people *Suomi* (meaning "the land of lakes"), has more than 35,000 lakes, and Ontario in Canada and the regions near it have many thousands. In both countries the lakes were formed by the great ice sheets which once covered the land. Some of the basins were formed by the ice scooping hollows in the surface rocks, but most were produced by the way in which rocks and soil were left on the ground by the melting ice sheets. This rubbish often formed low hills of boulders, clay and sand, which are called *moraines*. Many old river valleys were blocked by moraines lying across them, and the rivers were thus dammed back to form long narrow

lakes. Many lakes in mountain areas were formed in this way. Sometimes the moraines were dumped irregularly on low plains by the melting ice to form shallow basins of irregular shape. Some of the lakes in Canada and Finland are of this kind.

During the Ice Age the edges of the ice sheets often acted as moraines and walled in great volumes of water. One of these, called by geologists Lake Agassiz, covered much of what is now the rich prairie land of Manitoba and Minnesota in North America. All that remains of this vast sheet of water is Lake Winnipeg and some of the smaller lakes near it.

Most of the greatest lakes were formed by movements of the Earth's crust such as cracks, slips, collapses, and earthquakes. This is true of the chain of great lakes drained by the St. Lawrence River (see GREAT LAKES) in North America, although ice action also affected them. Lake Superior, one of the largest areas of fresh water in the world, is one of these. The Caspian Sea, which is the largest inland sea, and Lakes Victoria, Tanganyika, and Malawi in East Africa were all formed by movements of the Earth's crust. So too were the largest lakes in Europe (Onega and Ladoga in Russia), the Great Salt Lake in Utah, United States (see GREAT SALT LAKE), and Loch Ness in Scotland. Other examples of lakes formed in this way are Lake Baikal, the deepest in the world at about 1,525 metres (5,000 feet); the Dead Sea, which is the lowest lake; and Titicaca in Bolivia, which is the highest. The surface of the Dead Sea is about 400 metres (1,300 feet) below sea-level and that of Titicaca about 3,660 metres (12,000 feet) above it.

Volcanoes may bring about the formation of lake basins in two ways. The craters or cup-like hollows in the summits of extinct (dead) volcanoes may fill and form small lakes. Among the most famous of these is Crater Lake in the Cascade Mountains in Oregon (United States). In other cases, the flow of lava from a volcano may cross a valley and form a barrier which dams the river. The Sea of Galilee was formed by the damming of the Jordan River in this way.

A river flowing slowly through flat country usually follows a meandering, or winding, course. In time of flood the river may break across one of these meanders and leave it cut off when the flood goes down, thus forming a long narrow lake called an *oxbow* because of its crescent shape. Lakes of this kind are common along the lower Mississippi River. In Australia they are sometimes called billa-bongs. The Norfolk broads in England are lakes which were formed in the same way. (See NORFOLK.)

The drift of sand and pebbles along a coast may throw a narrow spit or bar across a bay or river mouth and in time enclose its waters. Lakes of this kind, usually called *lagoons*, are found where the shores are low and the sea shallow, as for example along the seaward edge of a river delta (see DELTA).The Nile delta has several lagoons of this sort.

Most lakes are dying. Their destruction starts from the first day they are formed. The stream taking the overflow from the basin deepens its channel and, as it does so, the level of the lake falls. In time, the lake disappears. The inflowing streams, however, are even more active in causing the death of the lake. They bring down mud and pebbles which settle on the lake bed, forming deltas at the mouths of the streams. These spread across

the lake, filling its basin and leaving a flat plain in its place.

The River Rhône enters Lake Geneva in Switzerland as a muddy yellow stream. It leaves as a clear, sparkling blue river, having left its mud on the bed of the lake. The deposits thus formed on old lake beds make fine fertile soil. The rich wheat-growing areas of Manitoba and Minnesota are on the bed of the ancient Lake Agassiz. Lakes are also valuable when they help to check the flow of rapid rivers, and reduce the risk of floods by spreading the flood water over their wide surface. In the dry season a lake of this kind prevents the level of water in the river below it from falling too low. An example is the Bodensee (Lake Constance) on the Rhine River. Many lakes serve as reservoirs supplying water to cities (see RESERVOIR).

LAMA. In the Tibetan language the word *lama* means "superior" or "great". It is the name for a priest or monk of Lamaism, a form of Buddhism, which is the chief religion of Tibet.

Since about the 7th century AD the Tibetans have been Buddhists (see BUDDHA AND BUDDHISM). Until the 1950s, when the Chinese took over Tibet, the monks had great power and monasteries were to be found all over the country.

Although the Chinese authorities have tried hard to discourage it, religion still plays an important part in the lives of Tibetan people and every devout Tibetan family hopes for one of its sons to become a monk. Life in a Tibetan monastery is simple and hard. Religious services, which all monks attend, are held daily, food is plain, and there are no luxuries. The monks are divided into several orders, each of which has its own rules. The largest order, the *dGe-lugs-pa* sect, are known as the Yellow Hat order because of the tall pointed hats that they wear. Often a monk goes away for long periods to live on his own in a cave, so that he may give himself up entirely to religious meditation. Some monks practise medicine or paint sacred pictures, while others are employed to drive away evil spirits.

Tibetan monks are expected to promote the welfare of both human beings and animals. They believe that they gain the power to help by becoming pure in mind themselves. In order to do this, and to drive worldly thoughts out of their minds, they repeat sacred sentences many thousands of times. Often the mystical sentences are written by the Tibetans on strips of paper and put into prayer wheels. The simplest form of prayer wheel consists of a small cylinder that is mounted on a handle and rotated by hand. Inside the cylinder are pieces of paper which have prayers and extracts from sacred books written on them. The object of the prayer wheel is to send out as many prayers as possible. Some prayer wheels are very large and are turned by machinery.

Camera Press

Two young lamas receive instruction. Religion still plays an important part in the lives of Tibetans.

Until 1959, the head of the state in Tibet was a monk called Dalai Lama, which is a Mongolian name meaning "Great Ocean". His palace stands on the Potala Hill high above the town of Lhasa, the capital of Tibet (see LHASA). The Dalai Lama is considered to be higher than all other human beings and through him forgiveness and mercy are spread over the whole world. When a Dalai Lama dies, the Tibetans believe that the merciful spirit that dwelt in him transfers itself to a baby, who then becomes the next Dalai Lama. First this baby has to be found, and as Tibet is a large country with a scattered population, this is not easy. However, oracles (see ORACLE) are consulted and with their help male children are found who fulfil some of the necessary rules. These children are then examined for signs that they qualify to be the next Dalai Lama; the signs include marks indicating an extra pair of arms. The most likely child candidate is shown the late Dalai Lama's rosary and bell, mixed with other exactly similar objects. If he picks the right ones he is accepted and taken to the Potala, where he is carefully trained for his future duties.

In 1959 the Chinese put down a rebellion in Tibet. Many Lamas were forced to leave, and they now live in exile in India, North America, and Europe. The Dalai Lama saw that his position was hopeless and fled on horseback over the mountain passes to Mussoorie in India.

See also TIBET.

LAMARCK, Jean-Baptiste de (1744–1829). In the year that the English scientist Charles Darwin was born, Jean-Baptiste de Lamarck, noted French scientist, published his famous book *Philosophie zoölogique (Zoölogical Philosophy)*. In it he developed fully his theories of evolution, and so became the first man to organize facts suggesting evolution.

Lamarck was born in a village in Picardy, France, and, in accordance with his father's wishes, studied for the priesthood. On his father's death in 1760, he left his studies to join the army. He served bravely during the Seven Years' War and, although only 17, he was given a commission. When he was forced by illness to resign from the army he began the study of medicine in Paris. He had already become interested in botany, how-

BBC Hulton Picture Library

The French biologist Jean-Baptiste de Lamarck, best known for his theory of evolution. He was the first scientist to distinguish animals with backbones (vertebrates) from those without (invertebrates).

ever. In 1778 he published a study of the plants of France, which secured him election to the Academy of Sciences, Paris, and an appointment as royal botanist. In 1788 he was put in charge of the royal botanical gardens. When that institution was reorganized five years later, he was appointed to the chair of zoology, thus being forced to turn his attention from botany to zoology. In spite of his late beginning in the latter department of science, and despite an approaching blindness, Lamarck became an authority on insects and worms and published a great natural history on the subject.

Lamarckism

From his investigations he came to believe that higher forms of life came up from lower ones which gave rise to his theory of evolution, known as Lamarckism, in which he said that plants and animals can take on new features that are then passed on to the next generation. For example, according to Lamarck, giraffes have long necks because for many generations, individual giraffes stretched their necks to reach the uppermost leaves of trees. In each generation the necks of giraffes grew slightly longer, and these differences were passed on to the offspring and so on, until the present neck size was reached.

The science of genetics was later to disprove Lamarckism because, on the whole, characteristics acquired during the life of a plant or animal cannot be inherited. Today, the generally accepted theory is that only genetic features can be passed on to the next generation (see DARWIN, CHARLES; EVOLUTION; HEREDITY AND GENETICS).

Despite being discredited, Lamarckism has its followers, including the 19th-century philosophers Henri Bergson and Arthur Schopenhauer, and more recently in this century the Russian plant scientist Trofim Lysenko.

LAMB, Charles (1775–1834) and Mary (1764–1847).

Probably the best example in English literature of an authors' partnership between brother and sister is that of Charles and Mary Lamb. For most of their lives they lived together; and together they wrote some books for children, the best and most popular of them being the *Tales from Shakespeare*. Charles's essays—short compositions in prose on all kinds of subjects—are among the most famous in English. They are called the *Essays of Elia*.

In daily life Charles was an accountant in the East India office in the City of London. But he might not have had to go on working so long in his rather dull office job if it had not been for a terrible event which happened in 1796, when he was 21. Mary suffered from fits of insanity and during one of these she stabbed and killed her mother. The rest of her life would have had to be spent in a mental hospital if Charles had not made an official promise that he himself would look after her and keep her safe. For much of the time Mary was well and they could enjoy each other's company,

National Portrait Gallery, London
A contemporary portrait of Charles and Mary Lamb.

but Charles could never be free of anxiety and sadness on her behalf.

He wrote busily in his spare time, however, and his poems and essays soon began to make his name known. In 1807 came *Tales from Shakespeare*. It was an introduction to Shakespeare to be read by children at a time when they might find the plays themselves rather difficult and boring. Charles wrote the stories of the tragedies, or sad plays, and the comedies were Mary's contribution. The other books they wrote together were *Poetry for Children* and *Mrs. Leicester's School*, a small book in which several girls at a school in the country tell the story of some part of their lives.

Charles gathered a great number of friends around him, many of them famous literary men of the day such as S. T. Coleridge and William Hazlitt. He used to entertain them at his home on Wednesday or Thursday nights, and the best part of the evening was always the conversation, for Charles was a good talker himself and also very good at getting other people to talk. In 1820 he began to write essays for the *London Magazine*, signing them with the name "Elia", and they were later collected into two volumes. Anyone who reads these delightful essays today feels that he knows their author almost as well as if he had actually met him.

When he retired from his office, Charles took Mary to live in the country, but he missed his friends very much and was often rather lonely in the last years of his life. He died suddenly in 1834 after a fall. Mary Lamb, whose illness became much worse, died in 1847. Charles left enough money for her to be looked after by nurses after his death.

LAMPREY is a fish-like parasite that bores into the bodies of fishes. Although it looks like an eel and is often called a fish, it is really neither. It belongs to a distinct group of animals called cyclostomes that include the hagfishes (see HAGFISH). Lampreys have round, jawless mouths and are ranked among the vertebrates below the fishes. There are about 22 species of lampreys. Some are found in fresh water and others in salt water. All have long, eel-like, scaleless bodies. On each side of the lamprey's head, behind the eyes, are seven round gill openings. On top of the head is a single nostril. With its sucking mouth the lamprey attaches itself to a fish, scrapes away the skin with horny knobs on the tongue which serve as teeth, and sucks out the blood. The commonest sea lamprey (*Petromyzon marinus*) is found in both European and American waters. It is about 90 centimetres (3 feet) long and is a mottled, brownish-greenish colour. In the United States there are several species of freshwater lampreys, 15 to 30 centimetres (6 to 12 inches) long.

Freshwater and saltwater lampreys go upstream to spawn and build nests for their eggs. The young lampreys, tiny worm-like

The sea lamprey grows up to 90 cm. (35 in.) long. It preys on other fish by sucking their body fluids.

creatures, burrow into the stream bed. In three to six years, when they are full grown, they swim downstream. Young sea lampreys that do not reach the ocean may make their home in fresh water. Sea lampreys entered the Great Lakes of North America when these were connected with the ocean by canals. They have become established in the lakes, where they kill great numbers of native fish. Scientists are trying both to trap them before they go upstream to spawn and to destroy the young in the streams.

Lampreys are caught for food in parts of Europe. Tradition has it that King Henry I of England died from eating too many of them in 1135.

LANCASHIRE is a county in northwest England. Its borders are with Cumbria to the north, with North and West Yorkshire to the east, and with the great city conurbations of Manchester and Merseyside to the south. To the west is the Irish Sea. Lancashire has an area of 3,064 square kilometres (1,183 square miles) and a population of 1,379,000 (1984 estimate).

Eastern Lancashire runs into the Pennine Hills, which here form high plateaus (tablelands). The highest point is Greygarth Hill which is 627 metres (2,058 feet) above sea-level. The northern region is also hill country, with beautiful river valleys. This is known as the Forest of Bowland. In the south are the heather moorlands of Rossendale, to the sides of which are deposits of coal beneath the surface. The flattest country is in west Lancashire, where peat bogs have been drained for farmland. Long stretches of the coast are fringed with sand-dunes and salt marshes.

The county's main river is the Ribble, which rises in the Pennines and flows southwest into the Irish Sea at Preston. The area between Morecambe Bay and the mouth of the Ribble is divided into three by two other rivers, the Lune and the Wyre. The Fylde coast, from Fleetwood to St. Anne's, has rich farmland fringed along the coast by residential development, popular with holidaymakers and retired people.

Industries and Towns

Lancashire's industries and large towns are concentrated in the southeast corner of the county, close to Manchester. The main industries were formerly textile manufacturing and coal mining, but neither is so important nowadays. Towns such as Blackburn, Burnley, and Colne, which once concentrated on weaving, are now turning to new industries, such as light engineering. Other towns include Accrington, Darwen, Leyland, Nelson, and Prescot.

The county town is Preston, which has been the centre of Lancashire government for some 600 years. Its industries include aerospace engineering, and it is also a port for ships sailing to it up the Ribble. The M6 motorway, one of Britain's busiest roads, passes to the east of Preston. Lancaster, on the River Lune, is the seat of a university and an ancient town founded on the site of a Roman fort. Its name means "camp on the Lune", and the county name is taken from it.

Courtesy, Blackpool City Council

The brilliantly lit streets of Blackpool by night; it is England's largest and most popular holiday resort.

While the south of Lancashire is adjusting to the changes brought about by the loss of older industries, the north and south of the county have seen fewer upheavals. These are the main farming areas, with dairying and livestock rearing in the Fylde, and market gardening around the Ribble estuary. The most famous landmark on the coast is the tower at Blackpool, one of Britain's most popular seaside resorts. Morecambe, Grange-over-

Sands, and Lytham St. Anne's are smaller resort towns. Fleetwood, at the mouth of the River Wyre, is a fishing port. In the southwest, near to the border with Merseyside, is Skelmersdale new town.

History

Lancashire was settled by people as early as the Bronze Age. It later became part of the kingdom of Northumbria, and parts of it were occupied by Danish invaders. During the Middle Ages there were large monasteries in Lancashire, but in spite of its royal connections (through the House, or noble family, of Lancaster) it was not a rich county. The Dukes of Lancaster were very powerful nobles; the best-known was John of Gaunt, son of King Edward III. (See JOHN OF GAUNT.) From the reign of his son, Henry IV, to that of Henry VI, the kings of England belonged to the House of Lancaster. The Lancastrians fought with the rival House of York for the throne, in the civil wars known as the Wars of the Roses. (See ROSES, WARS OF THE.)

Lancashire also saw much fighting during the English Civil War (1642–51). The north and west of the county mainly supported King Charles I, while the south and east supported Parliament.

Lancashire's history changed greatly from the beginning of the 19th century, with the coming of the Industrial Revolution. Its villages, situated in valleys with plentiful supplies of water, grew into industrial towns because of one product – cotton. Richard Arkwright, inventor of one of the earliest spinning machines, was born at Preston, and in fact the manufacture of linen and woollen goods had been local crafts since the Middle Ages. During the 18th century, cotton became Lancashire's main industry. Ships from the United States brought raw cotton to be spun in Lancashire's mills and then woven into cloth. The damp climate helped the industry, for cotton threads snap if they are spun in dry air.

With the cotton industry came steam power, and coal mining, followed by the railways. The cities of Manchester and Liverpool grew large and prosperous. (See LIVERPOOL; MAN-

CHESTER.) The Lancashire textile industry declined after World War II (1939–45), for it could not compete with cheaper goods being made in other parts of the world.

As its industries changed, so too did Lancashire itself. In 1974 its size was considerably reduced by reforms in local government. The cities of Liverpool and Manchester with their surrounding areas became separate counties.

Sir Ambrose Fleming, the electrical engineer who made the first thermionic valve in 1904, was born in Lancaster.

LAND RECLAMATION is the work people have done to transform unusable land into useful and productive areas. It has been going on for over 5,000 years. Originally, it mainly involved bringing water to dry places or draining water from marshy places. (See DRAINAGE; IRRIGATION.) In Ancient Babylon irrigation systems used the floodwaters of the great rivers to turn desert into fertile farmland. The ideas spread to Egypt, India, and China. The Chinese are still struggling with the "ungovernable" Huanghe (Yellow River) where a modern system of canals has created 26,000 square kilometres (10,000 square miles) of useful land.

Over the centuries, the Dutch have reclaimed huge areas of land from the sea. The Zuider Zee, Ijsselmeer, and Delta projects are the largest. In Hong Kong, a reclamation scheme has involved the removal of a whole mountain to help create urgently needed building land. The Pripet marshes in Russia, "Europe's largest swamp", now contain areas of productive farmland and forests, all due to reclamation work.

Both drainage and water supply systems require similar engineering works. They include the building of dams, dikes, drainage ditches, canals, reservoirs, and pumping stations. Large stretches of desert have been turned into good farmland by bringing water to them. Many of the biggest schemes, such as the Imperial Valley in California, are in the United States where reclamation has been financed by government grants for many years.

Reclaimed land (polders) in the Netherlands drained by a network of channels. The circular hill is not reclaimed. It would have been an island in the sea.

Land reclamation is of special interest to conservationists and today there are two other important aspects in addition to irrigation. One involves the use of modern fertilizers and farming techniques. The other is the restoration of land which has been damaged by building work or some industrial process such as mining.

In dry areas, water shortage is not the only problem. In California, for example, the high salt content of the soil is another critical factor (see IRRIGATION). In South Australia, the Ninety Mile Desert once supported only scrub vegetation. Soil analysis showed that small but vital amounts of zinc and copper were missing. After chemical fertilization this has now become good grazing land.

None of this reclamation work can be successful on land where the topsoil has been destroyed. Mining, quarrying, and digging for gravel all remove this life-giving layer, or it may be buried beneath dumps of industrial waste or building works. Industrial pollution, both airborne and waterborne, can kill vegetation and create wasteland a long way from the source.

In Great Britain, the government provides grants for work on reclaiming land that has been neglected or misused. Work on building sites now includes tidying up the surroundings and landscaping them. By law, mining companies must restore their sites after use. Some industrial waste is put back into the ground in old workings. This reduces the amount of surface "spoil heaps" and also helps to prevent subsidence, which can destroy land in itself. Waste heaps are reduced to a stable size and slope, then fertilized and seeded. This increases their stability and reduces their unsightly appearance. In Germany, progressive reclamation like this is practised, where vegetation and forestry are established on hillsides while at the same time waste is being tipped on another part of the slope.

On the east coast of Australia, a huge bauxite mining scheme involves the excavation of vast quantities of sand. After the extraction process, the waste sand is used to rebuild the sand dunes almost exactly as they were before, so that the original landscape is re-created.

Reclaimed land offers the opportunity to redesign an area for a particular purpose, either for building, agriculture, or amenities. Gravel pits have been flooded to create watersports parks. Cultivated waste tips have provided green space and recreation areas in built-up industrial districts. (See LANDSCAPE ARCHITECTURE.) Nature reserves and wildlife habitats have been established in secluded areas such as outworked quarries.

All types of reclamation need some aftercare. Irrigation schemes need constant attention to prevent breaches and silting. Fertilization must be done repeatedly to keep farmland productive. The levels of poisonous waste in soil and water systems must be checked regularly on old dumping sites, and, as reclaimed land often shrinks and sinks, all building work must be inspected and repaired. Land reclamation is a continuous process.

LANDSCAPE ARCHITECTURE is the art of arranging land and the objects upon it for human use and enjoyment.

A landscape architect takes a plot of land and must transform it so as to emphasize its good features and take away the bad ones. It is possible to create ponds and lakes, artificial hills and slopes, and to divert the course of streams and rivers. Marshy land can be drained and dry land can be irrigated (watered). On a small scale the landscape architect can create a garden around a private house. On a large scale he can design vast public parks and recreation areas, and provide a pleasing setting for roads, cemeteries, power stations, sewage works, and public buildings. Landscape architects may work with regular architects, engineers, town planners, traffic controllers, and economists and sociologists, when large projects are being planned.

Barnaby's

The park with the Lincoln Memorial at one end is part of the landscaped area of Washington, DC.

During most of its history, landscape architecture has been carried out on private land. Landscape gardening is a particular style of gardening, originally developed in England in the 18th century by designers such as "Capability" Brown. For the historical development of gardens, see GARDENS AND GARDENING. It was only in the mid-19th century that parks were first developed for public use in cities. Later, whole towns were designed with houses and public buildings surrounded by open land. Some well-known examples of planned cities

are Washington, DC; Canberra, Australia; and New Delhi, India.

Landscape design is not only an art but also a science, for the designer must have precise knowledge of all the materials he is dealing with as well as the natural features of the land he is working on.

Elements of Design

The main things to be considered in a landscape design are: space, mass, line, colour, light and shade, texture, scent, and time, climate and season.

Space is the air defined by physical features and man's imagination. A room is a space defined by the walls, floor, and ceiling. Outside space is defined by the earth, the sky, and trees, buildings, cliff faces, or whatever else limits the view. In the desert or the Great Plains in the Mid-west of the United States, space extends as far as the horizon.

Mass is the opposite of space, consisting of objects within a space. It may consist of rocks, trees, buildings, or streams and lakes.

Line means the edges and boundaries in a landscape. It may be the border between different surfaces or the outline of a rock or line of trees. It is important in the way a landscape is seen. Lines lead the eye to the distance or to a corner. The patterns made by lines change throughout the day and during the seasons as the light and vegetation change.

Colour gives the landscape interest and life. Bright, artificial colours may look out of place in a landscape, and it is the designer's job to use colour in such a way that it does not offend the eye.

Light and shade affect colour and line too, as shadows are cast in different places at different times and seasons. Light varies in intensity from the brilliant sunshine near the equator to the cool grey of northern climates.

Texture is the way things feel when they are touched. Through experience a person can imagine how they would feel. Looked at from a distance, a mass of vegetation or different surfaces of the Earth, like sand, gravel, or mud, can create textural effects.

Scent is a delicate element in landscape design. The pleasure of scent is often forgotten in cities with pollution problems. However, it should not be forgotten by the landscape architect when planning areas where people can get close enough to enjoy the scent of plants.

Time, climate, and season are some of the variable elements in landscape design. Creating a garden is not the same as creating a building or a painting, for it is a living thing and changes over a period of time. If a garden were to stay the same as when it was first created, maintenance would need to be constantly carried on. Shrubs, trees, and grass would have to be clipped to the correct size and beds of flowers constantly renewed as the blooms faded. Most gardens, however, are planned to allow for change as time goes on. Plants mature and reach their maximum size over a period of years, some grow far more slowly than others. Colours and textures change with the seasons. In a temperate climate where many trees lose their leaves in the winter the relationship of space, mass, and line also changes with the seasons.

Principles of Design

Design deals with the arrangement of the elements on a particular site, which may itself need reshaping. In the case of a town or city site, the required buildings, roads, and other structures must be placed on it in relation to the natural features. There must be a balance between unity and variety. Too many different building materials or kinds of plants will mean that none can be fully appreciated. There must be careful organization of all the elements to achieve a pleasing unity. A sequence or repetition of similar elements will help to achieve rhythm and balance. Accent and contrast help to enliven a landscape that may be well balanced but dull. Different coloured foliage can be used to create more interest.

Designed landscapes, by filling the open areas in cities, create a continuity in space between man-made structures and the countryside beyond.

LANDSLIP. A landslip happens when a mass of rock or earth slides down from a cliff or mountain. The scars caused by landslips and the rocks and earth brought down by them can often be seen at the foot of steep hills. Slipping sometimes takes place in road and railway cuttings too.

Landslips on a bigger scale occur in mountainous regions. They may be caused by very heavy rain or by melting snow, which moisten the beds of clay rocks and make them slippery, or an earthquake may start them. One of the great dangers is that the soil they bring down may dam up a river, thus forming a lake. As the dam of soil is not very strong it may easily burst under the weight of water behind it. If this happens a great flood will sweep down the valley and, unless warning has been given, much loss of life and damage may be caused. Another danger is that when great masses of rock fall into lakes they sometimes raise high waves, which may wreck boats and do great damage as they sweep across the shores.

When the landslip is formed of surface rocks loosened by melting snow, or merely of melting snow or ice, it is called an avalanche. (See AVALANCHE.)

LANGE, David Russell (born 1942). David Lange was prime minister of New Zealand from 1984 to 1989. He was the youngest prime minister of New Zealand since 1876.

David Lange was born at Otahuhu in South Auckland. His father was a doctor and his mother a nurse. The Lange home was a busy, sometimes chaotic household where people called in at all hours. Young David grew up enjoying the unpredictable, and disliking routine. Like his family, he loved jokes, talk and argument, and developed a booming voice. At Otahuhu College, and later at university, Lange excelled at public speaking and debating. His real passion as he grew older was wandering around New Zealand. He loved camping in remote places and often slept rough.

Lange graduated from Law School at the University of Auckland in 1967 and immedi-

New Zealand High Commission

David Lange, who became prime minister of New
Zealand in 1984 at the age of 42.

ately left for London. In England he married
Naomi Crampton. When he returned to New
Zealand in 1968 he became a lawyer,
specializing in criminal and family law. He
was also interested in politics. In 1977 he was
elected member of parliament for Mangere. In
1979 he became deputy leader of the Labour
Party, and in 1983 he was chosen to be leader.

In 1984 David Lange led the Labour Party to
victory in a general election. He became prime
minister and minister of foreign affairs in the
fourth Labour government. His strong concern for peace and fairness, and especially
his government's refusal to allow nuclear
weapons into New Zealand, quickly made him
an international figure. His refusal to allow
US Navy ships carrying nuclear weapons to
enter New Zealand ports disturbed his country's friendship with the United States. Lange
also keenly advocated making the Pacific
Ocean nuclear-free, and tried to halt the testing of nuclear explosions in the region. The
people of many small countries, including

other islands in the South Pacific, came to feel
that he spoke for them.

In 1987 Lange won a second term, but two
years later he resigned after a disagreement
with Labour Party colleagues about government policy.

LANGUAGE. A language is a system of
sounds which human beings use to communicate with one another. It is really a
collection of signs or symbols, in which the
words stand for objects or for actions or feelings. (See COMMUNICATION.)

In daily life, we all notice signs of some kind
all the time, and alter our behaviour according
to what they tell us. For example, a man sees a
large black cloud spreading over the sky, so he
puts on his raincoat when he goes out. A hunter
notices a broken twig and knows that an animal
has passed that way. A motorist sees a traffic
light change from green to amber and puts on
his brakes. A referee blows a whistle and the
players stop running after the ball. A boy
begins to cross the road when a friend calls out
"Stop!" In the first two examples the signs that
people noticed – the cloud and the broken twig
– were not deliberately made by one human
being to pass on a message to others. The traffic
light however was deliberately designed to
make a sign, and the referee blew his whistle
deliberately to make the players do something. Only in the last example, where the
sign was not only a deliberate one but also a
spoken one, was the message conveyed by
language.

Human beings are the only creatures in the
world that can communicate in a true language, although many other animals can
exchange information by sounds or movements of some kind. A sheep's *baa* calls its
own lamb to it; a dog barks at a strange noise
and the other dogs within hearing bark too;
a bee returning to its hive does a strange
dance which tells the other bees where the
food supply is. Although these sounds and
movements are much simpler than human
language, human beings do often use simple
signs of the same kind instead of speech. If
someone treads on your toe, for instance, you

make a sound such as "Ouch!" expressing pain. You may hold up your hand to stop someone, raise your eyebrows to show surprise or nod your head to show agreement about something.

It may not seem a very long step from these signs to a very simple piece of language like the cry of "Stop!" in the example mentioned earlier. It expresses a simple warning of danger almost as the bark of a dog might do. But the dog's bark could not explain what the danger was, nor why it is important not to run out in front of a moving motor vehicle, nor what happens if you do – this is the kind of thing that human language alone can do. By language we can exchange very complicated messages, describe things in great detail, and do things as different as giving someone instructions for making a radio set and reading a record of events that happened long ago. It is language of this kind that makes it possible for people to live together in large groups, co-operate in using tools, pass on skills and knowledge and share ideas and beliefs.

SOME OTHER ARTICLES TO READ ON LANGUAGE

ABBREVIATION	PARTS OF SPEECH
ADJECTIVE	PHONETICS
ADVERB	PREFIX AND SUFFIX
ALPHABET	PREPOSITION
ARTICLE	PRONOUN
CONJUNCTION	PUNCTUATION
DIALECT	RUNES
DICTIONARY	SENTENCE
ETYMOLOGY	SLANG
FIGURE OF SPEECH	TENSES
GRAMMAR	TONGUE TWISTERS
HIEROGLYPH	VERB
NOUN	VERSE

Language Families

There are in the region of 5,000 different languages spoken by the 5,000 million or so people in the world. One half of all the people in the world today speak only 15 of these languages. And more people in the world speak Mandarin Chinese (715 million) than any other language.

Not all languages are completely separate and distinct from each other. Scholars who have studied languages have shown that many of them are related to each other, related as if they were children and grandchildren and great-grandchildren of one parent language. The languages in each of these families have developed from a language used in earlier times, and this in turn may be related to other languages which all came from a still earlier one.

Nearly all the languages now and formerly spoken in Europe, as well as some languages used in Iran (Persia) and India, belong to one of these great families, called the *Indo-European* (see EUROPEAN LANGUAGES).

Within the Indo-European family are many smaller groups, each containing several languages very similar to each other. One group consists of French, Spanish, Italian, Portuguese, and Romanian, all of which in their turn developed from Latin, and they are usually known as the Romance languages. German, Dutch, English, Swedish, Norwegian, Danish, and Icelandic form another group, the Germanic languages. In all these languages there are likenesses in words, in grammar, and also in some of the changes that have come about in their sounds over the centuries. You will be able to notice a few likenesses if you look at the same sentence written in several languages belonging to the Germanic and Romance groups:

English	What time is it?	It is five o'clock.
German	*Wie spät ist es?*	*Es ist fünf Uhr.*
Dutch	*Hoe laat is het?*	*Het is vijf uur.*
Danish	*Hvad er klokken?*	*Klokken er fem.*
Swedish	*Vad är klockan?*	*Klockan är fem.*
French	*Quelle heure est-il?*	*Il est cinq heures.*
Spanish	*Qué hora es?*	*Son las cinco.*
Italian	*Che ora è?*	*Sono le cinque.*
Portuguese	*Que horas são?*	*Sâ cinco.*

Apart from the Indo-European family, about eight other language families have been fully worked out. For example, in Europe the languages of the Hungarians, Finns, Lapps, and Estonians form a separate group. Chinese, Tibetan, Siamese, and Burmese are related. Many of the languages of Africa belong to the Bantu language family (see AFRICAN LANGUAGES).

Some languages, such as ancient Greek and Latin, are well known but are no longer the native languages of any living people. They are called "dead" languages, and they are preserved in the books and writings that have come down to us from the times when they were "living" languages like our own today. These ancient languages are normally understood and used only by people such as scholars or priests, who study them for special purposes. Other examples of dead languages are Sanskrit, classical Arabic, Gothic, Old Norse, and Old English.

Language and Culture

A language is an important means of learning about different cultures. By learning the words of a language, one can learn what ideas and needs are important in that culture. For example, in one language there are no words for aunt and uncle. Instead, a person using that language calls his mother and his aunts by one name, his father and his uncles by another. From a study of such a language, one learns that these people must have a family life that is different from that of English-speaking people because they do not need to distinguish between their parents and their aunts and uncles. On the other hand, there is a language that has two words for uncle. One name is for uncles who are the mother's brothers, and the other is for uncles who are the father's brothers. Similarly, this language has two words for aunt. By knowing this fact, one can conclude that the people using this language make a great distinction between the father's and the mother's side of the family.

We cannot say that one language is more complicated, or more expressive, than any other. All human languages are equally complex. If a thought can be expressed in one language, the same thought can be expressed in another, even though the form of expression may differ.

The Spread of Language

There are many reasons why new languages form. As people who spoke a common language became separated from one another through migration, they gradually began to speak differently. New pronunciations developed, bringing about changes in the sounds of words. Some words no longer needed were dropped. New experiences caused the creation of new words. Ways of making sentences changed. If migrants settled in a land already occupied by people speaking another language, the two languages blended, hastening changes in each. At first, when the speech of the migrants changed only slightly from the original language, it was a dialect. After a longer time, when many changes in words, sounds, and grammar had occurred, an entirely new language had developed. In these ways Spanish, French, and Portuguese developed from Latin; and English, Norwegian, Swedish, Danish, and Dutch grew from an early form of German.

Language is constantly changing. Great social events introduce new words. During World War II, *blitz*, *radar*, and *jeep* became part of the English language. The civil rights movement of the 1960s in the United States added such words as *integrationist*, *sit-in*, and *desegregation*. New discoveries and new inventions add many words to a language. Since the exploration of outer space began in the late 1950s, English has gained such words as *astronaut*, *cosmonaut*, *spaceship*, *count-down*, and *blast-off*. In slightly more than 25 years, English has added such words as *television*, *Medicare*, *freeway*, *Salk vaccine*, and *laser*. These words come from various sources. *Television* and *Medicare* are made up from Latin and Greek words. *Freeway* is made of a combination of two familiar English words. *Salk vaccine* is called after its discoverer, Dr Jonas Salk. *Laser* is derived by combining the first letters of the following: Light Amplification by Stimulated Emission of Radiation. All languages can expand their vocabularies in this way.

The meanings of words change from time to time. In tennis, when a ball strikes the net, it is called a let ball. *Let* in this usage means stopped and is an old meaning of the word that is no longer used except in tennis. Today *let* means to allow or permit, almost exactly opposite to the older meaning of the word, to stop or prevent.

LAOS is a country in southeast Asia, in the region formerly known as Indochina. It is about the size of England, Scotland, and Wales together, with an area of 237,000 square kilometres (91,500 square miles). Laos is very mountainous, with deep valleys through which run tributaries of the mighty Mekong River (see MEKONG RIVER). Forests with valuable trees such as teak cover much of the land, and tigers, elephants, and water buffaloes are found. Rice, maize, and poppies for opium (see OPIUM) are grown and tin is mined. The main industries are rice-milling and forestry. The chief exports are timber, tin, coffee, leather, and hides. The main religion is Buddhism and most of the people are farmers, living in the Mekong valley. There are some Chinese traders, and the rest live in the mountains and forests. The capital is Vientiane (population 210,000) and the former royal capital is the picturesque town of Louangphrabang further north. There are no railways and few good roads, but air services link Vientiane with Bangkok (Thailand), Hong Kong, and Ho Chi Minh City (Vietnam).

The ancient kingdom of Laos was first unified in the 14th century by Prince Fa Ngum. Though this kingdom of Lan Xang ("a million elephants") enjoyed a short period of glory, Laos was often ruled by its more powerful neighbours, the Burmese, Thais, and Vietnamese. In 1893 the country became part of the French colony of Indochina. But when France was defeated in World War II (1939–45), Japan forced Laos to give the land west of the Mekong to Thailand. When the French returned after the defeat of Japan in 1945, the Laotian rulers were divided. The king, Sisavang Vong, supported the French, but Prince Souphanouvong formed a pro-Communist party called the Pathet Lao (Lao Nation). Laos became independent in 1949 but stable government was upset by the disagreements between the princes and their supporters. The Pathet Lao fought a guerrilla war against the government of Prince Souvanna Phouma.

During the war in Vietnam (see VIETNAM WAR), North Vietnamese troops used Laos as a base and supply route southwards. The United States assisted the Royal Lao army against the Communists, but with little success. In 1975 King Savang Vatthana abdicated and the Pathet Lao took over the government, declaring Laos a people's demo-

Courtesy, United Nations

Farm produce is sold in the open-air market-place in Vientiane, the capital of Laos. Rice, maize, and coffee are among the country's principal crops.

cratic republic. Short of money and trained people, Laos became an area of Vietnamese influence. Vietnam stationed some 40,000 troops in Laos.

The population of Laos is 4,290,000 (1991).

LA PAZ, in the Latin American country of Bolivia, is the highest capital city in the world, at an altitude of between 3,250 and 4,100 metres (10,650 and 13,450 feet) above sea-level. It is the largest city in Bolivia, and the country's administrative capital. (The capital by law and the seat of the supreme court is the city of Sucre.) La Paz has a population of 669,400 (1989).

La Paz lies in a deep, wide canyon made by the La Paz River as it flows southeast from Lake Titicaca, about 68 kilometres (42 miles) away. The canyon gives the city shelter from the cold winds that sweep across the Altiplano, the high plateau of the region. The climate is dry and cool.

La Paz (peace) was founded by Spanish explorers in 1548 on the site of an older Inca Indian village. For centuries it was used as a supply centre for mining, mostly for silver, that took place on the Altiplano.

La Paz developed into a major commercial centre in the 18th and 19th centuries. Today it is connected by railway and road to the surrounding countries of Chile, Peru, Brazil, and Argentina. Its airport, El Alto, is located on the plateau above the city.

The few remaining old streets in La Paz are steep and narrow, with colonial red-tiled buildings. But pressure for space in the canyon has led to the building of many modern skyscrapers. The snow-covered peaks of the mountains of the Cordillera Real loom over the city.

The Plaza Murillo, on the northeastern side of the river, is the centre of local government and culture. The modern cathedral, the government buildings, and the national museum of art are here. The huge, covered central market is a few streets away. The city also has two universities and an archaeology museum.

The chief industries of La Paz are food processing, and the production of consumer goods such as cloth, glass, furniture, and electrical equipment.

LAPLAND consists of the northernmost districts of Norway, Sweden, and Finland together with the western part of the Kola Peninsula in Russia. It is not a separate country, although the Lapps are a distinct people. Most Lapps live north of the Arctic Circle, where snow lies on the ground for more than seven months of the year.

Northern Lapland is a "land of the midnight sun", for between May 22 and July 23 the sun can always be seen, moving along the horizon at midnight before starting a new day's journey. Western Lapland is mountainous, much of the north is flat and barren, and the eastern part is hilly, with narrow valleys, rapid rivers and large lakes. In sheltered places there are often forests of pine, spruce, and birch, but farther north the trees are stunted and the land is stony or covered with moss, lichen, and berried plants.

Lapland gets its name from a people who are called *lappar* in Swedish, but who call themselves *Sameh*. They once roamed across the present frontiers with their herds of reindeer, having probably come to these empty stretches of Arctic Europe from Russia or central Asia.

Courtesy, Finnish Tourist Board

A young Lapp in traditional costume. Nomadic reindeer-herding is the way of life for many Lapps.

few of them still nomads (wanderers), and other Lapps who keep to the old way of life by herding reindeer feel they are the only "true Lapps". They more often wear the brightly trimmed woollen or reindeer-skin national dress. The reindeer pull sledges and they can also be ridden. Besides meat and skins they can supply milk and cheese. The reindeer herders often live in turf huts or tents, but many own boats with outboard motors or travel by bus, car, or aeroplane to markets and reindeer round-ups.

There is now a great deal of industrial and other activity in Lapland. At Kiruna and Gällivare in Sweden there are important iron mines connected by an electric railway with Narvik on the Norwegian coast, with Lulea on the Gulf of Bothnia and with Stockholm and Gothenburg far to the south. Tromso and Hammerfest, in Norway, are busy fishing ports, and the Swedes in their part of Lapland have built huge dams for water power.

Most of them were converted to Christianity about 300 years ago and are Lutherans (Protestants). The Lapps were originally short, sturdy people, with dark brown hair, but they have mixed with neighbouring peoples and many, especially in the far north, are fair and blue-eyed, of medium height or taller. They are tough and agile, have a good sense of direction and are expert skiers. The Lapp language is something like Finnish and Estonian, and includes many Scandinavian words. There are several dialects, so that Lapps from different districts sometimes cannot understand each other's speech. However a standard written language, based on northern Lappish, is taught in schools.

How the Lapps Live

Most of the Lapps make a living today by fishing, on the coast and in the lakes, or in forestry and other occupations. They live in timber houses which they own or rent, growing potatoes and cutting hay and often keeping sheep, goats, and cattle. Some are teachers. However, the Mountain Lapps, a

LAPWING see PLOVER.

LARCH. The larch is one of the most attractive of the conifers, or cone-bearing trees. Unlike other conifers, it sheds its needle-like leaves each autumn and remains bare throughout

LARCH
twig in spring
yellow male flowers
purple female flowers

old cone

the rounder Japanese larch cone

twig European Larch

new cone

summer foliage

summer   winter

bark

the winter. In spring, however, it stands out among the other trees of the wood because of its new, soft pale green needles and its female flowers, which are like little rose-coloured tufts. The yellow male flowers have pollen sacs inside their cones, and they appear after the female flowers, which later change into small brown cones. From these, winged seeds are shed a year later. There are about a dozen species of larch, native to cool regions of the Northern Hemisphere. The European larch (*Larix decidua*) averages a height of 30 metres (100 feet) and its bark is light brown, thick and rough. It is often attacked by a fungus, which plants itself in any cracks it can find, and by insects, the worst of which are the wood wasp and the larch miner.

The most widely distributed North American larch is the tamarack, hackmatack, or eastern larch (*Larix laricina*) which has blue-green needles that turn yellow in the autumn. It grows up to 42 metres (140 feet). Several species are grown as ornamental trees, especially the Japanese larch (*Larix leptolepis*).

Larch wood is coarse-grained, strong, hard and heavy. It is used for pit props in coal mines, for fences and gates, for telephone poles, in ship construction and for railway sleepers. Turpentine can also be obtained from larch wood and the bark is used in the tanning of leather.

LARK. There are about 75 species of songbird known as larks, mainly of the Old World. Most species are found in Africa. They generally have dull plumage but are noted for their high-pitched, melodious songs. The male common skylark (*Alauda arvensis*), like other larks, performs its courtship song high in the air. It rises up with fluttering wings until it is little more than a dot against the sky, while all the time its lovely, trilling song can be heard clearly from the ground. This skylark breeds across Europe, and has been introduced into Australia and New Zealand.

Australia also has its native species, the rufous songlark (*Cinclorhamphus mathewsi*) whose song is a light chatter, and the brown songlark (*Cinclorhamphus cruralis*) whose call consists of a series of curious creaking notes.

The only lark native to North America is the horned lark (*Eremophila alpestris*) found in Canada, the Great Plains, and the western

A European skylark showing the long hind claw typical of this group of birds. Larks live in open country.

United States. The bird is named because the male has two, sharp, well-defined horns, or tufts of feathers on the back of the head. It also has a black patch on the top of the head and under each eye. Like other true larks, it is distinguished by a long, straight back claw, called the "larkspur".

Larks build nests of woven grasses on the ground and feed on a mixture of seeds and insects.

LARKSPUR see DELPHINIUM.

LARVA. Many creatures go through different stages before they become adult, or grow up, and one of these is the larval stage, when the creature is known as a larva (larvae in the plural form). The word is a Latin one and means "mask". Many creatures change their shape and even their structure as they grow up, and it can be said that their appearance when young "masks" their adult form. Strictly speaking, a larva is an early stage of a creature which differs completely, or very greatly, from its adult stage. However, the word is now often used for almost any young form of many creatures. For example, in insects which, after hatching, pass through many stages (by moulting) before they are finally grown-up, these stages are often spoken of as the first, second, third larval stages and so on, whether they differ very much or very little from the grown-up forms (see LIFE CYCLE).

Caterpillars

A caterpillar is a good example of a larva, for there is nothing at all about it to suggest that when it is grown-up it will be a butterfly or a moth.

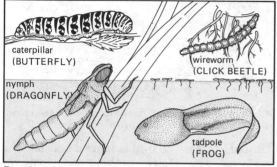

caterpillar (BUTTERFLY)

wireworm (CLICK BEETLE)

nymph (DRAGONFLY)

tadpole (FROG)

Four larval types that look very different from the adult tend to have different feeding habits. For example, most caterpillars feed on leaves while adult butterflies feed on the nectar of flowers.

One of the most obvious things about most caterpillars is the way their long bodies are divided into 13 segments, or rings. The first three segments behind the head eventually become the thorax of the butterfly—that is, the part which has the wings and legs attached to it—and the legs on these segments are hard and shiny. Those on the rest of the caterpillar's body do not reappear in the butterfly. They are soft and fleshy and their flat ends have tiny hooks, called crochets, which grip the surface they are standing on. Caterpillars often have less than five pairs of these hooked legs but never more than five, and if you find one with more than this number it is not a true caterpillar but the grub of a sawfly, an insect rather like a bee.

On each side of most of the caterpillar's segments there is a tiny opening leading to a network of air tubes through which the caterpillar breathes. Along the middle of the back runs the insect's heart, which can be seen beating in some thin-skinned kinds. It is little more than a thin tube through which the colourless

blood is pumped round the outside of the stomach and other parts of the body. The caterpillar has a very large number of muscles, as many as 900.

The head is the only really hard part of a caterpillar and the hardest parts of the head are the powerful jaws. On either side of the jaws there are also tiny antennae, or "feelers", which help the caterpillar to find and choose its food. Just below the jaws are the tiny openings from which comes the silk used by the caterpillar to make its cocoon. On each side of the front of the head there is a group of simple eyes, up to six in number, looking rather like tiny specks of dull glass.

Other Larval Types

Many different kinds of insect larvae have popular names. Gentles are the larvae of blowflies, though the larvae of most flies of this kind, such as house-flies, are generally called maggots. Leather-jackets are the larvae of the cranefly; bloodworms, often seen in stagnant water, are the larvae of a gnat. Wireworms, which do much damage to the roots of grass and crops, are the larvae of click beetles, and woodworms are the larvae of wood-boring beetles. The larvae of most flies, beetles, bees, and wasps, however, are simply called grubs. When young insects do not differ much from the adults (young plant-bugs, for example) they are often called nymphs.

Many sea animals have an active, swimming larval stage; among them are jellyfish, molluscs (limpets, oysters, cockles), starfish, and sea-urchins. Marine worms also have swimming larvae. Some larvae are so unlike their adults that at one time scientists mistook them for altogether different creatures, until they saw that one turned into the other as it grew up.

LA SALLE, Robert (1643–87). René-Robert Cavelier, sieur de La Salle was a French explorer and fur trader. He was the first European to travel down the Mississippi River to the Gulf of Mexico.

La Salle was born in Rouen, France, the son of a wealthy noble. He began to study for the

BBC Hulton Picture Library

In 1687 La Salle was murdered by a member of his expedition who had turned against him.

priesthood, but decided on a life of adventure in the New World. His older brother was a missionary in Canada. In 1666 La Salle joined him there and was given some land on the island of Montreal, which was then part of Canada's western frontier. But he was attracted by the stories Indians told of rivers to the west and south.

In 1669 La Salle joined a group of missionaries heading west. He explored the area south of Lake Ontario and claimed to have reached the Ohio River. On this trip he met Louis Jolliet, who soon afterwards explored much of the Mississippi Valley (see JOLLIET, LOUIS).

In 1672 a new governor arrived in Canada. He was Louis de Buade, Comte de Frontenac. He built Fort Frontenac where Lake Ontario flows into the St. Lawrence River. Frontenac

and La Salle became friends. They dreamed of building a French empire around the fur trade in North America. La Salle returned to France in 1674. He was given control of all the fur trade and he also commanded Fort Frontenac.

From Fort Frontenac, French fur traders headed across the Great Lakes in canoes. They gave the Indians brandy and other goods in exchange for furs. These furs were sold in Europe where they brought good prices. (See FUR AND FUR TRADE.)

After three years at Fort Frontenac, La Salle again returned to France in 1677. This time he was given permission to explore lands further west and to build forts. After returning to Canada, La Salle and his assistant, Henry de Tonty, built a boat, the *Griffin*, near Buffalo, New York, on the Niagara River. It was the first large boat to sail the Great Lakes. La Salle crossed the lakes to Green Bay, Wisconsin, on Lake Michigan. He was hoping to find a route to the east (see NORTHWEST PASSAGE), and he explored much of the area around Lake Michigan.

In 1680 La Salle built Fort Crevecoeur on the Illinois River near what is now Peoria. When it was destroyed he built another fort, this time on the upper Illinois River.

In 1682 La Salle and Tonty travelled down the Mississippi to the Gulf of Mexico. They were probably the first Europeans to do this. At the mouth of the Mississippi, La Salle claimed the whole river valley for King Louis XIV of France, naming it Louisiana in his honour.

Before La Salle returned to Canada, Frontenac had been replaced as governor. The new governor had taken away from La Salle the command of the forts in the Illinois country. So La Salle went back to France.

In 1684 he returned with four ships to set up a colony at the mouth of the Mississippi. Instead of finding the mouth of the Mississippi, they landed on the Texas coast. There La Salle built Fort St. Louis on the edge of Matagorda Bay. He made several efforts to find the Mississippi. In 1687, on his fourth trip, a group of his men turned against him. One of them shot and killed him.

LASER. The laser is an instrument which produces a bright light of a single wavelength and thus a single colour. (See COLOURS; LIGHT.) A laser usually gives out its light in a concentrated narrow beam (unlike a light bulb which gives out light equally in all directions). The word laser comes from the initial letters of "*L*ight *A*mplification by *S*timulated *E*mission of *R*adiation". This is a means of producing an especially strong form of light that was first suggested in 1958 by two American scientists, Arthur L. Schawlow and Charles H. Townes. To understand the process involved, we must first think about the atoms that make up the solids, liquids, and gases which are around us.

In every atom tiny particles called electrons circle a nucleus consisting of protons and neutrons. (For an explanation of subatomic particles, see ATOM; ELECTRON; ELEMENTARY PARTICLES; NEUTRON; PROTON.) Normally the atom is in the stable state. However, if the atom absorbs (takes in) energy from an outside source (an electric current, a bright light, a source of heat or a chemical reaction) this will have the effect of "exciting" one or more of the orbiting electrons and moving them into higher orbits with more energy. If left to itself, this "excited" atom goes back to its normal stable state in a fraction of a second. Its extra energy is given off as light which spreads out in all directions. It is this so-called spontaneous (natural) emission which makes a flame glow and which makes fluorescent paints (which absorb the invisible ultraviolet sunlight and give it out as visible light) seem so much brighter than ordinary colours.

However, if the excited atom is placed in a light beam of exactly the wavelength that it would naturally emit, it is stimulated to give out energy that is exactly in phase (in step) with the light beam. This energy travels in the same direction as the light beam amplifying it, that is making it brighter.

Since each type of atom can only have electrons in certain orbits with certain ener-

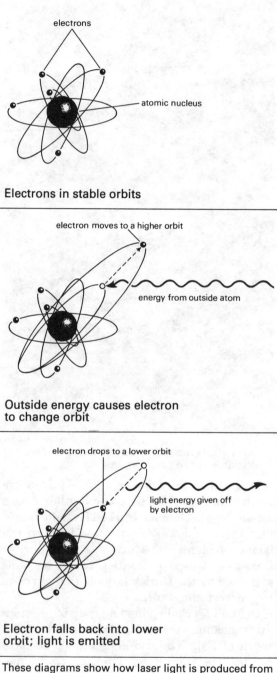

Electrons in stable orbits

Outside energy causes electron to change orbit

Electron falls back into lower orbit; light is emitted

These diagrams show how laser light is produced from "excited" atoms stimulated by an energy source.

gies, it follows that each type of atom can only absorb, emit, and amplify certain colours of light. Therefore each type of laser can only give light of one or two particular colours.

Types of Laser

Most lasers work by arranging to have a lot of "excited" atoms in a space between two mirrors. One of the mirrors is designed to let a small amount of light pass through it, so that spontaneously generated light from the excited atoms will bounce backwards and forwards many times between the mirrors. The light gets brighter on each bounce, before finally emerging through the mirror at one end as a narrow, intense (bright) beam.

One of the commonest types of laser uses a mixture of helium and neon gases in a glass tube between two such mirrors. When excited by an electric current passing through it, a narrow deep-red beam of light is produced. Argon gas gives the green, blue, and yellow laser beams which are used in spectacular laser displays and light shows. If carbon dioxide gas is used, a powerful beam of invisible infra-red radiation can be produced. This contains as much power as several electric fires concentrated into a tiny beam only millimetres wide which can cut through steel plates and burn objects at great distances.

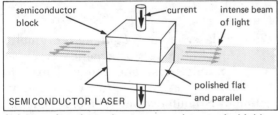

semiconductor block — current — intense beam of light

SEMICONDUCTOR LASER — polished flat and parallel

A tiny semiconductor laser uses a microscopic, highly polished crystal. Its light beam is intense.

At the other end of the scale are semiconductor lasers. These contain a block of a very pure crystal smaller than a pinhead, with each end polished to reflect light backwards and forwards inside it. Again, the atoms inside the crystal are excited by an electric current passing through, and the laser beam emerges as a cone of light from each end.

Although the lasers so far described are the ones most commonly used, many others are useful to scientists. There are, for example, lasers made from coloured liquid solutions, ruby crystals, the rare metal neodymium and coloured plastics. There has even been one laser made of a bright green jelly which could be eaten after it was used!

Uses of Lasers

Because laser light can be concentrated into a narrow beam, it can be seen and measured after travelling great distances. (An ordinary light beam spreads out as it travels.) This fact is made use of in laser range-finding equipment and laser radar (LIDAR), which can accurately measure the distance and position of a target by measuring the time taken by a flash of laser light to travel to the object and back again (rather like an echo-sounder). This method of measurement has been used to "bounce" laser light off the Moon and so measure the distance between the Earth and the Moon to an accuracy of within a centimetre (0.394 inch).

The concentrated laser beam can also be focused into a tiny spot and "scanned" across objects with a system of moving mirrors. In this way instruments can light up, weld or even burn away small areas of delicate objects with great accuracy. This technique is used for making and repairing electronic components. The laser beam can also be used to drill teeth painlessly.

Much lower-powered scanner systems with small helium-neon lasers are used in shops and supermarkets to "read" the striped "barcodes" on goods. Some video and hi-fi machines contain a small helium-neon laser, the beam of which focuses and scans across the surface of a special disc to read the music or video program encoded on it.

The narrow laser beam can also be easily shone into an optical fibre – a thin flexible fibre made of two types of glass and designed so that light will bounce down its length and emerge almost unaffected at the other end. Laser optical-fibre devices are used in medicine and engineering to light up awkward, inaccessible spots. (See FIBRE OPTICS.)

Computers have been built that use lasers to operate optical switches instead of the silicon-chip switches of normal electronic computers. The optical computer is much faster than the electronic one.

Very intense carbon dioxide lasers can be used in surgery to cut away damaged tissue while at the same time healing the wound and stopping bleeding. They have been used successfully to repair damaged retinas in eyes and in the treatment of certain cancers. In the future, scientists hope that extremely intense flashes of laser light, generated simultaneously from many neodymium lasers, will be able to heat and compress small balls of material to such a point that a controlled nuclear fusion reaction (similar to what happens inside the Sun and in an H-bomb explosion) will take place. This could produce almost limitless supplies of electricity from something like ordinary sea water. Lasers also provide the long-discussed "death ray", a high-energy beam capable of destroying missiles and aircraft.

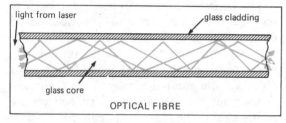

light from laser · glass cladding
glass core
OPTICAL FIBRE

Optical fibres let narrow laser beams be transmitted over distances without spreading or losing strength.

The purity of the colour of laser light means that it can be used to record three-dimensional pictures called *holograms* (see HOLOGRAM) and for measuring very small changes in distances, down to a millionth of a centimetre! Such laser measurements can be used to predict earthquakes by measuring tiny movements in the rocks and also to detect tiny faults in jet engine components. Architects and civil engineers use laser instruments to check alignment of such things as tunnels during construction.

Lasers and Communication

Perhaps the most exciting of all the uses of lasers, however, lies in the future of telecommunications. Already hundreds of separate telephone conversations can be simultaneously translated into a kind of code – a bit like Morse code – consisting of very short flashes of light generated by a semiconductor laser. These light pulses are shone into a thin optical fibre made of a special glass (so clear that a mile-thick window of it would appear almost totally transparent). At the other end of the fibre, the pulses of light are decoded back into the separate telephone conversations. (See TELECOMMUNICATIONS.) One optical fibre can do the work of hundreds of old telephone wires. Already optical-fibre laser communication systems are becoming the main means of transmitting both television pictures and telephone conversations, and are enabling computers to talk to each other.

Underwater radio communication is not possible because radio waves, which are infra-red in wavelength are absorbed by water. However, underwater communication is possible with a neodymium YAG (yttrium-aluminium-garnet) laser. This laser produces an infra-red beam but by passing the beam through a frequency doubler the colour of the beam is changed to green, which is not absorbed.

Masers

Whereas lasers amplify *light*, masers amplify *microwaves* – the electromagnetic waves used in radio, television, and radar. Thus, the word *maser* comes from "Microwave Amplification by Stimulated Emission of Radiation".

Where the laser operates primarily at light (visible and near-visible) frequencies, the maser operates at microwave (invisible) frequencies. Both solid-state and gas masers were developed from the early experiments. Solid-state masers are activated from energy stored in weakly magnetic crystals operated at very low temperatures close to absolute zero. These masers have resulted in greatly improved performance for many short-wave electronic devices.

LATIN is the ancient language of the Romans and the language on which the modern Romance languages (Italian, French, Spanish, among others) are based. It was originally spoken by a group of people who lived

Many examples of everyday Latin have been preserved in the city of Pompeii, which was buried by a volcanic eruption in AD 79. This photograph shows the remains of a shop in Pompeii selling hot drinks. The Latin word for a shop of this type is *thermopilium*. You can make out part of this word above the doorway. To the left of the door the names of girls working at the shop were written on the wall. Although the inscription is not perfectly preserved, experts have deciphered the names as Aegle, Maria, Arsellina, and Zmyrna.

Mansell Collection

in Latium, a small region in central Italy. Although it is no longer spoken in conversation, it is still taught in some schools and has not lost all its importance. Not only does it enable people to know about and understand the life of one of the great nations of the past and to read some of the wonderful books that were written by Romans, but it is also very important in the modern languages of Europe.

The Spread of Latin

As the Romans conquered the peoples of Europe and the Mediterranean coastal regions of Africa, beginning in the 3rd century BC, their language spread. It is partly because of this wide spread of Latin that the languages of modern Europe have a good deal in common, since they absorbed Latin words into their vocabularies and most of them still use the Latin alphabet. English, for instance, has many words which come from Latin— *superior*, *mile*, *juvenile*, for example. The Latin languages also took in words from the languages spoken by the people they had conquered, especially the Greeks.

In the Western provinces, conquered by Rome, Latin became the official language,

and soon the capital cities became centres of Roman culture. In the areas which are today France, Spain, and Italy, Latin was spoken by everyone. Latin was the language used in the courts, in schools, and in many of the homes. The Latin of ordinary conversation was simpler than that used in writing history or poetry or in official records. It also changed more rapidly. Poetry and prose themselves used different forms of Latin. There were words in Latin poetry that were rarely used in prose.

In time the spoken Latin of the different regions became so different that a person from Italy could barely understand someone from France or Spain. Gradually these various "dialects" of Latin developed into Italian, French, Spanish, Portuguese, and Romanian. They are called Romance languages because they developed from the language of the Romans; and the countries where they are spoken are often called Latin countries.

For centuries these popular languages were used only in speech and in private life. Literature and official records were written in Latin even in the Middle Ages. The church service was conducted in Latin. The Bible was read in the Latin version known as the

Vulgate. The hymns of the church were composed and sung in Latin. Not until the Renaissance were works of literature written in the language of the people; and even Dante and Petrarch wrote poems in Latin as well as in Italian.

The use of Latin declined after the Bible was translated into the various languages. But it continued to be the official language of the Roman Catholic church, and the ritual of the church is still sometimes conducted in Latin. The great musical versions of the Mass, by such composers as Bach, Mozart, and Beethoven, all use the Latin texts. Latin hymns are still familiar to many church choirs and congregations. Official pronouncements by the Pope are made in Latin, and in recent times the Vatican has published a magazine, *Latinitas*, in which the articles and editorial comments are in Latin.

The early European universities, such as the Sorbonne in Paris, France, Oxford in England, or Leiden in the Netherlands, trained their students to speak and write Latin. It was only in the 1960s that students were able to enter Oxford and Cambridge, the oldest and most famous English universities, without a knowledge of Latin.

Latin Literature

Around 240 BC, Livius Andronicus, a Greek prisoner of war who was captured by the Romans when they conquered the Greek cities of southern Italy, started the development of Roman literature by translating the *Odyssey* of Homer from Greek into Latin (see ODYSSEY). Livius also translated Greek plays, and directed their performance at a public festival. Through Livius the Romans became familiar with the Greek legends of the Trojan War. The earliest native Latin poets, Gnaeus Naevius and Quintus Ennius, wrote epic poems on Roman history, linking the beginnings of Rome with the legends of Troy. Both Naevius and Ennius also wrote plays. Little of their work survives, but they played a vital role in the growth of Latin literature.

The lighthearted comedies of Titus Maccius Plautus have often been compared with Shakespeare's. Plautus was familiar with the Greek comedies and used many of the same plots. The action always takes place in Athens and the characters are Greeks. But the plays were written for a Roman audience, and both characters and settings are actually taken from Roman life. A few of Plautus' plots and characters were later used by Shakespeare. The *Comedy of Errors* is based on the plot of one of Plautus' comedies.

Terence (Publius Terentius Afer) was a writer of comedies a little later than Plautus. His plays, also based on Greek originals, are more carefully written than those of Plautus, but not nearly so funny. Terence also gave his audience something serious to think about. His plays show the faults and follies of human beings and the evils of society, and he warns against the fashionable craze for Greek customs.

The only important prose work surviving from this period is a treatise on agriculture by Marcus Porcius Cato. It is a brusque, no-nonsense handbook on farming.

The Golden Age. The most fruitful and artistically excellent era of Latin literature began in the 1st century BC. In the period 80–42 BC, there were two great Roman poets. Lucretius (Titus Lucretius Carus) was a serious thinker and philosopher. He wrote a poem *On the Nature of Things*, which tells how the world is made of atoms of many different kinds, always moving, and combining with other atoms to produce all the things we see about us. Lucretius was intrigued by nature and its workings, and he illustrates his atomic theory with poetic images and descriptions.

Gaius Valerius Catullus was a young poet from northern Italy. Inspired by a beautiful and popular Roman lady named Clodia, his best poems are love lyrics, written to her under the name of "Lesbia".

The other important authors of the late Republic were statesmen as well as writers. They were Marcus Tullius Cicero and Gaius Julius Caesar (see CICERO; JULIUS CAESAR). Cicero rose to political power through his brilliant oratory. His powerful speeches managed to persuade the citizens to choose a particular course in public affairs. Caesar was also a good orator, but he based his political power on command of an army. His chief writings are his *Commentaries* on his war in Gaul (France) and on the war he fought against Pompey (Gnaeus Pompeius Magnus) for control of the Roman state.

Cicero was less active in politics in his later years and found time to write essays on many subjects, as well as speeches. He also wrote a great many letters to friends and acquaintances, using the less formal conversational Latin of an educated Roman.

Cicero and Caesar developed to perfection the art of Latin prose writing, making a Latin sentence express ideas clearly, simply, eloquently, and with beautiful rhythm. Their younger contemporary, the historian Sallust (Gaius Sallustius Crispus), developed a peculiar, journalistic style of his own.

The military upheavals of the 40s and 30s BC brought the destruction of the Roman Republic and the establishment of the Roman Empire under Augustus. Augustus knew the propaganda value of literature and encouraged writers to focus on the benefits of his reign. The greatest of the Augustan poets were Virgil (Publius Vergilius Maro, on whom there is a separate article) and Horace (Quintus Horatius Flaccus).

Horace wrote "Conversations" in verse called *Satires*. They contained anecdotes, criticism, and comments on literature and social customs. But his greatest work was a collection of lyric poems called odes and epodes, which express his thoughts and feelings on many subjects—friendship, how to enjoy life, and country pursuits. Some poems are lighthearted, while others are more serious. He also wrote a book on how to compose poetry.

Virgil's first two literary works are about the country, which he loved. The *Eclogues* are a collection of short poems, some written in dialogue, about shepherds and their flocks. The *Georgics* is about the art of farming. There are lovely descriptions of the country, the farm animals, the "society" of bees, and the happy contented life of the farmer. Virgil's most important work was the *Aeneid*, an epic poem full of patriotism about Aeneas' flight from Troy and his journey to Italy to found a new nation (see AENEID). The *Aeneid* was such a great poem that it could not be surpassed, and later Latin poets did little more than imitate Virgil.

The other great writer of the Augustan Age was the historian Livy (Titus Livius), who wrote the whole history of Rome from its founding in 753 BC to his own day. Less than a third of the 144 books that Livy wrote survive, but these are still the most important source of our knowledge of Roman history.

Among lesser writers of the Augustan period were the poets Ovid (Publius Ovidius Naso), who spent much of his life in exile, and Propertius and Tibullus, who wrote beautiful love poetry in elegiac verse.

The Silver Age (AD 17–130). The poets' hopes for a wise and just rule by the emperors was not found in Augustus' successors. During the first century AD there were four evil emperors, the worst of whom was Nero. Perhaps because the government was so evil, Latin literature turned toward satire, or writing which ridicules. With few exceptions, the best writers of the century were satirists.

The chief exception is Lucius Annaeus Seneca, a philosopher and writer of tragedies who was put to death by Nero in 65. His plays were not distinguished, perhaps because Seneca was more a moral philosopher than a dramatist. In his only satire, Seneca made fun of the Emperor Claudius.

A generation later, Martial (Marcus Valerius Martials) and Juvenal (Decimus Junius Juvenalis) wrote satires in verse, criticizing Roman society and customs. Martial wrote short witty poems called *Epigrams*, laughing at the evils of the times. Juvenal wrote longer *Satires*, filled with anger against the low morals, the greed, dishonesty, and injustices he saw about him.

The last important Classical Latin authors were prose writers. They were the two Plinys and Cornelius Tacitus. Pliny the Elder (Gaius Plinius Secundus) had one of the most inquiring minds of any man. He wrote an enormous amount, much of it lost. His most substantial surviving work is a vast treatise on natural history, written in 37 books. He died in the eruption of Mount Vesuvius in AD 79 (see POMPEII). His nephew Pliny the Younger (Gaius Plinius Caecilius Secundus) wrote *Letters*, which are really informal essays on various subjects. One letter, written when he was governor of a province, asks the emperor what to do about the Christians, who would not consent to worship the statue of the emperor. Pliny tells how surprised he was to learn that the Christians were not criminals, as everyone believed, but good honest people who did no one any harm.

Tacitus, the greatest prose writer of this period, wrote a history of Rome under the empire. He and his family had suffered greatly under the tyrants Nero and Domitian, and Tacitus paints a dark picture of the emperors' crimes. He also wrote about Britain and Germany. Tacitus' style, often taut and full of unusual words, is in marked contrast to that of Cicero and Caesar.

LATIN AMERICA is the region of the world that includes Mexico, Central America, the West Indies, and South America. It is called Latin America because most of the Europeans who settled the area were from Spain and Portugal. These Europeans are called Latin peoples because their languages developed from Latin. There are also many Caribbean countries such as Jamaica and Trinidad that are English speaking and were at one time British colonies.

Latin America accounts for 15 per cent of the land area of the world, and its population is about 8 per cent of the world's total. It spans 88 degrees of latitude, representing a north-south distance of more than 9,650 kilometres (6,000 miles). The Equator passes through Latin America, with the larger portion of the land area located in the southern hemisphere. Much of the area lies within the low latitudes (between the Tropics of Cancer and Capricorn), and the climates of Latin America are generally tropical and subtropical.

Some parts of the land area of Latin America

are extremely wide, and some parts are quite narrow. South America, for instance, is more than 4,830 kilometres (3,000 miles) wide at its widest point. The Isthmus of Panama, on the other hand, narrows to about 48 kilometres (30 miles) in width. Seven time zones cross the region. See also CENTRAL AMERICA; SOUTH AMERICA; WEST INDIES.

INDEPENDENT COUNTRIES OF LATIN AMERICA WHICH HAVE SEPARATE ARTICLES

ANTIGUA AND	GUYANA
BARBUDA	HAITI
ARGENTINA	HONDURAS
BAHAMAS	JAMAICA
BARBADOS	MEXICO
BELIZE	NICARAGUA
BOLIVIA	PANAMA
BRAZIL	PARAGUAY
CHILE	PERU
COLOMBIA	SAINT CHRISTOPHER-
COSTA RICA	NEVIS
CUBA	SAINT LUCIA
DOMINICA	SAINT VINCENT AND
DOMINICAN REPUBLIC	THE GRENADINES
ECUADOR	SURINAM
EL SALVADOR	TRINIDAD AND TOBAGO
GRENADA	URUGUAY
GUATEMALA	VENEZUELA

LATIN AMERICAN LITERATURE is that body of writing in Spanish and Portuguese that originates in Central and South America. It began with the reports sent to Spain by the Spanish conquerors of the New World. Christopher Columbus sent a joyful "Letter of Discovery" from the island of Hispaniola. In five long reports (*Cartas de relación*) sent to Emperor Charles V, Hernán Cortés told of his conquest of the Aztec empire (Mexico) and described its lands and peoples. Thirty years later, *La historia verdadera de la conquista de la Nueva España* ("True History of the Conquest of New Spain") was written by Bernal Díaz del Castillo (1492–c.1581). This former soldier of Cortés was past 60 when he wrote, but his memory was so keen that his story is the most vivid and accurate of the many chronicles.

The courageous deeds of the Spaniards and the bravery of the Indians inspired several long heroic poems. The greatest of these, *La Araucana*, by the Spaniard Alonso de Ercilla

(1533–94), described the fierce and noble resistance of the Indians of Chile and the hardships the poet himself suffered in these campaigns. This poem, of more than 20,000 verses, is the first real literary work of the new land.

By 1600 the conquest was over. The European invaders were now the masters and the Indians often slaves. Although life became more settled, the upper classes still thought of Spain and Portugal as home. Their writings, though often about American subjects, were usually poor imitations of those of the mother country. One excellent poet appeared in Mexico. She was the nun Sor Juana Inés de la Cruz (1651–95), a brilliant woman who wrote much poetry and plays. The greatest writer of the Portuguese colony of Brazil was José Basílio da Gama (1740–95). His masterpiece, *O Uraguai* (1769), described a Spanish and Portuguese campaign in 1756 against seven Jesuit missions along the Uruguay River and introduced the theme of the Indian into Brazilian poetry.

Freedom and Romanticism (1808–88)

The struggle of the Spanish colonies for freedom (1808–26) also marked the beginning of their cultural independence. From this time on, writers thought and wrote more as Latin Americans than as descendants of Spaniards or Portuguese. Their work was concerned with social issues. But cruel and oppressive regimes could make it very difficult for them to write freely. The war years produced much patriotic and political writing. The Ecuadorian José Joaquín de Olmedo's (1780–1847) ode to Simón Bolívar, *La victoria de Junín* ("Victory of Junín"), is still read with pride. Another excellent poet was José María de Heredia (1803–39) of Cuba. His descriptions of the forces of nature include a poem on Niagara Falls, written during a period of political exile in the United States.

Latin America's first real novelist was the Mexican José Joaquín Fernández de Lizardi (1776–1827), whose *El periquillo sarniento* ("The Itching Parrot") was published in 1816. This story of a *picaro*, or wandering rogue, was intended to criticize the customs of the time. It is still one of Mexico's most popular books.

The struggle to set up steady governments after the wars brought several dictators to power. Among the most hated was Juan Manuel Rosas of Argentina. During his bloody rule many writers were driven into exile. From nearby countries, they wrote against Rosas. *Amalia* (1851), a novel by José Mármol (1818–71), pictured the terrors of Rosas' rule. *Facundo* (1845), a long essay by the great teacher Domingo Sarmiento (1811–88), explained how unsettled conditions had helped these dictators rise to power and predicted their downfall when governments became stable.

Sarmiento and Mármol belonged to a group of writers influenced by the Romantic movement in Europe. In their search for material, the Romanticists often turned to the history of their countries or to the lives of simple people. The best historical novel is *Enriquillo* (1882) by Manuel de Jesús Galván (1834–1911), of the Dominican Republic, which describes the massacre of the Indians of Hispaniola by the conquering Spaniards. Many stories and poems were written about Indian legends and frontier struggles. The most popular novel of the time was *María* (1867), a love story by Jorge Isaacs (1837–95) of Colombia. Early Brazilian Romanticism produced the poet Antônio Gonçalves Dias (1823–64).

Latin American Romanticism produced the poems written about the *gauchos*, the cowboys of the *pampas* (grasslands). The picturesque gaucho was made a national figure by such writers as José Hernández (1834–86) and Estanislao del Campo (1834–80), both of Argentina. Hernández' most famous work was *Martín Fierro* (1872), a great poem which describes the gaucho's struggle against a society which destroyed his freedom.

Ricardo Palma (1833–1919) of Peru turned to the past for his subject matter. In the ten volumes of *Tradiciones peruanas* ("Peruvian Traditions") he told, in a delightful style, about the days before the conquest and when Peru was still under Spanish rule.

Realism and Naturalism

Latin America, like Europe, also had its Realist and Naturalist writers. Their works described urban life and changes in society, and people as they really were. But, like the Romanticists, Realist writers made use of *costumbrismo*—that is, the depiction of folk types and typical scenes. Law and order, middle-class virtues, honesty, and trust are upheld; greed and speculation denounced. The Argentinian Naturalist writer Eugenio de Cambaceres (1843–88) comments harshly on contemporary values in *Sin rumbo* ("Without Direction"; 1885).

In Brazil the first important Realist novel was *Memórias de um Sargento de Milicias* ("Memoirs of a Militia Sergeant"; 1854–55) by Manuel Antônio de Almeida (1831–61), which describes the street life of Rio de Janeiro. Joaquim Maria Machado de Assis (1839–1908) is perhaps the greatest of Brazilian novelists and short-story writers. His finest novel is *Dom Casmurro* (1900). In 1902 Euclydes da Cunha (1866–1909) published *Os Sertões* ("Rebellion in the Backlands"), inspired by a government military drive against the racially mixed people living in the dry cattle-country of the northeast.

Modern Literature (after 1888)

Before 1888, Latin American writers usually followed the literary styles of foreign countries. But the Cuban José Martí (1853–95) and the Peruvian Manuel González Prada (1848–1918), who wrote both poetry and prose, aimed to change things through a new, vigorous attitude to language. In 1888, however, one famous book of poetry caused a stir. The book, called *Azul*, was by a Nicaraguan, Rubén Darío, who coined the term Modernism. This new style aimed at a higher level of awareness and sensitivity, and to use language in a new and exciting way. Modernism had many moods. It embraced José Asunción Silva (1865–96) of Colombia and Manuel Gutiérrez Nájera (1859–95) of Mexico. But it reached its peak with Darío, a most fluent poet; Leopoldo Lugones (1874–1938) of Argentina; Amado Nervo (1870–1943) of Mexico; and Delmira Agustini (1886–1914) of Uruguay.

At first, the poets expressed only their own feelings in elegant and musical verse. After the Spanish-American War (1898), however, they began to write about the beauty, and the problems, of their own countries.

Later Realism and Regionalism

The Spanish American Realist and regionalist novels of the 20th century describe a hostile environment, strange peoples, and social injustice—especially the treatment of the Indians. The Mexican Mariano Azuela (1873–1952) wrote *Los de abajo* ("The Underdogs"; 1916), which brings home the horrors and suffering of the Mexican Revolution. Eustasio Rivera (1889–1928), of Colombia, in *La vorágine* ("The Vortex"; 1924), gives a powerful account of the tragic and violent lives of rubber workers in the jungle.

Barbarism and civilization are contrasted in *Doña Bárbara* (1929) by the Venezuelan Rómulo Gallegos (1884–1969), set among the cowboys and ranchers of the plains. In his short stories—many set in the tropical regions of northern Argentina—the Uruguayan Horacio Quiroga (1878–1937) pits man against unpredictable nature.

In an outstanding novel *Don Segundo Sombra* (1926), the Argentinian Ricardo Güiraldes (1886–1927) tells the story of an orphan boy who runs away from a provincial town and is taken in hand by a gaucho. He grows up learning the discipline and skills of the gaucho.

In Brazil, authors stressed how vital it was for the country's regions, especially the vast northeast, to defend their culture. José Lins do Rego (1901–57) in his *Ciclo de Cana de Açucar* ("Sugar Cane Cycle"), a series of novels, explores the way of life of what he considers typical Brazil. Erico Veríssimo (1905–75) in his multi-volume *O Tempo e o Vento* ("Time and the Wind"; 1948–63) lovingly re-creates the history of the province of Rio Grande do Sul. João Guimarães Rosa (1908–67) transferred regionalism to a higher plane. In his *Grande Sertão: Veredas* ("The Devil to Pay in the Backlands"; 1956), the

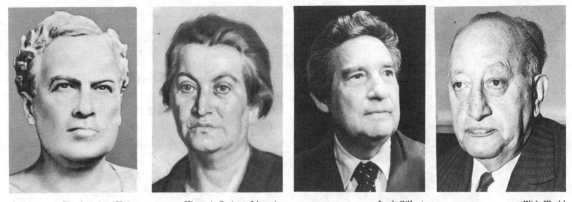

Left to right: Poets Ruben Dario of Nicaragua, Gabriela Mistral of Chile, and Octavio Paz of Mexico, and the Guatemalan novelist Miguel Angel Asturias.

sertão, a vast remote and inhospitable region of northeast Brazil, stands for the whole world.

Later Poetry

Poetry after Modernism has produced some fine writers. The message of Gabriela Mistral (1889–1957), of Chile, is simple and direct. Her collection *Desolación* (1922) is a moving expression of her longing for children. César Vallejo (1892–1938) is perhaps the greatest of all Spanish American poets. In his collections *Trilce* ("Triste", sad and "Dulce", sweet; 1922) and *Poemas humanos* (published after his death), he used the Spanish language in a daringly and startlingly new way. He left a close-knit family life in provincial Peru for political activity in Europe as a Communist during the Spanish Civil War in the 1930s.

Pablo Neruda (1904–73), of Chile, also embraced Communism. His poetry, above all his great epic *Canto general* (1938–50), is a burst of spontaneous personal experience. He writes on behalf of the persecuted and oppressed. The Mexican Octavio Paz (born 1914) writes on many subjects. His collection *Libertad bajo palabra* ("Liberty under the Word"; 1968) emphasizes his view that poetry is revelation and leads to human liberation.

In the 1920s Brazil had its own Modernist movement, unconnected with Spanish American Modernism. It centred mainly on São Paulo and its poets and novelists stressed sophisticated urban nationalism. They wanted a break with the past. *Memórias Sentimentais de João Miramar* (1924), a novel by Oswald de Andrade (1890–1954), typifies the new spirit. In contrast, the poet Jorge de Lima (1893–1953) celebrates black people and comments on their sufferings.

The Modern Novel

Modern prose-writing in Latin America has given the world authors of international reputation who have not hesitated to experiment. Jorge Luis Borges (1899–1986), who began his writing career in the vibrant intellectual atmosphere of Buenos Aires during the 1920s, wrote short stories and essays in which he explored the nature of self in a universe too difficult to understand. Borges, the outstanding Argentinian writer of modern times, is among the greatest of all writers in Spanish. Miguel Angel Asturias (1899–1974), of Guatemala, in his masterpiece *El Señor Presidente* (1946) writes of the misery caused by dictatorship.

The Paraguayan Augusto Roa Bastos (born 1917) treats a similar theme in *Hijo del hombre* ("Son of Man"; 1965), but in a tender and moving style. The published work of the Mexican Juan Rulfo (1918–85) is one short novel, *Pedro Páramo* (1955), and a slim collection of short stories, *El llano en llamas* ("The Burning Plain"; 1953). But these are enough to make his reputation as a master. Both are set in a hot, desolate valley.

Pan American Union

The Colombian writer Gabriel García Márquez
working at his typewriter.

Gabriel García Márquez (born 1928), of Colombia, was the winner of the 1982 Nobel Prize for Literature. His great novel *Cien años de soledad* ("One Hundred Years of Solitude"; 1967), is about the isolation and wonder of Spanish America. It is a mythical work, told in a traditional, sometimes humorous way. The novels and short stories of the Mexican Carlos Fuentes (born 1928) examine the ways of his huge, sprawling, and fascinating country. The leading Peruvian novelist is Mario Vargas Llosa (born 1936) whose *La ciudad y los perros* ("The City and the Dogs"; 1963) exposes the brutal life of a military academy and thus the weaknesses of Peruvian society.

Brazilian writing continues to reflect the tension between regional tradition and modernization. The loneliness of life in a big city is expressed in the novel *Angústia* (1936) by Graciliano Ramos (1892–1953). The poem *Vida e Morte Severina* ("Life and Death of a Severino"; 1955) by João Cabral de Melo Neto (born 1920) illustrates the tug between traditional roots and modern life.

LATITUDE AND LONGITUDE. The position of a place on the Earth's surface may be described by giving its latitude and longitude. On maps, charts, and globes the lines running east and west parallel to the equator are called parallels of latitude. The lines running north and south are the meridians of longitude and pass through the poles.

Latitude is measured in degrees north and south of the equator. The North Pole is at latitude 90 degrees north (usually written 90°N). London is at latitude 51.30°N, while Toronto is at latitude 43°N. The equator is at latitude 0°, Sydney is in about 33°S, and Auckland (New Zealand) at about 37°S.

Longitude is measured in degrees east and west of the meridian of Greenwich, which was chosen in 1884 by the nations of the world as

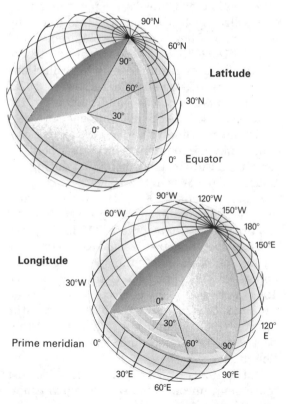

Degrees of latitude and longitude are the degrees of angles measured from the centre of the Earth.

the prime, or chief, meridian. Greenwich is a few miles east of London on the south bank of the Thames, and is itself at longitude 0°. New York is at about longitude 74 degrees West (74°W) and Melbourne at about 145°E.

Latitude and longitude are used for navigation by sailors and airmen who travel over the oceans and who therefore cannot always fix their positions by reference to some nearby landmark or town. (See NAVIGATION.) The latitude of a place can be found by observing with instruments the position of the Sun, stars or Moon. Longitude can only be found if the precise time is known.

The length of a degree of latitude is about 111 kilometres (69 statute miles, that is, miles on land), and exactly 60 sea miles (also called nautical miles). The length of a degree of longitude is the same as that of a degree of latitude *only at the equator*. It becomes less towards the poles, where it is zero.

LATVIA is a Baltic country that lies between the two other Baltic states: Estonia to the north, and Lithuania to the south. Russia lies to the east of Latvia, Belarus to the southeast, and the Baltic Sea to the west. Between 1940 and 1991 Latvia was part of the Soviet Union.

Much of Latvia is fairly flat, with large forests of spruce, pine, birch, and alder, and the country is crossed by numerous slow-moving rivers. The longest river, the Daugava, rises in Russia, and flows through Latvia to the Gulf of Riga. There are many sandy beaches on Latvia's Baltic Sea coastline. Winters in Latvia are long and cold, and summers short but usually warm and dry. The Latvians celebrate the longest day of the year at Midsummer (24th June) with bonfires and dancing. In June and July the summer nights are short and light.

Riga, the capital of Latvia, lies as far north as Aberdeen and Hudson Bay. It has been an important port for centuries. Before the coming of modern industry, it imported salt, spices, wines, and colonial goods from the West, and exported flax and hemp for rope- and sailmaking, as well as corn and timber.

Every spring, with the thawing of the wide River Daugava, thousands of rafts of timber would arrive in Riga, steered downstream all the way from Russia by fierce-looking bargemen. The coming of the railways ended this river traffic and Riga became a big industrial city. Before the coming of industry, most of the people living in Riga spoke German. As its industries expanded, thousands of Latvians flocked to the city from the countryside in search of work. By 1918, when Latvia became an independent country, the majority of the people in Riga spoke Latvian. Following the outbreak of World War II, in 1939, and the annexation of Latvia by the Soviet Union in 1940, almost all of Riga's German-speaking residents returned to Germany, to be replaced by Russians, who now form the majority in the city. Latvians still form the majority of the population of the country as a whole.

Present-day Latvia is an industrialized country. It manufactures heavy machinery, railway equipment, ships, and farm machines. During the period when it was part of the Soviet Union, Latvia was the principal manufacturer of refrigerators, radios, record players, and television sets for the whole of the Soviet Union. Latvian farmers rear cattle, pigs, and poultry, and there is a large food-processing industry in the country.

History

The Latvian tribes who inhabited the area around the River Daugava first came under foreign rule in the early 13th century, when

German crusaders built a castle and the town of Riga. These Teutonic knights ruled most of the territory inhabited by the Latvians, and the Estonians, to the north, until the middle of the 16th century. This territory was known as Livonia. In 1561 the last Master of the Teutonic knights swore obedience to the King of Poland. He became duke of Kurland, the land to the south of the River Daugava. The rest of Livonia came under Swedish control in 1626 and was conquered by Peter the Great of Russia in 1710. The Duchy of Kurland also became a part of the Russian Empire in 1795.

FACTS ABOUT LATVIA

AREA: 63,700 square kilometres (24,600 square miles).
POPULATION: 2,680,000 (1989).
GOVERNMENT: Republic.
CAPITAL: Riga, 915,000
GEOGRAPHY: The land is fairly flat, with large forests and numerous slow-flowing rivers.
CITIES: Daugavpils, Liepāja, Jelgava, Ventspils.
CHIEF PRODUCTS: Heavy machinery, railway equipment, ships, farm machinery, electrical consumer goods.
EDUCATION: Children must go to school between the ages of 6 and 16.

During this period the Latvian people were tied (not free) peasants working for German-speaking masters. In 1819 they were given their personal freedom and a prosperous farming community began to emerge. After the Russian Revolution, in 1917, Latvia became independent, and the large estates of the landowners were divided up into smaller farms, which were offered for sale to the peasants. But Latvian independence was short-lived, for in the summer of 1940, the country was taken over by the Soviet Union. A year later it was occupied by Germany, after that country attacked the USSR. In 1944 the Germans were driven out by the Soviet army. There was some Latvian resistance to the restoration of Soviet rule, and thousands of Latvians were killed or deported by force to Siberia.

In the late 1980s, when Soviet rule was relaxed, Latvians again campaigned for independence, which they achieved in 1991, shortly before the break-up of the USSR.

LAUD, William (1573–1645). This famous English clergyman, who became archbishop of Canterbury, was born at Reading, in southern England, on 7 October 1573. He was the son of a wealthy cloth merchant and was educated at the grammar school in Reading. He went to St. John's College, Oxford University, in 1589, became a Church of England clergyman in 1601, and president of St. John's College in 1611.

In England at that time, particularly in the universities, there were great arguments about religion. The Puritans wanted to follow the severe type of Protestantism that John Calvin had taught (see CALVIN, JOHN; PURITANS). At the other extreme were people who wished to bring back Roman Catholicism. The Church of England was midway between the two. Laud thought this was right. He believed that when England became Protestant at the time of the Reformation (see REFORMATION) it had returned to the teaching and form of worship of the early Christians. He was therefore pleased with the religious position in

Mansell Collection

Archbishop Laud died for his belief in a middle-of-the-road Church of England, neither Puritan nor Catholic.

England. He strongly opposed the Puritans, who wanted to do away with all religious ceremonies.

He found greater opportunities for enforcing his ideas when he became archbishop of Canterbury in 1633. He did not hesitate to use the courts of the Star Chamber to make people accept what he declared to be the rules of the Church of England.

Laud also played an important part in politics and believed in the Divine Right of Kings. (See the article JAMES (KINGS OF BRITAIN)). He therefore supported King Charles I against parliament and when Charles tried to govern without parliament Laud was one of his chief supporters. Laud thought that both religious and political affairs should be directed by the sovereign, who could be relied upon to govern for the benefit of all his people. He considered that anybody who had different ideas was wrong and even wicked.

These beliefs and his high-handed ways made Laud very unpopular with the Puritans. In 1640—just before the Civil War broke out, when the king was already losing his power—parliament had Laud imprisoned in the Tower of London. In 1644 he was tried and found guilty of supporting royal tyranny, seeking to bring back Roman Catholicism, and trying to destroy the rights of parliament.

He was condemned to death, and beheaded on Tower Hill on 10 January 1645. After the Civil War was over the Church of England became very much what Laud had wanted it to be.

LAUNDRY. Doing the washing or laundry is a problem that every household has to face. Clothes and household linen have to be kept clean to prevent the build up of bacteria, to remove dirt accumulated through wear, and to keep them looking attractive.

Before the use of machinery, laundry had to be done at home or be sent out to people who were paid to do it by hand. Water had to be heated over a fire, the clothes and linen had to be scrubbed with soap and thoroughly rinsed. Next they were wrung out and then dried outside in the sun or inside by a fire. The garments were then ironed with a flat iron heated on a stove. Garments that were not washable were brushed and beaten and possibly pressed with an iron. It was laborious work and much of it depended on there being good weather to dry the laundry.

The invention of labour-saving machinery, now operated by electricity, has reduced the time and effort needed. The chemical industry provides detergents, bleaches, fabric softeners and brighteners, and the textile industry provides fabrics which do not need ironing. So washing day no longer needs to dominate the household.

Washing Machines

The earliest washing machines had a central "agitator" to keep the soapy water and laundry moving. The machine had to be emptied and refilled with clean water for rinsing. The laundry was next put through a wringer or mangle, which was a pair of rollers set close together to squeeze out the water.

The first major development in washing machines was the revolving cylinder. At first it failed to work because the clothes were pressed against the side of the drum by centrifugal force and the dirt was not removed. The rotary washer with reversing action, patented in 1863 by Hamilton E. Smith of Philadelphia, solved the problem by constantly turning over the clothes into the suds. Centrifugal force is used to remove the water by "spin drying", and tumble dryers are now often used to toss the laundry in heated air for final drying. Automatic machines which combine both washing and drying are now used in many homes. All the operator has to do is put in the laundry and the washing powder and set the machine at the correct temperature.

If you do not have a washing machine, you can take your laundry to a launderette and do it yourself in the machines provided. The machines are coin-operated. There may also be machines for dispensing washing powder and bleach, as well as snacks or refreshments.

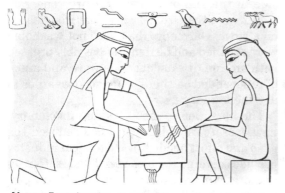

Above: Egyptian drawing showing early methods of laundering; **Below:** A 19th-century washing machine used a wooden tank; **Right:** Women in Belize, Central America, wash clothing on rocks in a stream.

Courtesy, (above) American Institute of Laundering; (below) Bettman Archive; (right) Paul Conklin/Pix from Publix; (bottom) Courtesy, Electrolux—Wascator

In a launderette, coin-operated automatic washers (left) and dryers (right) are available for anyone to use. Washing powder can be obtained from a coin-operated dispenser.

Laundries

The first commercial laundry in the United States was opened in 1835 for the laundering of detachable collars. In 1851 the Contra Costa laundry was established in Oakland, California. At first all the work was done by hand. Later a 12-shirt washing machine was built, powered by a ten-horse-power donkey engine.

In a modern commercial laundry bundles of clothes are sorted into different colours to be washed separately. Garments are placed in net bags to keep each customer's laundry separate. The suds go freely through the nets. Most laundries use water softeners to counteract "hard" water, which is water containing minerals such as calcium and magnesium salts that make sudsing and rinsing difficult. They also use bleach, which is added to the suds to remove stains and kill germs. Bluing or brighteners are added to white fabrics to keep them looking white and clean.

After washing and drying, the laundry is ironed. Flat pieces, such as table and bed linen are finished on huge ironers and then folded. Shirts and other garments are pressed on shaped, padded forms.

Large institutions such as hospitals and hotels often have their own laundries to clean the linen and staff uniforms. Special chemicals may be used in hospital laundries to kill bacteria, and all the equipment used is sterilized by steam to prevent the spread of diseases in the hospital.

A special kind of laundry provides linen and sometimes uniforms to restaurants, hotels, offices, large stores, and hospitals. The laundry owns the linen and keeps the customer supplied with clean items in return for the soiled ones on a regular schedule. The advantage to the laundry is that there is no need to identify the individual pieces for each customer.

Dry Cleaning

The dry cleaning industry started in the middle of the 19th century. There is a story about a French sailor who fell into a vat of turpentine. When his uniform dried it was clean. Camphene, which is produced from pinene, the main constituent of turpentine, is a liquid that was often used at this time to remove spots from garments, which were then washed. Gradually, more solvents were developed for dry cleaning, but many are highly flammable or have poisonous fumes. They all leave a strong smell which must be removed after cleaning.

Modern dry cleaning companies usually use either petroleum or synthetic solvents. The petroleum type can be used in an open machine like a washing machine, but synthetic solvents evaporate quickly in the air and must be used in closed, airtight machines. Items for cleaning are sorted according to their fibre and by colour. The process is similar to washing and rinsing, except that the solvent is used instead of water. Since the solvent evaporates quickly, cleaning by this method is "dry", or without water. After cleaning, garments are pressed with steam to return them to their proper shape.

LAUREL. Nowadays laurel bushes are often grown for ornament in gardens, but in ancient Greece and Rome poets and victorious warriors were crowned with wreaths made of laurel. Nowadays the phrase "winning laurels" is still used to mean success.

The laurel used for wreaths was sweet bay or bay laurel (*Laurus nobilis*) (see BAY). This and the other true laurel, Canary Island laurel (*Laurus canariensis*), which grows in the Canary Islands and in Madeira, belong to the family Lauraceae. However, there are many other shrubs called laurels which belong to different plant families.

The European cherry laurel (*Prunus laurocerasus*) and the Portugal laurel (*Prunus lusitanica*) of the family Rosaceae are both evergreen shrubs or small trees with dark green, leathery, glossy leaves. The leaves of the cherry laurel are poisonous and contain prussic acid. Its flowers are bright pink and white and appear in the spring, followed by red berries which later turn black. The flowers of the Portugal laurel are white and come out in summer.

There are several North American plants

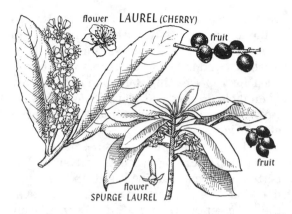

flower LAUREL (CHERRY)

fruit

fruit

flower
SPURGE LAUREL

known as laurels. The California laurel (*Umbellularia californica*) is an evergreen tree of the Pacific coastal region. Its yellowish-green flowers appear in the winter or early spring. Mountain laurel (*Kalmia latifolia*), of the heath family, is a rhododendron-like shrub. It forms dense thickets in rocky woods in eastern North America. The bowl-shaped blooms are made up of many small cup-shaped pink flowers.

The spurge laurel or garland flower, *Daphne laureola*, belongs to the thyme family, and is a shrub just over 1 metre (3.3 feet) high. It grows in woods in Europe, central Asia, China, Japan, and in India, where its bark is used to make paper. Because of the long tube formed by its coloured sepals it is only visited by long-tongued insects, such as bumble bees and some moths, which suck out the honey. The shiny, leathery leaves which grow in clusters remain on the plant for two years. *Daphne*, the name of its genus, comes from the Greek legend of Daphne, who was changed into a laurel tree when pursued by Apollo.

The Japan or variegated laurel (*Aucuba japonica*) belongs to the dogwood family and grows in the Himalayas and in Japan. It is cultivated for the leaves of the female plant, which are a mixture of dark and yellowish green, and look rather as though they have been splashed with distemper. The leaves of the male are plain green. The New Zealand laurel (*Corynocarpus laevigus*) is an evergreen shrub with extremely poisonous orange fruit.

LAURENTIAN MOUNTAINS. In the Canadian province of Quebec is the highland belt called the Laurentian Mountains, also called Les Laurentides, stretching for 1,600 kilometres (995 miles) from the Ottawa River to the Strait of Belle Isle. It has a steep margin overlooking the valley of the St. Lawrence River.

The Laurentians form the southeastern border of a huge block of the Earth's crust called the Laurentian or Canadian Shield. The Shield, so called because of its shape, curves round Hudson Bay and as far as Labrador. It was once a great mountain system and has been worn away by the ice sheets of the great Ice Age into a hilly country with many hollows which are now filled with lakes.

In many places the Laurentians do not rise above 300 metres (990 feet) and only north of the city of Quebec do they reach 900 metres (3,000 feet). They have a long severe winter but the parts in which people live are warm and sunny in summer. Bear, moose, caribou, and deer live in the forests, although the trapping of these animals for their fur and skin is now less important than it was in the past. The trunks of the spruce, pine, and fir trees are floated down the rivers to be made into sawn timber, wood pulp, and paper. The rivers are also used for making electric power.

The rocks are rich in minerals, and at some places at the western end of the Laurentians, such as Noranda and Kirkland Lake, gold and copper are found together. There are deposits of bauxite (from which aluminium is obtained). Mica is mined, and there are quarries for limestone, granite, and marble. Iron ore is mined at Schefferville in Labrador and the Laurentians contain the largest known deposit of titanium in the world. Around Lake St. John is a prosperous agricultural lowland.

Winter sports can be enjoyed in the Laurentian Mountains and many visitors come in summer to explore the beautiful scenery in canoes and to shoot and fish.

LAURIER, Sir Wilfrid (1841–1919) was the first French-Canadian prime minister of Canada. He was born in the French-Canadian village of St. Lin, in Quebec province. He attended French and English schools, which helped him to understand both national groups. When he was 30 years old he was elected to the Quebec provincial legislature. At 33 he entered the Canadian House of Commons, where he served the rest of his life. He was a brilliant speaker in French and English. At all times Laurier tried to get all Canadians to work together.

BBC Hulton Picture Library

Sir Wilfrid Laurier, Liberal prime minister of Canada, 1896–1911.

Not until 1887 did he become the leader of the Liberal party, though for years he had been leader of the French-Canadian group in the party. In 1896 he became prime minister, and in the next year he was made a knight by Queen Victoria.

During this period Canada was growing at its most rapid rate, especially in the prairie region of the west. Laurier saw the need for better transport, and he encouraged the building of the railways from coast to coast.

In 1900, when the Boer War broke out between the British and the Boers in South Africa, Laurier rallied Canadians to fight for the mother country. But though loyal to Britain, he also believed that Canada must be a strong, self-governing nation. He wanted his country to be held to Britain not by legal bonds but by friendship and common interests.

In the election of 1911 the Liberal party was defeated, and Robert Borden became prime minister (see BORDEN, SIR ROBERT LAIRD). In 1914, at the beginning of World War I, Laurier urged that Canada should help Britain against Germany. But when Borden wanted to conscript men into service, Laurier opposed him. The French-Canadians were with Laurier, but in the election of 1917 they were badly defeated. Two years later Laurier died.

LAVA is rock that has been forced from inside the Earth in a molten (hot fluid) condition. The lava comes out through holes or cracks in the solid crust of the Earth and its appearance depends to a large extent on the temperature and composition of the molten lava. Lava from a rounded hole spreads into a more or less rounded puddle and cools into rock. If more lava is forced out later, it flows over the earlier layer, making it higher. After this has happened many times, a mountain of rock called a volcano is formed (see VOLCANO). The rounded hole through which the lava flows is called the pipe.

Sometimes the crack through which the lava flows is a long thin one called a fissure, in which the lava forms a thin and fairly even bed over a large area. Sometimes a lava flow comes out of a pipe or fissure and spreads over the land, covering or burning everything it meets. These lava flows may vary in thickness from a centimetre to hundreds of metres.

Towns close to volcanoes are always in danger of being destroyed by a flow of lava or ash. In AD 79 the volcano Mount Vesuvius erupted and overwhelmed the towns of Pompeii, Herculaneum, and Stabiae not far south of modern Naples in Italy. Herculaneum and Stabiae were buried under lava but Pompeii was covered mostly by ash which, in modern times, it has been possible to dig away. (See POMPEII.) Sometimes the lava flow covers a forest, and the trees are buried under rock.

Courtesy, US Department of the Interior

Publishers' Photo Service

Aa lava, which has a clinker-like appearance, is formed when the hardening crust of the lava flow is broken up by a further eruption. *Pahoehoe* has a wrinkled or ropy surface, formed as the flowing lava solidifies. Both are common in Hawaii, where their names come from.

Later, water trickling down through the rocks rots away the tree trunks and replaces them with particles of silica and other minerals. After many years, the entire tree-trunk is replaced by silica. At the bottom of the Grand Canyon in Arizona (United States) there are 15 layers of these stone trees, those in the lowest layer being probably 15 million years old.

Different Types of Lava

The appearance of lava depends on the way in which it was pushed out of the Earth, on its chemical composition and on its rate of cooling. If the lava is forced out in a slowly flowing stream it is usually laid down in beds. If it is thrown out by a violent explosion from a volcano, the lava may cool as it flies through the air and form smooth almond-shaped lumps called bombs, or hot incandescent (glowing) dust. The smallest fragments fall as ash. If the lava is forced out under the sea, each outflow is rapidly cooled by the water and the lava solidifies in the shape of a pile of tumbled pillows, called pillow lava. The volcanoes in the Hawaiian Islands sometimes gush forth lava with such force that it spurts upwards in glow-ing fountains hundreds of metres high, cooling to fall as droplets and threads.

Most forms of lava contain a quantity of silica. Sand is usually composed of the mineral quartz, which is pure silica. Lava containing much silica is usually thick and sticky. It flows stiffly and does not spread out much. Lava of this kind tends to solidify as a kind of glassy rock, especially if cooled rapidly. The natural volcanic glass known as obsidian was long used by early peoples for knives and arrow heads. Other lava containing less silica and more of such substances as lime, magnesia, and iron is quite runny when molten and spreads out as it flows. Basalt is the common-est kind of rock formed from such lava. If it cools slowly, the lava sets as crystalline rock but if cooled more rapidly it forms a semi-glassy rock. Many islands in the Pacific Ocean, such as the Hawaiian Islands, consist of basaltic lava and have been formed by volcanoes under the sea building their lava higher and higher until the mound rose above the level of the sea.

The substance called pumice or pumice-stone is a kind of lava containing a large amount of silica and produced by violent eruptions. These occur when the gases dissolved inside the lava form bubbles which make it porous, or honeycombed with little holes. Some pumice floats in water, and the great eruption of Krakatoa Island (Indonesia) in 1883 produced a floating mass of pumice more than 30 kilometres (19 miles) long and more than 800 metres (2,600 feet) across. Most pumice is obtained from the Lipari Islands just north of Sicily, Tenerife (Canary Islands), and Japan. Pumice-stone is used in industry for grinding, smoothing and polishing.

LAVENDER is known for its sweet scent, which comes from oils produced by hairs all over the flowers and leaves. Lavender water is a solution of the oil in ethyl alcohol, with various essences, such as rose, added.

Common, or English, lavender (*Lavandula vera*) is a small bush with branches growing upwards, rather than spreading out. The tough, strap-shaped, grey-green leaves are crowded together in the lower part of the bush, while the long flower-stalks stand straight up. The small mauve flowers grow in dense clusters along the stalks and are darker inside than outside. English lavender has a delicate

Lavender grows as a round bush and makes an attractive garden plant. Lavenders smell sweet and attract bees and butterflies. **Right:** Closeup of the flower heads.

aromatic odour. It was once grown in southern England on a large scale for its scent and for its oil, used to scent soaps and as a perfume. The heads of lavender are often dried and placed in gauze bags to scent clothes. More than 25 species of lavender grow wild from the Canary Islands along the Mediterranean coasts to India. Common lavender grows wild in mountainous districts round the western half of the Mediterranean, sometimes as high up as 1,300 metres (4,260 feet). Lavender does best in sunny, stony places.

In the south of France oil is obtained from the wild French lavender (*Lavandula stoechas*), spike lavender (*Lavandula spica*), and a hybrid of the two called lavandin. The flowers are collected at the beginning of August and from 12 to 30 kilograms (26 to 66 pounds) of oil are extracted from 1 hectare (2.5 acres) of bushes. These cultivated plants often have to be grown from cuttings or by having the roots divided and planted out again.

LAVOISIER, Antoine-Laurent (1743–94). The great French scientist Lavoisier was born at Paris and had a very good education. He became a chemist at the Paris Academy of Science and in 1775 was put in charge of the French government's gunpowder factories, where he made great improvements.

Lavoisier showed in the 1770s that air was a mixture of gases (see AIR) and that burning could not take place if one of these gases were absent. The gas in question had already been discovered in 1774 by the British scientist Joseph Priestly, but it was Lavoisier who, in 1777, gave it its modern name. He called it *oxygen*, the acid producer, because he thought, wrongly, that it was found in all acids. He also showed that breathing was a form of burning for which oxygen is necessary.

His results owed much to his careful use of the chemical balance (an accurate pair of weighing scales for measuring the changes of weight that happen during chemical changes). For instance, he heated mercury in air and found it gained weight by combining with oxygen from the air, thereby forming mercuric oxide. Then he showed that this gain in weight

Lavoisier was a founder of modern chemistry.

was the same as the weight of oxygen given off when mercuric oxide was heated. Modern chemists refer to such changes in weights as *quantitive* changes.

In 1783 Lavoisier announced his discovery that water is made up of oxygen and hydrogen. He went on to draw up a new system for naming chemical substances, which is still in use, and was the first person to write out a table of the chemical elements. (See ELEMENT, CHEMICAL). He did much to explain the importance of the results obtained by others; many of the current principles of chemistry are based on his work, and he has often been called the "father of modern chemistry".

Lavoisier was more than a chemist. He helped to found the metric system of weights and measures (see WEIGHTS AND MEASURES), started a special farm where he showed how

the use of scientific methods would give better crops, and tried to introduce reforms in hospitals and prisons and to encourage savings banks, insurance, and canals. In fact, he was one of the first men of science to take an active part in public affairs. That did him no good, however, for during the French Revolution the revolutionaries treated him as an enemy and eventually beheaded him at the guillotine. "It took only a moment to cut off that head", said the French mathematician Lagrange, "and perhaps a century will not suffice to produce another like it."

LAW is the body of rules by which people live together in society. Law is enforced by governments through the police and courts. Without law, communities could not live peacefully because everyone could do as they pleased, regardless of others. Wherever more than one person is living, law is necessary for settling possible conflicts.

The purpose of law is to define and make clear the relation between individuals and between the individual and society. It tries to give to each person as much liberty of action as fits in with the liberty of others.

Early Law-makers

In early societies laws generally grew out of the customs that were followed in a particular community. Such laws are known as "customary laws". The customs became laws when they were given official recognition by the ruler of the community. The earliest known such legal system was set down in the 18th century BC by Hammurabi, King of Babylon.

The Romans were the first great law-makers. They made so many different laws that by the time the emperor Justinian came to power in AD 527, the law of the Roman Empire was in a complete muddle, Justinian appointed a team of expert lawyers, who weeded out all the old laws that were unnecessary or contradictory, made the remaining laws as clear and concise as possible, and wrote some new ones. The result was what we call today the *Code of Justinian*, which forms the basis of many modern legal systems.

In the 5th and 6th centuries AD, Germanic peoples conquered much of western and central Europe and for a time Roman law was forgotten. By the 11th century, however, it had begun to return. Trade was booming in western Europe and merchants and manufacturers needed expert lawyers to regulate their affairs. Scholars trained in Roman law at universities in northern Italy, especially Bologna, were considered far superior to untrained local lawyers and were much in demand all over Europe. This law came to be known as *civil law* in contrast to *canon law*, which was the law of the church and had largely governed people's lives during the Middle Ages.

Civil law is used today on the continent of Europe, and in the former overseas possessions of France and Spain, including Latin America and parts of Asia and Africa. It is not used, however, in England or, with one or two exceptions, elsewhere in the English-speaking world. In these countries the system is based on what is known as common law.

The Common-Law System

When the Normans invaded England in 1066 they brought their own laws with them. They firmly resisted any attempt to bring Roman law to Britain. Instead, Norman customary laws were adapted to local conditions. Later, certain laws were declared to be "customs of the realm" and applied in every locality. These laws soon formed a body of *common law* – that is, laws that were common, or general, to all the people wherever they lived.

The common law was administered by officials appointed by the king. Court decisions were based on *precedent* – that is, what had been decided by a previous court in a similar case. The decisions were published in reports which were printed and circulated. The study of decisions made by previous courts is known as "case law" and became a central part of a lawyer's training.

Statutory Law

A legal system based on precedent made it difficult to make new laws. In the 13th century two kings, Henry III and Edward I, introduced what is known as *statute law* to England. Statute law consists of written laws introduced by a parliament or other law-making body. Among the most famous statute laws was the one brought in by Edward I known as the first statute of Westminster. It made trial by jury compulsory in criminal cases (see JURY).

Equity

It was also apparent that the common-law system was inadequate to remedy many injustices. In a dispute between two people the king's courts could only award damages and

Mansell Collection

The Court of King's Bench in 15th-century England was one of the courts that laid down the foundations of the modern system of common law.

order property to be returned to its owner. They could not put right frauds, compel people to keep promises, or order someone not to carry out a harmful act.

In such cases the person with the grievance had to ask for help from the king. But there were too many cases for the king to hear, so after a time petitions were referred to the king's most senior adviser, the lord chancellor. He decided each case on its merits. The chancellor's court was called the court of chancery and the justice that he dispensed was known as *equity*.

Since this time the common-law system has contained a mixture of case law, statute law and equity. From the 17th century onwards there have been many reforms, most notably in the 19th century when laws were introduced protecting the rights of the accused in a criminal court.

Common law is today the legal system in those countries in which English law was established during British Rule. As well as England it is the system used in Wales, Northern Ireland (but not Scotland), the Irish Republic, the United States (except Louisiana), Canada (except Quebec), Australia, and New Zealand. Scotland, Louisiana, and Quebec have civil-law systems.

Law in the United States

Few people among the early settlers of the New World knew much about law, but by the 17th century lawyers had arrived from England. They brought with them the English system of common law and equity. After independence there were many attempts to introduce a code of United States law along the lines of the European civil-law codes, but the common-law tradition proved too strong.

Nevertheless there are today marked differences between the law of the United States and English law. Most United States law, for instance, is based on statute rather than on case law as in England. Another important distinction is that the United States has a written constitution, guaranteeing the rights of citizens (see CONSTITUTION OF THE UNITED STATES). England has no such document. The

Ewing Galloway

"Contemplation of Justice", a statue in front of the US Supreme Court Building in Washington, DC.

United States has both state and federal law. Individual states can often choose their own laws. Only federal laws (that is, laws passed by the Congress of the United States) apply to the whole country.

European Codes of Law

Beginning in the 17th century many European nations produced their own national "codes" of civil law (a code is a complete list of laws). The most famous is the *Code Napoléon*, or Napoleonic Code, which was established in 1804 by the French emperor Napoleon Bonaparte. Napoleon's aim was to express all the laws in a language that the average citizen could understand. Similar codes were introduced in Germany and most other countries of western Europe.

Branches of the Law

The law is generally divided into two main branches: public law and private law. Public law includes international law, criminal law, constitutional law (that is, the laws that control government), and laws dealing with such matters as the administration of justice and public health and safety. Private law covers the ownership of property, the management of businesses, employment, family law, and disputes between people.

There is a further importance distinction in common-law systems. This is the one between civil law and criminal law. In this case civil law does not mean the system of justice used in Europe but rather the law that is applied in settling disputes between people. Crimes are dealt with under the criminal law. This is explained more fully in the article COURT.

Other Kinds of Law

Constitutional law and *administrative law* are the bodies of laws applying to the conduct of government and the rights of persons as set out in the state and federal constitutions. In the United States, the Supreme Court is the final court for interpreting and applying the federal constitution. The highest court in each state decides the meaning and application of the constitution of that state. Australia and Canada have similar federal courts. In the United Kingdom there is only one court system, which hears constitutional as well as private cases. (SEE COURT).

Military law is the body of laws governing the personnel of the army, navy, and air force. It began as customs of the service, but has been developed and organized by legislation. It is applied in military courts which try and punish violations of its rules.

International law is a body of customary rules which regulates the conduct of nations in their relations with one another. It has differed from other kinds of law in having no force behind it, but it is hoped that in time the United Nations may correct that defect. (See INTERNATIONAL LAW.)

SOME OTHER ARTICLES TO READ ON LAW

ARBITRATION	INQUEST
BAIL	INTERNATIONAL LAW
CAPITAL PUNISHMENT	JUDGE
CONSTITUTION OF THE	JURY
UNITED STATES	LAWYER
CONTRACT	LIBEL AND SLANDER
COPYRIGHT	POLICE
CORPORATION AND	PRISON
COMPANY	PROBATION
COURT	PUNISHMENT
CRIME	TREASON
DAMAGES	TRIAL
FORGERY AND FRAUD	TRUST
INJUNCTION	WILL

LAWN TENNIS see TENNIS.

LAWRENCE, D. H. (1885–1930). Although his work was often misunderstood during his lifetime, D. H. (David Herbert) Lawrence is now recognized as one of the greatest English novelists of the 20th century.

National Portrait Gallery, London

A painting of D. H. Lawrence in 1920.

He was born in the coal-mining village of Eastwood, Nottinghamshire, England, on 11 September 1885. His father was a coal miner and his mother had been a school teacher. Lawrence won a scholarship to Nottingham High School and later trained as a teacher at University College, Nottingham. He took a job in London but gave up teaching after the publication in 1911 of his first novel *The White Peacock*. *Sons and Lovers*, the novel which first made his name known, appeared in 1913 and the following year he married Frieda Weekley, a German woman.

For the rest of his life Lawrence and Frieda travelled widely, visiting Europe, the United States, Mexico, and Australia. He suffered from tuberculosis and died in the south of France on 2 March 1930.

Lawrence's novels closely reflect his personal experience. *Sons and Lovers*, for example, describes a young man, Paul Morel, growing up in a home very much like Lawrence's own. Lawrence's childhood in a mining community made him hate industrialization, which he thought an unnatural way of life for men and women. In contrast he developed a love of nature. He wrote about the beauty and power of nature in a vivid manner and was very critical of the restricted lives which most people were forced to lead.

Probably his best novels are *The Rainbow* (1915) and *Women in Love* (1921), which deal with the relations between men and women in marriage. Some of his views were severely criticized and the ban on one of his books, *Lady Chatterley's Lover*, was not lifted until 1961. Other novels include *The Lost Girl, Aaron's Rod, Kangaroo* (which is set in Australia), and *The Plumed Serpent*.

Lawrence also wrote short stories, three travel books, and several volumes of poetry of which perhaps the most original and lively, *Birds, Beasts and Flowers*, a collection of nature poems, appeared in 1923.

LAWRENCE, T. E. (1888–1935).

One of the most famous figures of World War I (1914–18) was the British soldier and writer T. E. (Thomas Edward) Lawrence, who became known as "Lawrence of Arabia". He was born on 15 August 1888, at Tremadoc in Wales, but went to school in Oxford. He later studied history at Jesus College, Oxford. He first visited the Middle East in 1909 to study crusader castles and returned to work on an archaeological expedition to the Euphrates.

When war was declared in 1914, Lawrence came back from an expedition into Sinai to join the map department of the War Office. He was then sent to the British military intelligence unit in Egypt. In 1916 he went on a mission to the Arab ruler, Husain ibn Ali, who was leading a revolt against the Turks. Lawrence became military adviser to Husain's son, Faisal (later king of Iraq). Lawrence put new life into the Arab revolt. He adopted Arab ways and dress and organized Faisal's men into an effective guerrilla army. The swift

National Portrait Gallery, London

Augustus John's drawing of Lawrence of Arabia in Arab dress.

Arab attacks, particularly on the railway between Damascus and Medina, kept thousands of Turkish troops occupied. This greatly helped the British army in Palestine, led by General Sir Edmund Allenby, which went on to capture Jerusalem and Damascus. During the fighting Lawrence was captured by the Turks at Dar'a, and was brutally treated before he managed to escape.

After the war, Lawrence attended the 1919 Paris peace conference. He was disgusted when such countries as Syria and Iraq were put under French or British control and felt that the Arabs had been betrayed. By now he was a national hero and his book about his experiences, *Seven Pillars of Wisdom*, published in 1926, increased his reputation.

To escape the unwanted publicity on his return home after the war, he joined the Royal Air Force in 1922, using the name John Hume Ross. When his real identity was discovered he was discharged. But in 1923 he joined the Royal Tank Corps as T. E. Shaw (the name he took legally in 1927). He was transferred to the RAF in 1925 as an aircraftman. Shortly after he left the RAF in 1935 he had a motorcycling accident near his home at Clouds Hill in Dorset and died six days later.

LAWYER. A lawyer is a person who is trained in the law and advises others on legal problems. A lawyer may prepare legal documents, such as wills and contracts and papers to be used in court, as well as representing clients or the state in a legal action.

Most lawyers specialize in a particular type of work, which can be broadly divided into appearing in court (litigation), and advising clients on a variety of matters which may or may not result in a court case. Litigation lawyers are sometimes known collectively as the *bar* after the barrier that existed, in England, between the judge and the rest of the court. Lawyer who appeared in court were said to be called to the bar.

Litigation work includes giving opinions as to whether a case should be "fought", advising clients in pre-trial meetings (called conferences), preparing the papers to be used in court (called pleadings), and advising on calling witnesses and other evidence. A lawyer who specializes in litigation must be able to think quickly "on his or her feet" and must be prepared to become an expert on almost any subject at short notice in order to be able to cross-examine witnesses.

Lawyers who do not deal with litigation may advise clients on a great variety of matters or they may specialize in only one branch of the law, such as tax law, family law, or buying and selling property (called conveyancing). They may also draft contracts, wills, deeds, and other documents and may ask the opinion of litigation lawyers as to whether a case should go to court.

In the United Kingdom these two branches of the legal profession are separate. Litigation lawyers are called barristers (advocates in Scotland) and those who deal with out-of-court work are called solicitors. This separation is not, however, total. Solicitors have the right to represent their clients in lower courts. A person who wants to be a lawyer must choose which kind to become before qualifying and can only change by going through a further course of training and examinations. He or she must then renounce their first qualification. In the early 1990s plans existed to merge the two branches into one profession.

The divided system still exists in some Australian states, although in other parts of Australia and in Canada and New Zealand, where it was originally used, the two parts of the profession have now come together, or "fused".

In the United States there is a single profession. Lawyers are usually known as attorneys (which is an old name for solicitors in Great Britain). People who want to be lawyers go to law school after graduating from college. On completing their studies they must pass the examinations of the bar association in the state in which they wish to work before they can practise law. The United States has more lawyers than any other country.

The legal profession in every country has its own governing body which regulates the conduct of its members and governs their training and qualifications. In the United States every state has its bar association. In Great Britain barristers must be members of one of the four Inns of Court and solicitors must belong to the Law Society.

Many lawyers do not practise privately but work in the legal department of a large company or other association, or are in government service.

LEAD was one of the earliest metals discovered by the human race and was in use by 3,000 BC. The ancient Romans used lead for making water pipes and lining baths, and the plumber who joins and mends pipes takes his name from the Latin word *plumbum*, meaning lead. *Plumbum* is also the origin of the terms *plumb bob* and *plumb line*, used in surveying and also the chemical symbol for lead, Pb. In medieval times, lead came to be used for roofing churches and their spires, for coffins, cisterns, tanks, and gutters, and for statues and ornaments. Another early use of lead was for the strips joining the pieces of coloured glass in church windows (see STAINED GLASS).

The dull grey colour of lead pipes and cables is caused by the oxygen of the air combining

Courtesy, UK Atomic Energy Authority

Lead is used to make the shielding that protects personnel working with radioactive materials.

with the metal so as to form a very thin film or skin composed of an oxide of lead. This film resists attack by air or water or even by chemicals such as acids. For this reason lead is not at all easily corroded, or eaten away. Unlike iron and steel, it does not need protection by painting. Underneath the film, lead is a bright, shiny bluish-white metal, as is shown by scraping it with a knife. When you scrape it you notice how soft lead is. It is this softness that makes it easy to squeeze or roll into different shapes.

The ease with which lead can be shaped and its resistance to corrosion make it valuable as the outer sheathing or covering, for electric cables. It protects the insulated wires inside without making the cable too stiff to bend. As lead has become much more expensive, it is used for roofing less often than in the past, and for water pipes copper or plastics such as polythene (see PLASTICS) are preferred because we have learned that lead is poisonous. (This aspect is discussed in the last paragraph of this article.) Sheet lead is used to line tanks holding corrosive liquids, such as

acids, which would eat through other metals.

As lead is heavier than iron or brass, it is used for making weights that must not be too bulky – for example, the sinkers on fishing tackle and in the boots of divers. Lead also melts at a lower temperature (327°C, or 621°F) than most of the other common metals. Soft solder, an alloy of lead and tin, has an even lower melting point. It is used for mending and joining metal articles (see SOLDERING). Many large buildings have water sprinklers in the ceilings for extinguishing accidental fires. The water outlet from the sprinkler is blocked by a seal made with an easily melting lead alloy. If the room becomes too hot because of a blaze, the seal melts and the water sprays the fire. Pewter, an alloy consisting of lead, tin and a little antimony, was once much used for mugs and dishes (see PEWTER).

Lead is still used for making organ pipes, rifle bullets, type (in letterpress printing), and the shot fired from sporting guns. As pure lead would be rather too soft, however, it is hardened by having antimony or arsenic alloyed with it. When alloyed with bronze (copper and tin) lead is sometimes used for the bearings for the shafts of engines and machines.

About one-third of the lead used is made into the plates of the batteries used for storing electricity. Motor-vehicle batteries are of this kind, and are explained in the article BATTERY, ELECTRIC. Lead is very effective as a screen to block the rays from radioactive substances. The reactors in nuclear power stations are screened by lead shields and the operators who work X-ray machines in hospitals are also protected by the use of lead shields.

The substances obtained by combining lead with chemicals have important uses. Among these are "white lead" (lead carbonate) used for making paint, and "red lead" (lead oxide) used as a first coat to prevent rusting when painting steelwork and for making joints in plumbing. Red lead is also used for making glass and for glazing pottery. ("Glazing" means making the shiny surface on cups and plates.) Other lead compounds are also used for glazing and for making paints, varnishes, glass, and matches. Lead azide is a violent explosive used in detonators (see EXPLOSIVE).

The largest supplies of lead come from the Broken Hill in New South Wales (Australia), the United States, Canada, Peru and Mexico. Significant quantities are also obtained from South Africa, Russia, and Kazakhstan, in central Asia.

Most lead is obtained from galena, an ore consisting of a combination of lead and sulphur sometimes found in limestone. The lead is obtained by crushing the galena and then roasting it to drive off the sulphur. The roasted galena is mixed with coke and limestone and put into a furnace. Air is blown into the lower part of the furnace to make a draught for burning the coke, and the molten lead is drawn off from the bottom. The limestone helps to make the slag formed by the impurities run easily.

The lead thus obtained often contains small quantities of gold, silver, copper, and other metals, and requires further treatment to purify it. Sometimes enough silver is recovered to pay for the purification. The fin-ished lead is cast into lumps called pigs. Much lead is obtained from "scrap"; that is, from old batteries and pipes which are melted down.

Lead and the compounds which contain lead are poisonous. Lead poison is retained in the body, and if a person is exposed to lead over a long period, poison builds up and causes damage to the brain and nervous system. For this reason the adding of lead to petrol to give smoother combustion in engines is now discouraged in many countries, as the lead is given off with the exhaust into the air, where it is breathed in by people. Lead has also been extensively used for water piping. In hardwater areas this was quite safe as a thin coating of lead sulphate quickly formed on the insides of the pipes, shielding the water from the lead. However, in soft water areas no such deposit collected and small quantities of lead could get into the water. For this reason copper or plastic is now used instead.

LEAF. Leaves are food factories of green plants. They manufacture the food which plants must use to become full-grown and healthy. They also manufacture food for people.

Leaves of fruit trees manufacture the food which helps to make fruit. Both peaches and maple sugar, for example, are sweet. Peach and maple tree leaves must be able to make sugar. They do this by taking materials from the air and the ground. One of these materials is carbon dioxide, a gas which is taken from the air. The other material is water, which comes from the soil. From the water and carbon dioxide the leaves manufacture sugar. This process of making food is called *photosynthesis* (see PHOTOSYNTHESIS).

Many kinds of plants seem to have no sugar in them because the sugar is soon changed to other kinds of food, such as starch and protein.

Every factory must have both machines and power to run the machines. The machines of the leaf are many little green bodies called *chloroplasts*. They are green because they have in them a green matter called *chlorophyll*. Sunshine is the power that runs the machines.

Chloroplasts work inside a leaf. The leaf is made up of *cells*, which are like many little boxes

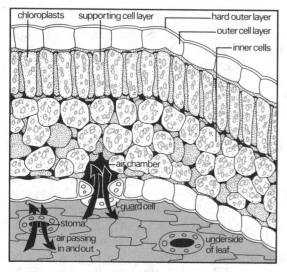

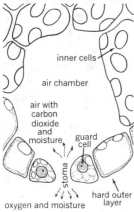

Top: An enlarged section through a leaf shows cells containing chloroplasts, used to make food by photosynthesis. This process requires carbon dioxide and moisture which enter the leaf through pores called stoma, mainly on the underside of the leaf; **Left:** A close-up of the stoma, flanked by guard cells and opening up into an inner chamber. The guard cells control whether the stoma is open or closed.

fitted closely together. Some of the cells have many chloroplasts in them. Other cells have few or none and are important for other reasons. *Guard cells* help regulate the size of the openings through which air passes. There are many of these cells on the underside of a leaf. A pair of guard cells and the opening between them is called a *stoma* (plural *stomata*).

The roots of the plant take water from the soil. The water goes through the roots, through the stems and branches, and then into the veins of the leaves. The veins in turn carry water to the cells. But veins do other work too. They carry to storage places such as roots, fruits, and seeds the food which the leaves have made and not used. There it is stored to be used at a later time.

Like factories, leaves must also get rid of waste materials. The air that goes into a leaf through the stomata has carbon dioxide in it. When the sun is shining the leaves use the carbon dioxide to make sugar. The rest of the air, with additional oxygen, is given off through the stomata. But when it is dark and the leaves are not making food, they do not need carbon dioxide. Then they give off air with carbon dioxide left in it.

Leaves give off water, too. Part of the water taken in through the roots is used to make sugar. The rest is given off from the leaves. A birch tree with 200,000 leaves, standing in open ground in hot weather, may lose 450 litres (120 US gallons) of water a day. A plant wilts when water goes out of the leaves faster than it comes in through the roots.

Autumn Colour

The leaves of many plants growing in the temperate, or mild, countries of the world, turn to brilliant colours in the autumn before they wither and fall off the plants. They fall because the lack of sunlight in the winter makes it unnecessary for leaves to remain on the plants. The leaves of beeches, oaks, and the sumach trees of North America become reddish bronze because of colouring matters (pigments) that develop in them. Others, such as chestnut and elm, do not make red pigments but instead become brilliant yellow as the chlorophyll separates into different parts and the yellows that have been hidden all the summer appear.

A layer of tissue grows across the base of each leaf stalk in the autumn so that the water supply is cut off and the leaf becomes dry. Before long, a gust of wind strong enough to separate the leaf from the stem comes and sends it fluttering to the ground. On the stem a scar is left, showing where the leaf has been. The scars vary in size and shape on different trees and are one way of telling one kind of tree from another in winter. In the case of a horse chestnut the scar is like a horseshoe.

Evergreen trees are those that do not shed their leaves all at once in the autumn but lose them gradually, and put out new buds while many adult leaves are still on the tree. In northern areas pines and other cone-bearing trees (except the larch) are the chief evergreens and their leaves are needle-shaped. Further south some broad-leaved trees, such as magnolia and ilex, are evergreen, and in the moist tropics practically all trees are evergreen.

Different Leaves

Leaves have been divided into groups to make it possible to identify plants more easily.

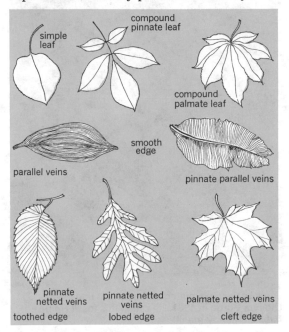

Each kind of leaf has its own shape and vein pattern.

It is important to notice whether a leaf is simple or compound. A simple leaf has a single leaf-blade, and a compound leaf has a blade divided into distinct leaflets. The leaflets of a compound leaf may be pinnate (like the parts of a feather, with one main vein and many small ones branching from it) or palmate (like the fingers of a hand, with several large veins spreading from the top of the leaf stalk). A fern leaf is pinnate and a lupin leaf is palmate.

Sometimes it is difficult to distinguish a simple leaf from the leaflet of a compound leaf. The surest way is to look for a bud at the place where the leaf stalk is joined on to the stem. Leaves have buds there, but leaflets do not.

Leaves, simple or compound, are arranged on the stem in a pattern so that they get as much light as possible. They are either alternate (growing first on one side then the other of the stem), like those of the elm; or opposite (growing in pairs up the stem, one on each side), like those of the lilac; or whorled (more than two growing from the stem at the same level), like those of the oleander.

The arrangement of the veins in leaves is important in dividing the flowering plants into two great orders. The long-bladed grass or wheat leaf shows the veins as long, straight, or slightly curved lines running the whole length of the leaf and parallel to one another, with only a few very small cross veins connecting them. Such leaves are said to be parallel-veined and are found on one of the two great orders of flowering plants, the monocotyledons. This order includes, besides lilies and orchids, the cereal grains such as oats, wheat, and barley, and all the grasses. Dicotyledons are plants which have the tiny veins in their leaves arranged in a network. Among them are peas, roses, potatoes, and all the broad-leaved trees. The network can be seen through a magnifying glass, and sometimes a "leaf skeleton" may be found, consisting only of the veins because an insect has eaten away the soft green part of the leaf.

Leaves vary also according to the parts of the world in which they grow. The prickly pear and other cacti have very small leaves, while the stem is large and green and carries on most of the sugar manufacture for the entire plant. Aloes are plants of dry regions that have thick, juicy leaves which serve as water-storage tanks.

The leaves of ferns develop strips or groups of powdery brown dots on their undersides in the autumn, and from them come tiny cells called spores, which are scattered into the air and later become little plants (see FERN).

Some kinds of plants, such as the sweet pea, climb by means of tendrils. The tendrils may be long, slender, twining leaves or leaflets that twist around a support and hold the plant up.

Perhaps the strangest leaves of all are those of carnivorous plants, which act as traps for the insects on which the plant feeds. The butterwort, bladderwort, and sundew are carnivorous plants. (See CARNIVOROUS PLANTS.)

Some leaves do not look like leaves at all, among them being those of the poinsettia, which are like large, brightly coloured petals. However, leaves can easily be identified by their position. They are always placed below a bud or the branch which develops from it. Anything that appears immediately below such a bud or branch is a leaf, no matter what shape it is or what function it performs.

LEAKEY FAMILY. Louis Leakey (1903–72), his wife Mary (born 1913), and their son, Richard (born 1944) are distinguished for their contributions to physical anthropology and palaeontology, which is the study of fossils.

Louis Leakey was the son of English missionaries to the Kikuyu people in Kenya, where he was born. He studied archaeology at Cambridge University, and in 1924, he began to do archaeological work in East Africa.

About 800 kilometres (500 miles) from Nairobi, where Leakey became director of the Coryndon Museum, was the Olduvai Gorge, in what was then Tanganyika (now Tanzania). German scientists worked at Olduvai about the time of the first World War and discovered huge numbers of fossil remains. In 1939 Leakey started making regular expeditions to Olduvai. His wife Mary was also an archaeologist, and she, and later their sons, accompanied him. The area was hot, very dry for many months of the year, and wild animals were plentiful. On one particular night, Leakey counted 11 lions close to his tents. But, he said, "We never bothered them and they never bothered us."

For almost 20 years, the Leakeys' excavations in the area yielded numerous tools, and they compiled a remarkable fossil record. But they did not manage to find any human-like fossils. Then, in July 1959, Mary Leakey discovered embedded in a rock a bit of bone and two teeth which she instantly realized were not animal teeth.

Over the months they were able to reconstruct a skull with the bits and pieces that they found. They named this fossil Zinjanthropus

Popperfoto

Louis Leakey examining an important find from Olduvai Gorge in 1961. He called this fossil *Homo habilis* ("handy man").

(*Zinj* means "East African" in Arabic). The Leakeys thought that Zinjanthropus was 600,000 years old, but they did not have accurate methods of dating at the time. Later, Californian scientists, using radiocarbon techniques, put it at 1,750,000 years. The Leakeys carried on excavating the area where the skull had been found and discovered an ancient camp site on the edge of what was once a lake, filled with tools and remains of dead animals that had been killed for food. It was firm proof that early man had been a toolmaker. In the 1960s, they discovered another fossil and another camp site. They called this new fossil *Homo habilis* ("handy man") and thought that it was a more direct ancestor of man than Zinjanthropus, for he walked upright, made stone tools, and although his brain was smaller than a gorilla's, his posture and his feet were more like man's than a gorilla's were.

The field of physical anthropology is full of guesswork, and scholars found it difficult to accept many of the Leakeys' interpretations of their fossils and the way they classified them. Their work was nevertheless extremely important. It indicated that human evolution was centred in Africa, and not in Asia, as early discoveries had suggested. It also put back the origins of man to a date roughly 2 million years ago, far earlier than anyone had previously believed.

Richard Leakey originally planned to do something completely different with his life from what his parents were doing. But he changed his mind after he discovered a near-human jaw in a region in northeast Tanzania in 1963. From 1967 to 1977 he uncovered about 400 fossils along the shores of Lake Rudolf (now Lake Turkana) in northern Kenya. This site, called Koobi Fora, has proved to be the richest human fossil find to date. Two fossil skulls, found in 1972, are thought to be about 2.6 million years old. This dated the beginnings of the use of tools back a million years earlier than Zinjanthropus. Richard Leakey's views are published in *The Making of Mankind*, published in 1981.

For more details on the origins of man, see MAN, ORIGINS OF.

LEANDER see HERO AND LEANDER.

LEAR, Edward (1812–88). The first and the most famous of all writers of nonsense verses was Edward Lear. This was how he described himself:

> How pleasant to know Mr. Lear!
> Who has written such volumes of stuff!
> Some think him ill-tempered and queer,
> But a few think him pleasant enough.
>
> His mind is concrete and fastidious,
> His nose is remarkably big;
> His visage is more or less hideous,
> His beard it resembles a wig.

His conversation was full of fun and he could draw pictures that were as funny as his poems. However, he was not just a humorous artist,

and much of his life was spent travelling in many countries, writing about his travels, and illustrating them with landscape paintings.

Edward Lear was born in London, the youngest son of a large family—he had 20 brothers and sisters. At the age of 15 he began to earn his living by doing drawings. Among his first drawings were rare parrots, and he spent a whole year (1831) drawing them in the parrot house at London Zoo. The Earl of

Courtesy, Vivien Noakes

MACROCERCUS ARACANGA.
Red and Yellow Maccaw

Edward Lear started his artistic career drawing animals at London Zoo. This fine drawing is of a macaw.

Derby, who had a zoo of his own, was very impressed by the drawings and asked Lear to illustrate a book for him. Lear spent four years drawing the Earl's animals and was soon a favourite in the family. He used to escape into the nursery, where he told the Earl's grandchildren the limericks that afterwards became the *Book of Nonsense* (see LIMERICK). They loved the odd people he described for them—the old person of Rye "who went up to town on a fly", the old lady "whose folly induced her to sit on a holly"! Here is one of them:

> There was an old man in a tree,
> Whose whiskers were lovely to see;
>   But the birds of the air
>   Pluck'd them perfectly bare,
> To make themselves nests in that tree.

The longer poems such as *The Jumblies* and *The Owl and the Pussy Cat* are also great fun. Some, *The Dong with the Luminous Nose*, for instance, are a little sad and show a streak of sadness in Lear's shy character.

Lear's own drawing of "the old man in a tree".

Lear published four books of nonsense verse between 1846 and 1877. They made his reputation and have been popular ever since. He also published three books of animal drawings. But the demands of detail and accuracy made on Lear's eyes caused him to give up zoological drawing, and he took to travelling and painting. He published seven travel books illustrated by his landscapes. They all deal with southern Europe (Italy, Greece, Albania, and so on), where he spent more and more of his time because of ill health. The last 20 years of his life were rather lonely, his only companion being Foss his cat, "who has no end of a tail—because it has been cut off!" He died at San Remo, in Italy, at the age of 75.

LEARNING is the process of acquiring habits, skills, and knowledge through experience. Some kinds of learning involve formal teaching, for example, when schoolchildren learn to read, write, and calculate with numbers. In other cases, learning involves deliberate effort and practice by the learner but no formal teaching—many people learn to ride bicycles or to play musical instruments by their own efforts alone. Most learning, however, takes place without formal teaching or deliberate effort on the part of the learner. Throughout our lives, we acquire beliefs and attitudes, personal habits, various skills, and general knowledge without even realizing that we are learning anything new.

Human beings are able to learn much more than other animals, and our highly developed spoken and written languages make it possible to hand down vast quantities of knowledge from one generation to the next. But the basic principles of *habit learning* are exactly the same in human and non-human species. Indeed, much of what we know about habit learning has come from experiments with rats, pigeons, dogs, chimpanzees, and other animals.

One important type of habit learning first studied in animals is called *conditioning*. The Russian scientist Ivan Pavlov discovered that if he rang a bell whenever he was about to feed a dog, the sound of the bell was soon enough on its own to make the dog salivate, because the dog had learnt to associate the bell with food (see PAVLOV, IVAN). American scientists later showed that if a hungry rat is rewarded with food whenever it presses a lever in its cage, it gradually develops the habit of pressing the lever even after the food rewards are stopped. Surprisingly, the habit is even stronger, and takes longer to disappear, if the reward for pressing the lever is given only occasionally instead of always. An animal conditioned with occasional feeding uses up more energy pressing the lever than it gets in return in food rewards. The same thing happens when human beings develop the habit of gambling with one-armed bandits, or fruit machines. These, too, are cleverly designed to reward the gambler only occasionally. People often end up putting much more money into these machines than they get back in prizes, yet they find the habit very hard to break. Psychologists often use conditioning methods to treat mentally ill patients by replacing harmful habits with healthier ones.

The *learning of skills* has been studied mainly in human beings. Some skills, such as mathematical techniques, are purely mental; others, for example, typing or playing tennis, are partly mental and partly physical. They all improve with practice, but the rate of improvement slows down as higher levels of skills are achieved. There are also often periods when the skill stops improving or even gets slightly worse before starting to improve again. Continuous practice is not as effective as short periods of practice with many rest periods. When you are learning to type, for example, six ten-minute practice sessions with short rest periods in between are worth more than an hour's continuous practice.

Memorizing names, dates, and foreign words are examples of *knowledge learning.* (See MEMORY.) Information of this kind is remembered better when the learning is active rather than passive. Take studying a book, for instance. If you think about what you are reading, relating it to things you know already, and practise remembering the key ideas or facts at least twice, straight after learning them, you will learn faster and remember much better than if you just read passively.

Material learnt in a certain mental state or situation is most easily remembered in similar circumstances. That is why, when people are depressed, they tend to remember depressing things from the past, which unfortunately makes them even more depressed. In one experiment, deep-sea divers who memorized information under water were better able to recall it under water than on dry land. People who are learning information for examinations should therefore try to do their preparation in circumstances as similar as possible to the examination conditions.

Everything that is learnt is stored somewhere in the brain, but the details of this process are not yet fully understood. Severe injury to certain parts of the brain makes it impossible to absorb any new knowledge, although nearly everything learnt before the injury may be retained. People with such injuries cannot hold normal conversations because they constantly forget what they said and what was said to them only minutes earlier. Sometimes they stop speaking in the middle of a sentence because they cannot remember how the sentence began. They often read the same newspaper or magazine article over and over again without taking anything in or realizing that they have read it all before. One patient who was admitted to hospital with this form of brain damage kept ringing the night nurse for an explanation of how he came to be in a hospital bed and what he was doing there. Brain-damaged patients who cannot absorb any new knowledge can still learn new habits and skills, which shows that these things are stored in different parts of the brain (see BRAIN).

LEATHER comes from the hides, or skins, of animals but much has to be done to change hide into the soft leather of a shoe or a handbag. The skins cannot be used just as they are when removed from the dead animal, because they would rot. Drying would prevent this, but if they were merely dried—without going through other processes as well—they would be too stiff to be of much use. There are in fact three kinds of leather—rawhide, parchment, and skins.

Any animal skin can be made into leather but most leather comes from the skins of cattle, horses, sheep, goats, and pigs. These are domestic animals, which are used in a variety of other ways. Their hides are additional and useful by-products. Certain wild animals have been hunted for their hides and have become rare as a result. The alligator is an example. Fortunately most people now realise that it is better to see a live wild animal than to have a handbag made from its skin.

Cattle hides come from the chief cattle-raising countries, such as Argentina, Australia, Brazil, and the United States. Goat skins come from the Middle East, Africa, and India.

How Leather is Prepared

Three-quarters of the weight of a skin consists of water and one-quarter of what is called collagen, or skin substance. Collagen is a protein (see PROTEIN) and is made of the same substances as meat and fish. This explains why

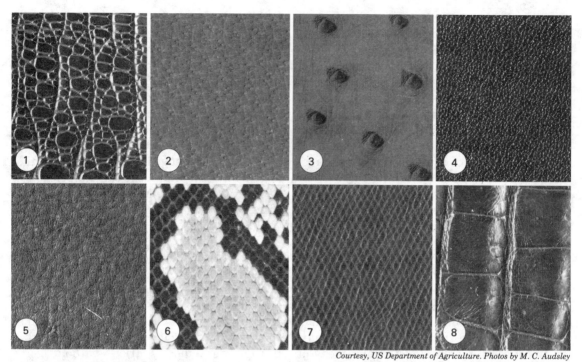

Courtesy, US Department of Agriculture. Photos by M. C. Audsley

Some of the patterns and textures found in leathers from different animals. **1** Lizard, **2** Pigskin, **3** Ostrich, **4** Morocco (goatskin), **5** Deer, **6** Python, **7** Elkgrain cowhide, **8** Alligator. Many are now rarely used because the animals are endangered.

skins rot if they are left just as they are. Therefore as soon as they come off the animal they are either dried or salted in order to prevent the collagen from rotting. This process is known as *curing*.

The skin has three layers. There is a very thin top layer called the epidermis, which consists of tiny cells, linked together like bricks in a wall, in which the hair roots are embedded. This layer is no use for leather and is removed. The hair is used in carpet manufacture. At the bottom there is the flesh layer, made of thin sheets, which holds the skin on to the body. This also is useless for leather and is removed. It is used in glue making. In the middle comes the main layer called the dermis, corium, or true skin. This is the layer that is made into leather. It consists of bundles of very long, thin but strong fibres woven together in a most complicated manner. (They can be seen sticking out from the ends of a broken strap.) It is the way in which they are interwoven that makes leather strong and flexible.

The skins are cured immediately they are removed from the dead animal. After this they are soaked in water to remove dirt, blood, and salt (if they have been salted) and to replace the water lost in curing.

In order to loosen the hair, cleanse the skin, and improve the texture the skins are limed; that is to say they are soaked in a mixture of water, lime, and sodium sulphide. The mixture eats away the hair roots and the top layer of skin, making it possible for these to be scraped off. With small skins such as sheepskins the wool is usually loosened separately by coating the flesh side with a paste of lime and sodium sulphide or by hanging for a few hours in a hot, damp room. After liming, the flesh layer is sliced off from the under side of the skin, leaving the corium as a rubbery, snow-white sheet.

Tanning

The corium has now to be *tanned*, or changed into leather. There are many ways of doing this. A process that has been known since ancient times is to treat it with a liquid obtained by soaking parts of certain plants in water. This is known as vegetable tanning. Oak bark, chestnut wood, or quebracho wood may be used. All these contain tannic acid, which changes the corium into leather. Tannic acid obtained from plants gives a yellowish or reddish brown leather, used for the soles of shoes, upholstering chairs, bookbinding, straps, and satchels. Synthetic tanning chemicals have now been developed, which makes tanning faster and a greater variety of leathers can be produced.

When leather is made for the soles of shoes the skins are rounded; that is, the belly and shoulder parts are cut off, leaving the oblong back parts only. These are put through a series of tanning liquids whose strengths gradually increase. The tannic acid slowly soaks into the collagen, turning it into leather. This process takes from one to six months, according to the methods used. When the leather is taken out of the tanning liquids it is scoured (to clean the surface), given a thin coating of oil, slowly dried and then placed under a roller in a machine, which hardens and solidifies the leather. The belly and shoulder parts are tanned separately for small things such as straps, and the welts and insoles of shoes.

Another method of tanning is mineral or chrome tanning. It is used for leathers such as box-calf, patent, and glacé (shiny) kid. The tanning substance is a bluish-green liquid containing a compound of the metal known as chromium (see CHROMIUM). After soaking for only a few hours the leather is washed and then pressed to squeeze out the loose water. If the leather is thick or uneven, it is split into two layers and the outer layer only is used. Then it is dyed and put through a process known as fat-liquoring, in which it is soaked with an emulsion of oil to make it soft. The dyed and fat-liquored leather is then hung up to dry. If a shiny leather is wanted it is coated with white of egg and placed in a press under a heated polished plate or rubbed in a glazing machine with a polished glass or metal roller. Many leathers are first vegetable and then chrome tanned (semi-chrome) or the other way

round (chrome re-tan). Leather for the uppers of heavy boots is first tanned with tannic acid and then with the chrome compound. Such leather is then made waterproof and soft by currying; that is, by applying a mixture of oils, fats, and waxes.

Special Kinds of Leather

Suede is usually made from calfskin or goat-skin. Its velvety surface is prepared by rubbing the inside of the leather on emery wheels.

Patent leather is made by coating the leather with layers of lacquer and then baking the finish so that it is like enamel.

The chamois leathers used for washing windows are made from sheep-skin, and not nowadays from the skin of the chamois antelope. To make chamois leather, the tanner splits the sheep skin into two layers, known as the grain and the flesher. The grain, or outer layer, is tanned with tannic acid and made into "skivers", used for shoe linings, book bindings, and fancy leather goods. The inner layer, or flesher, is tanned using cod or other fish oils before being cleaned, softened, and dried, and becomes the familiar yellow wash-leather. The dense fibres in a chamois leather enable it to absorb a lot of water, and also (when dry) to pick up dust efficiently. When treated with formaldehyde and cod liver oil, sheep-skin becomes a leather known as doe-skin.

The stiff, semi-transparent parchment and vellum on which people used to write before paper became common were made from animal skins – parchment from sheep skin and goat skin, and vellum from calf skin. (See MANUSCRIPT, ILLUMINATED.) Parchment and vellum are still used for important documents, known as charters. They are made of dried, untanned skins.

LEBANON. The Republic of Lebanon on the coast of the eastern Mediterranean lies between Israel and Syria. The Lebanon Mountains, which rise to 3,000 metres (9,800 feet), run down the middle of the country like a backbone, and between them and the Anti-Lebanon Mountains on the eastern border lies the fertile Bekaa valley drained by the river Litani which is the only river in Lebanon that flows during the whole year.

Unlike most countries of the Middle East, Lebanon has abundant rainfall. The climate is mild on the coast but deep snow covers the mountains in winter. Originally most of the country was forested, but today, after centuries of logging, forests only cover about seven per cent of the land. The famous cedar of Lebanon is confined to a few mountain groves protected by law.

Most Lebanese are Arabs, but there are many racial and cultural groups. Muslims make up more than half the population, while most of the rest are Christian. Both Muslim and Christian communities are divided into a number of different sects. About 88 per cent of the people can read and write. In proportion to its size, Lebanon has the highest number of skilled and professional people among Arab nations in the Middle East.

Civil war has disrupted all of Lebanon since 1974 and has almost destroyed its economy. Farming is concentrated in the coastal plain and Bekaa valley, but many farmers have lost their livestock and crop production has fallen. In the areas where farming is still possible the main crops are wheat, barley, fruit, and vegetables. Goats and sheep are the main livestock.

Before the war, Lebanon had small-scale manufacturing industries that were prosperous compared with most other Middle Eastern countries. By the early 1990s, however, the country's manufacturing had dwindled to a few products, among them cement, wheat flour, and paper. Tourism is another casualty of the war. Tourists from all over the world used to visit Lebanon's historical sites and beautiful seaside and mountain resorts.

FACTS ABOUT LEBANON

AREA: 10,230 square kilometres (3,950 square miles).
POPULATION: 2,897,000 (1989).
GOVERNMENT: Republic.
CAPITAL: Beirut, 1,500,000.
GEOGRAPHICAL FEATURES: The country consists of a narrow coastal plain backed by two parallel mountain ranges enclosing the fertile Bekaa valley.
CITIES: Tripoli, 500,000; Zahlah, 200,000; Saida (Sidon) 100,000; an-Nabatiyah, 100,000.
CHIEF PRODUCTS: Vegetables, fruit, textiles, non-precious metals.
EDUCATION: Education is free and compulsory between the ages of 6 and 10.

The increasing lawlessness that has resulted from the fighting has allowed smuggling and drug trafficking to take the place of the country's traditional industries. Lebanon is now a major centre of the heroin trade. The drug is grown in the Bekaa valley and exported illegally. Despite the war Lebanon remains an important trade and financial centre and its banking and insurance activities have survived.

The country has no oil and is short of coal and metals. The hydroelectric power stations on the Litani River provide electricty and water for irrigation. Oil pipelines from Iraq and Saudi Arabia run across Lebanon to reach the coast at Tripoli and Sidon. Beirut, the capital, is the main cargo and passenger port, although it has been severely damaged by the war. There is also a large international airport near Beirut, but it is frequently closed by the fighting and is no longer used by the major airlines. A railway system links Lebanon with other Arab countries, and through Turkey, with Europe.

History

The region that includes Lebanon has had many rulers – including the Phoenicians, who

Donkeys plod along a deserted road which runs through a densely populated area in Tripoli. The city is the second largest in Lebanon, and the country's chief sea port.

H. Gritcher/Peter Arnold Inc.

founded the cities of Sur (Tyre) and Saida (Sidon), the Greeks, Romans, and Byzantines. Christianity was introduced in the 5th century and Islam in the 7th. The region was ruled by the Turks from the 16th century until the end of World War I.

Then, with Syria, it became a French mandate. In 1920 France created the republic of Greater Lebanon, with boundaries the same as those of present-day Lebanon, and in 1943 the country became independent.

However, there were serious tensions between the Christian and Muslim groups. The Lebanese constitution laid down that the government should be shared between Muslims and Christians. In practice the Christians had more power. This caused considerable unrest among the Muslims because they were in the majority. By 1975 the strife between the two communities had become open warfare and Lebanon's neighbour Syria sent several thousand troops to restore order.

Ever since the foundation of Israel in 1948 the conflict between Muslims and Christians in Lebanon has been complicated by the presence of thousands of Palestinian refugees who fled to Lebanon from Israel during the Arab–Israeli wars (see PALESTINIANS). The Palestinians support their fellow Muslims against the Christians. In 1970 the Palestine Liberation Organization (PLO) made Beirut its base and launched raids across the border into northern Israel. Israel retaliated in 1982 by invading Lebanon and driving the PLO out of the country. Israeli forces occupied southern Lebanon until 1985. That same year a multinational peacekeeping force left Lebanon because of attacks by Muslim extremists.

Since then the country has been the scene of vicious fighting not only between Muslims and Christians but between rival groups within the Muslim and Christian communities. Thousands of innocent people have been killed in artillery fire and bombings. Western countries have been drawn into the violence by the acts of international terrorism carried out by Palestinian groups based in Lebanon. Their terrorist activities have included the hijacking of an American airliner and the taking of Western hostages.

The United Nations and many Arab and Western countries have tried to find a way of uniting Lebanon. In 1989 there were hopes of a reconcilation when moderate Muslim and Christian leaders agreed on a new constitution that would end Christian dominance. It was accepted by moderate Christians and Muslims but not by the extremists on either side.

See also BEIRUT; PALESTINIANS; MIDDLE EAST.

LE CORBUSIER (1887–1965) was one of the greatest architects and city planners of the 20th century. He was also a painter, sculptor, furniture designer, and writer. "Le Corbusier" is a pseudonym; his real name was Charles-Édouard Jeanneret, which was the name he used to sign his paintings. Le Corbusier was born in La Chaux-de-Fonds, Switzerland. His father engraved and enamelled watch faces, and his mother taught piano. Le Corbusier left school at 13 and planned to study the same trade as his father. At the local art school he started to become interested in architecture, which he mostly taught himself.

Between 1907 and 1911, Le Corbusier travelled in central Europe, and the Mediterranean countries, where he was impressed by simple square houses, painted in white. He worked for a time with two distinguished figures who were to influence his architectural ideas: Auguste Perret, the Parisian architect, who used reinforced concrete in his buildings, and Peter Behrens in Berlin, one of the first industrial designers.

In 1917, Le Corbusier settled in Paris. He painted and wrote, and in 1923 he published his first important book, *Towards a New Architecture*. In it he discussed his ideas about the machine. He said that machines could contribute to the development of architecture for the masses, and could create pure, simple forms, as opposed to the decorative forms popular at the time.

He thought that mass-produced houses should be "healthy and beautiful", and he started to put his ideas into effect. His early houses were partly raised above the ground and had roof decks. The large and very high living areas were lit by large windows, and the partitions were often curved and movable so that the space could be rearranged in various ways. The house frames were rectangular and made of reinforced concrete.

In 1925, Le Corbusier exhibited his first model of what he called a "living cell" at an international exhibition of decorative arts in Paris. This cell was one of many which could be stacked together to form a block. He held that blocks should be self-contained and com-

plete with facilities for the people living in them including nurseries and clinics for the children. They should also be surrounded by parks and recreation space. One of the most famous of his residential blocks is the *Unité d'Habitation* in Marseilles, France, built between 1946 and 1952. This was a "community" of 18 floors, which housed 1,800 people.

Le Corbusier liked furniture to be simple and preferred objects which were mass-produced by machines rather than made by hand. He designed some of his own furniture, using mainly steel tubes.

In 1953, Le Corbusier was invited to build a whole city in India. This was Chandigarh, the capital city of the Punjab. He planned the city and designed the more important government buildings. He also built some outstanding private homes in India. Among his other famous designs are the Swiss dormitory at the Cité Universitaire, Paris, the chapel of Notre-Dame-du-Haut at Ronchamp, France, the Carpenter Visual Arts Center at Harvard University in the United States, and the National Museum of Western Art in Tokyo.

There are illustrations of some of Le Corbusier's work in the articles ARCHITECTURE and FURNITURE.

LEE, Richard Henry (1732–94) was an American statesman who was one of the signatories of the Declaration of Independence.

Lee was born in Stratford, Virginia, one of 11 children in a wealthy family. He had private tutors and then completed his education in England. He returned to Virginia in 1752 and in 1758 became a member of the Virginia House of Burgesses. From then on he was almost always in the Virginia legislature or in the Continental Congress or in both.

Lee and Patrick Henry were the leaders in the demand for colonial rights in Virginia. In 1768 Lee suggested Committees of Correspondence to spread information between the colonies. This idea was adopted in 1773 and led to the first Continental Congress in 1774. Lee served in the first and second Congresses. In June 1776 he proposed that the colonies declare their independence. This led to the Declaration of Independence (see DECLARATION OF INDEPENDENCE).

From 1784 to 1786 Lee was president of the Congress. When the new constitution was written he was against it because it did not have a bill of rights. Lee wrote *Letters of the Federal Farmer* to give the reasons for his opposition. Lee was chosen one of Virginia's senators in the new government. His chief concern in the Senate was to pass the amendments which became the Bill of Rights. In 1792 he retired from public life because of illness.

LEE, Robert E. (1807–70) was the leading Confederate general in the American Civil War (see CIVIL WAR, AMERICAN). He was born at Stratford, Virginia, of a well-known but impoverished family. He graduated from West Point military academy and for some years worked on engineering projects for the War Department. He rose to superintendent of West Point and then lieutenant colonel of cavalry.

Although Lee was strongly against breaking up the Union over the disputed question of slavery, he felt he could not fight against his own state of Virginia, even though he favoured gradual freedom for the slaves, freeing many of his own. At the start of the Civil War in 1861 he refused the offer of command of the United States army. But when Virginia withdrew from the Union in April 1861 Lee was given command of its armies. The first important battle of the war, Bull Run, was won by the troops he sent to Manassas Junction, Virginia.

In March 1862 Jefferson Davis, president of the Confederacy, asked Lee to serve as his adviser in the state capital, Richmond. Shortly afterwards, in the spring, Union troops marched on Richmond. General Johnston, the Confederate commander, was badly wounded and Lee took over the armies in the east. In the Seven Days' Battle Lee, together with "Stonewall" Jackson, forced the Union army under George McClellan to retreat. Lee proved himself a brilliant strategist, moving his troops quickly to avoid superior forces and often making the northern armies attack him in territory he could defend. In autumn 1862 Lee invaded the North by crossing the Potomac River and marching into Maryland. But heavy losses prevented him from entering the state of Pennsylvania. In December he drove back the Union army at the Battle of Fredericksburg.

In the spring of 1863 Lee won his greatest victory at Chancellorsville, Virginia. But it was his last. His best general, Jackson, was

Paul's Photo

The home of the Lee family (left) at Stratford, Virginia, where General Robert E. Lee (right) was born.

killed in the battle, supplies were becoming scarce, and he had lost many men. He again invaded the North, however, only to suffer his worst defeat at the Battle of Gettysburg (see GETTYSBURG, BATTLE OF). Lee's men suffered badly in the winter of 1863. During 1864 the Union general Ulysses Grant hammered away at the Confederate forces. In February 1865 Lee was named commander-in-chief of all the Confederate armies. But by then his men were exhausted. At Appomattox Courthouse, Virginia, he was surrounded and had no alternative but to surrender.

After the war Lee set an example for the South by obeying federal laws and urging his soldiers to accept the outcome of the war. He spent the last five years of his life as president of Washington College, Lexington, Virginia— a loved and respected figure.

LEECH. Leeches are closely related to earthworms, and, like them, their bodies are made up of ring-like segments, or parts. Most leeches have flat bodies and are black, green, or brown in colour. They may be less than 2.5 centimetres (1 inch) long or almost 90 centimetres (35.5 inches). Their eyes are arranged along the back in pairs and vary in number from four to ten. On the head is a sucker-like mouth with small, saw-shaped teeth.

ARDEA

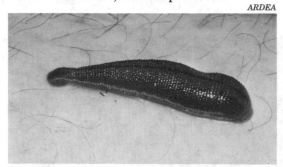

A jungle leech feeds on a human leg. Note how the leech's body is swollen with its blood meal.

Some leeches are scavengers; that is, they eat up rubbish and the flesh of dead animals. Others devour earthworms and insect eggs, but most are parasites, which means that they live on other animals, which are then called "hosts". The leeches fasten themselves on to their hosts with their teeth and suck blood.

Leeches need water to live. There are many in the sea, even in the Arctic and Antarctic, which attach themselves to fishes. They are also found in fresh water and in warm, wet climates. Some live entirely in water, others partly in water and partly on land and some only on land.

These last, the land leeches, are found only in Asia and on the islands of the Pacific Ocean from Japan to Australia. They are common in tropical forests on the ground and in the bushes, and drop on to passers-by from branches of trees.

Most leeches do not hurt when they fasten themselves to the skin, but from their mouths comes a substance called hirudin, which keeps the blood from clotting, and so it is difficult to stop the bleeding.

The horse leech (*Haemopis sanguisuga*), which is found in streams in Europe and America, is much less of a pest than the land leech. Though it sucks blood, it does not cling so persistently to its host. It is usually about 15 centimetres (6 inches) long and is black in colour.

It used to be thought that many illnesses were caused by too much blood in the body, and one kind of leech, the medicinal leech (*Hirudo medicinalis*), was specially bred for sucking away blood. The leech (*Limnatis niloticus*) of southern Europe, North Africa, and the Near East may enter the body in drinking water, or through the excretory openings of people who bathe in infested waters. When taken with drinking water they may attach themselves to the lining of the mouth or throat and work their way to the lungs where they can cause great loss of blood. Leeches can cause suffocation and death of the host animal and, in Asia in particular, domestic animals commonly die in this way.

LEEDS, in West Yorkshire, is the fourth largest city in Great Britain after London, Birmingham, and Glasgow. Its population is 714,000 (1983). Leeds stands on the River Aire, which rises in the Pennine Hills and flows through the city before joining the River Ouse at Goole.

In this region the water is soft and therefore suitable for washing and bleaching wool. In the 14th century Flemish workmen came to Yorkshire and helped to develop the clothing trade. Cloth weaving became an important industry and Leeds built up a large market for cloth. The clothing trade revived in the second half of the 19th century, and is still important today.

The engineering industry, which developed in Leeds during the 18th and 19th centuries, is now the city's most important occupation. Other important industries are printing, particularly colour printing, leather and furniture making, and electrical and metal goods production. Leeds is well placed for the main north to south motorway and railways, and there is an airport at nearby Yeadon.

The University of Leeds grew out of the Yorkshire College of Science, which was founded in 1874. Leeds has a fine museum and art gallery. The piano competition held there every three years is famous worldwide.

Some way from the centre of Leeds is Temple Newsam, the birthplace of Lord Darnley, the second husband of Mary, Queen of Scots. It is a great mansion in which are kept various treasures, including a collection of Chinese porcelain and Leeds and Staffordshire pottery.

LEE KUAN YEW (born 1923) became the first prime minister of independent Singapore. Lee was born in Singapore of a wealthy Chinese family. He studied at Raffles College in Singapore and then went to Britain to study law at Cambridge University. After qualifying he returned to Singapore where he acted as negotiator for several trade unions.

Singapore was then a British colony. Lee determined to bring self-government to the island. He formed and became secretary general of the People's Action Party (PAP). In 1958 Singapore became a self-governing state within the Commonwealth. Elections in 1959 gave Lee's PAP an overwhelming majority. He formed a government and set out a programme of social and industrial reform.

In 1963 Singapore joined Malaya and other countries in the newly formed Federation of

Topham

Lee Kuan Yew, Singapore's national leader, inspects a guard of honour during an official visit.

Malaysia (see MALAYSIA). But tension grew between the Chinese, who form the majority of the population, and the minority Malayans. Rioting broke out, and in 1965 the other members of the federation asked Singapore to withdraw. Singapore then became a completely independent country with Lee as its first prime minister.

Lee brought prosperity, efficient administration, and peace to his country in spite of its small size and its powerful neighbours. But he was also criticized for keeping too strict control of political life in Singapore. Since independence the PAP has completely dominated parliament.

See also SINGAPORE.

LEEUWENHOEK, Antonie van (1632–1723). Often called the father of modern bacteriology, Leeuwenhoek was the first to create microscopes capable of seeing tiny bacteria and one-celled animals. Born in Delft, the Netherlands, he left school at 16 to become an apprentice dry goods merchant. At 21, he set up his own drapery shop and at 28 became chamberlain of the town hall.

From this time, his income was sufficient to allow him to devote much of his time to his favourite occupation, grinding lenses and making microscopes, far better than anything known in his day. Unlike today's complex instruments, Leeuwenhoek's microscopes consisted of a single, tiny, short-focus lens, set between two pieces of metal. They could magnify 40 times, 100 times, and possibly even 300 times. These he turned on everything within his grasp—ox eyes, rain water, tooth scrapings. One day he saw "very little animicules" later known as bacteria and protozoa, which he described were found in all fresh water including street gutters. He also described how these small animals can be carried from place to place by the wind "along with bits of dust floating in the air". (SEE BACTERIA; PROTOZOA.)

In 1676, he wrote a letter to the Royal Society of England, telling of his discovery. The unschooled Dutchman was made a Fellow of the Royal Society along with other great scientists of his day. In later letters to the Royal Society—375 in all—he recorded his many findings on bacteria, yeasts, plants, etc. These included the first drawing of bacteria and the discovery of the tiny capillaries which join the veins and arteries. His observation of the life histories of various animals, including insects, described how they came from eggs, and did not, as was commonly supposed "arise spontaneously" from the substances they lived on or in. For example, weevils were supposed to come from wheat, and sea mussels from the sand of the seashore.

LEGUMINOUS PLANTS. The legume family is the second largest family of seed plants with more than 20,000 species, including herbs, shrubs, and trees which are found in most parts of the world. Examples of the most common legumes are vetch, clover, bean, and pea.

Most of the legumes appear to have nitrogen-fixing bacteria in their roots. While growing, the plants take nitrogen from the air and return it to the soil. The process adds to the fertility of the soil. For this reason the legumes are important in soil improvement programmes, especially in crop rotations.

The family is of great economic value, containing many plants that are widely cultivated. The seeds, which are rich in starch and proteins, form valuable foods. A few are rich in oil, and some yield strong poisons. Many legumes are useful fodder plants and some are valuable as green manures. This is a plant which when ploughed under while green enriches the soil.

Many tropical-tree members of the family supply useful timber; some yield fibre and some gums and resins. Dyes are obtained from a few, medicinal products are supplied by others, and a large number are important ornamentals, examples such as sweet peas, broom, and wistaria being favourite climbing plants.

An important leguminous tropical tree is logwood (*Haematoxylon campechianum*), which grows in Mexico, Central America, and the West Indies. The reddish brown wood is cut into large blocks from which a dye is extracted that ranges in colour from blue to black. It is used to colour silk and woollen goods, leather, and inks.

Lespedeza, Clover, and Vetch

Lespedezas are a group of approximately 125 species of the legume family. They are commonly known as bush clovers. All lespedezas are native to either eastern North America or eastern Asia. In addition to the value of some species for hay, forage, and green manuring, all lespedezas are important sources of food for wildlife, especially birds. Quail are very fond of the seeds and the various species supply an almost perfect cover for them.

The true clovers, members of the genus *Trifolium*, may be found all over the world. About 300 species are known. Numerous related plants are also called clover. The sweet clovers, members of the genus *Melilotus*, are the clovers often seen growing along roadsides. All the sweet clovers are excellent bee plants and the honey from them is especially prized. Most of the species contain coumarin, which gives the sweet odour and the bitter taste. Coumarin is used in medicine.

There are about 150 species of vetch, also called "tares". They are widely spread in the northern hemisphere and there are a few in South America.

(See ACACIA; BEAN; BROOM; CLOVER; LENTIL; LUPIN; PEA; SWEET PEA; VETCH; WISTARIA).

LEIBNIZ, Gottfried (1646–1716). The German scientist and thinker Gottfried Wilhelm von Leibniz was one of the few men in history who was a genius in many different fields of learning. He developed and made known important ideas in law, history, religion, mathematics, and philosophy. But unlike some other philosophers who could support themselves from private wealth or from fees resulting from university research positions, Leibniz depended on wealthy sponsors for an income. He spent most of his time working as a court librarian and as a diplomat. He often travelled about Europe, trying to bring about agreements between other governments and his own.

Leibniz was born in Leipzig, Germany. He taught himself by reading the books in his father's library. At the age of eight he could read Latin and within four years he had also learned Greek. He studied law at Leipzig University, obtaining his doctorate from Altdorf in Nürnberg in 1666. He entered the diplomatic and legal service of the Elector of Mainz. His employer died in 1673 and three years later Leibniz became librarian, historian, and legal adviser to the Dukes of Brunswick-Lüneberg, Electors of Hanover. He remained in this employment until his death, while continuing to travel as a diplomat, to write, and to develop his philosophical and scientific ideas. In 1711–14 he visited Vienna, where he was made Adviser to the Empire and given the title *Freiherr* (Baron).

Leibniz formed a complicated philosophy that tried to prove that God was the source of all things. He wrote books on many scientific subjects, such as the theory concerning motion and time. His best-known work was in mathematics. In 1673 he invented a calculating machine. In 1684 he published his invention of calculus, an important branch of mathematics, on which there is a separate article. The great English scientist Sir Isaac Newton, without knowing of Leibniz's work, published his own form of calculus three years later. In addition to his scientific work, Leibniz tried to find ways to unite the Protestant and Roman Catholic churches.

BBC Hulton Picture Library

The German philosopher and mathematician Gottfried Leibniz was a genius in many fields of study.

During his travels in Europe, Leibniz met many of the most important thinkers of his time. With his help an Academy of Science was started in Berlin in 1700, and he was its first president.

LEICESTER, Robert Dudley, Earl of (1532 or 1533–88). Robert Dudley, the favourite courtier of Queen Elizabeth I of England, was the fifth son of the Duke of Northumberland. He first met the young princess Elizabeth at the court of her brother, Edward VI. When Northumberland plotted to make Lady Jane Grey queen in 1553, Dudley was sent to the Tower of London. He was later freed and went to fight in France.

As soon as Elizabeth became queen in 1558 his career began to flourish. Dudley was tall, handsome, clever, and ambitious. The queen was very fond of him and granted him important appointments. Many people at court were jealous and he became even more unpopular after the mysterious death of his wife Amy Robsart. This seemed to leave the way open for a marriage between Dudley and Elizabeth. However, it did not take place, though in 1564 the Queen made him Earl of Leicester.

A miniature of the Earl of Leicester, painted by Nicholas Hilliard in 1575.

In state affairs he saw the power of Spain and Roman Catholics in England as a danger to the country and wanted quick, firm action against them. In 1585 Leicester was sent to the Netherlands to help the rebels fighting against Spain. Although his period of command there ended in confusion, in 1588 Elizabeth appointed him lieutenant general of the army waiting at Tilbury to fight the Spanish Armada. But that same year he died.

Like other great nobles, Leicester helped and encouraged learned men, and also supported a company of actors. Though he displeased Elizabeth by secretly marrying Lettice Knollys, she forgave him and he kept the queen's affection all his life.

See also ELIZABETH I.

LEICESTERSHIRE is a county in the eastern midlands of England. It is bordered on the north by Nottinghamshire, on the northwest by Derbyshire, on the east by Lincolnshire, on the southeast by Northamptonshire, and on the southwest by Warwickshire. It also touches Staffordshire on the west. After reorganization of county boundaries in 1974, the small separate county of Rutland was made part of Leicestershire. Leicestershire has an area of 2,553 square kilometres (986 square miles), and its population is 866,100 (1984).

Leicestershire is divided into two nearly equal parts by the River Soar, which rises in the south and flows north to join the River Trent in Nottinghamshire. Northeast of Leicester, the county town, the River Wreak flows into the Soar. In the northeast of the county is the fertile land of the Vale of Belvoir (pronounced "Beaver"), beneath which lies a recently discovered coalfield. West of the Soar the county is made up of clay and limestone. Hard rocks form barren ridges, particularly in the beautiful hilly regions of Charnwood, northwest of Leicester.

Industries and Towns

Leicestershire is well known as a farming county. Sheep and cattle are raised, and the county is the home of the Leicester breed of sheep, and of Longhorn cattle. These were varieties introduced by the stockbreeder Robert Bakewell (1725–95), who was born at Dishley and did much to improve British farm methods and livestock. As well as raising animals, the fertile pastures of the county are also ploughed and sown with a variety of crops.

Coal mining has been carried on in Leicestershire since the Middle Ages and was developed on a large scale during the Industrial Revolution in the 19th century. The working of ironstone, a kind of iron ore, in the northeast, and granite quarrying in the southwest, also developed at the same time. There are cement works and limestone quarries at Ketton, and from Clipsham in the east comes the mellow grey stone used for many public buildings, including the House of Commons. Oakham has shoe and clothing factories and light engineering, and there is a plastics industry at Uppingham.

The largest city in Leicestershire is Leicester, which stands on the River Soar. In Roman times its name was Ratae Coritanorum. The

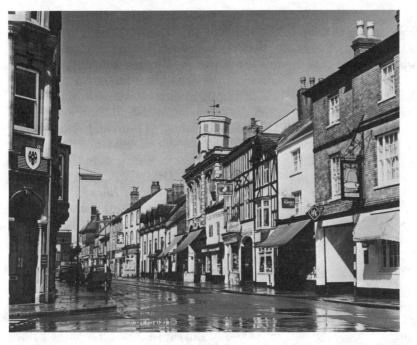

Barnaby's

The attractive old market town of Melton Mowbray stands on the River Eye in northeast Leicestershire.

remains of the forum, or market place, and pavements and a public bath of the Roman town can be seen. Through the city runs the Fosse Way, the road which the Romans built to link Bath and Lincoln.

Today Leicester is one of the largest industrial cities in Britain, with a cathedral and university. Traditionally it was famous for hosiery; that is, the making of socks, stockings, and knitted goods. Light engineering, boot and shoe making, printing, and plastics are also important today.

Loughborough, near the River Soar, also has engineering and hosiery factories, and bells are founded (made) there. Loughborough University is an engineering centre. The market town of Melton Mowbray, on the River Eye, is noted for its pork pies and as the home of Stilton cheese. Most of the county's towns and industries lie along the valley of the River Soar.

History

After the Romans left Britain, in the 5th century AD, Leicestershire became part of the kingdom of Mercia, and was later overrun by the invading Danes. Leicester itself was one of the five Danish boroughs, or army centres, in the 9th century.

Remains of 12th-century monasteries can be seen at Gracedieu and Ulverscroft, near Loughborough. The religious reformer John Wycliffe (see WYCLIFFE, JOHN) was parish priest at Lutterworth in the 1380s. Near the market town of Market Bosworth is the site of the battle fought in 1485 which ended the Wars of the Roses. (See ROSES, WARS OF THE.) Here King Richard III was slain by the forces of the Earl of Richmond, afterwards Henry VII, the first of the Tudor sovereigns. At Ashby-de-la-Zouch, in the west of Leicestershire, are the remains of a 15th-century castle that was destroyed by Oliver Cromwell's army during the English Civil War.

Famous people born in the county include Lady Jane Grey, the "nine days' queen" of England, who was born in 1537 in the now-ruined Bradgate House near the village of Newton Linford, on the edge of Charnwood Forest. George Fox, founder of the Society of Friends, or Quakers, was born in 1624 at Fenny Drayton, a village northwest of Hinckley. The historian Thomas Babington Macaulay (1800–59) and the scientist and writer C. P. Snow (1905–80) are two other people of distinction claimed by the county.

LEIF ERIKSSON was probably the first European to visit North America. He is sometimes called Leif the Lucky. Leif was one of the Norsemen, bold sea warriors also called Vikings (see VIKINGS). His father, Eric the Red, had founded a settlement in southern Greenland (see ERIC THE RED). When King Olaf Tryggvesson of Norway became a Christian, he sent Leif, in about AD 1000, to bring the new religion to the Vikings in Greenland.

Instead of sailing to Greenland by way of Iceland, Leif set off across the Atlantic Ocean, but he was blown off course. After many weeks he came to a fertile land of wild wheat and vines, which he valled Vinland (Wineland). Leif and his men noticed that the area was warmer and more fruitful than Greenland.

It is now believed that Leif landed either in Rhode Island, United States, or in Nova Scotia, Canada. If so, then he was the first European in the New World.

The following year Leif's brother Thorstein tried unsuccessfully to reach these new lands. The next Norseman to reach North America was Thorfinn Karlsefni, who left Greenland in 1003 with three ships to reach Vinland. He sailed down the eastern coast, naming the bleak northern Labrador coast Helluland (Flagstoneland) and the wooded lands further south Markland (Forestland). He tried to found a colony but trouble broke out with the Eskimoes and the Norsemen returned to Greenland in 1006. Later there were probably occasional visits to Markland for timber, but there was no settlement.

LEINSTER is one of the four provinces of Ireland and covers 19,633 square kilometres (7,580 square miles) in the southeast and central parts of the Republic of Ireland. It is the richest of the Irish provinces and contains Dublin, the capital of the Irish Republic (see DUBLIN). It also contains more counties than any of the others. They are Carlow, Dublin, Kildare, Kilkenny, Leix (Laoighis, in Irish), Longford, Louth, Meath, Offaly, Westmeath, Wexford, and Wicklow. The population of Leinster is 1,851,000 (1986).

On the west the River Shannon forms the boundary between Leinster and the province of Connacht (on which there is a separate article). Other rivers flowing through Leinster are the Nore, the Barrow, and the Slaney in the south, and, farther north, the Liffey, on which Dublin stands, and the Boyne.

Most of Leinster is flat, but there are small mountains in county Dublin and Wicklow, the lovely Slieve Bloom mountains in Leix and Offaly and others in Wexford. In the midland counties of Leix, Offaly, Kildare, and Westmeath is the great Bog of Allen. This is now being drained to provide turf (peat fuel) and land for growing crops.

Outside Dublin, in the rest of Leinster, there are breweries and distilleries, flour mills, sugar factories, and boot factories, besides the great electric power stations which have been established near Dublin and on the bogs. Black marble and coal are still quarried in Kilkenny and copper and other metals have been mined again in County Wicklow.

The Counties of Leinster

Carlow, in the southeast, is a small county. Its capital town, Carlow, has boot factories and flour mills and makes sugar from locally grown sugar beet.

County Dublin is also a small county. Besides the capital it contains Dun Laoghaire ("Leary's Fort"), southeast of Dublin, from which ships regularly cross to Holyhead in Wales. The coast of Dublin has beautiful scenery around the wide expanse of Dublin Bay, with Killiney and Howth bays on each side.

Kildare, southwest of Dublin, is one of the flattest of the Irish counties and includes some areas of bog. However, it also has rich pastures on which sheep and cattle are kept.

Kilkenny, the most southwesterly of the counties of Leinster, has a historic castle and a cathedral. It is a prosperous county.

Leix, or Laoighis, used to be called Queen's County and Offaly was King's County. The king and queen after whom they were named were Philip II of Spain and his wife Mary I of England. During the reign of these two monarchs many English people were given lands in Ireland.

A view across wooded hilltops of the distant Wicklow Mountains, which form part of the Leinster Chain

Lois Crighton

Longford is in the west, and between it and Roscommon, in Connach, is Lough (lake) Ree on the course of the Shannon. Longford contains some boggy country, but has large stretches of useful grazing land.

Louth, on the east coast, is the smallest county in Ireland. Its chief town is Dundalk and on the Boyne is Drogheda. County Louth is associated with the legendary Irish hero Cuchulainn.

Meath, west of Dublin, was once the centre of a province and at Tara the high king of Ireland was crowned. (The high king was the most powerful of the kings of the five provinces of ancient Ireland.) The wonderful Book of Kells, an illustrated copy of the Gospels from the late 7th century, was produced in the now ruined monastery of Kells in Meath.

Offaly (King's County) is between Leix and Westmeath. On the west the Shannon flows between Offaly, Galway, and Roscommon. Offaly is the chief centre of the bog drainage and the use of turf as fuel for power stations. It also includes the sacred place of Clonmacnoise, with the ruins of many ancient churches and abbeys.

Westmeath, west of Meath, was, until 1543, part of the old midland province of Meath. Mullingar, the county town, is a cattle market and a road and railway junction.

Wexford is in the southeast corner of Ireland and has been the scene of historic events for centuries. From Rosslare, near Wexford town, ferries sail for Fishguard in Wales.

Wicklow, north of Wexford and south of Dublin, is very beautiful, with rough mountainous country. Its east coast, bordered by the Irish Sea, has few harbours, but Arklow is a growing port.

LEIPZIG is the tenth largest city in Germany. Prior to the reunification of 1990 it was the second largest city of East Germany (the former German Democratic Republic). The city lies about 160 kilometres (100 miles) southwest of Berlin. It consists of an old inner city surrounded by modern districts. The old town has many steep-roofed houses of the 16th and 17th centuries and is a maze of narrow streets. A round tower is all that remains of the 13th-century citadel. Among its churches is the 13th-century Thomaskirche where the composer J. S. Bach, who was organist there, is buried.

Leipzig became important in Germany because of its great university founded in 1409 and as the centre of German literature and music. The composer Richard Wagner was a native of the city and the great poet J. W. Goethe went to its university.

Leipzig became famous abroad for its great trade fairs, held twice a year (at Easter and in September) since about 1170. Merchants and manufacturers from all parts of Europe and from Asia showed their goods at these fairs. The International Leipzig Fair today attracts businessmen and scientists from all over the world. Early in the 19th century Leipzig became the centre of the German book trade and has about 200 printing works as well as many bookshops. There are also factories making chemicals, paints, textiles, iron and steel, machinery, computers, and musical instruments. It is an important road and rail centre, with one of the world's biggest railway stations.

Leipzig takes its name from the Slav word *lipa* (meaning "lime tree") given to the first settlement there before the year AD 1000. It became an important trading town in the Middle Ages. It was often besieged or occupied by foreign armies and the great Battle of Leipzig, in which the Emperor Napoleon I and his troops were defeated by the Prussians, Austrians, and Russians, was fought around the city from 16 to 18 October 1813 (see NAPOLEONIC WARS). Because of its importance as a rail junction it was heavily bombed during World War II and about a quarter of its houses were destroyed. Although after the war East Berlin was made the capital of the German Democratic Republic, Leipzig became the chief centre of trade, learning, and the arts. Its population is about 559,000 (1984).

LEMMING. There are several species of lemming, small mouse-like rodents, which live in the mountains and polar regions of North America and Eurasia.

The Scandinavian lemming (*Lemmus lemmus*) is about 13 centimetres (5 inches) long, with a large head and a stumpy body. Its fur is yellow-brown, spotted with dark brown or black. The lemming eats leaves and bark and burrows under the snow in winter. It is a restless, brave, and quarrelsome little animal and if disturbed it sits upright against a stone and hisses. Lemmings breed very fast, and the females have at least ten young a year. They

NHPA/Brian Hawkes

A Greenland collared lemming blends in with the lichen-encrusted rocks of its tundra home.

make grass nests lined with hair for the young.

Every three or four years, lemmings become so numerous that there is not enough food for them and so they begin a mass migration and move outward in all directions from the central area. They usually travel mostly at night, feeding and sleeping by day, and nothing stops their march. Followed by birds and beasts of prey, they swarm all over the countryside. This population explosion makes the lemmings behave unusually. Normally they avoid water but on migration they will cross rivers and also pass through towns. When they reach the coast, thousands of animals plunge into the sea and swim until they become exhausted and drown.

There are various explanations for this. One is that, long ago, when the Baltic and North seas were narrower than they are now, lemmings were able to swim across them and reach land where they could find more food. The lemmings of today still become overcrowded because they breed so fast; they are compelled to move but they can no longer swim across to fresh pastures.

LEMON. Like the orange tree, to which it is closely related, the lemon tree (*Citrus limon*) is green the whole year round. It often bears buds, full-blown flowers, and ripening fruit at the same time. There is a period of the year, however, when there are greater numbers of flowers and fruits than at others. It rarely reaches a height of 9 metres (30 feet). The flowers, which are white, tinged with purple or pink at the edges, are less fragrant than orange blossoms. Lemon oil, used in flavouring and perfumes, is obtained from the outer peels of the fruit. Pectin, which is used to stiffen jellies, is made from the white inner rind. The juice serves many purposes. When fresh it is used for lemonade and other beverages and also as a flavouring in cooking. It is valuable as a protection against scurvy because of its high vitamin C content. From it is made citric acid which is used in calico printing and to fix dyes on other cloths.

The native home of the lemon tree is thought to have been in northwestern India, but it has been grown throughout southern Asia and in Asia Minor for centuries. During the 12th century it was introduced into Europe by the Arabs. Now it is grown in all warm countries from Zimbabwe in southern Africa to California in the United States. Spain, Portugal, and Italy are the chief lemon-growing countries of Europe. In the United States lemons are grown in Arizona, Texas, and Florida, as well as in California. Until 1895 Florida was the

ZEFA

A lemon tree laden with fruit in a Greek garden. Mediterranean countries export many of their lemons.

chief lemon-producing state. Now lemons are grown mainly in California.

The trees which bear the best fruit are often less strong. Therefore, shoots from these selected trees are usually grafted on sturdier stock or on the stock of the sour orange. The trees are set out in the orchards when they are about two years old and begin to bear fruit about four years later. Usually the rows of trees are about 6 metres (20 feet) apart. In California and other arid regions irrigation ditches run between the rows.

Lemons are picked while they are still green. The fruit must be handled very carefully, for it bruises easily. After they are picked, the lemons are stored in dark, moist, well-ventilated rooms until they have ripened. Then they are wrapped in tissue paper and packed in boxes for shipping. Since lemons which are ripened in this way can be kept for six months, the winter crop may be safely stored until it is needed in the summer.

See also CITRUS FRUIT.

LEMUR. Lemurs are primitive primates, the group of mammals to which apes and man also belong. They live only on the large island of Madagascar off the east coast of Africa.

About 15 species of lemur live in Madagascar. No true apes or monkeys ever reached the island, which millions of years ago broke away from the continent of Africa. So the lemurs filled the "gap" and flourished, free from competition. Lemurs look rather like dog-faced monkeys. They have large eyes, long, bushy tails, and slender limbs. They climb well, using their grasping hands, and spend most of their time in trees. Most lemurs live in groups, and eat plants or insects. The ring-tailed lemur (*Lemur catta*) is just over 1 metre (3.3 feet) long while the smallest members of the family are the mouse lemurs (*Microcebus*), about 30 centimetres (12 inches). They store fat in the rump and tail and sleep during the dry season.

The largest species of lemur is the indri (*Indri indri*), up to 70 centimetres (27.5 inches). It is found only in the northern part of the east-coast rain-forests. It has very long back legs, which allow it to make enormous vertical leaps from tree to tree. It lives in small social groups and communicates by far-ranging howls.

All lemurs are tree dwellers except the ring-tailed lemur, which lives in dry, rocky places.

The aye-aye (*Daubentonia madagascariensis*), a curious close relative of the lemur, is also found only on Madagascar. It has large forward-facing eyes, bat-like ears and a large bushy tail. It spends most of its time high in the larger branches of trees, where it extracts grubs from the bark, using its exceptionally long third finger.

Zoological Society of London

The ring-tailed lemur is one of the largest lemurs. It prefers open rocky land to forest areas.

Lemurs are a fascinating group of mammals that unfortunately are becoming rare as their forest habitat is being destroyed. They are of particular interest because, from the study of fossil remains, we know that lemurs first lived on Earth some 65 million years ago. This makes them among the very earliest primates.

See also MONKEY.

LENA RIVER. A major river in Russia and one of the longest rivers in the world, the Lena rises near Lake Baikal and flows for about 4,400 kilometres (2,730 miles) to reach the Laptev Sea, in the Arctic ocean. The Siberian lands through which it flows have very long and cold winters and the lower part of the river is frozen over from mid-October until June or July. Thus ships can use the Lena for only a short time in each year. However, as there are no railways in this part of Russia, the river traffic is important. Just east of the mouth of the Lena is Tiksi, one of the chief ports on the Northern Sea Route between the Atlantic and Pacific Oceans. The delta, at the mouth of the river, is a vast sandbank cut through by many channels of all sizes, which change their direction from year to year. Near the delta the people live by hunting and fishing. Further upstream along the middle river there are some farms where cattle are bred and crops grown, the centre of this district being the fast-growing town of Yakutsk. There are huge deposits of coal, natural gas, gold, salt, and diamonds in the Lena basin (see also SIBERIA). The leading modern port upriver on the Lena is Osetrovo, near Lake Baikal.

LENIN, Vladimir Ilich (1870–1924). Few people have brought about such great political changes as Lenin, who led the Bolshevik Revolution in Russia in 1917.

His real surname was Ulyanov but he took the name Lenin when taking part in secret political activities in 1901, and stuck to it ever afterwards. He was born on 22 April 1870, at Simbirsk, which was later renamed Ulyanovsk in his honour, on the River Volga. His father was an inspector of schools and his mother a doctor's daughter. In 1887 his elder brother was executed for taking part in a plot to murder the tsar (emperor) of Russia.

At this time there was much discontent in Russia, for many of the people had no political rights (the right to vote is an example of a political right) and many of the peasants were extremely poor, while the nobles and great landowners were very rich. Young members of middle-class families such as Lenin's began to form political groups to try to bring about changes, some believing in one method of trying to alter things, some in another. Lenin himself made a careful study of the works of

Camera Press

Lenin (right) as editor of *Pravda*, the Communist Party newspaper, with Molotov (left) and Stalin.

the German Karl Marx (see MARX, KARL), who was one of the founders of the political belief known as Communism. Marx stated that it was wrong for individual people to own shops, factories, land, and other property, and thought that the working people in each country ought to revolt and take over all these things, making them the common property of everybody. (See COMMUNISM.) These ideas appealed greatly to the young Lenin and he determined to bring about a Communist revolution in Russia.

In 1891 Lenin gained a degree in law and worked in the courts, representing mainly poor peasants and workers. In 1893 he moved to St. Petersburg (which was later named Leningrad after him), and soon became a leader of the revolutionaries; that is, those people who wanted to bring about a revolution. Two years later he was arrested because of his political activities, imprisoned, and then exiled to Siberia, in Asia. There he married Nadezhda Krupskaya, a revolutionary colleague from St. Petersburg, who helped in his work until his death.

In 1900 after his exile was over he visited Switzerland, Germany, Britain, and France. From Munich, in Germany, and London he published a revolutionary newspaper called

Iskra (The Spark), which was smuggled into Russia. In 1903 a Russian revolutionary party known as the Russian Social Democratic Workers' Party held a meeting in London (it could not be held in Russia because the members would have been arrested) and Lenin played a large part in its proceedings. The members soon quarrelled among themselves and the party split into two sections. Lenin and his supporters were known as the Bolsheviks. (They were the larger section, and in Russian *bolshe* means "more". In the same way the members of the smaller section were known as Mensheviks, from the Russian word for "less".)

In 1905 there were revolutionary outbreaks in Russia, and Lenin returned there in disguise and carried on his political activities secretly. In 1907 he escaped to Switzerland and remained abroad until 1917, but continued to direct political agitation in Russia.

In February 1917, while Russia was fighting Germany in World War I, a revolution broke out in St. Petersburg, Moscow, and other large cities. (See RUSSIAN REVOLUTION.) The tsar was deposed and a provisional government was set up. Much as Lenin wanted to have a hand in it he was unable to reach Russia without travelling through Germany. He could not do that because although he was against the Russian government he was a Russian citizen, and the Germans would have arrested him as an enemy. Then, unexpectedly, the German government came to his help. It was keen to add to the troubles of the Russian government and arranged for Lenin and some of his followers to be sent across Germany into Russia. He arrived in April 1917 and immediately set about organizing a campaign that would lead his party to power. In July he tried to seize power but failed and had to go into hiding. In November, however, he and his party were successful and Lenin became head of a new Russian government. This was the first Communist government in the world.

In August 1918 a member of an anti-Bolshevik party tried to murder him and wounded him severely in the spine. He recovered and for the next five years worked ceaselessly to put the Communists' plans into operation. He died on 21 January 1924. His body was embalmed to preserve it and Soviet citizens and others come to see it in its marble tomb in the centre of Moscow.

See also the article UNION OF SOVIET SOCIALIST REPUBLICS, which explains more fully the political events mentioned in this article.

LENS.

A lens is a shaped piece of glass or other transparent substance that helps to produce an image or picture of an object at which it is pointed. The eye itself uses a system of natural lenses, and lenses are used in most optical instruments, including the camera, telescope, magnifying glass, and spectacles.

How a Lens Works

Light travels in straight lines through space or through the air. This can easily be shown by making a small hole in two cards and holding them one in front of the other between your eye and a light bulb. The bulb can be seen only when it and the holes in the cards are directly in line. In the same way, light also travels in straight lines through clear water or glass. If, however, the light travels from one transparent substance to another – say, from air to water, or vice versa – it is refracted, or bent, and changes its direction unless it meets the surface of the new substance exactly at right angles (90°). You can find out more about the effects of refraction in the article REFLECTION AND REFRACTION.

John Howard/Science Photo Library

Lenses come in many forms and sizes. One of the most familiar types is the simple magnifying glass.

Like water, glass too has a bending effect on light. When light travels from air into glass it is refracted and when it comes out of the glass into air it is refracted again. But unless the two surfaces of the glass are parallel to each other (as in a window pane) the final direction of the light will not be the same as at first. These changes of direction happen because light cannot travel as fast in glass or water as it does in air. (See LIGHT.)

Light passing through a prism (a triangular block of glass) is refracted, just as it is when passing through a window pane. If two prisms are fixed with their bases together, the rays of light from the sun or a lamp will converge, or be brought together, after passing through them. If, however, the two prisms are fixed so that their points are together, an exactly opposite effect is produced and the rays will diverge, or spread out, after passing through the prisms. The first arrangement of prisms is the principle of the *convex lens* and the second that of the *concave lens*; but lenses are in practice usually made curved instead of angular. (You can always remember the difference between "convex" and "concave" shapes because concave ones are hollowed out like a cave.) If one side of a lens is flat, it is either a *plano-convex lens* or a *plano-concave lens*.

The ordinary magnifying glass is a convex lens. If it is held so that the face of the lens is at right angles to the Sun, the Sun's rays may be brought to a tiny spot on a piece of paper. In this way both the light and the heat from the Sun are concentrated on a small area, which becomes very bright and hot. This is the principle of the burning glass, which was used in the past for lighting fires. Heath and forest fires are sometimes started accidentally by bits of curved glass, such as from a broken bottle, acting in the same way.

If a magnifying glass is held up to light coming in through a window and a piece of white card is held behind it, a small *image* or picture of the window appears upside down on the card when the distance between the lens and the card is adjusted correctly. When an object, in this case the window, is far from the lens, the distance between the lens and the card is called the *focal length* of the lens. But but with near objects, the image distance is not the focal length. The smaller the focal length, the greater the magnifying power of the lens. If the card is held too far from the lens or too near it, a blurred picture of the window is obtained. Adjusting the distance between the card and the lens in order to obtain a sharp picture is called *focusing*.

Images through Lenses

If a convex lens is brought close to an object so that the distance between them is less than the focal length of the lens, a person looking at the object through the lens will see a magnified (enlarged) image the right way up. If, however, a piece of white card is held behind the lens, no image appears on the card as it did when the lens was held up to the window. The images that can be seen on a piece of card, film, or a screen are called "real" images. Those that cannot are called "virtual" images.

When using a magnifying glass or toy telescope, you can usually see coloured fringes around the objects viewed. This happens because rays of light of different colours are not bent through the same angle as they go through the lens. Rays of blue light, for instance, are bent more than those of red light. Since white light is a mixture of all the colours of the rainbow (see COLOURS), the result is that the image seen has a rainbow fringe. This can be corrected by making the lens in two layers each of a different kind of glass. A lens of this type is called a *compound lens*. It is difficult to make and costs more than a simple lens, which is why good cameras and binoculars are so expensive.

Lenses in the Eye

The eye uses a convex lens system to form images. The clear curved front part (the cornea) and the watery liquid behind it form a lens that focuses light as it enters the eye through the pupil (the small hole in the iris – see EYE AND EYESIGHT). The light then passes through an inner crystalline convex lens behind the pupil. Tiny muscles can change the curvature or shape of this lens, and in doing so focus the image. The image is formed on a light-sensitive area, called the retina, at the back of the eye. As the lens system is convex, the images are actually formed upside down, and it is the brain that turns them the right way up.

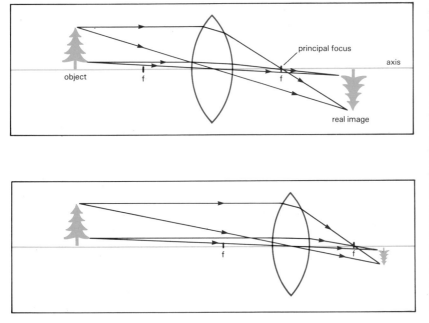

A convex lens produces a virtual image of an object that is located at a distance of less than the focal length of the lens. But if the object lies beyond the focal length of the lens a *real* image will be produced. **Top:** The object is just beyond the focal length of the lens and its real image, magnified and turned upside down, is formed by light rays at a point on the other side of the lens, just beyond the principal focus. **Bottom:** The object's distance from the lens is over twice the focal length, and its image, also real and turned upside down, is reduced in size. Real images are formed at the very point where they seem to be and can be projected onto film, a piece of white card, or a screen.

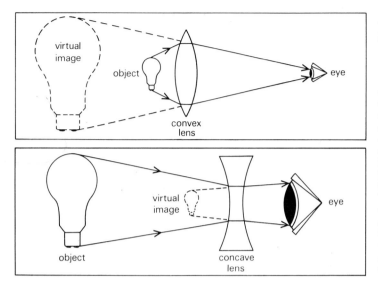

All lenses bend light to produce images of objects. **Top**: A convex lens bends light rays inwards, producing a magnified image behind the object observed. **Bottom**: A concave lens bends light rays outwards and produces a reduced image that appears between the lens and the object. The light bulb in each of these illustrations stands within the focal length of the lens. The image of the light bulb (the one with the dotted outline) is called a *virtual* image, because the light rays from the bulb only appear to form the image at that point.

Uses of Lenses

A convex lens is used in a camera to focus the image of a group of people or scene – which are quite far off compared with the size of the camera – into a small picture, upside down, on the film at the back of the camera. The "reflex" camera has a second lens exactly like the first to throw the same picture onto a ground glass screen, so that the photographer can focus correctly and see the exact picture that will be obtained. Zoom lenses consist of an arrangement of separate lenses set in such a way that the focal length can be varied. (See the separate article CAMERA.)

A cinema projector or slide projector uses a convex lens which projects, or throws, the rays of light from the brilliantly lit film onto a large screen. The film is only 35 millimetres (about 1.4 inches) wide but the picture on the screen may be many metres across.

Manufacture and History of Lenses

A lens is made from a block of glass by grinding it with carborundum or emery (very gritty powders) and by polishing it while wet with a kind of paste known as rouge. Although some of this can be done by machinery, the process is slow and expensive and the final polishing and testing need great skill. Plastic materials such as perspex (see PLASTICS) are nowadays sometimes used for such things as spectacles, contact lenses, and magnifying glasses.

The ancient Greeks and Romans sometimes used round glass flasks filled with water to act as burning glasses for lighting fires. Spectacles and magnifying glasses were invented before the year 1300. The telescope was invented in 1608; there are separate articles on it and on the microscope, which is a form of very powerful magnifying glass. Lenses range in size from a pinhead to about 1 metre (3.3 feet) in diameter (width), which is the size of the object glass in the big telescope at Yerkes Observatory in Wisconsin, in the United States.

LENT for Christians is the period of fasting and penitence in preparation for Easter, when Jesus Christ's resurrection (returning to life after death) is remembered. Lent is observed by members of the Roman Catholic and Eastern Orthodox churches, and some Protestant churches. The word comes from the Old English *lencten*, meaning *springtime*. Lent begins on Ash Wednesday and ends on Holy Saturday, the day before Easter. Although it lasts for 6½ weeks, only 40 days of that period are fast days. (See EASTER.)

Fasting in preparation for Easter is an ancient Christian tradition, perhaps inherited from the Jewish practice of fasting before certain religious holidays. Probably the 40 days were associated with the 40 days Jesus spent fasting in the wilderness in preparation for his ministry (see JESUS CHRIST).

In the early years of Christianity, fasting rules for Lent were strict. Only one meal a day was permitted, and certain foods could not be eaten at all. Today, however, Lent is more often observed by the sacrifice of certain pleasures or comforts; the sacrifice is intended to show one's sincere desire to repent and live a Christian life.

LENTIL. Lentils, which are the seeds of small plants such as vetches (see VETCH), were among the first crops to be cultivated. The "mess of pottage" in the Old Testament of the Bible, for which Esau sold his birthright to his brother Jacob because he was so hungry, was a meal made of lentils.

An old Hindu proverb says: "Rice is good but lentils are my life." Lentils contain more protein than rice and other cereals, and this protein is needed for the building and repair of muscles and other tissues of the body. They also contain vitamin B, iron and phosphorus, making them a nourishing food. They are often eaten in the form of soup.

The lentil plant ranges from 15 to 20 centimetres (6 to 8 inches) in height and usually has pale blue flowers. It belongs to the same

A lentil plant with a pod cut open to show the seeds.

family, Fabaceae, as peas and beans, and like them it can add nitrogen to the soil.

The pods contain only two seeds, which may be red, brown, black, or grey. The French lentil seed is ash-grey and is often sold without being split. The Egyptian variety has smaller, rounder seeds which are usually split into two reddish-yellow cotyledons, or seed leaves. Like peas and beans, lentils are sometimes called pulses when eaten.

Lentil plants like warm, sandy soils. They are widely grown in India, Pakistan, western Asia, North Africa, and in parts of southern Europe, including France.

LEONARDO DA VINCI (1452–1519) was one of the most amazing men who ever lived. Not only was he a great painter, whose pictures the *Mona Lisa* and *The Last Supper* are among

ZEFA

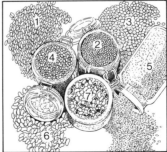

Lentils, beans, and peas.
1 Flageolet beans; **2** Mung beans; **3** Chick peas or garbanzo beans; **4** Yellow split peas; **5** Red lentils; **6** Kidney beans; **7** Black-eyed beans or peas.

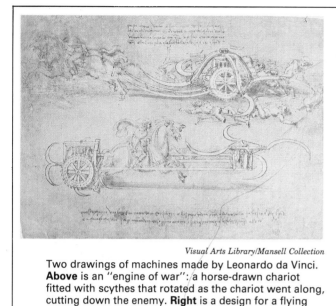

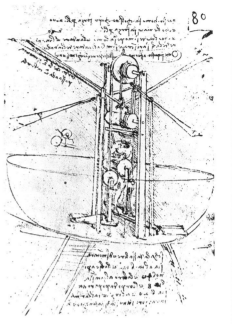

Visual Arts Library/Mansell Collection

Two drawings of machines made by Leonardo da Vinci.
Above is an "engine of war": a horse-drawn chariot
fitted with scythes that rotated as the chariot went along,
cutting down the enemy. **Right** is a design for a flying
machine. Neither of these two machines was ever built.

the most famous in the world, but also he was a sculptor and an architect, a poet and a composer of music. He was a scientist and inventor, whose ideas and discoveries were hundreds of years in advance of his time. Leonardo had a clear idea of his talents and in a letter to Ludovico Sforza, Duke of Milan, applying for a job, he described himself as an inventor of engines of war, a builder of movable bridges and chariots, and an engineer skilled in the science of artillery and sieges. He added as a postscript that he was a sculptor and could paint as well as any other man. Leonardo also studied the working of the human body, more deeply than most doctors of his day, and was already working on what we now call the science of aeronautics – that is, of flight. One of his designs was for a practical aircraft.

However, Leonardo wrote his notes with his left hand, backhanded, from left to right across the page, which made them very difficult to read and for many years his work was not understood.

Leonardo was born not far from Florence, Italy, near the village of Vinci, from which his father's family took its name. As a child he enjoyed music, drawing, and modelling. When his father showed some of his drawings to an artist named Andrea del Verrocchio, Verrocchio at once realized that the boy should be trained as an artist and probably took him into his own studio in Florence, where Leonardo is believed to have worked for several years. He was fascinated most by the appearance of real things, which he tried to draw accurately on paper. He attempted to portray the strange shapes of hills and rocks, rare plants and animals, and the unusual faces and figures of men, for example. Besides studying the outward appearance of nature, he also tried to find out how things were constructed and how they worked; for instance, how the human eye was made up, how plants grew, how light and water behaved, and how birds flew.

In about 1478 Leonardo started the painting called *The Virgin of the Rocks*, which is now in the Louvre museum, in Paris. It shows the Virgin Mary with the infant Jesus, the young John the Baptist, and an angel, against a strange background of caves and rock arches, tufted with flowers. (He painted another version of the same picture, later, which is in the National Gallery in London.)

Leonardo's second version of *Virgin of the Rocks* (finished 1508) hangs in the National Gallery, London.

Just when Leonardo was thinking of leaving Florence, in 1483, he was offered the chance of going to the court of Duke Ludovico Sforza, in Milan. He accepted and remained in the duke's service until 1499. During this period Leonardo invented new machinery for defence, built canals, and planned an extensive irrigation system. He made plans for the cathedral at Milan, and supervised the pageants and masques given at the duke's castle. Ludovico wanted Leonardo to do a great sculpture for him, a statue of his father, Francesco Sforza, mounted on a horse. The statue was to be in bronze, and Leonardo got as far as making a huge model of it, almost 8 metres (26 feet) high. But the bronze cast had not yet been made by the time French invaders captured Milan in 1500, and the model was later destroyed.

While at Ludovico's court Leonardo found time to organize the Milanese Academy, and there he continued his scientific studies, which were published in Paris in 1551.

In 1494 he began to work on what was to be his greatest painting, *The Last Supper*, for the monks of the church of Santa Maria delle Grazie in Milan. He painted the picture on the wall, but unfortunately the kind of paint he used did not hold firmly to the wall,

Visual Arts Library

Leonardo's *Mona Lisa* (Louvre, Paris), finished after 1513, is a portrait of a Florentine lady.

and even in Leonardo's lifetime it began to flake off. This wonderful picture of the groups of disciples, with Christ in their midst, has been partly restored, however, and the decay has been prevented from going any further.

In 1500 Leonardo returned to Florence to become architect and chief engineer to Duke Cesare Borgia. But he also continued to paint. Back in Florence he began a great battle-picture for one of the walls of the council chamber. In two years he completed his cartoon, or preliminary painting, which was breathtaking in its expression of battle frenzy. Unfortunately the magnificent work that Leonardo planned was never completed.

About this time, however, Leonardo did finish another painting, the *Mona Lisa*, which is among the best-known paintings in the world. It is a portrait of the wife of a Florentine official. It is said that he ordered music to be played at every sitting so that the beautiful

Mansell Collection

Drawings of the human head. Leonardo produced a great number of drawings of the human anatomy.

smile and expression should not fade from the lady's face. The *Mona Lisa* is now in the Louvre, in Paris.

From 1507 to 1513 Leonardo travelled around Italy, and then he met the young and brilliant King of France, Francis I, who invited the old artist to his country and promised him every honour. Leonardo accepted and in his last years he lived in a castle the king gave him at Cloux, near Amboise. He hoped to be able to set in order all his papers, the results of his life's studies, but he died before he could do so and his precious manuscripts were hardly known until quite recently.

About 5,000 pages of Leonardo's sketchbooks still survive. They are filled with drawings and comments. Some of his sketchbooks can be seen in the Royal Library at Windsor Castle, England, and also at the Victoria and Albert Museum, and the British Museum, both in London.

LEOPARD. The leopard (*Leo pardus*) is a member of the cat family, smaller than the lion and tiger, but fierce and cunning. It is also known as the panther, especially in India and Pakistan.

The leopard is a striking-looking animal, having a yellowish-brown coat with black spots arranged like rosettes. Some leopards have black coats on which the spots show up dimly. The body of the leopard is over 2 metres (6.5 feet) long, and its tail is usually half the length of its body.

Leopards live over nearly the whole of Africa south of the Sahara, and extend through Asia Minor and central Asia to India and China. They are found mostly in jungles and low rocky hills. In the jungles they are quite at home in trees, where they lie among the leaves, camouflaged by their coats, and spring upon monkeys or drop onto deer or antelopes passing beneath. They also ambush prey by stalking, then leaping on them from a short distance. Favourite prey include baboons, and young antelopes. Leopards sometimes boldly raid villages for goats, cattle, and dogs. Occasionally a leopard

NHPA/Peter Johnson

A leopard sits in a tree with its antelope kill, beyond the reach of marauding lions and hyenas.

attacks a human being, but it does this even more rarely than the tiger.

There is no definite breeding season; the female produces two to four, usually three, cubs.

Leopards are among the most vocal of large cats, communicating by a mixture of throaty growls and deep purring sounds.

In the high snowy regions of the Himalaya Mountains lives the snow leopard (*Leo uncia*). It ranges in summer up to altitudes of 5,500 metres (18,000 feet). It has a soft coat consisting of a dense insulating undercoat and a thick overcoat of pale greyish hairs with dark rosettes, and a dark streak along the spine.

The snow leopard hunts marmots and wild sheep at night. It is classed as an endangered species.

The clouded leopard (*Leo nebulosa*) lives in the forests of southeastern Asia. It is a rather short-legged cat with a long head and very long upper canine teeth. The coat is greyish-brown, beautifully marked with spots and large dark patches partly edged with black. It preys on birds and on small mammals such as monkeys.

Pictures of leopards are often seen on heraldic coats of arms (see HERALDRY) and some African tribes consider the leopard a royal animal. The beautiful fur has always been valued and the leopard has become rare because of the demand for its fur. Egyptian high priests wore leopard skins as a sign of their office.

LEOPOLD (Kings of Belgium). Three kings of Belgium have been named Leopold.

Leopold I (1790–1865) was the first king of newly independent Belgium. He was the fourth son of Francis, Duke of Saxe-Coburg-Saalfeld. At the age of 18 he joined the Prussian army as a cavalry officer. In 1816 he married Princess Charlotte, heiress to the throne of Great Britain. He was made a British subject and was given the title Duke of Kendall. In 1817 the princess died, but Leopold remained in England until 1831. The Greeks had wanted him to be their king in 1830, but he refused the offer. The next year the National Congress of Belgium elected Leopold king, and he was crowned on 21 July 1831.

Leopold governed firmly and wisely, and was highly influential in European diplomacy, strengthening Belgium's ties with France, Britain, and Austria through marriages. In 1840, for example, he helped to arrange the marriage of his niece, Queen Victoria, to his nephew, Prince Albert of Saxe-Coburg-Gotha.

Leopold II (1835–1909) was the son of Leopold I. He served in the Belgian army from the age of 11 until he became king, travelling a great deal in the East and North Africa.

Leopold came to the throne in 1865, aged 30, and ruled for 44 years. He was clever, politically, and persuaded his country to stay out of the Franco-Prussian War (1870–71).

Leopold was also a successful businessman. He organized the African International Association in Brussels in 1876, and in 1885 the Berlin Conference gave him personal control over the Congo Free State (see ZAIRE). He was later criticized for the way he ruled this territory and, in 1908, the Congo was taken over by the Belgian government. When Leopold died his nephew, Albert I, became king.

Leopold III (1901–83) was crowned king on the death of his father, Albert I, in 1934. In 1935 his wife, Queen Astrid, was killed in a car accident. In 1941 he married Mary Liliane Baels, the daughter of a former government minister. This was an unpopular marriage and the resulting children have no claim to the throne.

In World War II, during the German occupation of Belgium, Leopold was taken prisoner and held in Austria. At the end of the war, in 1945, the Belgian Parliament refused to let Leopold return to the country because he had ordered the Belgian army to surrender to the Germans in May 1940. His brother Charles had been made prince regent in 1944. This situation lasted until 1950, when a majority of the Belgian people voted in favour of Leopold's return. When he came back, however, there was great civil unrest, and in 1951 Leopold abdicated (gave up his throne). His son, Baudouin, then became king.

LEPROSY, also known as Hansen's disease, is a disease that damages the skin, the nerves of the limbs and face, the lining of the nose, and other parts of the body. The skin becomes patchy and lumpy, and the victim may lose feeling in the limbs and power in the muscles.

Leprosy is caused by tiny bacteria (*Mycobacterium leprae*) and is infectious, that is, it can be caught from those who suffer from it, while the sufferer remains untreated. But catching it is quite difficult and usually happens only after years of living in close contact with sufferers.

The seriousness of the disease depends on how resistant a person is to the leprosy germ. The mildest cases take the form of a skin infection that heals itself. However, if the victim has little resistance and the disease takes hold, then regular treatment is essential. Without medicine the victim may develop a claw hand or foot as his limbs stiffen up. Also, because of the loss of feeling, he cannot feel pain and so burns or cuts himself easily. Deformities often associated with leprosy are in fact the result of such accidents. Leprosy itself rarely kills, but long-term sufferers who

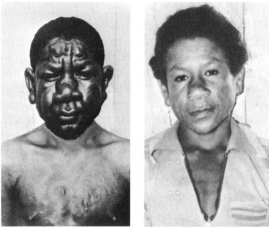

Courtesy, The Leprosy Mission
A 14-year-old Indonesian boy with leprosy is treated with drugs. **Left:** March 1979, before treatment; **Right:** Three years after commencing treatment.

are not treated become more likely to catch other diseases, which can kill.

Throughout the world there are from 10 to 15 million people suffering from leprosy. The worst-affected areas are West and central Africa, South America and Southeast Asia.

For many centuries people were particularly afraid of skin diseases because they believed them to be a punishment for evil. Leprosy sufferers were forced to live as outcasts and beg for their living. The old belief, mentioned in the Bible, that leprosy could be caught simply by touching someone who had it, is quite untrue.

Nowadays leprosy can be treated by several drugs, such as dapsone and rifampicin, although the damage already done to the body cannot be mended. A complete cure needs a long course of drugs, which is expensive, and leprosy sufferers tend to live in poor parts of the world. A campaign for widespread treatment of leprosy is high on the World Health Organization's list. With enough money, doctors, and drugs, the disease could, like smallpox, be banished from the world.

LESOTHO is a tiny landlocked country in southeast Africa which is completely surrounded by the territory of its powerful neighbour, South Africa. The entire country is 1,600

metres (5,250 feet) or more above sea-level. In the northeast are the high, bleak Maloti Mountains. The eastern border is formed by the Drakensberg Mountains, which include Thabana Ntlenyana—at 3,482 metres (11,424 feet), the highest mountain in southern Africa.

The Orange River rises in Lesotho, and its valley provides one of the two most fertile regions in the country. The valley of the Caledon River, which forms the western border with South Africa, covers a third of the country. The natural vegetation of Lesotho is sparse grass, shrub, olives, garlic, willows, and aloes. The grasslands of the mountain slopes provide excellent grazing.

The country has hot, moist summers and dry, cool winters during which there are overnight frosts. Rainfall varies considerably. For instance Maseru, the capital, has about 600 millimetres (23.5 inches) a year, while parts of the Drakensberg range have three times this much.

Lesotho, one of the poorest countries in the world, is heavily dependent on South Africa. Most of its trade is with that country, and over a third of the adult men are employed in South African mines and factories at any one time. The wages that they send back to Lesotho are a major source of income. The chief town is Maseru. Good roads are few. There is a rail-

ZEFA

Lesotho is a mountainous country; two-thirds of it lies over 3,000 metres (10,000 feet) above sea-level.

way link with South Africa and a number of airstrips.

Agriculture and Industry

Cultivated land is confined to the lowland areas of the two main river valleys. The country suffers from erosion, and so very little land can be farmed. The main crops are wheat, barley, sorghum, maize, peas, and beans. Lesotho has to import food when the harvests are poor, as well as livestock, drink, and tobacco. Sheep provide one of the most important exports, wool.

Industries, which include brewing, canning asparagus for export, furniture-making, and tourism, are all very small. Diamonds are found in alluvial deposits (that is, the material washed downstream by rivers); and there is a diamond mine at Letseng-la-Terai. Over 3,000 metres (9,840 feet) above sea-level in the Maloti Mountains, it is the highest diamond mine in the world. However, its resources are limited.

The People and their History

Most of the people living in Lesotho are Basutos, a Bantu-speaking people. Almost three-quarters of them are Christians. There is a small white minority, mainly South African, as well as some Coloureds and Asians. In Lesotho as a whole there is a high level of education and the people have one of the highest literacy rates in Africa. (Literacy means being able to read and write.)

FACTS ABOUT LESOTHO

AREA: 30,355 square kilometres (11,720 square miles).
POPULATION: 1,628,000 (1987).
GOVERNMENT: Independent kingdom; member of the Commonwealth of Nations.
CAPITAL: Maseru.
GEOGRAPHICAL FEATURES: Mountains, highlands and sources of the Orange, Caledon and Tugela rivers.
NATURAL PRODUCTS: Sheep, cattle, horses, goats, poultry, maize and wheat.
INDUSTRIAL PRODUCTS: Diamonds, wool and mohair.
EDUCATION: Most children attend primary school.

The Basuto nation was founded early in the 19th century by King Moshesh whose African name was Moshoeshoe. He united various groups of Basutos who had been resisting the invading Zulus. In 1868, as his people fought the advancing Boers (Dutch pioneers who were settling in the country), Moshesh agreed to accept British rule, and Basutoland became a British protectorate in 1884. South Africa wanted to incorporate the area into its territory, but this move was resisted by the British, and in 1966 Basutoland became independent as Lesotho.